11/10

D0205214

20th CENTURY BATTLEFIELDS

20th CENTURY BATTLEFIELDS

PETER AND DAN SNOW

BBC
BOOKS

To the memory of Captain Jim Philippson, an outstanding
soldier and friend, who gave us valuable help. Like so many
other young men in this book he died in action far from home.

10 9 8 7 6 5 4 3 2

This book is published to accompany the television series entitled *Twentieth Century
Battlefields*, first broadcast on BBC2 in 2007.

First published in hardback in 2007.
This edition published in 2008 by BBC Books, an imprint of Ebury Publishing,
A Random House Group Company.

The Random House Group Limited Reg. No. 954009

Addresses for companies within the Random House Group can be found at
www.randomhouse.co.uk

A CIP catalogue record for this book is available from the British Library

ISBN 978 1 846 07286 4

Mixed Sources
Product group from well-managed
forests and other controlled sources
www.fsc.org Cert no. TT-COC-2139
© 1996 Forest Stewardship Council

The Random House Group Limited supports The Forest Stewardship Council (FSC),
the leading international forest certification organisation. All our titles that are printed on
Greenpeace approved FSC certified paper carry the FSC logo. Our paper procurement policy
can be found at www.rbooks.co.uk/environment

Commissioning editor: Martin Redfern
Project editor: Eleanor Maxfield
Designer: Martin Hendry
Production: David Brimble
Maps: HL Studios

Set in Adobe Garamond and Frutiger
Printed in the UK by CPI Cox & Wyman, Reading, RG1 8EX

CONTENTS

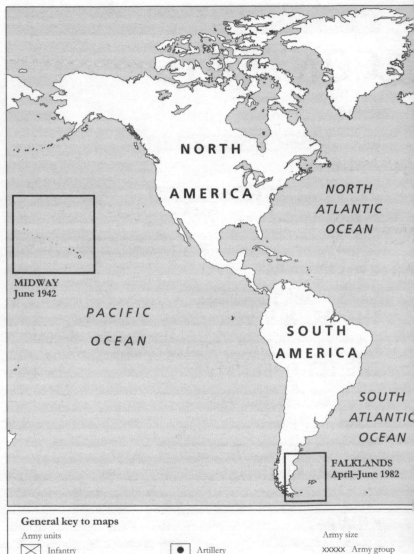

NORTH AMERICA

NORTH ATLANTIC OCEAN

MIDWAY
June 1942

PACIFIC OCEAN

SOUTH AMERICA

SOUTH ATLANTIC OCEAN

FALKLANDS
April–June 1982

General key to maps

Army units

⊠ Infantry

⊠ Mechanized infantry

▭ Armour

◿ Light armoured/recce

● Artillery

⊠ Airborne infantry

◀▶ Air assault

◀▶ Helicopter assault

Army size

XXXXX Army group

XXXX Army

XXX Corps

XX Division

X Brigade

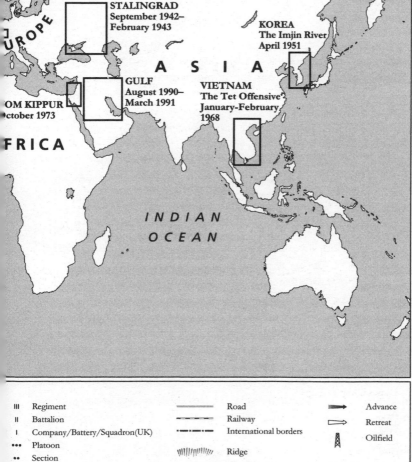

MIENS
gust
8

STALINGRAD
September 1942–
February 1943

KOREA
The Imjin River
April 1951

ROPE

A S I A

OM KIPPUR
ctober 1973

GULF
August 1990–
March 1991

VIETNAM
The Tet Offensive?
January-February
1968

FRICA

INDIAN
OCEAN

III	Regiment		Road		Advance
II	Battalion		Railway		Retreat
I	Company/Battery/Squadron(UK)		International borders		Oilfield
•••	Platoon				
••	Section		Ridge		
•	Squad	▲	Spot heights		

INTRODUCTION

Antibiotics, artificial intelligence and the internet: the twentieth century was one of unimaginable progress in so many ways. At no previous time in history has the human condition been so radically transformed. A Briton born in 1901 could expect to live half as long as one born today. He or she would be expected to defer to his or her betters. The world of 1901 was one of empires and monarchies, where class, ethnic and racial hierarchies were part of everyday life. Only a tiny number of states had yet embraced universal suffrage. Self-determination and democracy were not yet widely accepted as desirable forms of government. It was a world without air travel. The motor car was only a decade old and utterly primitive. The first radio broadcast was still years away. The vast majority of the world's population had never used a telephone or travelled more than 50 miles from where they were born. Yet 100 years later an explosion of scientific progress resulted in a fivefold increase in the world's population, astonishing medical advances, the discovery of the very building blocks of human life (DNA) and the projection of man-made objects beyond the limits of our solar system.

These changes revolutionized every aspect of life on earth, but they were powerless to curb the all too human propensity to resort to violence in order to settle differences. Indeed, it might be said that warfare flourished: in no field has the progress of science had a more striking effect than in combat. The destructive capacity of weapons increased so much during the twentieth century that any comparison has become meaningless. By the last third of the century, mankind had the ability to destroy the human race many times over. Satellites orbited the planet providing vital military intelligence and communications support to combatants on the ground. Jet aircraft could travel at over 2000 miles per hour and deliver weapons to within a few inches of their intended targets. Nuclear-powered submarines could stay on the bottom of the world's oceans almost indefinitely and packed enough of a punch to eradicate a medium-sized nation state. The ability of governments to enlist, motivate, train, equip and maintain enormous numbers of men and women in the armed forces was no less impressive. Changes in education, communications, healthcare, financial systems and transport were seized upon by warriors to revolutionize warfare as surely as they were transforming civilian society.

As a result, warfare reached unprecedented levels of intensity, scale and cost. Entire societies laboured under the yoke of war. Civilians were deliberately targeted in an attempt to crush the enemy population's will to fight. Armies of tens of millions fought along fronts the width of continents. Ethnic and state groups used all the machinery of the industrial age to carry out slaughter, sometimes of entire peoples. Tens of millions were murdered in Eastern Europe, Russia, China, Cambodia and sub-Saharan Africa.

It is a vicious paradox that the century which witnessed the scaling of such stunning scientific heights also saw the darkest chapters in the long and terrible story of man's inhumanity to man. Whenever a new field was opened to human development, militarization would immediately follow. In previous centuries, humans had restricted themselves to fighting largely on the surface of land and sea. By the end of the twentieth century, war had moved into the air, underground, under the sea and had made the first tentative steps into space and the ether as well. And as with many advances throughout human history, it was often military considerations that drove the pace of technological advance.

This is not to say that the increasing scale and destruction of warfare was not matched by some well-meaning attempts to prevent states fighting each other. Abhorrence at the devastation of the First World War prompted the creation of the League of Nations, and the United Nations was set up after the Second World War. The Kellogg-Briand Pact was signed in the White House on 27 August

1928 and nations including Germany, Japan, the UK, America and France agreed upon the 'renunciation of war as an instrument of national policy'. The spirit of the Pact was evident two decades later in the wording of Chapter 2 of the United Nations Charter: 'All Members shall refrain in their international relations from the threat or use of force.' The growth of other supranational organisations, such as the European Union, also encouraged dialogue and provided a framework for reducing tensions. The century also saw attempts at arms control. Awareness of the awesome power of nuclear weapons led to the Nuclear Non-proliferation Treaty. But neither the existence of the treaty nor the United Nations did much to deter states that perceived a threat to their existence from using force or pursuing the development of nuclear weapons.

In this book we chart the course of eight of the most striking and dramatic battles of the twentieth century. They vary in scale from possibly the biggest battle in history, fought at Stalingrad in the winter of 1942–3, to the relatively minor struggle over the Falkland Islands in 1982, but they all had a critical impact on the course of history. They had one feature in common: they changed the future. The world would have been very different if the outcomes of these battles had been reversed

Any list of decisive battlefields is subjective and we make no claim that what follows is a military history, let alone a full history, of the twentieth century. Instead, we examine eight of the great punctuation marks of the century. We acknowledge the importance of the Boer War and particularly the Russo-Japanese War, which saw the eclipse of Russian power in east Asia, shook the Tsarist regime to its foundations and gave birth to a modern Japanese empire. But we decided to begin with the First World War. This global clash destroyed the old world order based on the hegemony of the ancien regime European empires. During this conflict, 65 million men from around the world were mobilised, 8 million of them were killed and 21 million wounded. Contrary to the popular view, the men who presided over this unheard of carnage were not stupid, blinkered or lazy. Generals of all nationalities wrestled with a military situation that had been transformed by the introduction of new weapon systems and a revolution in communications. Rarely in military history have armies adapted so quickly. By 1918, the British army bore almost no resemblance to the small, professional imperial police force it had been in 1914 and the changes to the American, French and German armies were no less dramatic.

The first battle in the book, the Battle of Amiens, is oddly little remembered. In fact, it marked a key turning point in the First World War. It also witnessed the birth of modern all-arms warfare. The British, Canadian, Australian and French troops who fought in it would not have been out of place in the Falklands, whereas their counterparts of just four years earlier, in 1914, used tactics reminiscent of their forebears at Waterloo. If any battle illustrates the reasons for the Allied victory in the First World War, it is the Battle of Amiens in August 1918.

The untidy outcome of the First World War provided a crucible for the ideologies and conflicts that blighted the rest of the century. In Europe it toppled four ancient multinational empires and spawned a torrent of radical ideas that promised Utopian solutions to a shattered continent. After a vicious civil war, Communism took hold across the several time zones of Russia, while in central Europe and east Asia charismatic fascists won populations over with promises of racial domination and economic self-sufficiency.

The Second World War was even more terrible than its predecessor. Millions of combatants died on battlefields of a titanic scale, millions of civilians were tortured, raped and murdered in campaigns of racial annihilation. Cities were systematically destroyed from the air and their inhabitants incinerated. Men and women fought in a striking variety of conditions. Off the North Cape of Norway life expectancy was measured in seconds if sailors ended up in the icy water. In the deserts of Egypt the oven-like intensity of heat during the day tormented sunburnt soldiers at the very extremity of long and often dysfunctional supply chains. On the Kokoda Trail in New Guinea the strongest boots fell to pieces after only a few days of clambering over razor-sharp volcanic rock, wounds took an eternity to heal and cannibals lurked around the margins, waiting to pick off any Japanese or Australian stragglers.

We chose two battles from the Second World War, each one decisive in its own theatre of the war. The destruction of the Japanese carrier fleet at the Battle of Midway in June 1942 spelt absolute disaster for Japan's strategy in the Pacific. After Midway, all Japan could do was pray for a miracle while hundreds of thousands of her servicemen fought with suicidal bravery, trying to delay the inevitable: total defeat of their country. In the war between the Soviet Union and Germany, which saw the most critical struggle of the Second World War in Europe and 90 per cent of its casualties, the Battle of Stalingrad was the turning point. Although the reverse in front of Moscow in December 1941 effectively spelt the end of Hitler's dream to destroy the Soviet Union, the capitulation of the 6th Army in early 1943, among the ruins of Stalin's city, was the moment at which people around the world believed that Hitler's hitherto invincible *Wehrmacht* could and would be defeated.

The Second World War finally ended with the ultimate product of the marriage of science and warfare, as nuclear bombs obliterated Hiroshima and Nagasaki. But the halt in fighting was no more than a hiatus. The eclipse of a great power more often than not led to fighting over the spoils among its successors. Civil wars flared up where broken European empires shrivelled, and in the areas vacated by the Japanese in the Far East. Opposing groups could appeal to one of two ideologically opposed 'superpowers': the United States and the Soviet Union. The two countries stood at the head of respective coalitions that eyeballed each other across the shattered remnants of central Europe, each determined to stop the other from gaining any advantage.

It was the beginning of four decades of Cold War, no less bloody for being undeclared. Ten million people are estimated to have lost their lives as the two superpowers wrestled for influence from Greece to Malaya and from sub-Saharan Africa to Cuba. One civil war became a test, and a success, for the new United Nations as North Korea's Communists, hoping that the international community would not care, attempted to annex the American-backed south. Despite the desire by war-weary societies to rebuild after the Second World War, nations gathered in a vast alliance that was to secure eventual stability and lasting partition on the Korean peninsula. Another such conflict in Vietnam saw France humbled and then America bogged down in military operations quite unlike the mobile operations of the Second World War or the positional slogging match in Korea. During the Tet Offensive of 1968, the American military scored a notable success over the North Vietnamese and the Communist insurgency in South Vietnam, but lost the wider political battle for the hearts, minds and votes of the American electorate. As generals were to discover, instant news and television pictures broadcast almost simultaneously around the world would raise challenges as dramatic as the development of the tank, bomber or machine gun. Of all the eight battles in this book, it is the Tet Offensive in Vietnam that most markedly illustrates the central importance for modern nations at war to match success on the battlefield with the careful maintenance of popular support at home.

In the Far East, it was the collapse of the Japanese and French empires that encouraged competing parties to wage war to fill the void. In the Middle East, it was the British who withdrew when the financial cost of empire outweighed any gain. Since the British left Palestine, Arabs and Israelis have been fighting to control it. In 1948, 1956 and 1967, major wars broke out between the State of Israel and its neighbours. But it was in October 1973 that the most hard-fought battles took place. The conflict that began on the Jewish holiday of Yom Kippur hung in the balance for some time and at one point seemed almost to threaten the very existence of Israel.

Declining British power was also responsible for the attempt by the military junta of Argentina to seize the Falkland Islands in the South Atlantic. The Argentinian regime took a gamble. Its leaders judged that a weak Prime Minister, Margaret Thatcher, presiding over a nation that appeared to be in terminal decline, would not be in a position to recapture the islands. Margaret Thatcher surprised them and the world by doing just that. The success was to allow her to push through reforms that changed Britain radically and established her as one of the most influential figures of the late twentieth century.

The last chapter of this book deals with a conflict that to some looked like the dawning of a new era of international law and collective punishment for those who flouted it. When Saddam Hussein invaded Kuwait in 1990, he did not imagine that he would be faced with a coalition that spread from Syria to the United States preparing military action to force him out. In a stunning display of force, the US led the coalition and deployed the troops and weapon systems that NATO had been preparing to use against a Soviet thrust into Western Europe. The result was a shattering defeat for Iraq and its Soviet-supplied arsenal of weapons while the American military recovered the pride and prestige it had lost in Vietnam. But the high hopes were soon dashed when Saddam Hussein increased the repression inside Iraq itself and continued to defy the outside world. Iraq was a crisis that would continue well into the twenty-first century, even beyond the American invasion of 2003 and the execution of Saddam Hussein himself in January 2007.

Many of these conflicts were waged on such a gigantic scale that it is hard to believe that individuals could have had any impact on their outcomes. The history of the twentieth century can give the impression that we humans were adrift in a raft on a mighty river, where ferocious paddling was, at best, able only to have a slight effect on our course. But leadership retained its pivotal power to decide events throughout the century. What if Tsar Nicholas had kept his fragile empire out of the First World War, or Admiral Jellicoe had led the British fleet to disaster at Jutland? What if Halifax had become Prime Minister rather than Churchill, or Hitler had not halted Army Group Centre in front of Moscow in the autumn of 1941? What if Stalin had not recovered his nerve after his breakdown during Barbarossa, or his subordinates had not been so efficient at relocating Soviet factories in the teeth of the German advance? What if the Japanese commanders had prioritized the destruction of the aircraft carriers or oil tanks in Pearl Harbor, or Israel's leaders had not mobilised so effectively when caught by the surprise Arab attack in October 1973? The world today would be a very different place.

During the course of writing this book and making the television programme for BBC2, we have covered all of these battlefields on foot. We argued with each other about the Domino Theory inside the walls of the Imperial Palace at Hue, which has never been fully rebuilt since the Tet Offensive; we have peered through the finger-sized bullet-holes in the blue glass of the big hangar on Ford Island in Pearl Harbor; we have been moved by the litter of pathetically inappropriate plimsolls left on the hills of East Falkland by the boy soldiers of the Argentinian Junta. Dan stood on the 'Bridge of No Return', between North and South Korea, with two South Korean soldiers standing by in case soldiers from the North attempted to abduct him, with the words of the American area commander still ringing in his ears: 'Don't worry about the North Korean snipers. They'll be covering you alright, but if they shoot, you'll be dead before you hear the shot.'

As much as possible, we have tried to see the stories of these battles through the eyes of those who fought them. We have trawled through diaries and other eyewitness accounts and spoken to survivors, from generals, admirals and statesmen to ordinary soldiers, sailors and airmen on all sides, in order to bring alive for the reader what it must have been like to experience the horror of war. We have met a number of veterans. Particularly memorable were the survivors of Stalingrad: we listened to their tales of the battle and the lasting psychological damage it did to them as they plied us with freezing vodka and chilled pig fat. In a village on the Russian Steppe, a man remembered seeing General Paulus in autumn 1942, when as a boy he was allowed to play on the street outside the German army's headquarters. We asked him what Paulus had looked like: he pointed at Peter and replied, 'Like him.' In Vietnam, a middle-aged man showed us around a tunnel complex which he had built as a boy: he remembered the ground shaking as American bombs landed noisily but harmlessly above. He told us, 'The Americans owned the day; we owned the night.'

Many of these battles have not simply left physical scars on the landscape and dreadful memories for the survivors. They remain open wounds, threatening to erupt all over again. Along the Korean frontier, the third and fourth largest armies in the world still eyeball each other across a ceasefire line. On the Golan, Israeli positions are maintained in case the Syrians try again to seize back their lost lands. It is a standoff that threatens to poison the relationship between Islam and the West for years to come, as extremists on both sides try to engineer a wider clash of cultures.

It will take more than a naive faith in the continuing advancement of the human condition to ensure that the unfinished business of the twentieth century does not pollute the 21st. One thing that can be said is that we are unlikely to see warfare on the scale of the gigantic struggles of the twentieth century again. With the dropping of the nuclear bomb on Hiroshima on 6 August 1945, the age of internecine industrial warfare between the great powers came to an end. There will be nothing like Verdun, Stalingrad, Kursk or the Leyte Gulf in the foreseeable future, if ever again. This does not mean an end to violence. Regional struggles will continue and ethnic conflicts are all too intractable. And wars will not be confined to the developing world. The overwhelming military might of the great powers will not save them from future conflict. But it will not be warfare on the massive industrial scale of the twentieth century. Al-Qaeda opened the twenty-first century with a devastating example of what is called 'asymmetric' warfare. The unprecedented military dominance of the USA and its vast nuclear arsenal were impotent in the face of a small, highly motivated group of terrorists who struck at targets in New York and Washington. Two years later, the aftermath of the invasion of Iraq in 2003, massively mismanaged by the invaders, left Britain, America and their allies facing an insurgency that brought back fearful memories of earlier unconventional conflicts. As in the war in Vietnam, guerrillas will respond to overwhelming military power by simply side-stepping it. The revolution in communications, the internet and a 24-hour media, as well as the vast destructive potential of small amounts of biological, chemical or radiological materials, mean that small groups can strike at the very heart of an enemy. Thus the past century has witnessed a slow and inexorable extension of the battlefield. It began with opposing sides trying to crush the enemy's frontline troops and then slowly crept back to include their command and control and logistics. Now a highly motivated force, even if it is immeasurably weaker in conventional military hardware, can erode the other side's will to fight by targeting its political will to fight. The wars in Iraq, Afghanistan and Vietnam demonstrate how important it will be for armed forces to adapt to a quite different kind of conflict.

By 2007 this new form of warfare was having a discernible impact on the structure and doctrine of the world's armed forces. Half a decade into the wars in Afghanistan and Iraq, the United States was being compelled to abandon plans for a move to lighter armed and more streamlined forces. Urban warfare against a hidden enemy and the threat of roadside bombs demanded heavier rather than lighter armoured vehicles and more weighty body armour and personal weaponry. A new counterinsurgency code emphasized the need for tactics that would win the hearts and minds of the population.

However, contrary to expectations, the student of military history in the twentieth century need not become an inconsolable pessimist. There are grounds for hope, and even optimism, about the future. There was more to the twentieth century than rampant and colossal violence. The major wars were brief, if horrific, interruptions in a century that became progressively less violent. The dawning of the nuclear age has effectively put an end to warfare between the great powers. Nuclear proliferation will bring new dangers. It will increase the risk of nuclear weapons falling into the hands of irresponsible leaders or terrorists, but it will also increase the number of nuclear-armed states who may be mutually deterred from fighting each other. Other changes too seem to have eroded the root causes of conflict. The advancement of democracy, growing prosperity and a revolution in communications have improved understanding and empathy between peoples widely separated by geography. A globalized economic system allows individuals and states to pursue their legitimate ambitions without having to use force to secure natural resources and markets. While many challenges lie ahead, it can reasonably be hoped that the twentieth-century battles we describe in this book, in which states threw the full weight of their industrial might at each other, represent the peaks of high-intensity warfare. We may very well be looking back at the most violent century in the history of mankind.

AMIENS

At 4.20 a.m. on a summer's morning, the dark, quiet countryside around the River Somme in northern France was shattered by the sound of thousands of guns. Jets of flame erupted from British artillery barrels, sending high-explosive shells racing towards an enemy caught utterly by surprise. Countless flashes of light illuminated the desolate landscape, pitted with shell holes and already covered with the corroding debris of war. Here and there the remains of villages could be seen, once backwaters, now on the front line of the greatest conflict in history. Forward of the guns, thousands of men, mainly from Britain and its empire, crouched in trenches knowing that it would soon be their turn. They checked and rechecked equipment: the magazines for their rifles, the chinstraps on their helmets. Some said prayers; many wished they could be anywhere in the world but here. They were part of a push to beat back the German invaders. But unlike the apparently futile offensives which had gone before, this attack would have a profound impact both on the First World War and on military tactics. It bore little resemblance to the struggle fought along the same river two summers earlier; instead this battle, begun on 8 August 1918, would mark the emergence of the art of modern warfare. The tactics used on this battlefield would be the blueprint for the way battles were fought to the present day. Indeed, the soldiers who took part in the attack were to have more in common with the servicemen described in the final chapter of this book than they had with their unfortunate predecessors of two years before. This battle would take its name from the nearest city, Amiens, and, although now largely forgotten, it is one of the most significant milestones in British military history.

THE GREAT WAR

Just over four years earlier, the heir to the throne of the sprawling Austro–Hungarian empire had been shot and killed in Sarajevo, Bosnia. The assassination of Franz Ferdinand was seized upon in Vienna as an opportunity to reassert Austrian mastery of the Balkans and punish its bellicose neighbour, Serbia, who it guessed was behind the assassination. But Slavic Serbia was protected by its mighty mentor, Imperial Russia. Austria could not risk war with Russia before checking that its Teutonic equivalent, Germany, would offer support to the Austrian side. The German leadership believed a pan-European war was probably inevitable sooner or later and that Germany stood a better chance of winning it now, while it still had a sizeable industrial lead over a fast-modernizing Russia. So Germany's Kaiser, Wilhelm II, handed Austria what has become known as 'the blank cheque': Austria could do what it wished to Serbia, even if those actions precipitated a much wider war.

Austria began to bombard the Serbian capital, Belgrade, after only the most perfunctory attempt at reaching a peaceful solution. Russia mobilized while its Tsar, Nicholas II, sent frantic telegrams to his cousin the Kaiser begging him to defuse the situation. Instead Germany declared war on Russia, and in doing so dragged in France, which was treaty-bound to come to Russia's defence. The German plan called for a lightning defeat of France in the West followed by a campaign against Russia. Britain was not treaty-bound to come to the aid of Russia and France, and the Kaiser hoped that, with its massive global empire, Britain would avoid continental entanglements. But Britain had one foreign policy aim older even than the preservation of its empire: to prevent a single European power dominating the continent. Added to this was the fact that German troops were sweeping through Belgium to outflank French fortifications. The British government decided that its national interest and honour obliged it to stand by its treaty commitment to protect Belgian neutrality. Just before midnight on 4 August 1914, Britain declared war on Germany.

And so it was that this elaborate web of events and strategic calculations led to the most destructive war the world had yet seen. In the course of four long years the nature of war was to undergo a radical transformation, but it was not until the last 18 months of fighting that a new pattern of tactics would emerge. For most of the war it seemed that the overwhelming weight of firepower and the constraints that it imposed on mobility and attack would condemn all sides to be mired in trench warfare that neither side could break.

At the beginning of the war the Royal Navy, the biggest and most modern fleet in the world, sealed off the North Sea and cut Germany off from raw materials and other vital supplies. This would have a slow but decisive effect on German agriculture, industrial production and eventually civil society itself. But in western Europe the war on land soon settled down to a bloody stalemate on virtually immobile front lines. The small but professional British Expeditionary Force (BEF) crossed into northern France and played its part in trying to reverse the German advances in the fighting of autumn 1914. But from the end of that year until the end of the war an unbroken line of trenches ran from the Channel ports to the Swiss border.

The prospect of either side freeing itself from the tyranny of positional warfare had been extinguished by recent radical technological changes. The industrial revolution had altered the way human beings fought each other as surely as it had changed the way they travelled, built and communicated. But there had not been a corresponding revolution in military tactics. In 1914 officers and men went into battle in ways that would not have been out of place 100 years before, when an infantryman could fire just three rounds a minute. But by 1914 a small number of men could fire an almost infinite number of bullets, far more accurately, over a far greater range. It was said that during an attack on High Wood on 24 August 1916 ten Vickers heavy machine guns fired in excess of one million rounds over a 12-hour period. Indeed, First World War weapons such as these remained in use until the middle of the twentieth century. These breech-loading, rapid-firing weapons were reinforced by quick-firing artillery which could deliver a murderous weight of accurate fire. The critical feature of these new weapon systems, as with other more low-tech innovations such as barbed wire and underground concrete bunkers, was that they benefited the defending side far more than the attacker. Charging men had to cross a killing zone of greater depth and lethality than ever before. At the 1916 Battle of the Somme British troops climbed out of their trenches hoping that the preceding ferocious British artillery bombardment would have destroyed the German positions. Instead, once the Germans heard the barrage lift they emerged from their dugouts, set up machine guns and caught the British in the middle of no man's land, walking in tightly bunched lines behind a belt of largely unbroken barbed wire. The first day of that battle, 1 July 1916, was the worst day of slaughter the British army has ever experienced: 57,470 officers and men were killed, wounded or captured, and 32 battalions each lost over 500 men.

Technology favoured the defence in other ways, too. Although railways benefited both sides, it was the defenders who gained the most: they could rush supplies and reinforcements to any point on their railway line. Attackers could not lay track as they advanced; instead, every step took them further away from their logistical chain. Nor could most machine guns and artillery pieces be easily moved forward. Machine guns weighed too much in 1914 and artillery required teams of horses, themselves vulnerable to enemy fire. Battlefield communications were a constant problem. Radio was in its infancy and too bulky to be carried by infantrymen. Even if the attackers were still within range of their own artillery, there was no way quickly to call in fire support.

Contrary to an all-too-persistent popular misconception, it would be quite wrong to assume that commanders made no attempt to overcome these enormous problems. Soldiers, scientists and engineers tried every conceivable experiment. From 1914 onwards the Western Front was a seething hotbed of new ideas and wild strategies and a testing ground for new technology. Both sides were constantly developing weapons and tactics in an attempt to break the deadlock of trench warfare.

In 1915 the British Expeditionary Force in France came under the command of Sir Douglas Haig. He was a veteran of campaigns in Sudan and South Africa and in 1905 he had married, after a few days' acquaintance, a lady-in-waiting to the Queen. Thereafter, he enjoyed useful access to King George V, which helped strengthen his position in the face of increasing hostility from the politicians in London. A cavalryman through and through, he always believed that trench warfare was an aberration and that the day of the horseman and the cavalry charge would return. Although he did encourage technological development during the war, in 1915 he is alleged to have said that the machine gun was 'over-rated', and as late as 1925 he maintained that 'some enthusiasts today talk about the probability of the horse becoming extinct and prophesy that the aeroplane, the tank and the motor car will supersede the horse in future wars.... I am sure that as time goes on you will find just as much use for the horse – the well-bred horse – as you have done in the past.'[1] Haig is, without doubt, one of the most controversial figures in British military history – to some a butcher, to others a great strategist who presided over a British army that was evolving more rapidly than at any time in its history.

The size of the BEF that Haig commanded had grown from 100,000 regulars in 1914 to over 1.8 million by 1917.[2] Nearly all of these men had come into the army from civilian life – they were everything from students and bakers to office workers and tradesmen. A mix of volunteers and conscripts, they had to be taught the art of modern warfare. The attacks of 1916 and 1917 along the Somme and in Flanders are often written off as futile, but they had in fact been a valuable learning experience for these men, albeit a bloody one. Raw troops, if they survived, were slowly turned into veterans. By late 1917 the BEF had made huge strides: its best units were as good as any in the French or German armies.

There was one British attack in 1917 that stands out as an example of the BEF's rapid improvement and its willingness to embrace new technology. In March the Germans had made a tactical withdrawal to a massively fortified position known to the British as the Hindenburg Line, after the new commander of the German forces, General Paul von Hindenburg. In November Haig decided to fight a limited battle to break the Hindenburg Line at the town of Cambrai. It would be a completely new form of offensive: he decided to use innovative artillery tactics to stun the German troops, and then send in tanks in massed formation for the first time. The British were pioneers of tank warfare, which they saw as a way to alleviate the slaughter on the Western Front. It was their naval experience that encouraged them to develop the tank. It seemed, to nautical-minded Brits, akin to a heavily armoured gunboat ploughing through oceans of mud. Indeed, for its first few years the tank was named the 'landship'. The early tanks were slow, prone to breakdown and, with no separation between the crew compartment and the engine, they tended to asphyxiate their crews. But they could crush barbed wire, their tracks ensured that they could cross a shattered landscape, their machine guns could bring fire to bear on enemy positions and their armour made them invulnerable to enemy small-arms fire. The Germans had not embraced mechanized warfare, partly because the blockade had prevented them from getting enough of the requisite raw materials and partly because their traditions led them to put a priority on aggressive infantry attacks.

On 20 November, 1000 British guns fired a short barrage and then 476 tanks rumbled forwards. German defenders were stunned by the shelling and then panicked as they saw tanks roll out of the gloom. That night the British advanced as much as 5 miles (8 km), a great distance when ground was typically lost or won in terms of mere yards. When the news reached the United Kingdom, church bells were rung for the first time since the beginning of the war. But it was not to be an unqualified success. Haig decided to push on with the attack over the next week, and it bogged down. The Germans took the opportunity to counter-attack, and the battle ended with no clear advantage to either side. During the counter-attack the Germans displayed new tactics of their own – another of their constant innovations to try to break the deadlock on the battlefield. Elite units of men armed with lighter than normal weapons moved forward quickly, infiltrating British lines and searching out weak points. These men were called *Strosstruppen*, Stormtroopers, and their presence on the Western Front would prove revolutionary.

Cambrai hinted that change was coming, but by New Year's Day 1918 a number of factors away from the battlefields of north-east France had made a dramatic transformation inevitable. After a string of military defeats, Russia had collapsed. The Tsar had been ousted in early 1917 and the government that replaced him was in turn toppled eighteen months later. The new Bolshevik leaders withdrew Russia entirely from the war. France was near breaking point: mutinies had ravaged the French army as morale dropped to a new low after a number of failed offensives. But Germany was feeling the effects of prolonged warfare too. Its people's suffering at the hands of the British naval blockade was increasing. In early 1917 Germany had taken the huge gamble of declaring unrestricted U-boat warfare in the Atlantic, which came close to starving Britain of supplies. But inevitably American ships travelling to and from Britain were torpedoed, and many American citizens killed. The United States, the world's largest economy, was now forced to join the war against Germany.

America would take a long time to make its presence felt on the battlefields in France. In 1916 the US army numbered just 100,000 men.[3] America effectively had to build a modern army from scratch: the British experience had already shown just how long it took to turn civilians into professional soldiers. The war was now a race. Russia's collapse meant that Germany could rush its troops from the Eastern to the Western Front. The question was whether Germany could win the war before America's bottomless pit of manpower and its financial and industrial might could be brought to bear. The year 1918 would be a decisive one.

The men in the trenches sat through the fourth winter of the war on the frost-covered plains of Flanders and northern France with a sort of grim fatalism. Desmond Allhusen, an officer with the 8th King's Royal Rifle Corps, wrote, 'The future seemed to be an end-less vista of battles, each one worse than the last. We still felt that we would win, but had stopped saying so. The war was the only real and permanent thing, thriving and increasing in a world that was going to ruin … our destinies were clear enough. We would be hit, and if we recovered we would be hit again, and so on until we were either dead or permanently disabled.'[4] Hubert Essame, from a Northamptonshire battalion in the 8th Division, wrote years later : 'The mood of these men in their forward posts on this bitter New Year's Day could be summed up as stoical endurance combined with bewilderment. Any desire they ever had to attack the Germans had long since vanished: now they counted the minutes and hours to be endured before relief came.'[5]

The Germans had more to celebrate. Russia had been knocked out of the struggle, and there were rumours of a planned attack in the West that would win the war. Herbert Sulzbach, a German artillery officer, wrote in his diary, 'Once more a year reaches its end, in which we can be proud of each other, since what we have stood firm against on this Western Front can never be described in words…. People are talking a lot just now about a big offensive which is supposed to be coming off in France; we are already keyed up, and hardly dare hope for it.'[6]

THE LUDENDORFF OFFENSIVES

Germany had to win the war in one campaign. Further attrition and another winter of shortages caused by the Royal Navy's blockade could only end in defeat. Erich von Ludendorff was Hindenburg's quartermaster general and the *de facto* commander of Germany's armies; Hindenburg's calm solidity provided the cover for his subordinate's brilliant if abrasive personality. The time had come, Ludendorff decided, to use the men no longer needed on the Russian front to strike a series of blows that would break the Allies in France. Those blows were to be aimed initially at the British, because he was convinced that Britain was the central power in the alliance. Beat Britain, he calculated, and France, deprived of its paymaster and supplier, would collapse. The British armies had their backs to the Channel: he would drive them into the sea.

The attack would be made in Picardy, over the terrain of the old Somme battlefield. It was drier here than in Flanders, so there was less risk of getting bogged down in bad weather; and the British had recently taken over a section of line from the French, which meant that the available forces were spread a little more thinly. Everything that the Germans had learnt in the previous three years of fighting would be put into effect. It would be an attack quite unlike any other.

In mid-March a trench mortar operator, J.W. Gore, wrote in his diary, 'There is an ominous feeling about, as if something is about to happen.'[7] Haig too believed that something was afoot. In fact, he was feeling rather bullish about it. On 2 March he confided to his diary that the British 'plans were sound and thorough, and very much work had already been done. I was only afraid that the enemy would find our front so very strong that he [would] hesitate to commit his army to the attack with the almost certainty of losing very heavily.'[8] Two weeks later he wrote to his wife that 'everyone is in good spirits and only anxious that the enemy should attack.'[9] At 4.40 a.m. the next morning, 21 March, he got his wish. Six and a half thousand German guns roared along a front of 70 miles (110 km). That day they were to fire 3 million shells. Half of their entire artillery strength on the Western Front had been secretly moved to support this push. Winston Churchill, visiting that portion of the front in his capacity as Minister of Munitions, called it, 'The most tremendous cannonade I have ever heard'.[10] Gas and high-explosive shells pounded British troops, bunkers, railways, communication centres, supply dumps and any other target, no matter how apparently insignificant. Historian Malcolm Brown characterized it as 'the greatest utterance of modern industrialized warfare to that date'.[11] The offensive was Germany's bid to win the war and it was named after the country's patron saint, Michael.

The Michael Offensive was not based just on massive and accurate use of artillery. The entire German army had been scoured for the best men, who had been retrained as *Strosstruppen*. Among the new weapons they carried was the world's first sub-machine gun, the MP18, which increased the infantryman's firepower without

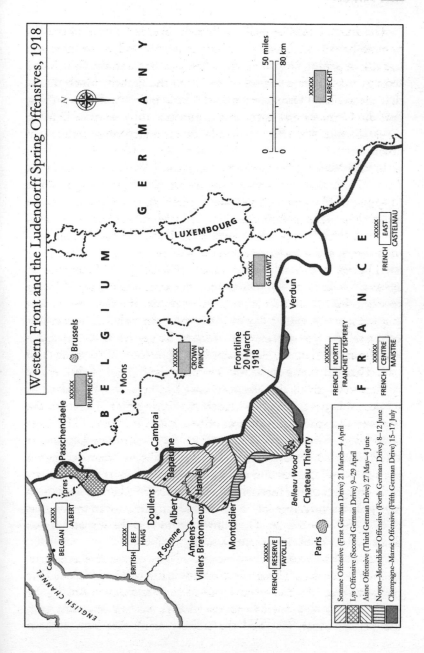

Western Front and the Ludendorff Spring Offensives, 1918

ENGLISH CHANNEL

Calais

BELGIAN
BELGIAN
ALBERT
XXXX

BRITISH
BEF
HAIG
XXXXX

FRENCH
RESERVE
FAYOLLE
XXXXX

Ypres
Passchendaele

RUPPRECHT
XXXXX

B E L G I U M

Brussels

Mons

Cambrai

Doullens
R Somme
Albert
Bapaume
Hamel

Amiens
Villers Bretonneux

Montdidier

Belleau Wood
Chateau Thierry

Paris

CROWN
PRINCE
XXXXX

Frontline
20 March
1918

G E R M A N Y

LUXEMBOURG

Verdun

GALLWITZ
XXXXX

F R A N C E

FRENCH
NORTH
FRANCHET D'ESPEREY
XXXXX

FRENCH
CENTRE
MAISTRE
XXXXX

FRENCH
EAST
CASTELNAU
XXXXX

ALBRECHT
XXXXX

N

0   50 miles
0   80 km

Somme Offensive (First German Drive) 21 March–4 April
Lys Offensive (Second German Drive) 9–29 April
Aisne Offensive (Third German Drive) 27 May–4 June
Noyon–Montdidier Offensive (Forth German Drive) 8–12 June
Champagne–Marne Offensive (Fifth German Drive) 15–17 July

burdening him with weight. Two men in each squad carried a flame-thrower: compressed nitrogen expelled fuel oil which was ignited as it left the nozzle and could envelop whole stretches of trench in a blazing fireball. Others carried grenade-launchers or light mortars which had a range of just 3300 feet (1000 metres). British Lewis light machine guns, captured on the battlefield, were popular with the Germans; weighing just over 28 lb (13 kg), they could be carried forward quickly. Assisted by massive artillery support, these squads would dash forward and exploit any weakness in the enemy line. If they met opposition they would either destroy it or bypass it and sow confusion further on, leaving follow-up troops to deal with the obstacle.

According to a German medical officer, Stephen Westman, 'The men of the storm battalions were treated like football stars. They lived in comfortable quarters … they did their jobs and disappeared again, and left it to the poor foot sloggers to dig in, to deal with counter attacks and to endure the avenging artillery fire of the enemy…. They moved like snakes over the ground, camouflaged and making use of every bit of cover, so they did not offer any targets for artillery fire … dangerous people to come up against.'[12] As they prepared to move forward towards British positions on the 21st, the most famous storm trooper of them all, Ernst Jünger, wrote, 'This gigantic roar of annihilation from countless guns behind us was so terrific that, compared with it, all preceding battles were child's play. What we had not dared to hope came true. The enemy artillery was silenced, put out of action by one giant blow…. We got out on top [of our dugouts] and looked with wonder at the wall of fire towering over the English lines and the swaying blood-red clouds that hung above it.'[13] As he led his men to attack he 'was boiling with a fury now utterly inconceivable to me. The overpowering desire to kill winged my feet. Rage squeezed bitter tears from my eyes … the English jumped out of their trenches and fled by battalions across the open. They stumbled over each other as they fled, and in a few seconds the ground was strewn with dead.'[14]

On the first day, the Germans captured nearly 100 square miles (255 square km) of British-held territory. It was an unprecedented advance. Some British units were wiped out. The war diary entry of the 9th Battalion, the Kings Royal Rifle Corps recorded: 'By the evening of the 21st, the battalion ceased to exist.'[15] Many accounts speak of men being pummelled senseless and not really caring whether they lived or died.

The British lost 40,000 men in that one day, including 21,000 men captured by the Germans. But Ludendorff's men suffered too. Private Arthur Wrench of the 51st Highlanders wrote on the night of Friday, 22 March, 'It is absolute hell here. Cold blooded murder and mass slaughter. The Germans in their mass formations get it from our Lewis and machine guns while they give it to us unmercifully with their artillery. The fatigue is awful and the strain of holding on tremendous, and God knows how long it will go on. Our line is getting thin while the Germans seem to be coming on in inexhaustible numbers and must surely get through.'[16] The Germans were indeed capturing territory, but they were paying heavily for it: their casualties on that first day were around 40,000 as well. In fact, most of the German gains had been against General Sir Hubert Gough's 5th Army, where they had taken over French positions that were in poor condition. North of it was Sir Julian Byng's 3rd Army, which had much more success in holding back the German advance.

By 27 March Ludendorff's forces had seized Montdidier, and in doing so briefly divided the French and British armies. The situation was so bad for the Allies that they made some long overdue changes in the unsystematic way they were fighting the war. The day before the Germans captured Montdidier a conference at Doullens established a unified command on the Western Front. The French general Ferdinand Foch was appointed to coordinate the Allied armies, and on 3 April was formally entrusted with the 'strategicdirection of military operations'.

Meanwhile, the British Prime Minister, David Lloyd George, released from the UK another 170,000 men who were in a reasonable state of readiness. Three divisions were summoned from other fronts. The age bracket for conscription was widened: now men from 17 up to 50 or even 55 years old could be called up. It was the supreme moment of crisis for the BEF. On 1 April Churchill telegraphed Lloyd George: 'It is considered certain here that the Germans will pursue this struggle to a final decision all through the summer and their resources are larger than ours.... Every effort must be made to avoid destruction.'[17] But even this great offensive was stalled by the inexorable logic of the Western Front. As the Germans advanced across shattered countryside they moved too fast for their artillery, supplies and reinforcements. These had to be dragged, hauled and marched along shell-cratered roads. Meanwhile, the British and French, who had railways and undamaged roads behind their positions, were able to move rapidly and plug the gaps in their defences. On 4 and 5 April Amiens, the critical railroad junction, was saved by British and Australian troops fighting 10 miles (16 km) to the east at Villers Bretonneux. On the 5th Ludendorff bowed to the inevitable and closed down the Michael Offensive. When Churchill realized it had stopped he wrote, 'It has been touch and go on the front. We stood for some days within an ace of destruction.'[18]

Ludendorff now expended his reserves of men and munitions in a series of further strikes along the Western Front. Each time he achieved some initial tactical success, but each time it failed to turn into a strategic breakthrough as his losses mounted and the French and British scrambled to construct new defensive lines further back. On 27 May the last major offensive, known as Blücher Yorck after two Prussian field marshals of the Napoleonic era, crashed into British and French troops in Champagne. It quickly turned into an all-out assault on the French capital.

On the 29th German forces entered Château Thierry, just 55 miles (90 km) from Paris. Here they were met by a new presence on the Western Front, the Americans. Much sooner than expected, the United States had raised and equipped an astonishing 4 million men, and by the early summer of 1918, 2 million of them were already in France and many were ready for action.[19] Their commander, General Pershing, could now offer Foch the men he needed to help defend Paris. At the end of May American troops established positions just west of Château Thierry. They held off German attacks for two days, and then counter-attacked in a battle known as Belleau Wood. This timely action by fresh, well-supplied and energetic troops brought Ludendorff's offensive to a halt. American inexperience was costly: they suffered nearly 10,000 casualties. But the effect of their involvement was great on both sides. Ludendorff launched two other limited attacks but each of these petered out. By the middle of July the Ludendorff offensives were over. The Germans had lost nearly a million men in their attempt to win the war. Overwhelmingly these casualties were among the most motivated and highly trained troops in their army. They now had more territory to hold with fewer men, and Allied retaliation was inevitable.

COUNTERSTRIKE

There was one man on the Allied side who was determined to launch an attack and thought he had worked out just how to do it. Sir Henry Rawlinson's career had not recovered from the disaster of the first day of the Battle of the Somme in 1916, when his 4th Army had sustained the worst losses ever recorded by a British army. After the battle he had been sidelined and posted to a liaison job with the French. But Sir Hubert Gough's failure to stem the German advance enabled Rawlinson to be given another chance. Gough was sacked and Rawlinson was appointed to command the 5th Army. He was lucky: by the time he had taken up the reins on 28 March the German offensive had run out of steam. He managed to secure the city of Amiens and its vital railhead and he began to look for opportunities to attack. He knew that the 4th Army, as the 5th was redesignated in April, was perfectly placed to go on the offensive. In part this was because he had under his command some of the best troops in France: the Australian Corps, commanded by Lieutenant General John Monash.

Under Monash the Australians had gone a long way towards solving the problems of trench warfare. They had spent the summer carrying out raids and small-scale attacks. Emphasis was placed above all on cooperation by all the different arms: machine-gunners, tanks, artillery, aircraft and infantry. Monash wrote that, 'A modern battle is like nothing so much as a score for a musical composition, where the various arms and units are the instruments, and the tasks which they perform are their respective musical phrases. Each individual unit must make its entry precisely at the proper moment, and play its phrase in the general harmony.'[20] At the Battle of Hamel in July, for example, tanks and artillery were used to break the German lines and as a result fewer men needed to be sent forward to capture the ground; they were then reinforced by the first-ever air drop. The Hamel operation was so successful and at such minimal cost that Rawlinson now wanted to use these tactics on a much larger scale. He felt that the wide, rolling terrain of Picardy, dotted with small woods and villages, would favour an attack with massed tanks. He and his staff got to work. They were the same men who had planned the Somme, but now they were working under quite different circumstances. In 1916 they had been afforded little leeway, but two years on Rawlinson was determined to give them the opportunity to think freely about how best to break through the German defensive positions. Drawing on their earlier experiences, his team put together a meticulous plan which attempted to correct past mistakes and inflict a decisive defeat on the German army.

On 17 July Rawlinson went to the commander of the BEF with his idea. He asked Haig for the elite Canadian Corps: with them and the Australians as his main strike force he would punch a hole in the German lines in front of Amiens. The land was dry and suitable for tanks. Rawlinson wanted to concentrate them in huge numbers and, after the briefest of artillery bombardments, throw them at the enemy. This, he said, would 'save casualties to the infantry'.[21] As the infantry and armour advanced they would be protected by a creeping barrage which would provide a screen, moving forward just ahead of them, of shrapnel and high explosive. In the skies, aircraft would direct artillery fire and support the infantry by dropping bombs and machine-gunning enemy positions. It would be the BEF's opportunity to demonstrate 'all-arms warfare' on a huge scale. Haig and Foch liked the sound of the plan. Foch, as on most occasions, wanted the offensive to be bigger and start sooner: he insisted the attacking force should include the French 1st Army and that the whole plan should be advanced by two days. Rawlinson was furious: the hastening of the date would involve a huge amount of work. But Haig sided with Foch and had to issue his reluctant subordinate a direct order: zero hour would be 4.20 a.m. on 8 August.

SECRECY AND STRENGTH

As with Cambrai and the German Michael Offensive, surprise was absolutely critical. If the Germans had time to rush in reserve divisions to shore up their line, the chance of success would be much reduced. Even a few hours' warning would be disastrous: the Germans would have time to move their artillery to different positions. To maximize secrecy, Amiens, from which most of the population had fled in the spring, was emptied of its remaining civilians. Planning meetings were held up and down the Western Front so that too many staff officers weren't continually seen in the same place. Divisional commanders weren't informed until as late as possible, and the infantrymen who were going to be at the tip of the spear were not told until 36 hours before. Officers were ordered not to peer over the parapet of a trench looking at maps and pointing out objectives. Artillery was only to be moved into the area at night and would be well camouflaged in daytime. In this way, 1000 artillery pieces were covertly assembled into the area. They had a strictly coordinated firing schedule: each gun would fire individually to check its range and accuracy, in order to promote the illusion that there was no increase in the overall volume of fire.

Overhead, RAF aircraft checked that the British guns were well hidden. Haig had always been an enthusiastic advocate of military airpower, which provided invaluable reconnaissance and during battles could even 'spot' for the artillery. Pilots would tell artillerymen via wireless how to adjust their fire to hit the target directly. Rawlinson's push would have as many aircraft supporting it as Haig could scrape together. The British fighters such as the Sopwith Dolphin and Camel were not quite as good as the latest German Fokker DVII, but they enjoyed a considerable advantage in numbers.

The Canadians were left out of the front line till the last moment. The Germans had so much respect for them that their presence in any part of the line would be taken as a sure sign that the next attack would fall there. This prompted Rawlinson to divert two Canadian battalions, two casualty clearing stations and Canadian wireless operators to the 2nd Army front in Belgium. British commanders were ready to mislead their own troops to make the whole deception campaign more convincing: the two battalions were ordered to 'prepare the front for attack pending the arrival of the remainder of the Canadian Corps'.[22] The Germans were so fooled by the presence of the Canadians in the north that they even began building new aerodromes to prepare for the imagined assault. In fact, the Canadian Corps was moving south towards Amiens, always travelling by night. Herbert Witherby, a sergeant in the Canadian artillery from Lethbridge, Alberta, wrote, 'The night marches were most fearfully hard on us.... I had to keep riding up and down, shaking the drivers and gunners to keep them awake.'[23] When they arrived in the line, their artillery was not allowed to fire but had to employ new methods of what was called 'silent registration': they would use aerial photographs, sound ranging and the latest meteorological reports to achieve accurate fire without having to fire any practice rounds.

From 27 July, the number of men and horses in the 4th Army doubled. Rawlinson would have 441,588 men available for the battle and nearly 100,000 horses. The latter were not just for transport. Haig, always the cavalryman, insisted that they should be on hand to exploit the gaps in the enemy lines. As for the infantry, the Canadians and the Australians, recognized as second to none in the BEF, had been spared the worst of the spring offensives and were raring to show off their expertise. The British troops alongside them were not as effective: they had been gravely weakened by the German offensives from March onwards, and many units were struggling to incorporate inexperienced men who had replaced the casualties. Even so, all the infantry were trained in the new methods of attack. The assaulting forces were going to fight a 'combined arms' battle in which artillery, infantry, air, tanks and cavalry would act in a closely coordinated way to overcome the enemy.

Critical to the plan was the use of unprecedented numbers of tanks: Amiens was to be the largest armoured battle of the First World War. The main thrust would consist of 342 heavy tanks, Mark Vs and Mark V*s, both capable of around 4 mph (6 kph). They were parcelled out equally between the Canadians and the Australians, with a much smaller number going to the British III Corps. The tanks' job was to seek out and destroy enemy machine gun nests which the artillery had not dealt with, and which the infantry could not take on alone. Behind them were 72 Whippet tanks, lighter and faster – capable of 8 mph (13 kph). They would move ahead of the assault after the initial breach in the enemy's lines had been made and sow confusion in their rear. These would be joined by 12 even more lightly built armoured cars. Supply tanks, 120 of them, would ply to and fro, bringing the attacking infantry and armour everything they needed to keep up the pace of the advance. Altogether around 530 tanks, effectively the whole strength of the British Tank Corps, would be involved in the offensive. However, the frequency of mechanical failure and very slow speed of these early tanks made them vulnerable to German artillery. So far they had been a great help on the battlefield but had not yet proved a decisive breakthrough weapon. Success at Amiens would depend on how well the tanks could work together with the other 'arms' of the attacking forces. Rawlinson judged deception vital to keep the presence of the tanks a secret. The 1st Army, 100 miles (160 km) away, trained ostentatiously with a tank battalion in broad daylight to delude the Germans into believing that that was where British armour was concentrating.

These huge numbers of men and machines were assembled with painstaking stealth. Planes flew low overhead to drown out the sounds of tractors and tank engines as they moved into their positions. Some German troops did warn of increased activity in their sector, but were told that it was unsoldierly to be nervous. On 4 August Ludendorff was forced to issue a statement quashing fears that there was an Allied offensive in the offing: 'There is nothing to justify this apprehension, provided our troops are vigilant and do their duty.'[24]

At the last possible minute the Canadians were moved into the front line. Herbert Witherby wrote, 'We were very close to the line and had to be careful to cover up the guns and equipment against enemy observing planes. The woods were shelled all night, stopping about daybreak, but no one else was hit; all day of the 7th we rested well, had the last orders and lay low. This was all we had to do; keep out of sight.'[25] The last Canadians arrived in the front line only 120 minutes before zero hour. Even the rest of the 4th Army was caught by surprise. One Australian infantryman wrote, 'A few officers and NCOs went to the front line to view the ground. They returned round-eyed with wonder. The woods on the right were full of Canadians. Canadians? We thought they were at Arras.'[26]

The 7th was hot and sunny. The temperature had plunged during the cloudless night that followed, and by the early hours of the 8th there was the thickest of ground mists. It was eerily similar to the night of 21 March, when the Germans had attacked and come so close to breaking the British army.

Through the hours of darkness the tanks completed their slow journey to their start positions just 1000 yards (920 metres) behind the forward trenches. Captain Henry Smeddle, who commanded three Mark V* tanks at Amiens, wrote about the huge effort to ensure surprise: 'Our tankodrome consisted of a long line of elms on the bank of a canal; their leafy foliage aided by our camouflage nets amply protected our tanks from the prying of any scouting aeroplane.'[27] After a briefing at Company HQ he returned to give the men a rough outline of the proposed action, 'excepting the actual date, time and location, which would be given at the last moment'. He got a 'good look over the ground which we were to pass with our tanks on the following day'. On the approach 'there was to be no smoking, or flashing of electric torches, and no shouting, whistling or unnecessary noise during the march. Only tank commanders would be allowed to smoke; the glow of their cigarettes was to be the method by which they would guide their tanks whilst walking in front without undue attention.' The tanks rumbled into their final positions, following white tape laid out along the ground, and things went so smoothly that they all arrived on time. Herbert Witherby wrote, 'About midnight the tanks started to go by, such countless numbers of them, tank after tank, lumbering and creaking along, it's a wonder the Huns never heard them.'[28]

To disguise the noise of the tanks the RAF had been supposed to fly over British positions. But the heavy ground mist made flying conditions so bad that very few pilots managed to get airborne. Major Donald Dunbar Coutts, a medic with the 2nd Australian Division, remembers that 'a few of our aeroplanes were flying overhead with the throttles open, to make as much noise as possible, so that the Hun could not hear our tanks'. He was up with the infantry, poised right at the front of the assault, and wrote that 'everybody was excited and very optimistic about the possibilities of the stunt'. His men had been told to withdraw 'from the front line to leave it free from troops, 10 minutes before zero. Everybody was to keep in the trenches because our guns at first would be firing at such short range that the shells would be skimming the ground.'[29] The Canadian Witherby 'never slept a wink that night ... I was too busy, and had not the inclination, we had some hot tea and something to eat about 2 a.m.'[30] An Australian gunner, J.R. Armitage, later wrote in his diary, 'It was utterly still. Vehicles made no sound on the marshy ground.... The silence played on our nerves a bit. As we got our guns into position you could hear drivers whispering to their horses and men muttering curses under their breath, and still the silence persisted.'[31]

BATTLE IS JOINED

At 4.20 a.m. precisely, 2000 barrels roared as one. Armitage wrote simply, 'All hell broke loose and we heard nothing more. The world was enveloped in sound and flame, and our ears just couldn't cope.

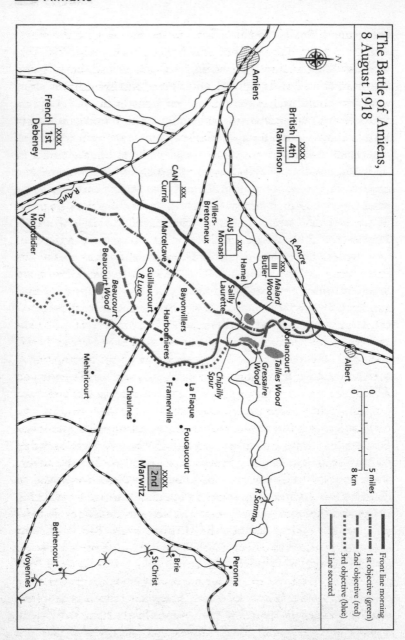

The Battle of Amiens, 8 August 1918

British 4th xxxx Rawlinson

French 1st xxxx Debeney

CAN Currie xxx

AUS Monash xxx

III Butler xxx

2nd xxxx Marwitz

Amiens

Albert

R. Avre

R. Luce

R. Ancre

R. Somme

To Montdidier

Villers-Bretonneux

Marcelcave

Guillaucourt

Beaucourt Wood

Beaucourt

Méharicourt

Harbonnières

Bayonvillers

Chaulnes

Hamel

Sailly Laurette

Malard Wood

Morlancourt

Tailles Wood

Gressaire Wood

Chipilly Spur

La Flaque

Framerville

Foucaucourt

Bethencourt

Voyennes

St Christ

Brie

Péronne

0 5 miles
0 8 km

Front line morning
1st objective (green)
2nd objective (red)
3rd objective (blue)
Line secured

The ground shook.'[32] Senior officers to the rear watched the whole horizon light up. On the front line, Major Coutts wrote, 'The battery of 18-pounders just behind us which had been firing intermittently all night, opened with a burst, and immediately afterwards we could hear every gun on our front open up.'[33] Captain Smeddle was impressed by the suddenness of it: 'It broke the silence with a terrific crashing roar, flashes were spurting up from all around where we were standing. It was still dark, but the flashes of the guns gave out sufficient light to distinguish the forms of the gunners and guns, the nearest of which was twenty-five yards from where I was standing, and so quietly had everything been prepared that I was not aware of its presence until it started firing.'[34] Rawlinson had been determined to concentrate as much artillery as he could for the attack. There were around 2000 guns in the 4th Army sector against just over 500 on the German side. There was a light gun every 29 yards (27 metres) along the front and a heavy gun every 59 yards (54 metres). New methods meant that it was one of the most sudden, accurate barrages of the war so far. German artillery pieces had been identified by aerial photography and their positions fixed by the latest sound-ranging microphones. Meteorological information and data about each barrel's wear and muzzle velocity were taken into account, as were measurements of propellant charge temperature and variations in shell weight. The result was a precision unimaginable only a year or two before. Two-thirds of the heaviest artillery, around 650 barrels, were targeting German guns in a 'counter-battery programme'. Before the attack, 504 out of 530 German guns had been identified. It was vital to destroy them because they could do immense damage to attacking troops and they were the only German weapons capable of destroying tanks. Against them, the British guns had sufficient high-explosive and phosgene gas shells to fire four rounds a minute for four hours. As Witherby the artilleryman passed through one position, 'I could see the gunners sweating and heaving to their work, hard work too, as well I know.'[35] German gunners were killed, dazed or forced to abandon their guns. The rest of the British artillery pounded other identified strongpoints, such as machine gun nests. The lighter guns, or field artillery, began to fire a creeping barrage to shield the advancing infantry, moving forward at the same speed: 100 yards (90 metres) every three minutes.

As soon as the barrage started to roar overhead, the infantry clambered out of their positions and pushed into no man's land. Their first objective was what was called the Green Line, about 3500–4000 yards (3200–3700 metres) into German-held territory. This was the limit of the 'creeper'. Once they had secured this line, the front-line soldiers would wait. They would be protected from counter-attacks by a wall of high explosive and shrapnel from their artillery while other guns were dragged forward and another creeping barrage could be laid down. Following this barrage, a second wave of troops would 'leapfrog' the first and push on for another 2000–5000 yards (1800–4600 metres) towards the Red Line. The final objective, the Blue Line, lay 4000–5000 yards (3650–4600metres) beyond the Red Line. The plan was to push on towards that line if resistance was not too stiff. On the northern edge of the battlefield, on the north bank of the Somme, the British III Corps attacked. It was difficult ground, dotted with thick woods and steep gullies which made it unsuitable for tanks. To make matters worse, two days previously an elite German division had raided British trenches and upset preparations for the attack. Perhaps warned by news brought back from this raid, the German troops seemed ready and British progress was slow. German batteries fired gas and the British troops were forced to attack wearing their gas masks.

THE AUSTRALIANS

To the south of the river, things were different. The Australian troops 'hugged' their creeping barrage tightly: they believed that if you weren't sustaining friendly casualties from your own 'creeper', then you weren't close enough behind it. 'It was just getting light, but there was a heavy fog, so thick you could not see more than ten yards in front of you,' wrote Major Coutts. It was made even more opaque by the smoke shells fired as part of the barrage to confuse the Germans. The Australians were highly motivated and straining to get at their enemy. Coutts attended to a soldier who had sustained a leg wound, but could not stop him from rejoining the fight: 'He wanted to go back – he said he wouldn't miss the stunt for anything.'[36] The four advancing Australian brigades had 12 tanks each to help them deal with any serious opposition. The initial wave of men was only lightly armed, and some of them laid white tape for the tanks about 100 yards (90 metres) behind them. Behind the tanks came sections of eight men walking in single file, with plenty of space between each file. The following waves brought machine guns, so that if the first troops found a strong-point, they could bypass it and leave it to the men behind. At first there was no danger from German artillery. In the words of the 4th Army's Chief of Staff, Major General Sir Archibald Montgomery, the German guns were 'deluged by a hurricane bombardment and neutralised to such an extent that hostile artillery retaliation was almost negligible'.[37]

Deprived of vital artillery support, caught totally by surprise and terrified by the rumble of the tanks, the German infantry was over-whelmed. The effectiveness of the 'creeper' was such that, by the time it had passed over a German dugout and the occupants could climb out into the open, the Australians were on top of them and there was little option but to surrender. Occasionally the Australians lost their way in the murk and pockets of German resistance flared up as a result. Coutts remembers that the advancing troops 'had evidently missed some machine gun positions in the fog, and the Huns were still firing'. But each time they were dealt with by the available Lewis guns, rifle grenades and portable trench mortars.

Tank–infantry cooperation varied greatly along the line. Some Canadian infantrymen (who had less experience of working with tanks than the Australians) claimed after the battle that the tanks had not been much help – they were slow, kept breaking down and were too vulnerable to German guns. Others were full of praise for the tanks: the official account by a battalion in the 1st Canadian Division stated after the battle that, 'it is very doubtful if we would have been able to have gotten forward without considerable manoeuvring and reinforcements if it had not been for the timely intervention of a tank, which exterminated a series of machine gun nests which held up the whole battalion'.[38] The Australians seemed particularly pleased with their tanks. One infantryman wrote, 'Whenever we found ourselves in trouble we signalled to the tanks, and they turned towards the obstacle. Then *punk-crash, punk-crash*! … another German post was blown to pieces.'[39]

In some cases, though, the Germans put up bitter resistance until the end. D.G. Denison of the Royal Tank Corps remembers 'firing the gun as fast as I could put the belts of ammo on it. I could not see any Germans, but I knew we were over their trenches, on account of the stick bombs they were flinging at us.' Minutes later, 'I was firing my gun, when something hit it with a crack and it was smashed completely on the outside. The butt hit me in the mouth and split my top lip open. Blood poured from my mouth and I felt a bit queer.'[40] While tanks appeared terrifying enough to the enemy, the experience of being in one was no less dreadful. After a day of exhausting noise and asphyxiating fumes, their crewmen often had to be hospitalized. When Denison's crewmate went quiet and Denison 'thought he had been hit. I switched on the lights for a few seconds. There was poor Taffy on his knees praying or weeping like a child. I remember shouting to him "Taffy, get your gun going or we are all killed." But it was of no use, his nerve had completely gone.'[41]

By 7.15 a.m. on 8 August the Australians had reached their first objective. The troops stopped and reorganised for two hours. Two fresh divisions pushed through and were ready for the next phase of the move forward. It was one of the most spectacular advances ever seen on the Western Front. But to the south the Canadians were not having quite so easy a time.

THE CANADIANS

The ground over which the Canadians were attacking was rougher and more broken than the Australians' patch; in particular the River

Luce was a serious obstacle. To make matters worse, their artillery barrage had been slightly less effective than that of the Australians, thanks to all the guns having had to register silently: photographs and maths were still not as efficient as a few trial shots. In addition, the Canadians' flank was exposed to German fire because the French 1st Army, to the right of the Canadians, did not move off the start line at the same moment. The French, rather conservatively, insisted on firing a 40-minute artillery barrage before they advanced. Nevertheless the robust Canadians, who had had no chance to reconnoitre the ground over which they were attacking, made good progress. The 4th Brigade ran into fierce resistance from a trench about 1000 yards (900 metres) east of its start line. Tanks were successfully called in and the Germans killed or captured. Witherby passed over the ground just after the infantry. 'I remember seeing 4 or 5 men with a sergeant lying in a small bunch, cut down by the Huns' machine guns, just in front of his trenches, but in the trenches and a little way back, the German dead lay thick, I never saw anything like it…. they had certainly been caught on the jump by our barrage, and our infantry.'[42] The village of Marcelcave proved to be a centre of fierce German resistance. The Canadians attacked frontally from the west and in a left hook at the village's northern flank, but it took three quarters of an hour to clear: one tank had to move from machine gun to machine gun-crushing weapons and crews beneath its tracks. The tank commander wanted to prove that it was he who took the village: so before handing over responsibility to the infantry he made sure, rather incongruously, that he had obtained a receipt.

On the far south of their advance the Canadians had to straddle the River Luce. It could not be forded and there was a marsh stretching for up to 200 yards (180 metres) on either bank. The Canadians controlled only a small bridgehead on the south side of the river. To expand it, the 43rd Battalion, supported by some tanks, was tasked to seize some higher ground further from the river. The 43rd was therefore at the southern edge of the entire army. It was thought that a full-frontal assault would be too costly, so they enveloped the objective and attacked from flank and rear. It was a superb set-piece attack. With the high ground seized, the rest of the Canadian 3rd divisions could move eastwards along the line of the Luce. As the sun burned off the mist between 7 and 8 a.m., the Canadians reached the Green Line. They were a little behind schedule but felt that it was excusable.

Behind both the Canadian and Australian sectors the artillerymen strained to get their guns moved forward and support the next phase of the advance. Herbert Witherby was part of that desperate effort but had time to notice that, 'It was a fine hot day, a typical August morning, just such a day that in Western Canada puts the finishing touch to the ripening wheat.... We were travelling fast, the sweat was rolling down my face, the shells were bursting everywhere.... Machine gun bullets also whistled over us from the left flank.... there was no time to consider anything at such a time.... the mist and smoke was lifting fast now, and we could see further around us. On our right was a shallow trench, used by the Germans that morning, and some dead Germans were lying there.' Throughout the morning they would stop the advance every so often, unlimber the guns and provide artillery support. Witherby's fire was being directed by, 'our forward observation officer, still in touch with the infantry, [who] sent word back to us all day by means of mounted men of the battery.... and at times by signallers using their flags'. As the hours passed, he noticed groups of prisoners heading back to the British lines, 'in some cases absolutely unattended, only too glad to get out of battle'. Witherby's main impression of the day was, 'of tanks, infantry, cavalry and transport, all going forward, a wonderful sight.... Here indeed was true open warfare.'[43]

By now, too, the RAF could make itself felt on the battlefield. There had been a huge build-up of aircraft for the offensive, in all 800 British and over 1000 French. They would perform a wide range of tasks. At dawn RAF bombers had hoped to attack German aerodromes, supply dumps and railway stations but the mist had prevented them doing so. Other planes observed the progress of the battle and tried to keep Rawlinson's staff up to date with the advance. One squadron had been specially trained to cooperate with tanks. Others tried to direct artillery fire. Eight squadrons scoured the battlefield, attacking ground targets with bombs and machine guns. Some RAF planes attempted to drop ammunition to advancing troops. Between 9 a.m. and midday the RAF were at their best. There were too few German planes in the air to stop them machine-gunning, bombing and dropping smoke to screen the allied advance. German staff cars were shot up and lorries blown off the road by phosphorus bombs. But as the afternoon progressed the Germans were able to redeploy aircraft from other fronts and the two sides were caught up in giant dogfights above the battlefield.

BRITISH SETBACKS

The British III Corps in the north found the difficult terrain and lack of tanks too much for them. By the time they cleared Mallard Wood their creeping barrage had disappeared ahead of them. As they emerged from the wood at around 9 a.m. to attack the imposing Chipilly Spur, they were pinned down by intense machine gun fire and could make no progress. The open fields offered no cover against well-sited German defences on the Spur, which was protected by a steep ravine between them and the attacking British. One battalion, the 10th Essex, comprised overwhelmingly of teenagers, took advantage of the fog and made an impressive advance of over 2000 yards (1800 metres) beyond their Green Line objectives. However, they found themselves attacked from their right and left by seasoned German troops and had no choice but to conduct a fighting retreat to the Green Line. At the end of it all, the battalion, which had gone into battle with around 500 officers and men, was reduced to a pathetic group of about 15.[44] The battle here, north of the Somme, was getting bogged down into an old-fashioned stalemate. The whole of III Corps, which should have reached the initial Green Line by 8 a.m., had only just made it by the end of the day.

The British delay was to jeopardise the Australians to the south of them. As their northernmost units pushed on from the Green Line at 8.20 a.m. they came under fire from German guns on the other side of the Somme, which the British had failed to silence. Despite this setback, the rest of their attack was going well. The Australians were supported closely by an artillery brigade that would fire in support then limber up and dash forward. The two attacking divisions had 30 Mark V tanks which had not yet been used and also a number of Mark V* tanks: the latter were longer and transported a squad of infantry armed with Lewis light machine guns – part of the relentless quest to get firepower forward safely and quickly. But on account of the fumes and noise inside the tank, the machine-gunners were virtually unable to fight once they alighted.

BREAKTHROUGH

The Australians moved forward at a rate that no unit of the BEF had managed since 1914. The battle became the sum of hundreds of small actions as these experienced veterans advanced. When resistance was encountered, there would be a vicious localized fight. Sergeant G.H. Robertson remembers one vividly: '[We] had reached our objective and were lying and crawling about in a shallow sunken road and Wylie lifted his head to look at a machine-gun position opposite when he was hit right in the throat. Within a few minutes Wylie, a man named O'Mara ... Davies ... and Curly Hendry ... were killed and Male was also mortally wounded ... they were buried at Harbonnières. Wylie was a short chap, slightly bow-legged. I think he came from Scotland. He had his leave there a short while before. He was a good soldier and a decent little chap.'[45]

Such encounters usually ended with the Australians destroying the enemy position themselves or with the help of the tanks. The infantry used Lewis guns, of which there were now as many as 50 in a battalion, to pin the Germans down.[46] Their comrades would then work around the flanks and attack from the rear, often finishing the job with grenades. The 4th Australian Division was held up by the fire from across the Somme, but to their south the 5th Australian reached the Red Line at 9 a.m., well ahead of schedule. Coutts remembers, 'About 9 o'clock all the roads on both sides of us were crammed with traffic lines of motor lorries pulling guns and loaded with ammunition, armoured cars, field guns ... moving slowly forward in long lines.'[47]

The tyranny of the trenches had, for a moment, been lifted. The light armour streamed into the open countryside. Behind the heavy tanks the mounted cavalry, light Whippet tanks and armoured cars looked for their opportunity to burst through and thrust deep into the enemy's rear. Twelve armoured cars of the Tank Corps' 17th Battalion made a dash through enemy lines along the Amiens–Brie road, and when they reached the village of La Flaque they were greeted by the kind of spectacle that was soon to become every tank commander's dream: the road was choked with transport vehicles, reinforcements, horse-drawn carts and staff cars. The crewmen in the armoured cars fired until their barrels glowed hot. Horses panicked and bolted. Lorries smashed into each other. Collisions blocked the road. The British cars moved on to the road itself and progressed along it, some going north, others south towards Framerville. Men stationed in the rear, used to being well away from the fighting, suddenly found their offices being machine-gunned. At Framerville, the British Whippets surprised the headquarter staff of the German 51st Corps as they ate lunch. They fled, leaving behind documents that contained crucial details of the Hindenburg Line defences. The cars patrolled until dusk, when they returned to British lines. Almost half of them were too damaged to be of further use; but, remarkably, there were no serious casualties among their crews.

The Canadian infantry set off at 8.20 a.m. from the Green Line and headed for the second objective, the Red Line. Resistance varied, but shortly after midday they achieved their Red Line goals, although just beyond the village of Guillaucourt the remaining 1500 yards (1370 metres) to the Red Line cost them 200 casualties. The Canadians also sent their more mobile units into the German rear. One ambitious attempt to give infantrymen extra mobility ended when the Canadian Cyclists' Battalion pedalled forward but were held up by German machine guns. More success was enjoyed

■ AMIENS

▲ General Sir Douglas Haig, commander of the BEF, reviewing Canadian troops after the Battle of Amiens. Although blamed by many for the losses of the previous two years, he was quick to see the merits of Rawlinson's plan for Amiens and gave him all the troops and armour he needed.

▲ Hauling British 60-lb guns into position, Amiens 9 August 1918. Artillery was vital at Amiens; the advancing infantry needed the constant support of heavy weapons like these. The teams had to manoeuvre the guns forward to new positions as quickly as possible.

and petrol had leaked down into the crew compartment. The floor was flooded and the toxic fumes threatened to overwhelm the crew. By 2 p.m. the heat was unbearable and the crew could only breathe using their box respirators. Arnold was further forward than any other unit in the 4th Army except the armoured cars, which were operating 2 miles (3 km) away to the north. Musical Box now stumbled on a road packed with transport. For a whole hour it cruised up and down this road, machine-gunning and causing mayhem.

At 3 p.m. the inevitable occurred: a glancing blow from a field gun caused the fuel washing around inside the hull to catch fire. Arnold forced the door open and dragged two members of his crew out into the fresh air. They rolled on the ground, trying to put out their burning clothes. Germans rushed up, killed the driver and beat the others severely – no doubt expressing a sense of frustration at their impotence against the British tanks. Arnold was put in solitary confinement for five days before being sent to a POW camp.

The tank action was a glimpse into the future of warfare. Musical Box had shown how armour could penetrate deep into the enemy's rear and cause chaos. Overhead, that other new arm of Britain's forces, the RAF, was demonstrating what it could do. However, the day was to highlight airpower's limitations as well as its advantages. As the fog cleared during the morning, the RAF was dominant on the battlefield, strafing, reporting to HQ on the position of friendly troops and helping spot for the artillery. During the afternoon, however, German reinforcements were rushed to the battle zone. The fight that ensued was one of the most intense fights of the entire war. Eighteen-year-old pilot Harold Taylor was making his first combat flight: 'So far, we had had the sky to ourselves, but as we turned for home I became aware of a number of black specks on our left, rapidly growing into a flight of enemy scouts. They did not dive on us, but hung behind, peppering away at the end machines of the V formation. Everyone of us opened up with his two Lewis guns, and I had my first sight of a machine sent down in flames. As he got closer to the British lines he noticed a number of machines carrying out most wonderful evolutions. There must have been twenty, twisting and turning like worms writhing in a fisherman's bait tin.'[49] He was witnessing a giant dogfight. But his job was not to get involved. He and his comrades were bombers: they had just struck an ammunition dump and they had to get back to base to be rearmed.

By mid-afternoon RAF commanders decided to focus over-whelmingly on bombing the bridges over the Somme at Peronne, Brie, St Christ, Voyennes and other places which were swarming with retreating German troops. If the bridges could be destroyed, the Germans would be cut off from escape and no reinforcements would get through. It was hugely ambitious. The small bombs car-ried by the British biplanes probably would not have been able to blow up the big stone bridges, even if they had scored direct hits. To try to hit them, the pilots had to fly low, straight and steady towards the structures, making them easy prey for the ever-increasing num-bers of German planes. It was thought worth the risk. All other bombing raids were cancelled and 205 sorties flown against the bridges; some pilots flew as many as three missions. German aircraft hammered the British from their airbases right next to the bridges, and the RAF did little damage to make up for their serious losses. That day 45 British aircraft failed to return to base and a further 52 were so badly damaged that they had to be written off. This was about 13 per cent of their total strength – too much for one day's fighting. They also lost 80 trained personnel, who died because their commanders had been over-ambitious. One day airpower would become the decisive force on the battlefield, striking deep into enemy territory and delivering accurate munitions which would change the course of the battle on the ground. But not in 1918, and not with wood and canvas biplanes and 25-lb (11-kg) bombs.

The French attack south of the Canadians had been successful too. They advanced up to 5 miles (8 km) and took a good haul of German prisoners. Their action made the Canadian advance far more secure than it would have been otherwise. As the sun set on 8 August, it was clear that this had been one of the most successful days the Allies had yet seen on the Western Front. The Australians had pushed 6 miles (nearly 10 km) into the German lines, the Canadians up to 8 miles (nearly 13 km). The exhausted troops dug holes in the ground to provide a little warmth and cover from German shells and bombs. Witherby's battery stumbled across a loft full of carrier pigeons and they all had two each for dinner. Coutts grabbed a few hours of sleep on a stretcher in a captured German trench; it 'was very comfortable there, except [it] smelled very strongly of Hun cigars, and butts were lying about everywhere'.[50]

CARRYING ON THE OFFENSIVE

But there was to be no let-up in the fighting. Haig visited Rawlinson during the 8th and became so excited by the progress made that he ordered a further push on the 9th. Outposts should be 'thrown forward' and 'touch maintained with the enemy'.[51] Clearly he thought the Germans were in headlong retreat. In fact, the German machine was rumbling into action. Nine new divisions would arrive at the front before the end of the 9th. Meanwhile, the exhausted Canadians, French, British and Australians had not slept properly for two consecutive nights. As so often, Haig's imagination was running away with him. Artillery plans had to be drawn up fast to combat German batteries which had not been identified by aerial reconnaissance. Reinforcements were promised and then withdrawn. Planning was not done with the meticulous care that had launched the original assault. Fewer than half the tanks of the day before were still available, because of battle damage and exhausted crews.

Even so, 9 August was more successful than most second-day offensives on the Western Front. Although RAF support was reduced because of its preoccupation with the Somme bridges, the British line moved forward a further 3 miles (5 km). It was a ragged advance: 16 brigades attacked, but they did so at 13 different times. Some received good artillery support, others very little. The whole affair was far less coordinated than it had been on the 8th. The Americans made an outstanding contribution. A regiment from the 33rd division was thrown into battle to help the struggling III Corps north of the Somme, and assisted the British in taking the

Chipilly Spur and Gressaire Wood which had held them up the previous day.

On the 10th the impetus of the 4th Army's offensive drained away. It had not been planned as a sustained push, and there is evidence that even the staff did not want to continue: they had succeeded in their intention to inflict a short but costly defeat on the German army. By the 10th tank strength was a small fraction of what it had been at dawn on the 8th and many of the troops were in no state to fight. Even so, the Canadians advanced 2 miles (3 km), and in front of the French the Germans carried out a planned withdrawal. Alarmingly, the old 1916 battlefield of the Somme now stretched in front of the 4th Army. Shellholes pock-marked the ground, while rusting wire and old trenches criss-crossed the terrain. The German reinforcements had arrived and were exacting a heavy price for any ground they gave up. Divisional commanders asked Haig to halt the offensive. On the 11th only 38 tanks were in action and the Australians and Canadians took very little ground. Rawlinson talked to Haig and advised a pause so that they could

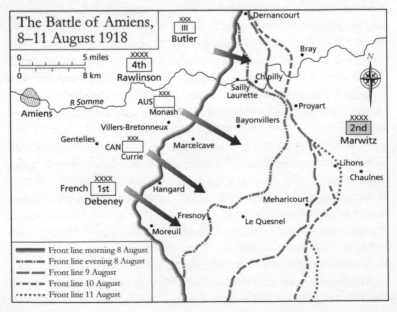

The Battle of Amiens,
8–11 August 1918

0   5 miles
0   8 km

XXX III Butler
XXXX 4th Rawlinson
R Somme
Amiens
AUS XXX Monash
Villers-Bretonneux
Gentelles
CAN XXX Currie
XXXX French 1st Debeney
Hangard
Marcelcave
Moreuil
Fresnoy
Dernancourt
Bray
Chipilly
Sailly Laurette
Proyart
Bayonvillers
XXXX 2nd Marwitz
Lihons
Chaulnes
Meharicourt
Le Quesnel

N

Front line morning 8 August
Front line evening 8 August
Front line 9 August
Front line 10 August
Front line 11 August

plan another set-piece battle. That afternoon Rawlinson told his corps commanders that there would be a halt to combat operations. The Battle of Amiens was over.

Just after it ended Rawlinson wrote to a fellow general, Sir Henry Wilson, 'I think we have given the Boche a pretty good bump this time.'[52] They certainly had. The German casualties on the first day were nearly 30,000 – about 9000 men killed or seriously injured and a remarkable 18,000 taken prisoner. During the rest of the battle, the British and French captured nearly 10,000 more men. General von der Marwitz, commander of the German 2nd Army, is said to have admitted the loss of 400 guns on 8 August alone. The 4th Army had made a hugely impressive 12-mile (19-km) advance at the cost of only 4000 men killed and around another 5000 wounded. But the most important result of the battle was that it marked a watershed in the relative performances of the British and German armies. The BEF had found a way to break the stalemate on the Western Front, and its skilful use of all-arms tactics limited the cost to itself. It would now be able to do something the Germans had failed to do earlier in the year: it could keep hammering away at the enemy line with these kinds of limited attack almost indefinitely. For their part, the German troops had collapsed in an unprecedented fashion. Six entire divisions had fallen apart under the British onslaught. The fighting spirit of German units differed greatly. In some cases whole companies had surrendered to single men.[53] Retreating troops even abused and jeered at reinforcements, accusing them of prolonging the war. Tanks too had played a big part. One German prisoner said of his comrades, 'Their sense of duty is sufficient to make them fight against infantry, but if tanks appear, many feel that they are justified in surrendering.'[54] Yet in other sectors, as Witherby witnessed, 'nearly every hole had a dead German machine-gunner in or near it, proving how they stuck to their post and died at it. We remarked "what a pity they were not fighting for a better cause."'[55]

Winston Churchill visited the front on 9 August and saw files of prisoners heading for captivity. As an ex-prisoner of war himself he felt sorry for their lot, but he noticed that 'the woe begotten expression of the officers contrasted sharply with the almost cheerful countenances of the rank and file'.[56] Hindenburg was appalled by the news from the front. 'I had no illusions,' he wrote later, 'about the political effects of our defeat on August 8th.... The failure of August 8th was revealed to all eyes as the consequences of an open weakness. To fail in an attack was a very different matter from being vanquished on the defence.'[57]

THE BLACK DAY

It was Germany's worst defeat of the war. Even the Austrians came close to panic: a German representative at the Hapsburg court in Vienna wrote that the news of Amiens hit the Austrian people like a 'sledgehammer' and 'the emperor himself is profoundly affected'.[58] When Ludendorff read the reports of the collapse of his men he was left in no doubt. He later wrote, 'August 8th was the black day of the German army in the history of this war. This was the worst experience I had to go through ... it put the decline of our fighting powers beyond all doubt. The army had ceased to be a perfect fighting instrument.'[59] Ludendorff's belief in victory had been shattered; he offered his resignation to the Kaiser, who refused to accept it. In the days that followed he had seizures and became uncontrollably neurotic and unable to make complex decisions. A psychologist told him to get plenty of rest and sing German folk songs first thing in the morning.[60] Ludendorff refused to sanction the sensible step of withdrawing his forces to the Hindenburg Line, because he was worried that during the retreat the army might collapse totally. Amiens had shown him that he could not win the war, and the best the Germans could now hope for was a compromise peace which left them in possession of some of their wartime gains. On the 11th he told the Kaiser simply, 'The war must be terminated.'[61]

The men of the BEF knew that this was a decisive moment. Captain Oliver Woodward of the 1st Australian Tunnelling Company wrote, with forgivable bias about the role of his own corps, 'Only those present can understand the great feeling of relief which followed the glorious attack of the Australian Corps. For some months we had seemed to be living under the fear that the enemy might at any moment launch another great attack, which possibly might be as successful as his early one. We were up and about before zero hour on the 8th, wondering what success would be ours in the coming attack. We were to measure swords with the enemy. Failure might mean anything. Yet at 9 a.m. we felt once again we were on top, and that we would eventually win the war ... all recognized that we had the game well in hand and eventually the winning goal would be kicked. Our whole viewpoint has been changed in a few hours.'[62]

King George V visited the 4th Army on 12 August. He decorated several men from the American 33rd division as their band played 'The Star Spangled Banner' and 'God Save the King'. He then knighted John Monash, the commander of the Australian Corps who had contributed so much, both with the outstanding performance of the men under his command and in his development of tactics that would break the stalemate of the trenches. The real achievement of Amiens had been the triumphant coordination of an all-arms attack. It was the first truly modern battle.

It was also the beginning of the 'hundred days' in which German forces in the West were driven back and brought so close to total destruction that on 11 November their government was forced to ask for an armistice. The BEF was the main engine of this offensive, which in terms of scale remains the greatest campaign in British history. As Professor Harris has argued, it is also probably the campaign in which forces under British command exercised the most influence on the history of the world in the twentieth century.[63] After Amiens, blow after blow forced the Germans back. Not even the mighty Hindenburg Line could protect them: it was penetrated by British divisions, largely without the help of tanks, in October. British war reporter Philip Gibbs followed the army from Amiens: 'It is now the enemy who is on the defensive, dreading the hammer blows that fall upon him day after day, and the initiative of attack is so completely in our hands that we are able to strike him at many different places.'[64] But these victories came at a high price.

In 1918 the British suffered more casualties than in any other year in history – more casualties than during the whole of the Second World War.

As for the Germans, Ernst Jünger is unambiguous about their morale by the end of August: 'There was not a man who did not know we were on a precipitous descent, and the fact was accepted with an equanimity that only the moral force, which in every army accompanies its armed force, can explain. Every man knew that victory could no longer be ours. But the enemy should know that he fought against men of honour.'[65]

The fighting in the first half of 1918 almost ended in German victory and British withdrawal from the European continent. But the BEF and its Allies had clung on and by late summer they had developed the tactical skill to combine their various arms and inflict a series of crushing defeats on the Germans. Armies of tradesmen, office clerks and factory workers had come of age. The Battle of Amiens was the beginning. From 8 August onwards they took on, and defeated, the best army in the world, bringing to an end what had been the most terrible war in history.

MIDWAY

The crews woke well before dawn, breakfasted quickly and then hurried to their stations. On each of the four great carriers, aircraft were filled with fuel. Type 80, 800 kg (1700 lb) land attack bombs rolled along on carts, together with torpedoes, each weighing well over three-quarters of a ton (nearly 700 lb). Once armed and fuelled, each plane weighed up to 4 tons and it took a team of a dozen or more men to push it along the hangar deck to the elevator that would hoist it to the flight deck. The pilots were allowed to sleep till 2.45 a.m. The climb from the lower decks in heavy cotton flying suits and helmets had them sweating. They gathered round the air officer, who issued them with a final brief on the weather and their mission. When he had finished he looked up and said curtly, '*Kakare!*' (Get to it!)[1] On the illuminated flight deck the crewmen revved the engines of the planes to 1000 rpm. At 4.26 a.m. the signal lights on the longest carrier began blinking instructions to the other three. Together they formed four corners of a huge square – 5 miles (8 km) apart and protected by a screen of cruisers and destroyers. This was *Kido Butai*, the Imperial Japanese Navy's First Carrier Strike Force, the finest unit of its kind in the world. From the bridge of his flagship, the *Akagi*, Vice Admiral Chuichi Nagumo nodded solemnly to a staff officer. His order was transmitted to the flight deck where an officer swung a red lantern in a great circle. The pilot of the first plane yelled, '*Ikimasu!*' (I'm going!). His aircraft tore along the length of the deck and lifted off, clearing the bows of the ship, out over the vast Pacific Ocean. The jubilant crew cheered and waved their white caps wildly.

It was the beginning of one of the most decisive days of warfare in history. By the battle's end the balance of the Second World War in the Pacific would be irretrievably reversed. Some of the world's mightiest ships would be sunk and thousands of men would die. The battle took its name from an island which is, appropriately, halfway between Japan and the United States of America; a small atoll that was about to be the target of *Kido Butai's* dawn strike: Midway.

THE NEW POWER IN THE EAST

This attack on Midway Island on 5 June 1942 represented the culmination of half a century of imperial expansion. During that time, Japan had carried out a remarkable series of advances across mainland Asia and vast swathes of the Pacific. In the 1890s it had wrested control of the Korean peninsula from China. It had surprised Russia's Far East fleet at Port Arthur in 1904, and destroyed another Russian fleet in a decisive naval encounter in the Tsushima strait, between Japan and Korea, the following year. By 1937 radical nationalists had taken over the Japanese government, and the incursions into northern China that had started in 1931 escalated into a full-scale war that was to last eight years. But it was an expensive affair. Far from providing the Japanese with resources not available in their home islands, the war in China only put their own meagre reserves of oil, rubber and timber under huge strain. There were, however, plentiful supplies elsewhere in the region. European-owned territories such as Malaya and the Dutch East Indies had enough of these commodities to make Japan self-sufficient. Japanese ambitions began to extend into South-East Asia, and the theory of *nanshin-ron*, 'advance in the south', was born.[2]

The USA viewed the rise of Japan with growing unease. The American people had no stomach for foreign entanglements, but their President, Franklin Delano Roosevelt, did what he could to help China. His alarm at Japan's expansion was heightened by the early progress of the Second World War in Europe. Hitler was allied with Japan, and in 1940 his rapid occupation of France and the Netherlands and his threat to invade Britain made their empires in Asia vulnerable. The door to South-East Asia was wide open to Japan's armies, which were already rampant in eastern China. Roosevelt refused to tolerate further Japanese expansion, and announced a trade embargo on the country.

Japan's economy was reliant on American trade, but its reaction was defiant. Its leaders, thoroughly indoctrinated with the spirit of *bushido*, a chivalric warrior code dating back to the twelfth century and now enjoying a revival, could accept an honourable defeat on the field of battle but not slow strangulation by American business-men. There was to be no caving in; Japan would continue to fight China and would become self-sufficient by seizing the oil and other resources of South-East Asia, even if that meant having to defeat the Americans.

The United States was not a mighty military power when the Second World War broke out in Europe. After the First World War it had retreated into isolationism and slashed its armed forces. Its army was now small and lacked armoured vehicles. In an era of rap-idly evolving aviation, most US aircraft were obsolete. For their defence, the Americans relied on the vast Atlantic and Pacific Oceans and on the ships of the US navy which patrolled them. But although America may have been militarily weaker than Japan, its economy was infinitely stronger. The USA produced 4.5 million automobiles in 1941, Japan just 48,000. Even more worryingly for the Japanese, in response to their aggression and that of Germany, Roosevelt had launched a massive programme of rearmament in the summer of 1940. He was now spending billions of dollars on new ships and aircraft for the US navy. Japan's leaders realized that if they were to strike at America it would have to be soon.

The architect of Japan's assault was Admiral Isoroku Yamamoto, a veteran of the Japanese victory over the Russians at Tsushima in 1905, when he lost two fingers on his left hand. Subsequently, he studied at Harvard and become naval attaché in Washington. During that time, he travelled the country and advised his fellow diplomats not to take taxis but to catch the bus in order to get the measure of the American people. He was a proponent of naval air-power since the 1920s, and helped develop some of the most advanced aircraft in the world. Yamamoto was an inveterate gambler, addicted to poker, and believed that to beat America he would have to stake everything on one hand: he would destroy the US fleet with a pre-emptive strike, followed by a 'decisive battle' if necessary. Yamamoto threatened to resign if the reluctant naval general staff did not go along with his plan. They capitulated, and gave the admiral the go-ahead to plan a giant assault on America's Pacific fleet.

PEARL HARBOR

Roosevelt had moved most of the ships of this fleet from US mainland bases to the base at Pearl Harbor on the Hawaiian island of Oahu. This move was supposed to beef up the US presence in the Pacific, but it also had the unintended effect of bringing the entire fleet within range of Japan's most potent naval strike weapon – its fleet of aircraft carriers. Yamamoto planned to use the combined airpower of no fewer than six of his carriers to attack Pearl Harbor and destroy the American Pacific fleet.

Pearl Harbor was, and still is, a great posting. The warm climate, the beaches that line the shore and the bars of Honolulu ensure that there is rarely a dull moment. In early December 1941 the naval base was humming with activity. For the first time in months all the battleships were in port. But the fleet's carriers were not. Two of them, the *Enterprise* and the *Lexington*, were on special missions. USS *Saratoga* was having a refit in San Diego, California. The US navy's other four carriers, the *Hornet*, the *Yorktown*, the *Wasp* and the *Ranger*, were in the Atlantic.

The commander of the fleet, Admiral Husband Kimmel, was perturbed that his staff did not know the whereabouts of the Japanese carriers. But it was not a disaster: they had lost touch with them twelve times in the last six months. When he asked his operations officer in the first week of December what the chances were of a surprise attack on Pearl, the reply came back instantly, 'None.'[3] Lieutenant General Walter Short, commander of the land forces in Hawaii, was worried about the 158,000 civilians on the islands who were of Japanese blood: strange phone calls to Tokyo had been intercepted. Washington was issuing vague warnings of the need for increased vigilance at Pearl. On the night of 6 December Short discussed the latest intelligence and ordered that all the island's aircraft be taken out of their hangars and lined up neatly on the runways so that they could be guarded against sabotage. On his way home he looked down on the blazing lights of the naval base and said, 'Isn't that a beautiful sight? What a target they would make.'[4]

At that moment, less than 300 miles (just under 500 km) to the west, 6 Japanese carriers, with 22 escort ships, were steaming towards the Hawaiian islands. Takeshi Maeda, a torpedo bomber pilot, remembered, 'In the briefing room on *Akagi*, for the first time it was announced that we were to attack Pearl Harbor. There was a large model of it on the table. I thought to myself, "Oh my God, we are going to go to war with America!" I felt a bit afraid, but I couldn't show it as I was a military man.'[5] Yamamoto issued a final, stirring radio message to the men of the *Kido Butai*, the First Carrier Strike Force: 'The moment has arrived. The rise or fall of our empire is at stake.' Cheers echoed through the hulls of the ships. In the engine room of the *Akagi*, chief engineer Tanbo heard the cheers on the voice tube and wept with pride.[6]

At 6 a.m. on 7 December 1941, the carriers swung into the wind and the pilots of the first wave took off. Their uniforms were freshly pressed. Many wore traditional *hashamaki* headbands. They had eaten a special ceremonial breakfast of *sekihan* rice boiled with tiny red beans washed down with saki. The first wave of 183 planes was followed just over an hour later by a further 167 aircraft – a mix of fighters, dive bombers, torpedo bombers and high-level horizontal bombers.[7] Sailors on the decks cheered. Commander Tsukamoto, the navigation officer on the carrier *Shokaku*, decided it was the greatest moment of his life.[8] But the commander of *Kido Butai*, Chuichi Nagumo, was less euphoric: he had always worried that Yamamoto's plan was too risky. Now he watched impassively from the bridge of the *Akagi*. The die was cast.

On the north tip of Oahu the army's mobile radar station was having a quiet morning. The system had been running only since November and it was plagued by faults. When a giant blip appeared at 7.02 a.m. the operator assumed at first it was a malfunction, but a further check revealed a swarm of planes coming in from the north, 137 miles (220 km) from Oahu. A call went back to a situation room where Lieutenant Tyler was on duty. His entire staff had gone to breakfast and he had only drawn this duty once before. He was not concerned, assuming it to be a group of US B-17 bombers flying in from the mainland, or some of the carriers' aircraft returning to Hawaii. 'Don't worry about it,'[9] he said.

A few minutes before, gunfire had rumbled around the harbour. A destroyer, the USS *Ward*, had spotted a submarine periscope and had fired on it and dropped a depth charge. The incident was reported to the naval district HQ, where everybody thought it was training or a case of mistaken identity. At 7.03 a.m. the *Ward* picked up another sub on her sound apparatus. Admiral Kimmel was informed at 7.45 a.m., cancelled a planned round of golf and headed towards his headquarters.

The leader of the Japanese first wave, Mitsuo Fuchida, tuned into civilian radio as he headed in towards Oahu. It was a useful navigational tool: the clearer the signal, the more accurate his course. But it was also good enough to give him a weather forecast. He was relieved to hear that although it was cloudy over the mountains, it was clear over the naval base.

In all there were 96 naval ships in Pearl Harbor that Sunday. Although there was supposed to be a 'number 3 condition of readiness', no one recalls that it was any different from a normal peacetime weekend. On board, men were rolling out of their bunks or listening to the Dodgers–Giants football game underway in New York. On the *West Virginia*, machinist's mate Hooton sat looking at some photos he had just received from his wife; among them were shots of the eight-month-old son he had never seen. On land, 62 of the army's brand-new P-40 fighters were lined up neatly on the runway at Wheeler airfield. The only two men awake at the base

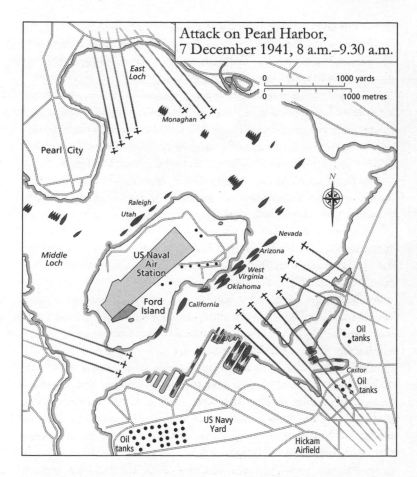

Attack on Pearl Harbor,
7 December 1941, 8 a.m.–9.30 a.m.

were Lieutenants Welch and Taylor, who had come for a Saturday night out and stayed up all night playing poker.

At 7.55 a.m., the morning colours ceremony was the chief concern. On every ship signalmen gathered to hoist the 'jack'. On the big battleships, moored in twos along the east side of Ford Island, a band prepared to play the national anthem. On the USS *Nevada* the bandsmen heard explosions and noticed some specks in the air far off to the south-west. The destroyer USS *Helm* had been sent out to join the *Ward* and investigate the reports of submarines. As she steamed down the channel, quartermaster Frank Handler noticed a group of low-flying planes coming towards him from the south. They passed 100 yards away, heading into the naval base. One of the pilots waved, and he waved back.[10]

From his cockpit, Fuchida looked down on the unsuspecting Americans with satisfaction. He spoke into his radio, '*Tora! Tora! Tora!*' It was the prearranged signal to let *Kido Butai* know that surprise was total. Hundreds of miles away, Nagumo turned to his chief of staff. In silence the men exchanged a long handshake.[11]

On the *Nevada*, band leader Oden MacMillan and his men struck up 'The Star Spangled Banner'. As they did so, a plane launched a torpedo at the *Arizona* and peeled off over the *Nevada*, spraying the deck with machine gun fire. The band and the marine guard were unharmed, but the deck was splintered and the ship's flag was shredded. The musicians kept playing. Only when the last note had sounded did everybody dive for cover. [12]

At first people assumed it was a US army air force exercise gone horribly wrong. Then, as more planes screamed overhead and more and more ships were hit by torpedoes, it became clear what was happening. The executive officer on the *Castor* shouted into the PA system, 'The Japs are bombing us! The Japs are bombing us!'[13] First to attack were low-flying torpedo planes carrying the deadliest weapon the Japanese navy possessed. They had been experimenting all year with specially modified torpedoes for use in the shallow waters of Pearl Harbor: wooden stabilizers had been fitted to stop the weapons diving too deep and hitting the muddy bottom. They worked superbly. Within minutes, the *Utah* and *Raleigh* had been hit at least once. They were unlucky enough to be docked where the Japanese expected the US aircraft carriers to be. On 'battleship row', the mighty ships barely realized that they were under attack before torpedoes were slamming into them. The *Oklahoma* took five hits, the *West Virginia* six, the *California* and the *Arizona* two each. On the *Oklahoma* the lights went out and the sea poured into her port side. There was a stampede for the ladders. Men were shoved aside, trampled and drowned. Some were caught on the wrong side of watertight doors and screamed for help as the water rose. There was little organized response. So unprepared were they on the *Monaghan* that boatswain's mate Thomas Donahue threw wrenches at low-flying planes because the locks to the ammunition boxes needed to be sawn off.[14]

Eight minutes after the *Oklahoma* had first been hit, she capsized. Meanwhile, Fuchida led his high-level bombers over the battleships. His aircraft were carrying 15- and 16-inch (38- and 40-cm) armour-piercing naval shells which had been fitted with fins to keep them falling straight. They sliced through the upper decks and exploded deep inside the ships. One of them crashed through the *Arizona*'s forecastle and ignited her forward magazines. Smoke, flames and chunks of steel mushroomed 500 feet (150 metres) into the air. A thousand men died instantly. High above it all, Fuchida felt his bomber shaking like a leaf.

Kimmel watched his fleet being annihilated. The story goes that a spent bullet smashed through a window in his HQ and hit him lightly in the chest. He picked it up and said, 'It would have been merciful had it killed me.'[15] The first raiders had finished their work by 8.30 a.m., but only ten minutes later the second wave arrived. Dive bombers hit Pearl Harbor while high-level bombers attacked US airfields all over Oahu. Lieutenants Welch and Taylor managed to get two P-40s in the air and shot down several Japanese planes. Both landed three times to replenish their ammunition. But they were the exception. Nearly all the US aircraft were destroyed on the ground: the neat lines on the runways were too good a target to miss.

Eventually, the second wave of Japanese aircraft returned to the carriers, leaving behind them a terrible scene. Eighteen ships had been sunk or seriously damaged, nearly two and a half thousand sailors, marines and soldiers killed, 188 aircraft destroyed on the ground and another 159 damaged. The Japanese lost only 29 planes and 55 men. Fuchida's was the last plane to land. He immediately reported to Nagumo and begged him to launch another attack because there were so many tempting, undefended targets. But the cautious Nagumo had no wish to push his luck. He told Fuchida, 'We may then conclude that the anticipated results have been achieved.'[16] At 1.30 p.m. Nagumo ordered *Kido Butai* to withdraw. He could rejoice that he appeared to have reduced the bulk of the US Pacific surface fleet to scrap. But cancelling a third wave was a grave mistake – it could have destroyed port facilities, command structures and the submarine base. The destruction of the oil tanks in particular would have forced the US fleet to withdraw to California.

The next day, democratic President Roosevelt went to Congress. As he entered the chamber, the Republicans applauded their sworn enemy for the first time in nine years. He told his audience, 'Yesterday, December 7th 1941 – a date that will live in infamy – the United States of America was suddenly and deliberately attacked.'[17] His speech took just six minutes. Congress needed only one hour to vote for war. American isolationism had been swept away in an instant.

The shattering attack on Pearl Harbor was just one part of a giant offensive which was launched simultaneously on a great arc from Hawaii to the Indian Ocean. Japanese troops carried out amphibious landings in Malaya, Thailand, the Philippines and Hong Kong at the same time as the bombs fell on Oahu. By spring 1942, Yamamoto had achieved most of his aims. Japan now controlled the oil of the Dutch East Indies and the rubber of Malaya. The British had been humiliated by the surrender of Singapore. Australia had been bombed. The Japanese had seized the strategically placed islands of Guam and Wake from the Americans.

WOUNDED GIANT

Roosevelt needed a victory. After Pearl Harbor he promoted Admiral Chester Nimitz to Commander in Chief Pacific Fleet, with orders not to return until the war was won. Nimitz had enjoyed a highly respected if unspectacular career. He was 57 years old, with white hair and steely blue eyes, and his hobby was pitching horseshoes. To his wife he bemoaned the fact that while the new command was his dream job, 'all the ships are at the bottom'.[18]

However, he quickly came to realize that the fleet had been lucky. He later said it was 'God's mercy'[19] that the Americans had not been alerted to the approaching Japanese. If they had been, Kimmel would have ordered his battleships to put to sea: they would have been sunk in deep water and many thousands more would have died. As it was, most of the ships sunk or damaged by the Japanese were salvaged from the shallow waters of Pearl Harbor. Besides, Nimitz still had his most highly prized warships – the carriers, which had been out of port. One of them, the *Enterprise*, had actually been due back at 7 a.m. on the day of the attack, but had the great good fortune to be delayed by rough seas.

His Japanese opposite number knew that he couldn't secure Japan's empire in the Pacific until he destroyed America's carriers. However, Yamamoto believed that they were inferior in numbers and in quality to his own, so he decided to try to lure them into battle. He would strike at the base on Midway Island, 1000 miles (1600 km) north-west of Hawaii. The US fleet would be sure to come to the base's rescue.

Yamamoto's decision to target US carriers was reinforced when one of them launched a spirited attack on the Japanese mainland on 18 April. Sixteen modified B-25 army bombers were carried by the USS *Hornet* from California to a point about 650 miles (1000 km) from Japan. Led by Lieutenant Colonel Jimmy Doolittle, the heavy aircraft, never intended for use on carriers, lumbered down the flight deck and just managed to lift off. Flying at wave height, they reached Japan undetected, then attacked military targets in Tokyo and other cities before the majority of them ran out of fuel and landed or crashed in China. The impact of this 'Doolittle raid' went far beyond the minimal material damage it caused. The fact that America was able to attack the heart of the Japanese empire with impunity was a stunning psychological blow to Japan's leaders. Yamamoto felt ashamed that his navy had been unable to protect the homeland and had endangered the life of the Emperor. The seizure of Midway would help shield Japan and would be a useful springboard for an invasion of Hawaii. As part of the Midway operation the naval staff insisted on an additional, diversionary strike at the Aleutian Islands, 1500 miles (2400 km) to the north, off the south-western tip of Alaska. Yamamoto reluctantly agreed.

On 29 April the First Air Fleet's officers gathered together and Yamamoto revealed his plan. Strategically it was simple enough; but the details were elaborate. The Aleutian expedition consisted of two carriers and many other surface ships and submarines. This force, codenamed AL, would attack three of the islands in the Aleutian chain to distract the Americans. The rest of Japan's fleet would head in the direction of Midway. Nagumo's six aircraft carriers would launch a strike force at the US base from the north-west. An amphibious force would be despatched from Guam and Saipan to assault Midway's beaches. Yamamoto himself, with the main body of battleships and one aircraft carrier, would linger 300 miles (almost 500 km) behind Nagumo in order to swoop down on the Americans when they came to Midway's rescue and engage them in a decisive battle. The Japanese fleet would be one of the largest collections of naval power ever seen, an immense force of nearly 200 vessels spread across 1000 miles (1600 km) of the Pacific Ocean. This would keep the Americans guessing where the main blow would fall, but allow all the ships to concentrate for battle when the US fleet arrived.

The mood of the meeting was supremely self-confident. Commander Watanabe, who served on Yamamoto's staff, remembers, 'Practically everyone thought that the battle was already won'. Someone asked what would happen if the Americans attacked the carriers while their fighters were away escorting the bombers to Midway. Commander Genda, Nagumo's operations officer, retorted, '*Gaishu isshoku!*'[20] which translates roughly as, 'We'll brush them off.' Yamamoto was exasperated by this atmosphere of euphoria and issued a warning: 'It is like a disease to think that we're invincible because of past successes.' Yet in spite of the admiral's words of caution the only thing that really worried everyone in the room was the possibility that the Americans might not show up.[21] Yamamoto was also concerned about Nagumo: he had not been entirely happy with the Vice Admiral's performance at Pearl Harbor. Some believed he would like to have removed Nagumo, but feared that his number two would take it as a personal disgrace and, in time-honoured fashion, commit suicide.

The US carriers were in fact already at sea and, while the Japanese planners played war games in early May, the Americans claimed their first significant scalp of the Pacific war. In spring, 1942, the Japanese had entered the Coral Sea to attack Port Moresby on the south coast of Papua New Guinea and from there to threaten Australia. They were intercepted at the end of the first week of May by Admiral Jack Fletcher with two US carriers, *Lexington* and *Yorktown*. It was the first sea battle in history in which neither fleet saw the other. The Japanese sank the *Lexington* and heavily damaged the *Yorktown*; but the Americans sank the Japanese light carrier *Shoho* and hit the *Shokaku* three times. The Japanese turned back their invasion transports. Port Moresby was safe, so, although tactically it was a Japanese success, the strategic victory was American.

The Japanese misread the Battle of the Coral Sea as another triumph for their *nihon seishin* – innate Japanese martial spirit – and superior naval aviation. They assumed they had sunk two major US carriers. But faulty aerial observation and damage assessment misled them into believing that the *Yorktown* had been destroyed as well as the *Lexington*. In fact, the Americans kept the stricken *Yorktown* afloat. And Japan's losses were worse than they seemed. *Shokaku* would need months in dry dock, and the depleted air crews of yet another carrier, *Zuikaku*, could not be quickly replaced. Nagumo's force for the Midway operation had just lost two carriers.

Nimitz, for his part, did not enjoy the luxury of having carriers to spare either. The *Yorktown* had been hit by an 800-lb (360-kg) bomb which had killed or seriously wounded 66 men. But the crew had managed to extinguish the flames and the ship limped back to Pearl. Minutes after she entered dry dock the *Yorktown* was swarming with 1400 men who worked around the clock to make her seaworthy again. Her captain, Elliot Buckmaster, was told he had two days to carry out several months of repairs. The *Yorktown* would go to sea with timber supports strengthening damaged compartments and watertight doors unable to close in their buckled frames.

What mattered was that the *Yorktown* was battle-ready: she could launch and retrieve aircraft.

Nimitz's haste was prompted by a spectacular intelligence coup. By April 1942 his signals intelligence team in Hawaii under Commander Joseph Rochefort had partially broken the Japanese navy code JN25. Nimitz had already come to trust Rochefort after he had predicted the Japanese move into the Coral Sea, and his intelligence chief now came to him with details of the Midway plan. Nimitz saw his opportunity and concentrated all his available forces to lay a trap for Nagumo. He had just appointed Rear Admiral Raymond Spruance to command Task Force 16, comprising the carriers *Hornet* and *Enterprise*. Spruance had no experience as a carrier commander, but he had not earned his nickname, 'Electric Brain', for nothing: he had a keen intellect and could make quick decisions. Nimitz despatched him from Pearl Harbor on 28 May. A day later, Fletcher, who would have overall command of the operation, followed with Task Force 17 centred on his patched-up *Yorktown*.

Nimitz packed Midway with 115 aircraft, which would help his carriers inflict a devastating hit-and-run attack on the Japanese. He would rely on surprise and speed to make up for the fact that the US fleet was vastly outnumbered. His plan was simple: to 'inflict maximum damage on the enemy by employing strong attrition tactics'.[22] He chose a rendezvous point for his three carriers 325 miles (520 km) north-east of Midway and named it 'Point Luck'.

Navy Day in Japan, the anniversary of the crushing victory over the Russians in 1905, was celebrated on 27 May. Appropriately enough, it was also the day on which *Kido Butai* slipped out of Hiroshima harbour to begin the Midway operation. The sailors were dressed in whites and cheered as they lined the ships' rails: it was an unforgettable scene, a snapshot of Japanese naval power at its zenith. Nagumo himself was in high spirits as he watched from his flagship *Akagi*. The final intelligence estimate suggested that the enemy was unaware of his presence and 'would remain so until after our initial attacks on the island'.[23] The officers and men of *Kido Butai* might have been less confident if they had had access to an

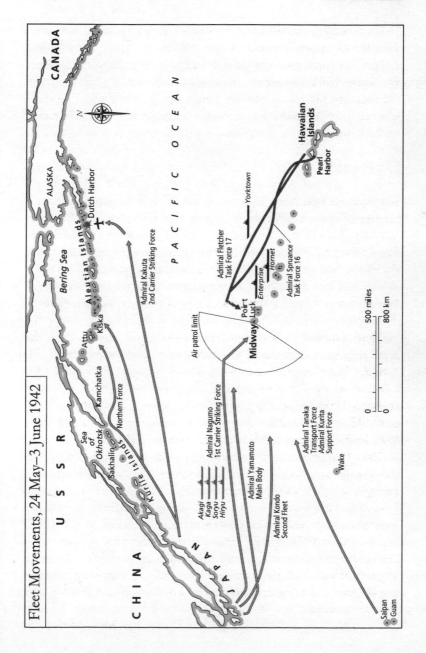

Fleet Movements, 24 May–3 June 1942

updated intelligence assessment sent by Tokyo on 2 June. It warned that the Americans had pre-empted them and that a carrier force was possibly present in the eastern Midway area. Thanks, however, to Yamamoto's insistence on radio silence at all costs, Nagumo had no idea of this change in the situation. He ploughed towards Midway, convinced that the Americans were still in Pearl Harbor.

BEGINNINGS

The Aleutian Islands are high in the northern hemisphere, and on 3 June 1942 dawn came early. By 3 a.m. the sun was up: 23 bombers and 12 fighters left the Japanese carriers *Ryujo* and *Junyo* and made straight for Dutch Harbor on Amaknak Island. Some got lost in the fog; those that got through inflicted some damage but hit no ships of importance. Crucially, Nimitz maintained his dogged faith in his intelligence team and was not drawn into sending his forces north. He restated his belief that this was just a diversion and told his forces in Midway to be on the lookout for the Japanese. With the battle only hours old, one half of Yamamoto's plan had totally failed.

Some hours after the attack on Dutch Harbor, Ensign Charles Eaton, flying a Catalina flying boat from Midway, spotted two cargo vessels. It was the first sign of the Japanese amphibious invasion force. Army B-17 bombers with extra fuel tanks were scrambled, and attacked the Japanese from high altitude at 4.40 p.m. The raid produced some dramatic waterspouts, but failed to hit a single ship. Nimitz reined in Fletcher: 'This is not, repeat not, the enemy striking force. That is the landing force. The striking force will hit from the northwest at daylight tomorrow.'[24] Fletcher and Spruance zigzagged around Point Luck, waiting. At nightfall Fletcher moved the three carriers further west so that they were almost directly north of Midway. Yamamoto received the grim news of the discovery of his invasion fleet and the fact that Midway seemed ready for them, but refused to break radio silence and inform Nagumo.

ATTACK ON MIDWAY

Early the next morning, 4 June, *Kido Butai* staged its aerial assault on Midway. The first aircraft to take off from the carriers were the Zero-Sen fighters, which would fly above their bombers and pounce on any enemy interceptors. Nagumo was being cautious. The men sent against Midway were younger, replacement pilots, some flying their first combat mission; he was holding back the majority of his veteran flyers and more than half his strike aircraft in case the US fleet appeared. These aircraft had already been armed with torpedoes and armour-piercing bombs for attacking ships. Nagumo had no reason to believe enemy ships were anywhere near, but even so he was determined to avoid the nightmare scenario of his carriers being attacked without air cover or any means of striking back.

The strike force of 36 Zeros, 36 dive bombers and 36 level bombers took off. They circled overhead for 15 minutes until the launching was complete. At 4.45 a.m. the signal was given and all 108 aircraft turned south-east towards Midway.

Mitsuo Fuchida was the pilot who had led Japan's assault on Pearl Harbor. A recent appendectomy meant he couldn't fly on this mission, but he was aboard the *Akagi*. The lack of resources assigned to scouting, which he put down to over-confidence and the Japanese obsession with going on the offensive, dismayed him. A plane sent scouting, in the official view, was one fewer to drop bombs and torpedoes. Nagumo's chief of staff, Ryunosuke Kusaka, later admitted this: 'I neglected the scouting, trying to save planes for the offensive.'[25] Only seven scout planes were used to cover hundreds of square miles of ocean.

On Midway, the defenders waited for news of the mighty assault that they knew was coming. At 5.34 a.m. a flying boat scout aircraft radioed the words that everybody in Hawaii and on the US carriers had been anticipating: 'Carrier bearing 320, distance 180.'[26] A quarter of an hour later another one reported, 'Many planes heading [towards] Midway.'[27] The pilots on the airfield raced to get off the ground before the Japanese bombers arrived overhead. Grumman F4F Wildcat and Brewster Buffalo fighters took off to hunt down the approaching enemy planes. Behind them, 37 US bombers of different types climbed into the air. The American bombers' orders were simple: 'To attack the enemy carriers.'[28] By 6.20 a.m. the air-field on the eastern of the two islets that make up Midway was deserted. Its motley collection of largely obsolete planes had taken off just in time: the Japanese were just 22 miles (35 km) away.

At 6.16 a.m. the American fighters spotted them. They had climbed higher than the Japanese bombers and now pushed their planes into steep dives, firing short bursts at the enemy and trying to

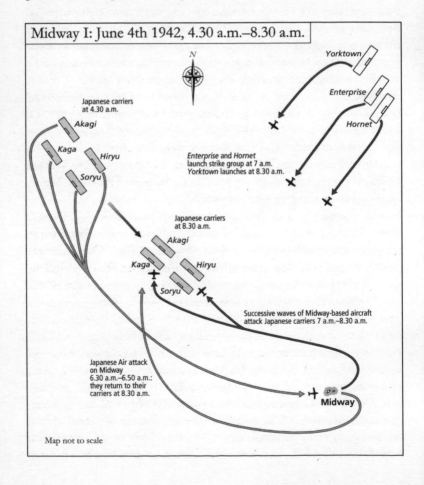

Midway I: June 4th 1942, 4.30 a.m.–8.30 a.m.

N

Yorktown

Enterprise

Japanese carriers
at 4.30 a.m.

Akagi

Kaga
Hiryu

Soryu

Hornet

Enterprise and Hornet
launch strike group at 7 a.m.
Yorktown launches at 8.30 a.m.

Japanese carriers
at 8.30 a.m.

Akagi

Kaga
Hiryu

Soryu

Successive waves of Midway-based aircraft
attack Japanese carriers 7 a.m.–8.30 a.m.

Japanese Air attack
on Midway
6.30 a.m.–6.50 a.m.:
they return to their
carriers at 8.30 a.m.

Midway

Map not to scale

make every round of their limited ammunition count. In no time, the Japanese Zero fighters which had been behind and above their bombers were diving into the attack and a huge, confused mêlée had broken out. The Americans were fighting at a hopeless disadvantage, for the Mitsubishi A6M3 Zero-Sen was the best carrier-borne fighter in the world. Its light airframe made it manoeuvrable and gave it a long range, but it also had a fierce punch: it carried two machine guns and two heavy-calibre cannon. However, all this speed, manoeuvrability and firepower came at a cost: the planes had no armour and no self-sealing fuel tanks. In keeping with the Japanese mindset, they were built for out-and-out offensive flying. They were lethal, but ultimately vulnerable. Even so, they totally outclassed the tubby Buffalos, every one of which was destroyed or damaged by the end of the dogfight. The Wildcat gave a better account of itself. Its pilots found that a couple of rounds fired into a frail Zero were often enough to finish it off. The Wildcat could take far more punishment. Lieutenant Cranfield's fighter was peppered with machine-gun fire and he was shot through both legs, but he still managed to land his machine back on Midway, despite almost passing out from the pain. Unable to brake, he skidded off the end of the runway.[29]

The Americans managed to shoot down only 3 bombers and 2 Zeros for the loss of 13 Buffalos and 2 Wildcats (with several more seriously damaged) and 14 of their 26 pilots killed. One Japanese pilot reported when he landed back on his carrier, 'Enemy fighters are lousy. I think they were almost wiped out.'[30] Having chased the US fighters away, Zeros flew low over the islands, strafing anybody caught in the open. The bombers attacked aircraft hangars and fuel tanks, starting fires that lasted for days. There was heavy anti-aircraft fire. Pilot Taisuke Maruyama wrote later, 'The fragments from those shells, along with the blast waves, just flew all over the place and tore into the planes in my formation.'[31] When one bomber was hit, the pilot opened his canopy, waved farewell to his comrades, then closed it and waited for death. One bomb landed in a rearming pit and detonated eight 100-lb (45-kg) bombs and 1000 rounds of .50-calibre ammunition. Electrical power was knocked out. The Post Exchange was hit: cans of beer tore through the air like shrapnel and US marines whooped as they scooped them up.

At 6.43 a.m. the Japanese commander ordered his aircraft to withdraw. Below, black smoke swirled around flattened buildings. The damage looked impressive, but he knew the job was not finished. The airstrip was still intact; so was much of the heavy weaponry that would oppose a Japanese amphibious landing. His radio was broken, so he held up a sign for his number two to radio back to Nagumo. It read: 'There is need for a second wave.'[32]

THE AMERICAN CARRIERS LAUNCH

It had been a tense morning on board the American carriers. Fletcher and Spruance waited for news of their enemy. Below decks, pilots had breakfasted early. Lieutenant Gray ordered that *Enterprise* delicacy, the 'one-eyed sandwich': a fried egg between two slices of toast, the top slice with a hole cut in it for the yolk. Then he joined the other pilots in ready rooms. Some managed to snooze. Others played cards or read dog-eared paperbacks that were doing the rounds. The tension in the room heightened when either the tele-type machines or the ship's PA system crackled into life.

Fletcher, cautious after his mauling at the Battle of the Coral Sea, had sent up ten scout planes at 4.30 a.m.; they would check the ocean to the north, just in case Nimitz's intelligence was wrong. At 5.34 a.m. the *Enterprise* had picked up the Midway-based flying boat's report of the enemy carriers. But the report had not specifically said that all four carriers were together: Fletcher feared throwing everything he had at only two of them and finding himself vulnerable to counter-attack by the other two. This had happened at the Coral Sea and he wasn't going to be stung twice. Just after 6 a.m. he flashed a message to Spruance: 'Proceed SW and attack enemy carriers when definitely located.'[33] Fletcher would wait for further information from his scout planes.

Spruance had to make a tough decision. He had planned to be 100 miles (160 km) away from the Japanese before making an all-out attack. He was now 200 miles (320 km) away. But the flying boat had reported that the Japanese strike force was heading for Midway. Spruance's staff estimated that these aircraft would arrive back at the Japanese carriers at around 9 a.m. The ships would then be at their most vulnerable, their decks and hangars crammed with planes, fuel lines and ordnance. He had to choose whether to launch immediately at extreme range in order to catch the Japanese in this condition, or wait, close the range and attack them later in the day. Spruance made his decision. He instructed his chief of staff, 'Launch everything you have at the earliest possible moment and strike the enemy carriers.'[34] His own carriers' Devastator torpedo bombers only had a combat radius of 175 miles 280 km) and by launching at such a distance he was condemning some of his pilots to ditching in the sea. After the battle he said, 'I figured if I was going to hit the Japanese I should hit them with everything I had.'[35]

General Quarters was sounded on the *Enterprise* at 6.15 a.m. with a staccato buzzer and on the *Hornet* at 6.26 a.m. with the ship's gong. Immediately, the air was filled with the noise of feet pounding up and down ladders. On the *Enterprise*, pilots queued up at water coolers to gulp down deep draughts, in the hope that should they be shot down, they might last longer in the sea if they were fully hydrated. They abandoned their customary coolness and embarked on a sudden frenzy of shaking hands. The previous evening, the aggressive and slightly eccentric commander of the *Hornet*'s Devastators, Lieutenant Commander John Waldron, had handed each of his men a message: 'Just a word to let you know I feel we are all ready. We have had a very short time to train ... but we have truly done the best humanly possible. I actually believe that under these conditions we are the best in the world.... If there is only one plane left to make the final run in, I want that man to go in and get a hit. May God be with us all. Good luck. Happy landings and give 'em hell.'[36] At their final briefing he told his men simply, 'Just follow me. I'll take you to 'em.'[37]

The aircraft elevators lifted Dauntless dive bombers, Wildcat fighters and Devastator torpedo bombers on to the flight deck. As they did so, Spruance's two carriers moved some miles apart, and at around 7 a.m. Spruance gave the order to launch. The carriers turned into the wind. *Hornet* launched 60 aircraft: 15 torpedo bombers with their 'pickle' slung underneath, 35 dive bombers carrying either a 1000-lb (450-kg) or 500-lb (230-kg) bomb; support would be provided by just 10 Wildcat fighters. The *Enterprise* started launching six minutes later. Its strike force was almost identical in composition: 14 torpedo bombers, 37 dive bombers and just 10 fighters. Spruance was holding on to the bulk of his fighters in order to protect his carriers.

Once each plane had taken off, it climbed and circled the carriers while the rest of the force formed up. But the launch took the best part of an hour, and Spruance became so frustrated by the delay that he ordered his lead aircraft to head for the Japanese carriers before all the planes were airborne. Bad visibility meant that the groups were further separated. As a result, the Americans set off not in one cohesive strike force, but as an uncoordinated series of mini-waves.

While Spruance was sending planes aloft, Fletcher was now hurrying to catch up. He had changed his mind. The Japanese were too good a target to miss. He would launch half of his aircraft and hold back the other half in case he came under attack. At 8.38 a.m. 17 dive bombers, 12 torpedo bombers and 6 Wildcat fighters took off from the *Yorktown*. Fletcher and Spruance now had 156 aircraft flying towards Nagumo's presumed position.

JAPANESE CARRIERS UNDER ATTACK

While all this was going on, after just under an hour's flying, the US bombers that had taken off from Midway to attack the Japanese fleet were spotted by lookouts on the *Akagi* at 7.05 a.m. The Japanese ships increased speed and turned to face them, so as to present a smaller target. The escort vessels put up a barrage of anti-aircraft fire to protect the carriers, and Zero fighters prepared to pounce. Six TBF Avenger torpedo bombers approached the *Hiryu*. Four B-26 bombers headed for the *Akagi*. This was their first combat mission. Second Lieutenant Ernest, flying an Avenger, had never flown out of sight of land before and had only dropped one torpedo in training. He had to travel on a steady course at an altitude of 200 feet (60 metres) at a speed of 200 knots. Flying low, straight and slow is the worst possible combination. Lieutenant Fukuoka watched from a returning Japanese reconnaissance aircraft as, 'like hawks pursuing a flock of doves, the Zeros shot down one plane after another'.[38] The Avengers succeeded in loosing off several torpedoes, but the Japanese carrier captains dodged them all – the helms of the *Hiryu* and *Akagi* were thrown hard to port, which got them out of harm's way and brought all the anti-aircraft batteries on one side of each ship to bear. Only one of the Avengers limped back to Midway, its hydraulics shot to pieces and its rear gunner shot dead in his turret. Next, the four B-26s came skimming over the waves. One exploded as a Zero poured fire into it. Another narrowly missed the bridge of the *Akagi* and ploughed into the sea just beyond. The Zeros were swarming all over them: Lieutenant Fujita from the *Soryu* found it was virtually impossible to get a clear shot. Back on Midway, Lieutenant James Muri estimated that his B-26 had been hit by several hundred rounds. Bizarrely, both he and Fujita were employed as pilots for Japanese airlines after the war and became firm friends.[39]

The US attacks on his carriers caught Nagumo as he pondered the message that a second strike was required against Midway. The American raid decided him. If the B-26, which had just missed the bridge of the *Akagi*, had flown 10 feet (3 metres) lower, he and his staff would have been killed. His scout planes, which should have reached the furthest points of their search by now, had found no sign of American ships. Why hold back his second wave in case a phantom enemy showed up, when he was under very real attack from the Midway-based planes? Orders rang out. The planes that were armed with anti-ship weapons would be rearmed with ground-attack bombs and sent to attack Midway. It was 7.15 a.m.

The hangar decks seethed with activity. The armourers had to remove the torpedoes, as well as changing the mounting hardware on the belly of the aircraft. While they worked, other crewmen pushed the torpedoes on carts towards the ordnance elevators.

But the elevators were busy bringing up land-attack bombs from the magazines. The bomb handlers in the magazines had their hands full getting the bombs up to the hangars, and couldn't handle torpedoes being sent back down. So the armourers simply stacked the torpedoes in the holding racks next to the elevator.

At 7.40 a.m., half an hour later, the Japanese cruiser *Tone's* scout plane sent a vague but devastating report back to Nagumo. It had stumbled across 'what appears to be 10 enemy surface units, in position bearing 10 degrees distance 240 miles (450 km) from Midway'.[40] This news sent a shockwave through the bridge of the *Akagi*. It was the first Nagumo had heard of an American fleet in the area, and he immediately requested clarification on whether there were aircraft carriers with the enemy force. His chief of staff apparently said, 'There couldn't be an enemy force without carriers in the area.'[41] Nagumo now had to make one of the most momentous decisions of the Second World War. But it was not an ideal environment for careful thought. There was so much noise that the public address system was barely audible. He and at least a dozen other people were crammed on to a bridge 15 × 12 feet (4 ⁄2 × 3 ⁄2 metres). There was no privacy for a frank discussion with his staff, and he did not wait to debate with them in public because he feared looking indecisive in front of the crew of the *Akagi*.

Time was everything. His Midway force was returning. The aircraft were running low on fuel, some were damaged and many carried wounded airmen. The carriers could not launch and recover aircraft at the same time. He either had to send a force against the American ships immediately, or wait until the Midway force had landed and been taken down to the hangar decks. An immediate strike could only consist of those aircraft that still carried anti-ship weapons – in other words, 64 aircraft from different squadrons on different ships. If he waited for all his aircraft that were still onboard to change back to anti-ship munitions, he would be able to launch nearly 80 planes – not a huge difference. But an immediate strike would also ruin the fleet's much-prized organization. Squadrons would be broken up. Efficiency would suffer.

As Nagumo wrestled with his decision, his carriers came under attack by another wave of planes from Midway. The ships rocked from side to side as their captains threw them into sharp turns. Deploying aircraft on deck under these conditions was dangerous, and the new situation seemed to decide Nagumo. He would not attack immediately, but would first beat off the American attacks and recover his Midway strike force. Only then would he send up a bigger, properly organized attack against the American fleet – with, he hoped, much clearer intelligence on its whereabouts. It was in perfect keeping with Japanese carrier doctrine, but it was a terrible mistake. He compounded it by ordering his ships to set a course towards the Americans. Aggressive as always, the Japanese wanted to close the range.

Over the next 40 minutes, waves of American aircraft from Midway attacked. First up were 16 dive bombers. Their pilots were so inexperienced that, instead of making a steep dive, they took a gentler 'glide bombing' approach that made them more vulnerable. The Japanese only had nine Zero fighters available because the rest were landing to refuel or rearm. But they were enough. They tore into the American formation, sending six aircraft down in flames immediately. One pilot, Daniel Iverson, had a close shave as he felt a bullet sever his neck microphone. But he and the surviving aircraft held their course. As they closed on the *Hiryu,* her anti-aircraft batteries roared into action, and streams of tracer hurtled towards the incoming planes. The Americans managed to land a few bombs in the water near the carrier, one only 150 feet (50 metres) away. Huge waterspouts drenched the Japanese sailors manning the anti-aircraft guns. Only half of the 16 American dive bombers made it back to Midway, and all of them had been badly shot up.

Finally, at 8.20 a.m., after constant requests, the cruiser *Tone*'s scout plane gave Nagumo the one piece of information that he most desperately needed to know: 'The enemy is accompanied by what appears to be a carrier.'[42] Nagumo had been ambushed.

At the same time, yet another threat appeared. The US submarine *Nautilus* fired a torpedo at the battleship *Kirishima*. The Japanese ship evaded it and a cruiser, the *Arashi*, stayed behind the fleet to drop depth charges.

By now, Rear Admiral Yamaguchi, commander of the Second Carrier Division comprising the *Hiryu* and the *Soryu*, was getting nervous. He was desperate to attack the American fleet and signalled to Nagumo on the *Akagi*, 'Consider it advisable to launch attack force immediately.'[43] Bringing the strike force up to the flight deck and launching them would mean that the returning Midway aircraft would have nowhere to land and would have to ditch in the sea. Nagumo didn't even bother replying to his jumpy subordinate. Instead, at 8.37 a.m., *Akagi* hoisted a white flag with a black ball, the signal to the Midway force to land. Unlike the Americans, the Japanese took all the planes down to the hangar decks to rearm and refuel because it afforded more protection to both machines and mechanics. But the process was slow and risk was still present since flammable fuel and munitions were loaded down in the heart of the ship.

Once the Midway force was back on board, Nagumo would need just over half an hour to get his strike force on deck, start their engines and launch them at the US fleet. The planes were already armed with torpedoes and armour-piercing bombs. But no sooner had he recovered the Midway force than more enemy aircraft appeared. To Genda, an air officer on the *Akagi*, they appeared 'like waterfowl flying over a lake far away'.[44] The planes from the American carriers had arrived. It was 9.18 a.m.

CARRIER VERSUS CARRIER

True to his word, Lieutenant Commander John Waldron led his 15 torpedo bombers from the *Hornet* straight to the Japanese carriers. In fact, he broke away from the rest of the *Hornet*'s aircraft which missed the Japanese altogether and ended up landing on Midway.

Twenty-one Japanese fighters were still airborne, and they tore towards Waldron's slow-moving bombers. Lieutenant Commander Mitoya watched from the *Kaga*: 'We were too many for them. None of the American planes got through to our carriers. We watched one speck after another, high in the sky, spark into flame and plummet down, trailing black smoke.'[45] In fact, one pilot, Lieutenant Gay, managed to drop a torpedo, even though he had never flown with one before. Seconds later he was shot down, but survived the battle by hiding in the wreckage; every single one of his comrades was killed.

Their sacrifice was not entirely in vain. During Waldron's attack, Nagumo was unable to bring his strike aircraft on to the flight decks. Instead, Zeros were constantly landing and rearming before taking off again to defend the fleet. Nagumo's bombers were waiting in the hangars, fully armed and fuelled, but the attacks gave him no gap in which to launch them.

Another attack followed Waldron's. This time it was torpedo bombers from the *Enterprise*. They got quite close to the *Kaga*, but then the Zeros sliced through their formation. The Devastators' rear gunners had two machine guns and they fired back as the Zeros streaked by. The *Kaga* made a series of turns, dodging two torpedoes. After using up their 60 rounds of exploding cannon shells the Zeros switched to their machine guns to down the torpedo bombers. Desperate for assistance, the American pilots screamed into their radios for help from Wildcat fighters which were circling high above. But patchy cloud and very poor radios meant that the fighters never heard or saw their hard-pressed comrades. The Wildcats headed back to the American carriers without witnessing the doomed attacks of the two torpedo squadrons. In the end, only four battered Devastators made it back to the *Enterprise*.

The utter destruction of the two attempted torpedo attacks seems to have given Nagumo renewed confidence. The American flying had been poor: his fleet had nothing to fear. Once he had a clear 40-minute window in which to launch his strike force, he would smash any enemy ship within range. But high above him yet more American aircraft had spotted the Japanese carriers. By an extraordinary stroke of luck, two separate formations had arrived at the same time – the pilots in each had no idea that another squadron was even in the area.

THE DESTRUCTION OF *KIDO BUTAI*

Flying at 19,000 feet (5800 metres), Lieutenant Commander Wade McClusky Jr was leading 33 Dauntless dive bombers from the *Enterprise*. At 9.55 a.m., after 30 minutes of fruitless searching, McClusky spotted a solitary Japanese ship through a gap in the clouds. It was the cruiser *Arashi*, which had stayed behind to depth charge the US submarine *Nautilus* and was now steaming north to catch up with the fleet. McClusky guessed that the ship would lead him to *Kido Butai*. He was right, and five minutes later he radioed Spruance, 'This is McClusky. Have sighted the enemy.'[46] Fifteen miles (24 km) to the east, the *Yorktown*'s strike force had also arrived. Unlike the aircraft from the other carriers, *Yorktown*'s – 17 dive bombers, 12 torpedo bombers and 6 fighters – had stayed close together. For the first time the Americans were in a position to make a coordinated attack.

The Japanese had no radar, and relied on the human eye for early warning. Therefore there was no way of predicting the direction or altitude of incoming attacks. Nor was there any way to control the Zeros in the air, as their radios were short-range, difficult to use and deeply unreliable. Fighter pilots judged for themselves where the threat was greatest, and were usually drawn to whatever fighting was going on rather than to where it might develop. At 10.10 a.m. there were about 40 Zeros in the air, most of them chasing off the remnants of the last torpedo attack. Then the *Akagi* spotted yet another squadron of Devastator torpedo bombers coming in low. Again Zeros attacked, but this time the Americans had six Wildcat fighters flying in support. Jimmy Thach, their commander, shot down three Zeros. Even this couldn't protect the Devastators completely. Lieutenant Fujita Iyozo had flown three sorties that morning and had not eaten, and still shot down three Devastators. The five survivors headed towards the *Hiryu*. She dodged their torpedoes and three more Devastators were shot down. Only two made it back to the *Yorktown*.

Nearly all the Zeros were sucked into this fight with the Devastators and Wildcats, and few were covering the rest of the

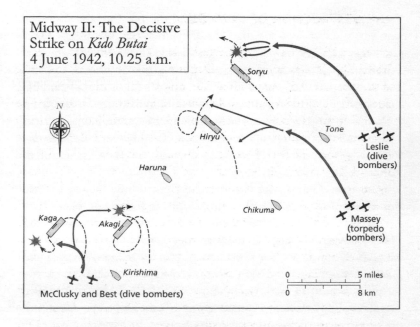

Midway II: The Decisive
Strike on *Kido Butai*
4 June 1942, 10.25 a.m.

fleet. *Kido Butai* was so preoccupied with this latest, dramatic torpedo attack that nobody noticed McClusky's dive bombers high above. But McClusky saw *Kaga* and *Akagi* below. On the decks of both ships, Zeros were warming up and preparing to launch. On the *Akagi,* one of them was piloted by Kimura Koreo: his would be the last plane ever to leave the deck. Undeterred by the fact that he had never dropped a bomb from a Dauntless before, McClusky opened his dive flaps and yelled at his wingman, the pilot flying alongside him, to follow. It was the decisive moment of the Second World War in the Pacific.

While *Kaga*'s PA system was triumphantly announcing the beating off of yet another torpedo raid, dive bombers were suddenly spotted directly overhead. The crews of the 5-inch (12-cm) guns desperately spun handles to elevate their barrels, and some flak was belatedly sprayed into the path of the bombers. The Americans came in fast and steep – Japanese pilots couldn't help admiring their technique. Captain Okada desperately threw his lumbering ship into a starboard turn. Her guns blazed at the sky. One dive bomber was hit; the rest kept coming. The first three bombs missed. Then one after another they hit. The first landed near the aft elevator. Another hit the forward elevator, detonating among the planes below. Another was a direct hit on the bridge: *Kaga's* captain and his senior officers died instantly. More bombs rained down, throwing jagged foot-long (25-cm) splinters through the air and twisting steel like tin foil. On the *Hiryu* the navigator, Commander Cho, remembers, 'It was like a horrible dream in slow motion; to see such a great carrier done in this easily.'[47]

Above the *Kaga*, Lieutenant Richard Best realized that two whole squadrons were attacking the same ship. He pulled out of his dive along with his two wingmen, and this meagre force flew towards the *Akagi*. Staying in their V formation, they dived at the Japanese flagship. Best aimed for the superstructure. The *Akagi* didn't see the planes coming until the last minute. Her captain quickly threw the helm over hard to starboard and presented her beam to the dive bombers. The first bomb landed 15 feet (5 metres) to port, sending up a waterspout which drenched everyone on the bridge. Another bomb grazed the flight deck and landed in the water. But Lieutenant Best's bomb dealt *Akagi* a mortal blow as 1000 lb (450 kg) of high explosive struck the aft edge of the elevator in the middle of the ship. Mitsuo Fuchida recalled, a loud crash and blinding light. When his eyes recovered enough to view the damage, Fuchida started to cry.[48]

The onslaught was not over. Four of *Yorktown's* 17 dive bombers had developed a fault which caused them to jettison their bombs in the ocean, but the rest aimed for the *Soryu*. Her gunnery officer, Commander Ryoichi, was absorbed in the torpedo attack on the *Hiryu* when suddenly a lookout screamed, 'Enemy dive bombers!' Ryoichi yelled to open fire. But it was too late. Three small groups of bombers attacked from different angles. He watched the first bomb drop. It landed near the bridge. 'Next thing I felt was like my hands were skinned and an ice pick rammed into my neck. It was the sensation of burning alive.' Around Ryoichi 'was one raging sea of fire'.[49] Another bomb detonated deep inside the ship and ruptured the steam pipes, scalding everybody nearby to death and stopping the engines dead.

Of all the great naval powers, Japan gave the least thought to damage control. A typical carrier had a dozen fuelling points for high-octane gasoline on the flight deck and on its two hangar decks. Armour protection for the magazines was minimal. Japanese hangar decks were not open-sided like those of the Americans, and therefore magnified the effect of an explosion. And at this moment the hangar decks were stuffed with fully armed and fuelled planes.

On the hangar deck of the *Kaga,* hundreds of men were blown to pieces by the initial blasts. Pilot Haruo Yoshino remembers that 'the scale of these detonations was beyond imagination, and with each explosion, the ship shook violently'.[50] The crew had been wearing only shorts and T-shirts, and any exposed flesh was badly burnt. Fire soon stretched from stem to stern. The *Kaga*'s water mains had been knocked out. Her damage control mechanisms – fireproof roller curtains and a carbon dioxide suppression system – were all destroyed. There was no means of stopping the spread of the flames. A pathetic bucket chain ran from the ship's latrines to the hangar deck. Below deck, trapped men listened to explosions rocking the ship above their heads. As smoke began to pour through ventilation shafts, sailors gathered round any ducts that brought in fresh air and took deep breaths. Above them on the hangar deck around 80,000 lb (more than 35,000 kg) of explosives littered the floor: torpedoes and bombs that had been switched during the morning had not been sent back down to the magazines. Pools of fuel were vaporizing and the gas was trapped in the confined hangars. It did not take long to ignite. Minutes after the attack, *Kaga* was torn apart as oxygen in the air reacted with the fuel: the resulting explosion was so violent that witnesses on other ships were certain that no one could have survived.

Soryu too was incapable of being saved. Only on *Akagi* had the damage been localized. She had taken just one direct hit: a 1000-lb (450-kg) bomb had landed among the 18 torpedo planes waiting to be launched on the strike against the Americans. Concerted action would probably have saved the ship, but on the crowded hangar deck the dazed crew did not respond in time. Three minutes later, secondary explosions rocked Nagumo's flagship. The crew fought the fire for nine hours; but unlike the Americans, who trained all non-aviation crew in firefighting techniques, the Japanese only had 350 specialists out of 2000 or so men on board a carrier. Damage control parties were not spread throughout the ship, the breathing gear was primitive and there were no portable pumps.

Captain Aoki of the *Akagi* begged Nagumo to leave the ship. 'I urge you, commander in chief ... to leave this vessel as soon as possible, so that command of this force may be continued.'[51] Nagumo and his staff had to climb down a rope to escape. Mitsuo Fuchida was halfway down when an explosion made him fall and he broke both legs and ankles. Two sailors carried him to Nagumo's launch. The oarsmen wept as they rowed the tiny boat away from the carrier. It was a stark illustration of the calamity that had overtaken *Kido Butai*. Two officers talked quietly, and one said to Genda, 'The outcome will surely decide the fate of Japan.'[52]

Behind them, on the *Akagi,* the crew fought against the inevitable. Crawling through dark corridors, they stuffed wet rags, some soaked in their own urine, into their mouths to block the smoke. The elevator shafts were now giant furnaces, sucking in the air at the bottom to feed the towering flames that vented out at the top. Some of the wounded were suffering such pain that they threw themselves into the fires. At 10.45 a.m. Captain Yanagimoto ordered his men to abandon the *Soryu*. Survivors jumped into the water. On the *Kaga*, those who survived the massive blast found the rubber soles of their shoes melting as they crossed the glowing decks. Incredibly, she continued travelling at two or three knots. Deep in the heart of the ship, cut off from rescue, engineers must have kept one engine going. What they endured while waiting for the end in burning heat under flickering emergency lights is unimaginable.

Yanagimoto shouted '*Banzai!*' from the bridge to encourage his men in the water.[53] His crew could not bear to see their beloved captain go down with his ship and so Chief Petty Officer Abe, the navy wrestling champion, was sent to bring him down – by force if necessary. He climbed to the bridge and urged, 'Captain, I have come on behalf of all your men to take you to safety. They are waiting for you. Please come with me to the destroyer, sir.' Yanagimoto ignored him. Abe advanced towards him, but a long, calm look from his skipper halted him in his tracks. He saluted and left. As he climbed down he heard Yanagimoto quietly singing '*Kimigayo*' – the national anthem.[54]

Six hundred miles (nearly 1000 km) away, Yamamoto's main force was enveloped in an impenetrable fog. Someone handed him a signal. He groaned. Then he sat, still as stone, gazing into the gloom.

HIRYU STRIKES BACK

But all was not yet lost. One carrier survived, *Hiryu*, and on it Admiral Yamaguchi raced to bring his strike force up to the flight deck and launch them against the Americans. *Hiryu*'s dive-bombing unit, commanded by Lieutenant Kobayashi, was believed to be the best in the fleet. His 18 Aichi D3A dive bombers had a superb record: in an Indian Ocean operation against the Royal Navy, 80 per cent of their bombs had hit their targets. The planes carried a mix of 550-lb (250-kg) armour-piercing bombs which would explode below decks and 530-lb (242-kg) high-explosive bombs to knock out anti-aircraft guns on deck. Six Zero fighters would escort them, and torpedo bombers would follow. The pilots received their final briefing in a mood of grim determination. One witness said, 'I had never seen such an impressive scene before.' Kobayashi was shaking so hard that his teeth rattled, not from fear but from a 'fierce determination' to fulfil his mission.[55] His small force left the deck at 10.58 a.m. The planes circled upwards through the thick black smoke from the raging fires that had killed so many of their comrades. The fleet watched them depart, praying that they would be able to snatch a victory of sorts and stave off utter defeat.

When Nagumo arrived on the cruiser *Nagara*, he immediately ordered his depleted fleet to head with all speed for the Americans

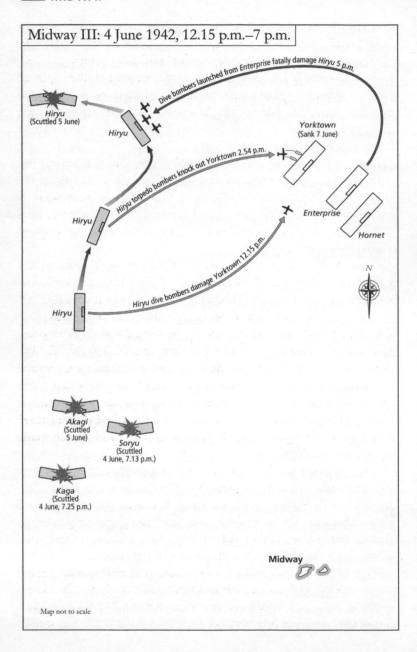

Midway III: 4 June 1942, 12.15 p.m.–7 p.m.

Dive bombers launched from Enterprise fatally damage *Hiryu* 5 p.m.

Hiryu
(Scuttled 5 June)

Hiryu

Yorktown
(Sank 7 June)

Hiryu torpedo bombers knock out Yorktown 2.54 p.m.

Hiryu

Enterprise

Hornet

N

Hiryu dive bombers damage Yorktown 12.15 p.m.

Hiryu

Akagi
(Scuttled
5 June)

Soryu
(Scuttled
4 June, 7.13 p.m.)

Kaga
(Scuttled
4 June, 7.25 p.m.)

Midway

Map not to scale

and engage them in a surface action. Word was received that the other Japanese units sprinkled around the Pacific were on their way. The men of the fleet felt a modicum of confidence return.

As the strike force headed towards the Americans, they spotted dive bombers returning to the US fleet. Unable to resist, the Zeros attacked them. But none of the Americans were shot down and the Zeros then had to try to catch up with the bombers they should have been supporting.

The *Yorktown*'s radar spotted incoming planes at 11.52 a.m., and 20 fighters were scrambled to deal with them. They charged at the Japanese bombers head on and scattered their neat V formations. A mêlée broke out and the American fighters shot down several of the Japanese bombers. The Zeros escorting the bombers arrived late and joined the fight.

The surviving Japanese bombers flew through the hail of anti-aircraft fire coming from the seven escort ships circling the *Yorktown*. The first aircraft released its bomb, but was shot down seconds later. Incredibly, the bomb landed on the machine gun which had shot the plane down and killed the crew. The second and third bombers just missed. Finally, *Yorktown*'s luck ran out. A 550-lb (250-kg) bomb went through her flight deck, ignited in the stack and snuffed out many of her boilers. The carrier's speed decreased and black smoke belched out from the jagged wound. Another bomb smashed into the forward elevator. Kobayashi's squadron had secured three hits, but they had paid a terrible price: only 6 of his 24 aircraft made it back to the *Hiryu*.

The *Yorktown* had both prepared for and responded to the attack magnificently. A fuel bowser that had been on deck was tipped into the sea just before the Japanese arrived. Fuel lines had been flooded with carbon dioxide. After the bombs tore through the ship, damage control parties fought their way through the black smoke and tried to patch up the flight deck with wood and steel plates.

On the *Hiryu*, a second wave of attacking aircraft was assembled on the deck, and Admiral Yamaguchi himself was giving the pilots a briefing. At 1 p.m. a downed American airman had been plucked out of the water and interrogated. He finally made up for the woeful

Japanese scouting and told them that there were three American carriers present. Yamaguchi passed this information on to the pilots, who listened to him solemnly. There were 16 of them: 10 were to fly Nakajima B5N torpedo bombers, and 6 Zeros would escort them. Yamaguchi told them that it was absolutely imperative to hit one of the three carriers that had not already been damaged. As the commander climbed into his bomber, Yamaguchi shook his hand and told him, 'I will gladly follow you.'[56] Overhead, a dive bomber returning from the previous raid dropped a message giving them the position of the *Yorktown* and confirming that it was on fire. But this latest intelligence never made it to the pilots who were about to take off. They launched at 1.30 p.m., a pitiful shadow of the force which had left *Kido Butai* at dawn.

If Yamaguchi and Nagumo had moved the *Hiryu* further away from the Americans after launching the second wave, the carrier might have escaped detection. But an American scout at the very limit of its range spotted her and got off a message to the US fleet. Aboard the *Hiryu*, Yamaguchi was scraping together a third wave. Far from thinking about the bigger strategic picture and the importance of preserving the *Hiryu*, he appeared to be possessed by a short-sighted fatalism. He is reported to have said, 'We with *Hiryu* alone are going to sacrifice ourselves to kill the damned enemy force.'[57] Stirring words, perfectly in keeping with the Japanese warrior code, but no way to win a war.

Just after 2.30 p.m., *Hiryu*'s second wave of strike aircraft spotted a US carrier surrounded by escort vessels. It looked unharmed and they prepared to attack it. But this was not an undamaged carrier; it was the battered *Yorktown*. Her radar and boilers were back on line and her speed was 19 knots. The ship had been warned by radar that another attack was impending, so fuel lines had been drained and fighters scrambled. Wildcats jumped on the incoming torpedo bombers and were, in turn, attacked by Zeros. The Japanese bombers streaked in at 200 knots, only 200 feet (60 metres) above the water. Jimmy Thach brought down the lead Japanese plane only seconds after he had left the *Yorktown*'s deck. The Japanese bombers were fast but, like the Zeros, the trade-off was a lack of armour for the fuel tanks and crew. Several planes exploded in midair.

Two Japanese aircraft flew in very low and dropped their torpedoes only 2000 feet (600 metres) out. Seconds later, two white plumes of water lifted out of the ocean alongside the carrier. The first torpedo knocked out three of the ship's boilers; the second flooded the forward generator room, killing *Yorktown*'s power. Water surged into the hull through the two holes. Soon the *Yorktown* was heeling badly; the carrier that had been America's great survivor was at last sinking. Fletcher ordered that the *Yorktown* be abandoned. Captain Buckmaster toured the ship thoroughly to make sure he was the last living person on board and then lowered himself into the sea. But the Japanese paid a high price for their attack: only 9 of the 16 planes returned to the *Hiryu*.

DEFEAT

In spite of their crippling losses, both sides struggled to prepare their aircraft for what they each believed could be the final blow.

Admiral Yamaguchi, on the *Hiryu*, believed that instead of hitting *Yorktown* with a second wave, he had now hit two of America's three carriers and only one remained. He managed to scrape together 5 bombers, 5 torpedo planes and 10 fighters for a final strike. But at the briefing it became clear that the pilots were too exhausted to fly – they had not eaten since before dawn, 12 hours or so earlier, and some had been flying almost continuously. They were given stimulant pills and the launch was pushed back by 90 minutes to allow them food and rest; many of them fell into a deep sleep in the ready room. The Americans, for their part, had lost 70 planes, 40 per cent of their strength. But they still had more than enough aircraft to overwhelm the depleted forces of just one Japanese carrier. *Enterprise* sent 26 dive bombers aloft. *Hornet* only managed to launch 16.

At 4.45 p.m. the *Enterprise*'s dive bombers found the *Hiryu* and came in from the west with the sun behind them. The exhausted

Zero pilots guarding the fleet failed to spot them until they were right over the carrier, and the *Hiryu*'s helm was hurriedly thrown into a series of sharp turns. The Zeros' pilots attacked with a sense of desperation: they knew that the carrier below them was the only one left for them to land on. They shot down two bombers, but there were too many US planes to stop. The American pilots aimed for the large rising sun of Japan painted on the flight deck. Four 1000-lb (450-kg) bombs smashed into the ship within metres of each other, and 19 Zeros in the forward hangar were instantly destroyed. The front of the flight deck was peeled back like the lid of a can, while the forward elevator was hurled into the air and large sections of it hit the superstructure, throwing everybody on the bridge to the floor. Below decks, pilot Toshio Hashimoto tried to get to safety: 'tripping over the limbs of my brothers-in-arms, I gasped and struggled through the darkness until I finally managed to escape onto the side of the bridge through a hole caused by one of the bombs.'[58]

Sailors used buckets on ropes to try to scoop seawater up to the flight deck to fight the fire. Escort vessels closed in and sprayed water. But the fire crept below, eventually knocking out the engine room and warping her hull plates, letting in water.

Over the next few hours, the pride of the Imperial Japanese Navy slid below the waves. According to a nearby destroyer captain, the *Kaga* had been 'like a huge bonfire. There surrounded by the flames stood the bridge looking like a volcano that had melted down; a lava slag.'[59] She was scuttled, and sank at 7.25 p.m. Minutes later, the *Soryu* followed her. The *Akagi* and the *Hiryu* did not sink until the early hours of the next morning. The *Akagi* rang with the noise of machinery crashing around as her bows rose out of the water. To one witness, 'It sounded like the shrieking of some living creature.'[60] At around 2 a.m. a mighty explosion on the *Hiryu* forced Yamaguchi to abandon ship. But he kept his promise to the young airman. The pilot had not returned from the strike and now Yamaguchi would indeed follow him to his death. He and the captain of the *Hiryu* lashed themselves to the helm and waited for the end.

The loss of all his carriers meant that Yamamoto's fleet was gravely exposed to air attacks from Midway and the US carriers. After some agonizing, he realized he had no option but to order a wholesale retreat. He knew that he had lost the naval war: without his First Carrier Strike Force, offensive action in the Pacific was impossible. Before Midway, Japan had had six carriers in the Pacific to America's four. After the battle, the balance shifted: three American to two Japanese. The Battle of Midway had transferred the strategic initiative from Japan to the United States. These carriers had been the most expensive ships ever built by Japan and had taken years to mould into a strike force. Their loss was a national tragedy. Japan's shipyards could never replace them. But the losses went beyond the ships themselves. Japan had entered the war with around 2000 highly trained naval aviators. It was standard practice to put veteran flyers on the front line rather than keep them back to train new pilots. The aviators lost at Midway were all irreplaceable. Perhaps even worse was the loss of the support staff. Armourers, engineers and maintenance crews were difficult to find and train in Japan, and 2000 had died on the carriers.

Victory for the Japanese at Midway would not have won them the war. The American economy was six times bigger than that of Japan and was to expand by a further 50 per cent during the Second World War. But victory would have bought the Japanese more time, perhaps allowing them to inflict fatal damage on the British in the Indian Ocean, to attack Hawaii again, or even to raid the US continent. Instead, the destruction of *Kido Butai* made the end of the war in the Pacific and of Imperial Japan itself only a matter of time.

STALINGRAD

Fires from the other side of the Volga cast a flickering light on the faces of the men as they waited for the boats. They were exhausted after marching all day, and one in ten of them lacked a rifle. But these men were the best the Red Army had. They were Guards, battle-tested veterans, and their commander, Major General Aleksandr Rodimtsev, a hero of the Soviet Union, had learned his trade in the vicious street fighting of the Spanish Civil War. He and his men were about to be thrown into the most savage urban battle in the history of warfare. Scores of Guardsmen crammed on to barges and the overloaded vessels were ferried in the dark to the western side. Shells crashed into the river, soaking them. One or two barges took direct hits and disintegrated. As the men approached the far bank, they stared at what had once been a model city. Now it was an apocalyptic vision of hell. The glow of countless fires and the bright flash of explosions illuminated shattered apartment blocks and the twisted steel innards of factories. For miles in either direction there was nothing but conflict. A thousand battles were being fought on street corners, in cellars and in attics. Two mighty and utterly irreconcilable empires, one Nazi, the other Communist, were locked in a titanic clash which could have only two outcomes: victory for one, annihilation for the other. Rodimtsev's Guardsmen were a last hope, a final desperate attempt to stop the Nazis seizing this strategic city and delivering a possibly fatal blow to Soviet morale. They knew they faced almost certain death. As the first units reached the landing stage they hurled themselves at the Germans. Fighting with knives and fists, they clawed back enough space for their comrades to land. No price in blood was too high to pay because this wasn't just any city; it bore the name of the Soviet leader himself, and in the eyes of the whole world it had come to symbolize the entire struggle for European domination. The city's name was Stalingrad.

The Battle of Stalingrad lasted from September 1942 to February 1943. It was one of the biggest, bloodiest and most decisive battles of all time. Its outcome determined the course of the Second World War in its most important theatre, known simply as the Eastern Front: it was here that hegemony over the Eurasian landmass was won and lost.

BARBAROSSA

On 22 June 1941 the code word 'Dortmund' was issued by the German High Command. It was the signal to begin the largest single military operation in history. Barbarossa. Three million men, grouped in 210 divisions, backed by 2000 aircraft, 7000 pieces of artillery and 3350 tanks (supported by over 600,000 horses)[1] attacked the Soviet Union along a thousand-mile (1600-km) front from the Black Sea to the Baltic. Hitler's aim was to destroy Bolshevism and Judaism, which he equated, and seize *Lebensraum* or 'living space' in the east. German colonists would be settled and the abundant natural resources would underpin his thousand-year Reich. The Slavic peoples of the east were *Untermenschen*, subhuman. Some would be left as slave labourers: Hitler announced that, 'Our guiding principle is that the existence of these people is justified only by their economic exploitation for our benefit.'[2] The rest were earmarked for genocide.[3]

The expectation was that the *Untermenschen* would collapse after a series of massive blows from the German *Wehrmacht*. No plans were made for a long campaign and no winter clothing was provided for the troops.[4] Hitler announced: 'You only have to kick the door in and the whole rotten structure will come crashing down.'[5]

Through the summer of 1941, it seemed that Hitler was right, as German forces routed the Red Army. The *Wehrmacht* encircled whole Soviet armies, inflicted millions of casualties, took millions more men prisoner and demonstrated tactical brilliance in the use of tanks and aircraft. The Soviet forces enjoyed huge reserves of manpower, but they were led by political appointees, they relied on largely obsolete hardware and their tactics were totally out of date. The man responsible for the woeful state of the Red Army was the General Secretary of the Central Committee of the Communist Party of the Soviet Union: Iosif Vissarionovich Dzhugashvili, or, as this *de facto* dictator called himself, Stalin. The name was derived from the Russian phrase for 'man of steel', but the German invasion came close to breaking him. His purges in the late 1930s had rooted out any Red Army officer with talent or an independent mind. In 1941 he wilfully ignored blatant intelligence and even ordered the execution, for disinformation and provocation, of a German soldier who had crossed the frontier on 21 June and told the Russians that the Germans would attack the next day. A week later Stalin seems to have come close to breakdown and told his companions, 'Everything's lost. I give up. Lenin founded our state and we've fucked it up.'[6] For two days he stayed in his country dacha and government was paralysed. In the middle of July, things had become so bad that he ordered an approach to the Bulgarian ambassador to see whether he could take Hitler an offer: if the Führer halted his *Wehrmacht*, he could have the Ukraine, the Baltic states, White Russia and Moldavia. The canny Bulgarian refused to act as a go-between, saying, 'Even if you retreat to the Urals, you'll still win in the end.'[7]

By 1 August, the Germans were only 250 miles (400 km) from Moscow and had captured or killed 2 million Red Army soldiers. But the Soviet Union's massive distances were starting to sap the vigour of the German advance. The *Wehrmacht* was not strong enough to encircle Soviet troops everywhere at once. Yet rather than launch the final assault on Moscow, Hitler wasted vital summer weeks by targeting Kiev, successfully, in the south and Leningrad, unsuccessfully, in the north. It was not until the autumn that he launched his armies against Moscow, whose capture he belatedly saw as the key to ultimate victory.

Operation Typhoon was launched on 30 September. Seventy *Wehrmacht* divisions, with 1 million men, 1700 tanks and 1000 aircraft, were hurled towards the Soviet capital. Within a fortnight they had shattered the Soviet front line and captured 600,000 Russians. Then the skies opened. Planes were grounded and tanks foundered as the dirt tracks of Russia turned into bogs. But the Germans pressed on through the increasingly bad weather and by mid-November they were in the suburbs of Moscow, 20 miles (32 km) from the Kremlin.

In early December, with the temperature at minus 35°C the Red Army stunned the world by counter-attacking. The 1st Shock Army drove the Germans back, and Army Group Centre came close to collapse. Hitler removed Field Marshal von Brauchitsch, the commander-in-chief of the German army, and took the job himself. He ordered a halt to all retreats: German troops were to stand and fight, regardless of the threat of encirclement. Isolated groups were to be resupplied by air until rescued by counter-attacks. Stalin, however, frittered away the chances of a major victory by ordering attacks up and down the line, rather than concentrating on completing the rout of Army Group Centre. Thanks to German tenacity and poor Soviet strategy, by March the line had stabilized. Hitler was convinced that it had been his insistence on not retreating that had saved the *Wehrmacht*.

By March 1942, Germany had lost nearly 1 million men, but had inflicted 3 million casualties on the Red Army and had taken another 3 million men prisoner (most of whom died after a short period in captivity). The Soviets had been denied precious resources too. The Germans had seized the fertile farmlands of the Ukraine, thereby halving the Soviet Union's bread supplies for 1942. Coal, steel and iron ore production for the beleagured Soviets had been cut by three-quarters.[8] But the Soviet Union had survived Hitler's onslaught. The Red Army had not collapsed. Indeed, despite its horrific casualty figures, massive conscription meant that the Red Army had swollen to 8 million by the end of 1941. The Soviet

Union now had the full backing of the USA, the world's biggest economy, which had been in the war since December 1941, and of the United Kingdom, at the head of the world's biggest empire. Hitler could not risk a long war against these three powers. In 1942 he had to finish the job he had begun in 1941: the destruction of the Red Army and the Soviet Union, and the securing of sufficient economic resources to take on Britain and America in a final struggle for global hegemony.

OPERATION BLUE

Hitler's strategy for the 1942 campaign was underpinned by his desire to deny resources to his enemy. He lacked the manpower to attack everywhere at once. But he ignored his generals' plea for a renewed onslaught against Moscow, the capture of which might topple the Soviet regime, and decided to concentrate on the south. Nazi Germany now had four times more industrial capacity at its disposal than the Soviet Union, but it lacked the one thing that it most needed: oil. Cut off by the Royal Navy on the seas, Hitler was totally reliant on the only oil in continental Europe, the Ploesti oilfield in Romania. But if he could seize the rich oilfields of the Soviet Caucasus he would both guarantee his own supplies and starve the Soviet Union of oil. So convinced was he of the importance of oil to the war effort that he told a group of officers from Army Group South in June, 'If I do not get the oil of Maikop and Grozny, then I must end this war.'[9] The Red Army, which the Germans believed to be on its last legs, would be forced to protect the oilfields: it could be encircled and crushed, as it had been the summer before.

Operation Blue was the name given to the offensive. The plan was to sweep east, encircle Soviet forces penned in between the rivers Don and Volga, and then cut the Volga in or near the city of Stalingrad to halt the flow of supplies up this vital waterway. Stalingrad itself was not particularly important. Hitler's original orders were to 'reach Stalingrad itself, or at least to cover it with heavy artillery, so that it will no longer be an industrial or transportation centre'.[10] Then the offensive would swing south towards the mountains of the Caucasus and seize the precious oilfields. Field Marshal von Bock's Army Group South had been reinforced by borrowing heavily from other German formations. Tanks along the rest of the front had been cannibalized for parts, so that southern panzer units could be brought up to full strength. Army Group South could call on 46 infantry divisions, 9 panzer divisions, two SS divisions and 11 others. These 68 divisions would be supported by 25 from Germany's allies: 1 million German soldiers would be backed up by 300,000 men from Italy, Romania and Hungary. Air Fleet Four would provide support in the skies from 1500 planes. With far fewer men than the year before, Hitler was about to launch an equally ambitious offensive along a 500-mile (800-km) front. The logistics of the operation, across terrain with no serious roads, would be difficult enough, even without the opposition of the Red Army. *Wehrmacht* officers hoped that the Soviets were as weak as the German High Command seemed to think.

Again, Stalin stubbornly misread intelligence reports. He was certain that Hitler would strike at Moscow rather than hundreds of miles to the south. Even when, on 19 June, a plane carrying a precise order of battle for the coming offensive crashed behind Soviet lines, Stalin believed it to be clumsy disinformation. The British government showered the Soviets with warnings gleaned from their breaking of Germany's Enigma code, but they were ignored.

On 28 June Operation Blue slammed into the Soviet lines. A huge dust cloud could be seen for miles as panzers raced across the dry open plains of the southern Ukraine. Soviet opposition disintegrated under the onslaught. Rostov-on-Don fell less than a month into the attack. The ease with which the city fell horrified the Soviets and gave heart to the Axis soldiers. William Hoffman, fighting in the 94th division of the German 6th Army, wrote in his diary, 'Today, after we'd had a bath, the company commander told us that if our future operations are as successful, we'll soon reach the Volga, take Stalingrad and then the war will inevitably soon be over. Perhaps we'll be home by Christmas.'[11] Many Ukrainians and

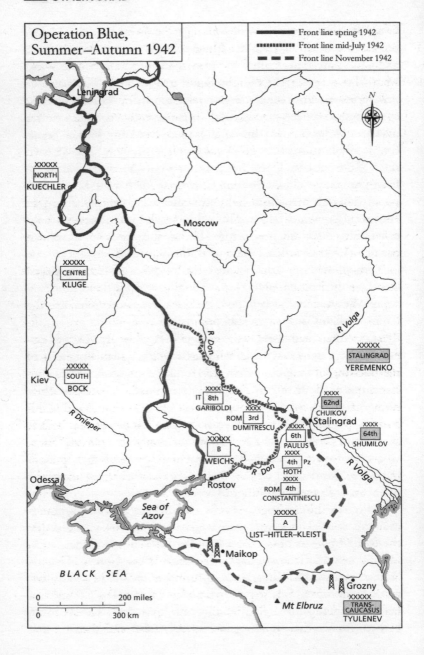

**Operation Blue,
Summer–Autumn 1942**

	Front line spring 1942
	Front line mid-July 1942
	Front line November 1942

Leningrad

XXXXX
NORTH
KUECHLER

Moscow

XXXXX
CENTRE
KLUGE

R Don

R Volga

XXXXX
STALINGRAD
YEREMENKO

Kiev

XXXXX
SOUTH
BOCK

R Dnieper

XXXX
IT 8th
GARIBOLDI

XXXX
ROM 3rd
DUMITRESCU

XXXX
62nd
CHUIKOV

Stalingrad

XXXXXX
B
WEICHS

XXXX
6th
PAULUS

XXXX
4th Pz
HOTH

XXXX
ROM 4th
CONSTANTINESCU

R Don

Rostov

XXXX
64th
SHUMILOV

R Volga

Odessa

Sea of
Azov

XXXXX
A
LIST–HITLER–KLEIST

BLACK SEA

Maikop

Grozny

Mt Elbruz

XXXXX
TRANS-
CAUCASUS
TYULENEV

0   200 miles
0   300 km

N

Cossacks even greeted the *Wehrmacht* as liberators, for Stalin's regime was widely hated. Children offered Nazi soldiers flowers and the traditional gifts of salt and bread. Little did they know what Hitler's plans for the Ukrainian people were. The previous year, Erich Koch, a veteran Nazi, had been made Commissar of a sprawling province encompassing these conquered lands. At his inauguration speech he declared, 'I am known as a brutal dog.... Our job is to suck from the Ukraine all the goods we can get hold of.... I am expecting from you the utmost severity towards the native population.'[12] By the end of the war, 250 villages and their populations had been singled out and deliberately destroyed to encourage good behaviour. The Ukrainian people were systematically beaten, starved, murdered and raped while under German occupation. Jews were rounded up and slaughtered.

Throughout July and August, the German armies rampaged across the wide open lands of the Ukraine and southern Russia. It seemed like a repeat of 1941, but there was one vital difference. On 6 July Stalin gave his generals permission to make tactical withdrawals rather than stand their ground and allow the Germans to encircle large numbers of Russian troops. Stalin had finally accepted the doctrine of swapping space for time.[13] As a result, while Axis forces plunged deeper and deeper into Russia, stretching their supply chains to the limit, they were unable to surround and eliminate big pockets of Soviet troops as they had done the year before. By the end of August, the Red Army had 'only' lost 600,000 men, an acceptable cost for such a vast machine. By refusing to present themselves for destruction, the Red Army was frustrating one of the main aims of Operation Blue.

Hitler saw things altogether differently. The absence of big encirclements with their large haul of prisoners suggested to him that the Red Army was now unable to offer any serious resistance. On 20 July he told General Halder, the chief of the German General Staff, 'The Russian is finished.'[14] In confident mood, he made a far-reaching decision. Echoing his disastrous intervention of the year before, he changed the plan for Blue and split Army Group South in two. Rather than heading east to the Volga and then turning south, his forces would now do both at the same time. One thrust, designated Army Group A, was told to head south immediately and seize the oilfields. They were given priority in terms of fuel and other supplies and took nearly all Army Group South's armour. The other thrust, Army Group B, was stripped of its panzers and told to keep going east towards Stalingrad. The two groups would now pursue entirely different goals without being able to support each other.

Army Group B consisted of Axis troops spearheaded by the 6th Army, one of the best in the *Wehrmacht*. Its commander was General Friedrich Paulus; he had been the 6th Army's chief of staff, but when its commander, General Walther von Reichenau, died suddenly in January 1942 he had been promoted. A thinker and a planner rather than a fighting general, Paulus was uncomfortable in the field. He hated dirt, and washed himself and changed his clothes several times a day. Unlike his tough, extrovert predecessor, Paulus was a quiet man who was at his happiest listening to Beethoven. Before the war, a senior officer described him as 'a typical staff officer of the old school. Tall, and in outward appearance painstakingly well groomed. Modest, perhaps too modest, amiable, with extremely courteous manners, and a good comrade, anxious not to offend anyone. Exceptionally talented and interested in military matters, and a meticulous desk worker, with a passion for war games and formulating plans on the map-board or sand-table.'[15]

Paulus now had to push deeper into Russia without the support of the tanks of the 4th Panzer Army which Hitler had sent south. Lacking transport and supplies, his advance slowed dramatically. In late July he was forced to halt altogether because of fuel shortages. Hitler realized his mistake and sent 4th Panzer back northwards on 1 August. Yet more time was wasted criss-crossing the vast Russian steppe: huge traffic jams clogged the single-track roads and crucial momentum was lost. The Soviets used the breathing space to bulk up the defence of Stalingrad. More and more divisions were deployed, and counter-attacks were ordered on the flanks of the German advance. On 19 July the city of Stalingrad itself was put on a war footing.

STALIN'S CITY

For hundreds of years the city of Tsaritsyn had stood at the point where the Tsaritsa River flowed into the mighty Volga. The tsars had established it as a garrison town to defend the southern frontier of the Russian empire from the wild tribesmen of the Caucasus. In 1918 Josef Stalin had found himself in charge of the city's defences during Russia's bloody civil war. Here, in the words of a biographer, 'he had gained his confidence as a man of action'.[16] Here, too, he had first discovered the efficacy of terror in government, won Lenin's trust and met his second wife, Nadya, and many of his closest friends. After the Bolshevik victory Tsaritsyn became Stalingrad, and in the 1920s it was designated a model socialist city. In the industrial district in the north, thousands of members of the Communist Union of Youth constructed the Dzerzhinskii tractor factory, which originally built farm machinery for use in the Ukraine and had recently switched to building T-34 tanks. Alongside it stood a chemical plant and the Krasnii Oktyabr (Red October) metal plant. All of them had their own schools and accommodation for the workers. Further south along the river bank, public buildings, municipal spaces and parks made up the city centre. A giant opera house provided entertainment for the workers, and in the summer they could saunter through the terraced formal gardens built along the river. But beneath the concrete of this socialist utopia lay an unruly physical geography. Several rivers flowed off the steppe into the Volga, carving into its banks deep ravines enjoyed by pre-war courting couples. In the centre a huge hill towered above an otherwise low-lying city. At 337 feet (103 metres) high, Mamayev Kurgan (named after a commander of the Tartar Golden Horde which in the Middle Ages ruled this region of Russia) dominated the terrain.

Men, women and children were set to work digging anti-tank ditches. Anti-aircraft batteries were set up to combat German tanks and planes. Stalin forbade the evacuation of civilians, believing that Red Army soldiers would fight with more zeal for a living city. August was a month of extreme crisis for the Soviet Union. Paulus's forces were once again on the move towards Stalingrad, and in the south it looked as if it was only a matter of time before the Caucasus fell into German hands. On the 9th they captured the oil wells of Maikop; Soviet demolition teams, however, had done their job well and the Germans never managed to extract more than a few barrels a day. Even so, approximately half the Soviet Union's population and resources were now under Nazi control. On 23 August German Lieutenant Spindler, closely followed by a film crew, reached the summit of Mount Elbruz in the Caucasus. At 18,500 feet (some 5600 metres), and taller than Mont Blanc, it is the highest mountain in Europe. There he planted a swastika flag. It was, give or take a few square miles, the point of maximum extent of the German empire, which now stretched from Brittany to the Caucasus mountains and from the North Cape of Norway to North Africa.

The same day, far to the north, elements of the 6th Army arrived at Stalingrad. German tanks found the open, flat steppe the ideal place to conduct armoured warfare and they smashed through the Soviet 64th Army outside the city. Inexperienced women manning artillery and anti-aircraft batteries fought bravely but hopelessly. The 16th Panzer Division actually reached the banks of the Volga north of the city, and fulfilled the original objectives of Operation Blue. But the advance had raised expectations even higher. By late August, anything less than the capture of the city itself would be seen as a failure, and Paulus decided to launch an all-out assault.

INFERNO

On the 23rd and 24th the Luftwaffe, the German air force, unleashed bombing raids against Stalingrad on a titanic scale: 2000 sorties were flown. In the almost total absence of Soviet interceptors, German pilots had a free run over the city. Their bombers smashed every kind of target: roads, railways, factories and public buildings. In an attempt to kill or demoralize the civilian population, the wooden buildings of the residential district in the south of the city were attacked with incendiary bombs. Firestorms swept through mile after mile of housing. One Soviet commander wrote, 'The huge city, stretching for nearly 35 miles [56 km] along the Volga, was enveloped in flames. Everything was blazing, collapsing. Death and disaster descended on thousands of families.'[17] The large oil containers on the river bank were obvious targets; when they caught fire a funeral pyre of black smoke stretched thousands of feet into the sky and burning oil spewed out on to the surface of the river. Fedor Leontevich Shatravko was a tank crewman who had been wounded badly in the defence of Moscow the year before. He remembers being in hospital 'when they came to find men for Stalingrad'.[18] Hauled out of bed and taken south, he fought through that winter. Today he lives in a tiny apartment in the city, surviving on his meagre pension and telling schoolchildren about his memories of the battle. Of those first few days all he says is, 'Everything was burning, everything was on fire.' Marshal Yeremenko, commander-in-chief of the group of armies that made up the 'Stalingrad front', wrote, 'We'd been through a lot in the war up to that time, but what we saw in Stalingrad on August 23rd was like a nightmare … the entire city was burning … the oil reservoirs appeared to be volcanoes throwing up their lava.'[19] Approximately 30,000 civilians were killed in two days, caught between their leader's refusal to evacuate them[20] and the Luftwaffe's deliberate attempt to kill and terrify the people of Stalin's city. After two days of apocalyptic destruction, General Wolfram von Richthofen, distant cousin of the First World War ace known as the Red Baron, and the commander of Air Fleet Four, flew over the city. He was the Luftwaffe's leading expert on dive bombing, with experience stretching back to his command of the Condor Legion in Spain, where he had ordered the pulverizing strike on the Basque town of Guernica in 1937. He made an inspection of the city and wrote in his diary that night that Stalingrad had been 'destroyed and [was] without any further worthwhile targets'.[21]

It was now the turn of the ground assault forces. Paulus, with support from the 4th Panzer Army advancing from the south, had something like 200,000 men, 500 tanks and around 4000 guns at his disposal. Facing him were approximately 54,000 Red Army troops, supported by 100 tanks and fewer than 1000 artillery pieces.

The Soviets were a hastily assembled collection of men divided into under-strength divisions. But taking the city would not be easy. The Germans' favourite and well-tested tactic of encirclement with armoured pincers was ruled out. The city may have been 30–40 miles (50–65 km) long but was only about 5 miles (8 km) in width, backing directly on to the broad Volga River. Encirclement was not an option. Instead, the thinness of the city invited four or five frontal attacks which would break through to the river, divide the Soviet defenders and reduce pockets of resistance one by one.

Stalin realized that the point of crisis had arrived. He began sleeping in his office in the Kremlin and insisted on being woken every two hours; soon he looked exhausted and gaunt. The strategic and psychological value of Stalingrad was too great to the Soviet Union and to him personally to let it fall with the ease of Rostov. Setting aside his suspicion of professional soldiers and his preference for Bolshevik stooges, he summoned the Soviet Union's greatest general to the Kremlin. Georgy Konstantinovich Zhukov had been born into a peasant family in 1896, but rose to command an army group that crushed the Japanese during a border incursion in August 1939. His armoured forces had outflanked the enemy and plunged deep into their rear, demonstrating precisely the tactics that the Germans would use to stun the world in the next few years. Zhukov was also one of the few men who spoke his mind to Stalin, and had consequently been removed in the summer of 1941 from his position as the Red Army's chief of the general staff. However, later that year he had halted the German thrust towards Leningrad and won the gratitude of millions at home and abroad with his counter-attack outside Moscow in December. Stalin, the Supreme Commander, now asked Zhukov to be his deputy.

The general at first refused, saying, 'My character wouldn't let us work together.'

Stalin replied, 'Disaster threatens the country. We must save the Motherland by every possible means, no matter the sacrifice. What of our characters? Let's subordinate them to the interests of the Motherland. When will you leave?'

Zhukov said, 'I need a day.'[22]

The Germans had been reduced to a crawl through the outskirts of Stalingrad, as the Luftwaffe's raids had only thrown up impediments to their advance. Collapsed buildings and twisted steel supports made the devastated city very different terrain from the open steppe. The Communist apparatus called on its people to build 'impassable barricades' on every street and ordered, 'Everyone who can carry a gun – to the barricades!'[23] Civilian levies made suicidal attacks and were mowed down in neat ranks. By 10 September, Stalingrad was totally cut off from Soviet forces to the north and south. The fighting had been tough, harder than any that summer. On the last day of August Wilhelm Hoffman from the 94th division of the 6th Army wrote in his diary, 'Are the Russians really going to fight on the very bank of the Volga? It's madness.'[24] Little did he know that he was about to be plunged into one of the harshest battles in the long history of warfare.

As always, Hitler was impatient. Soviet resistance had seemed to stiffen through August, and the autumn rains loomed large in the minds of his planners. But the Führer was growing obsessed with the symbolic. On 2 September he ordered that when the city fell every male was to be liquidated and every female deported. Stalin's stubborn city would be wiped off the face of the planet. The seizure of a city with little strategic value was, because of its name and the stubbornness of its defenders, taking on its own dynamic.

Stalin had relented somewhat and allowed people to leave the city if space could be found on the boats going backwards and forwards across the Volga. Vital machinery was dismantled and evacuated, all part of the hugely impressive programme of industrial relocation: from the first days of the war, key factories had been disassembled, evacuated and then rebuilt far to the east, where workers endured horrific conditions to get tank, shell and weapon production back on line. By 14 September, around 300,000 civilians had been sent east, all of them braving the trip across the Volga under almost constant fire from German artillery and air attack. As they scrambled towards the river crossing, they pinned notes to trees and buildings: 'Mama, we are all right. Look for us at Beketovka. Klava.'[25] Others stayed in the city throughout the fighting. Fedor

Shatravko remembers people staying in the factories for months at a time: 'They never went home. Parents brought them food and a change of clothes.'[26] In the German-held areas, many Russians were shot arbitrarily out of hand or deported for slave labour.

RATTENKRIEG

The defence of Stalingrad now fell to the 62nd Army. Cut off by the Germans from its neighbouring Soviet forces on either side, and by the river to its rear, it was ordered to hold its ground and keep a Soviet presence on the west side of the Volga. Its commander, General Lapotin, was a broken man who told his superiors that there was no way the 62nd Army could hold the city. He was fired, and replaced on 12 September by Vasilii Ivanovich Chuikov. In many ways Paulus's opposite, Chuikov was a rugged street-fighter, aggressive, crude and outspoken. He cared so little about his appearance that in his unkempt state he was often mistaken for an ordinary soldier, and his scarred and lined face made him look much older than his 42 years. British war correspondent Alexander Werth called him 'a tough, thickset type of Red Army officer but with a good deal of bonhomie and a loud laugh. He had a golden smile. All his teeth were crowned in gold and they glittered in the light of the electric lamps.'[27] In the month before taking command he had been in both serious car and plane crashes and for the next few months his HQs were always in the line of fire. Although he never lost his belief in victory, he was under such stress that he developed acute eczema: his hands were constantly bandaged.

Chuikov quickly developed a simple doctrine for his troops to inflict maximum casualties and delay on the Germans. Debris-filled streets, battered brick buildings and collapsed concrete walls ruled out the kind of free-flowing battle which the Germans craved. Mobile attacks by combined air, tank and infantry units were impossible. Chuikov ordered his forces to make a virtue of this constricted battlefield. They must get as close as possible to German troops, no further away than 'the throw of a grenade'.[28] This strategy

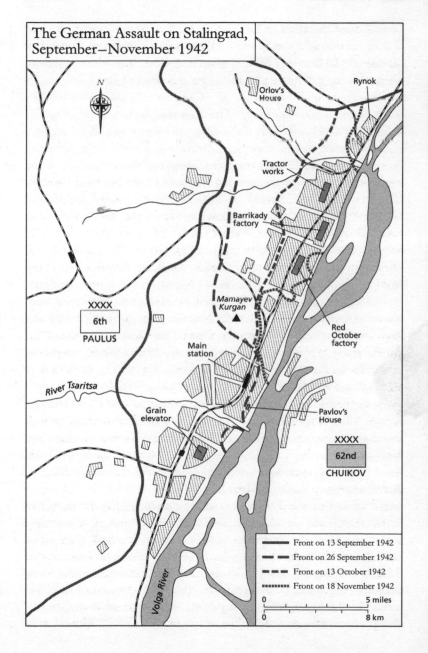

The German Assault on Stalingrad, September–November 1942

N

Rynok

Orlov's House

Tractor works

Barrikady factory

Mamayev Kurgan ▲

XXXX
6th
PAULUS

Red October factory

Main station

River *Tsaritsa*

Grain elevator

Pavlov's House

XXXX
62nd
CHUIKOV

Volga River

Front on 13 September 1942
Front on 26 September 1942
Front on 13 October 1942
Front on 18 November 1942

0   5 miles
0   8 km

would draw the fangs of German air strikes, because the Luftwaffe would be unwilling to bomb its own men. The German infantry would also be forced to fight in ways that were new to them. Rather than waiting for air attacks to soften the opposition and tanks to provide them with protection, the German soldiers would have to push forward by themselves. The Russians would be waiting for them with steel, rifle and club. Each encounter would be a close-quarters brawl, in which victory would go to the toughest and most committed. Chuikov ordered his men to build mini-redoubts and fortresses, with loopholes and tunnels to the rear for supplies. These strongpoints would be 'capable of all-round fire if sur-rounded'. This feature would allow them to hold the Germans and counter-attack their rear if they tried to bypass them. Chuikov would force the Germans to fight on his terms. Out on the steppe they were masters; in the city Chuikov would teach them a different kind of war. He told his men, 'Every German soldier must be made to feel he lives under the muzzle of a Russian gun.'[29] His men were to defend their corner, tunnel, attic or pile of rubble, with no thought of withdrawal or surrender. The Soviet Union was in mortal danger; it needed a breathing space to construct new defensive lines and amass reserves of men and equipment. As Chuikov said, 'Blood is time.'[30]

At 6.30 a.m. on 14 September Paulus began his all-out assault. Von Seydlitz-Kurbach's 51st Corps tore into the northern and central parts of the city in two pincers. These would attempt to reach the Volga and then turn to advance towards each other along the bank until they met, thus surrounding the defenders. Below the Tsaritsa River, southern Stalingrad was assaulted by the 4th Panzer Army using similar tactics. Despite ferocious Soviet resistance and heavy losses, the Germans crept closer to the river. In Germany, newspapers were printed with '*Stalingrad gefallen!*' splayed across their front pages. At the last minute they were held back as officials working for Hitler's propaganda chief, Goebbels, sought Paulus's absolute assur-ance that the Russian city had fallen. Paulus declined to give it. He deflected their questions, saying airily, 'Any time now, any time.'[31] In the city, it seemed that Paulus was right. Chuikov's HQ on top of

Mamayev Kurgan was knocked out, and he had to set up another one in a bunker on the banks of the Tsaritsa. He threw his last reserves into the battle and called for as much artillery support from the far bank as he could muster. At dusk a tank brigade with only 19 tanks was holding up the 51st Corps' advance. Chuikov begged his superiors for more men.

In response, the newly arrived 13th Guards Division under Major General Aleksandr Rodimtsev were sent across the river that night. The Luftwaffe had no night bombing capability and so the boat journey, almost suicidal by day, was threatened during the hours of darkness only by German artillery fire. Rodimtsev's first units had to clear the landing stage with bloody, hand-to-hand fighting. This done, they were assigned by Chuikov's staff to various vital points. Some were sent to retake the summit of Mamayev Kurgan; if the Germans held on to this single piece of high ground in the area it would spell destruction for the 62nd Army. Chuikov later wrote, 'If the enemy took it he could command the whole city and the Volga.'[32] Despite exhaustion and a shortage of rifles, the Guards rampaged through the city, halting the Germans in their tracks and even driving them back. Somehow they stormed the summit of Mamayev Kurgan and, although driven off it again by artillery and aerial bombing the next day, managed to turn it into a no man's land and deny it to the Germans.

Other Guardsmen were ordered to retake the main railway station, just to the south, where they fought using wrecked carriages as cover. All around them the buildings were on fire. Twisted steel girders fell among them, and shards of glass flew through the air as shells and small arms smashed windows. The station changed hands four times on the 15th and had done so 15 times by the 19th: both sides launched counter-attacks as soon as possible to stop the enemy digging in.

In this desperate situation, Guardsmen shot holes in drainpipes in case they contained any water to quench their thirst. Survivors of one unit lasted days with no food or water and threw rocks at the Germans when their ammunition ran out. Surrounded by dead and dying comrades, they fought on until the Germans brought up tanks and brought the building down on top of them. Another group of survivors was to include some of the most famous Stalingrad heroes. Sergeant Jacob Pavlov found himself in command of a platoon and decided to fortify an L-shaped apartment block in the middle of the city. There he and his men held out for 58 days against everything the Germans could throw at them. Pavlov's defenders fired anti-tank guns through holes in the walls, while the basement provided cover from air attack; civilians brought food, water, vodka and ammunition through tunnels and drains. The building became a permanent feature of the battlefield – its name, 'Pavlov's House', appeared on Soviet maps. Today it still stands: an apartment block with a museum in the basement.

By the end of their first day in the city, the Soviet 13th Guards had suffered 30 per cent casualties. After a week that figure had risen to 80 per cent. Only 320 Guardsmen survived the Battle of Stalingrad. Their sacrifice had stopped the Germans for a vital week, denied them control of Mamayev Kurgan and secured the area around the main landing stage. Chuikov wrote in his memoirs, 'Had it not been for Rodimtsev's division the city would have fallen completely into enemy hands approximately in the middle of September.'[33] But they were only the first of several divisions which suffered almost total extinction. Another such division was the 284th Siberian, who arrived on 23 September. It was made famous by the former shepherd Vasilii Zaitsev, who survived the initial attack to become a sniper responsible for the deaths of around 300 German soldiers. Modern books and the film *Enemy at the Gates* have given credence to the story that a crack German sniper was sent out to deal with him. In reality, there is no evidence of a duel between the two men.

South of the Tsaritsa, the German attack had reached the Volga, and by 17 September only a giant grain elevator kept two German pincers from closing around the entire 62nd Army position in the south. The grain elevator was manned by 30 marines and 20 Guardsmen, only one of whom survived to tell the tale of their ferocious resistance. Andrey Khozyaynov wrote that, 'In the elevator the grain was on fire, the water in the machine guns evaporated, the wounded were thirsty but there was no water. This is how we defended ourselves 24 hours a day for three days.' When they ran out of grenades, they hurled back those that were thrown at them. 'On the west side of the elevator the Germans managed to enter the building, but we immediately turned our guns on to the parts they occupied…. We sensed and heard the enemy soldiers' breath and footsteps, but we could not see them in the smoke. We fired at the sound.'[34] The diary of Wilhelm Hoffman, who was among the Germans attacking the grain elevator, is full of amazement at the tenacious defence being conducted by the Russians, whom he calls 'fanatics'. 'The elevator is occupied not by men but by devils that no flames or bullets can destroy…. Barbarians, they use gangster methods … Stalingrad is hell … our old soldiers have never experienced such bitter fighting before.'[35] By the 24th, the battle for the grain elevator was over. The Germans had taken the city south of the Tsaritsa.

On 26 September Paulus announced to the world that he had captured the south and centre of the city and that the 'battle flag of the Reich flies over the Stalingrad party building!'[36] It was an exaggeration. The landing stage was not secured; neither, infuriatingly, was the summit of Mamayev Kurgan. Nevertheless, Hitler flew from his forward HQ in the Ukraine back to Berlin to prepare for a speech announcing the fall of Stalingrad.

Privately, Paulus was worried. The supposedly subhuman Judaeo–Bolsheviks were holding on, despite everything he could throw at them. So great were his losses that he was obliged to bring more and more troops into the city from his flanks in the steppe. His mood was not improved by an acute attack of dysentery, although his discomfort paled in comparison to the suffering of the men under his command in the city. The length and vulnerability of the supply line from the west meant that rations were not getting through. Crawling through a wrecked city, measuring gains in mere metres and sustaining dreadful casualties sent morale plummeting. The Germans called this ordeal *Rattenkrieg*, war of the rats. A growing number of junior officers and NCOs were killed as they tried to lead their men forward. Some units refused to move unless they had

Sturmgeschütze, the self-propelled guns which would give them close support during any assault.

Any coherent attack soon broke down into a series of murderous small-scale actions as men fought above ground and below for alley-ways, rooms and sewers. Rather than concerning himself with the now inappropriate formalities of battalions and divisions, Chuikov ordered that 'shock groups' play the central role. These were groups of 50 to 100 men who armed themselves with flamethrowers, knives, Tommy guns and grenades, using stealth to ambush groups of Germans and surprise enemy outposts. Unlike the Germans, who attempted to combine artillery, aircraft and tanks in their attacks, the shock groups were opportunistic. They made optimum use of the terrain, sent in fast hit-and-run attacks and fortified defensive strongpoints. Chuikov later described these tactics in his book: 'Get close to the enemy's positions. Move on all fours, making use of craters and ruins. Carry your tommy-gun on your shoulder. Take 10 or 12 grenades. Timing and surprise will then be on your side.... Into the building – a grenade! A turning – another grenade! Rake it with your tommy-gun! And get a move on!'[37]

Chuikov was running the battle as he pleased, for Stalin was now giving his generals increasing autonomy. By the beginning of October, he downgraded the detested commissars, political appointees serving with every unit who would report on the reliabil-ity of military officers and who had a huge say over strategy. They were now restricted to maintaining morale.

In a neat contrast, while Stalin was letting his generals fight the war themselves, Hitler was increasingly interfering. For two and a half months in late summer he commanded the Army Group A himself and dictated day-to-day operations. Now his military advis-ers told him that the obsession with Stalingrad was denying men, munitions and fuel to the other Caucasus thrusts. Furious, he stopped dining with these generals and spoke to them only through intermediaries. On 24 September he removed the Chief of the German Army General Staff, Franz Halder, and gave the job to the more pliable Kurt Zeitzler. Even Zeitzler recommended that the battle for Stalingrad be terminated. But Hitler would not hear of it.

By the end of September, southern and central Stalingrad had been secured; the battle would now shift to its industrial heart in the north. The eyes of the Soviet Union, and indeed of the world, were now on this struggle. Two reporters wrote jointly in *Pravda* on 28 September: 'On the banks of the Volga the roar and thunder of the street fighting resounds like an echo. The ceaseless chaos of ear-splitting noises, fire, and smoke remind me of a gigantic infernal smithy ... the whole city shakes with the explosions of shells and mines. The streets are smothered in smoke and clouds of dust that never seem to have time to settle down before another bomb or shell falls.'[38] Sentries could see their breath on the night air. Winter was on its way and the battle showed no sign of abating.

Paulus's attack in the north of the city was based on the same throttling tactics as his previous thrusts in the south. Two pincers, one around the foot of Mamayev Kurgan and towards the metal plant and the other to the north through the tractor factory, would push towards the Volga. On reaching it they would turn north and south respectively along the bank and join up, surrounding most of what was left of the 62nd Army.

At 10.30 a.m. on 27 September, 11 German divisions tore into the factory district. Dive bombers hammered Soviet positions. As soon as the bombs had been dropped, tanks rolled forward with lines of infantry behind them, with the aim of finishing off the dazed defenders. But again the debris and rubble in the streets broke up the impetus of the attack. Well-protected defenders in upper storeys successfully knocked out vehicles, causing a traffic jam. For tank crews, immobility meant death: Soviet artillery spotters called down a lethal barrage on any group of German troops or vehicles that remained static for more than a minute. On the far, eastern bank of the Volga the Red Army had parked artillery almost wheel to wheel: there were 160 guns per mile (100 per kilometre), and they included around 200 heavy, long-range weapons. Well-camou-flaged spotters observed the impact of the shells from countless vantage points in the ruins of the city on the west bank. Groups of German infantry massing for an attack were gravely exposed, and air-burst shells wiped out whole companies of men. Soviet trucks on the west bank carried Katyusha rocket launchers, capable of firing a volley of 16 rockets which delivered 4 tons of explosives over a 10-acre area (40,000 square metres). The trucks would shelter under the steep bank of the river to reload, reverse to the water's edge, fire a salvo and then drive back under cover. One observer of the battle, Konstantin Simonov, wrote, 'We could certainly not have held Stalingrad had we not been supported by artillery and katyushas on the other bank all the time. I can hardly describe the soldiers' love for them.'[39]

Even so, by nightfall on the 27th the Germans had made strong gains. Despite the fact that, after constant capture and recapture, the summit of Mamayev Kurgan had reverted to a no man's land, elsewhere the Germans had advanced almost 2 miles (nearly 3000 metres). Two of Chuikov's divisions had been virtually wiped out. He wrote in his diary that night, 'One more day like this and we'll be in the Volga.'[40] But the Germans too had lost huge numbers of men, especially among the ranks that mattered most: as ever, junior officers and NCOs suffered by far the highest proportion of casualties. German units were being 'decapitated', and as a result their attacks on the 28th were noticeably less effective.

Thousands of small boats crossed the Volga from the eastern bank, bringing the supplies that would allow the 62nd Army to fight on. The priority was ammunition, next men and lastly food. Thousands of gallons of vodka were also sent into the city to provide the troops with moments of relief from the horror of their predicament. Most of this traffic moved by night, when the Luftwaffe was unable to fly; any boats that ran aground and could not be shifted faced deadly attacks at sunrise.

The fighting raged on in the industrial district and soon turned into a confusion of tiny, murderous mêlées. Fedor Shatravko had taken to living in the tractor factory, where soldiers and civilians were desperately repairing battle-damaged tanks and sending them straight back into the fray. When asked about his relationship with his tank crewmates, he holds up his clenched fist and says, 'Like fingers in the same fist – one Ukrainian, one Uzbek, one Tartar.' While they changed the tracks on their tank one morning in late

September, German tanks approached the factory. 'I was very frightened, but then I became fierce.' Shatravko fired three shells, two of which scored hits, and the other German tanks pulled back; the Germans apparently lacked good armour, so the sensible thing was, he recalled, to remain calm and 'You'll be fine.' Shatravko noticed two field guns further away which he tried to crush with his tracks, but his tank got stuck between them. It attracted enemy fire and soon burst into flames. Badly injured, and with his uniform alight, he was dragged to safety; his crewmates, less fortunate, were shot by the Germans. Ferried back across the Volga at night, Shatravko was taken to a makeshift hospital where his bed was a hay bale and his covering a greatcoat instead of a blanket. His ears rang for weeks.[41]

In the tangled mess that had been the factory district German troops came to fear the Soviet snipers more than ever. Their favourite targets were German soldiers carrying insulated food containers to the front-line troops. The supreme sharpshooter Vasilii Zaitsev also told his students to kill people carrying water. This would force the Germans to drink polluted water and they would contract dysentery. During one attack, Lieutenant Joachim Stempel of the 108th Panzer Grenadier Regiment remembered, 'Snipers, who, with their fire that hits us in the flank, inflict bloody losses, are lurking everywhere. They are hiding all around but cannot be spotted.'[42] Germans forced Russian children to collect water for them; when the Soviets realized this, they shot the children.

Another huge push by the Germans took place on 5 October, when bombers delivered 700 attacks on the tractor factory alone. But thanks to lack of supplies and fierce fighting, the Luftwaffe was running out of bombs, so some of the planes dropped scrap metal instead. As the German infantrymen clambered over twisted machinery following the raids, they noticed ruefully that much of it was German-made. The attack petered out as massive, saturating fire rained down on them from the Soviet artillery on the far bank.

Chuikov had been lucky to survive early October: his HQ had been almost buried under a flood of burning oil from punctured containers, and his eczema had got a lot worse. On the other side,

Paulus was aloof and taciturn; a nervous tic in his left cheek became more pronounced. Hitler's orders to him became ever more hysterical while the *Wehrmacht* High Command watched the decimation of the 6th Army with horror. Desperate for fresh men, Paulus ordered the Romanian 3rd Army to take up positions on the left flank of the German 6th Army, freeing up the VIII Corps to join the fighting in the city.

Winter was imminent. Soon ice floes would make the Volga impassable for weeks until it completely froze over. The cloudy skies would make air operations difficult. The 6th Army was about to make its final bid. The world watched.

At 8 a.m. on 14 October the Germans launched a furious onslaught. After a massive air and artillery bombardment, three infantry divisions, two panzer divisions and four elite combat engineer battalions rushed forward: 90,000 men and 300 tanks attacked along a front of only 3 miles (5 km). Chuikov later called it 'the bloodiest and most ferocious day in the entire battle…. That morning you could not hear the separate shots or explosions; the whole thing merged into one continuous deafening roar…. In a dugout the vibration was such that a tumbler would fly into a thousand pieces. That day, 62 men in my headquarters were killed.'[43] Buildings collapsed, masonry tore through the air like shrapnel, detonating bombs sucked the air out of men's lungs and thick concrete dust clotted in their ears, mouths and eyes. The Soviets cowered in slit trenches, unable to move or even think as around 3000 airstrikes pounded them continuously. German tanks broke through at 11.30 a.m., but as a panzer commander wrote, 'It was a terrible, exhausting battle on and below ground, in ruins, cellars, and factory sewers. Tanks climbed mounds of rubble and scrap, and kept screeching through chaotically destroyed workshops and fired at point-blank range in narrow yards. Many of the tanks shook or exploded from the force of an exploding enemy mine.'[44]

By midnight the Germans had surrounded the tractor factory on three sides and advanced over a mile (about 1.6 km). Assault groups had made it through to the Volga. For the next week, the Soviet presence on the west bank hung by a thread. Wilhelm Hoffman wrote in his diary during this time, 'October 17. Fighting has been going on continuously for four days, with unprecedented ferocity. During this time our regiment has advanced barely half a mile.... Men and officers alike have become bitter and silent.... October 22. Our regiment has failed to break into the factory. We have lost many men; every time you move you have to jump over bodies.... Soldiers are calling Stalingrad the mass grave of the *Wehrmacht*.... October 27 ... the Russians are not men, but some kind of cast iron creatures; they never get tired and are not afraid of fire....'[45]

Lieutenant Weiner of the 24th Panzer Division wrote in his diary, 'We have fought during fifteen days for a single house, with mortars, grenades, machine guns and bayonets ... this is a ceaseless struggle from noon to night. From storey to storey, faces black with sweat, we bombard each other with grenades in the middle of explosions, clouds of dust and smoke, heaps of mortar, floods of blood, fragments of furniture and human beings ... animals flee this hell; the hardest of stones cannot bear it for long; only men can endure.'[46]

On the second day of the assault, the 15th, yet another German division was fed into the carnage at the tractor factory. One of its toughest defenders was Olga Kovalova, the first female steel foundry worker in Stalingrad, with 20 years' experience and a foul mouth. She would shout at militiamen whom she considered lazy and, after refusing to obey an order to go to the rear, was killed at her post. Colonel Wilhelm Adam, a German staff officer with the 6th Army, referred to people like her in his diary: 'The population took up arms. Lying on the battlefields were workers in overalls still clasping a rifle or pistol in their stiff hands. The dead in workers' clothes leaned over the controls of smashed tanks. Never ever have we seen anything of the kind.'[47]

Soviet soldiers frequently found themselves cut off. A light artillery officer called Babachenko sent out a message: 'Guns destroyed. Battery surrounded. We fight on and will not surrender. Best regards to everyone.'[48] Chuikov's HQ was now a mere 1600 feet (500 metres) behind the front line. From there he ordered that support troops on the east bank – cobblers, mechanics and horse handlers — be formed into infantry units and fed into the city. Paulus too was scraping the barrel to keep up the attacks. While panzer crews grabbed a few hours of sleep, cooks and maintenance crews stood guard and beat off counter-attacks. The German obsession with Stalin's city surprised the Russians. Chuikov wrote, 'Fresh infantry and panzer units appeared and, regardless of losses, they rolled towards the Volga. It seemed as though Hitler was prepared to destroy the whole of Germany for the sake of this one city.'[49]

By 20 October, the tractor factory was in German hands. Inside other factories, and even inside their derelict furnaces, fighting continued amid the giant industrial machinery that had been smashed and upended by continuous bombing. The Soviet wounded crawled towards the river; the dead stayed where they lay. Around Pavlov's apartment block, destroyed German equipment piled up as the Soviets' guns fired down on enemy tanks from the upper storeys; German tank guns lacked the elevation to fire back. During the fighting around this one building, only 1300 feet (400 metres) from the river, the German army lost more men than it had done when it captured Paris in 1940.

Lieutenant Stempel recalls the fighting in the steel works, 'We're attacking. Metre by metre we crawl forward, following the bombs that the Stukas are dropping in front of us. The howling of sirens, explosions, breaking, splitting, fountains of mud by the exploding bombs! ... unbelievable ... one cannot understand anything any more ... the Russians are hanging tough and bitterly contest every hole in the earth and every pile of rubble.'[50]

The almost supernatural tenacity of the Russians has been written off by some recent historians as a product of coercion and use of terror. It is true that many Soviet attacks included blocking units of NKVD soldiers with orders to shoot any men who did not charge forward with sufficient enthusiasm; during the battle at least 15,000 Soviet troops were killed by their own side. It is also true, however, that millions of Russians all along the Eastern Front fought and died willingly. The atrocities committed by the Germans during their advance, the certain death that awaited them if they surrendered, and the horror that would be visited upon their loved ones if they were to let the Germans plunge deeper into the USSR seem to have given many Red Army soldiers an often suicidal resolution to fight to the end. Lieutenant Charnosov wrote to his wife saying, 'I am in good health. I have been wounded twice but these are just little scratches and so I still manage to direct my battery all right During these days of hard fighting I am avenging my beloved birth-place of Smolensk, but at night I go down to the basement where two fair-haired children sit on my lap. They remind me of Slavik and Lyda.' The letter was found on his corpse. So was one from his wife telling him to 'fight to the last drop of blood, and don't let them capture you, because a prison camp is worse than death'.[51] A German letter, from a Leutnant Otten, strikes a different note: 'I often ask myself what all this suffering is for. Has mankind gone crazy? This terrible time will mark many of us forever.'[52]

By 24 October, the attacks had petered out. Cold, exhaustion and lack of supplies were undermining the German advance. During the day the temperature had plunged to below minus 20°C; at night it was even colder. Winter clothes were inadequate and slow to make it up the long and slender supply lines. Despite the fact that the 6th Army controlled 90 per cent of the city, with Soviet sectors only hundreds of metres wide and under constant fire, and despite the fact that Paulus had destroyed 75 per cent of Chuikov's army, the truth was that he had inflicted fatal damage on his own German forces. Combat troops now made up only a small proportion of his overall numbers. Doctors in Berlin were shocked by cases of men who were unaccountably dropping dead, and concluded that it was caused by cumulative stress. The Russians had lost a greater number of men than the Germans, but they had plenty more to feed into the city; Paulus did not.

On 8 November Hitler spoke to Nazi party veterans to celebrate the anniversary of the Munich Putsch of 1923, the Führer's first attempt to seize power in Germany. He announced that Stalingrad had fallen: 'I wanted to take it and, you know, we are being modest, for we have got it! There are only a few small places left not cap-tured…. I do not want a second Verdun there but I prefer to do it with quite small detachments of assault groups.'[53] He was referring to the First World War attack by the Germans on the symbolically important French fortress of Verdun, which, after huge losses on both sides, did not fall. The shivering, lice-ridden, exhausted troops huddled in the ruins of Stalingrad listened to their radios in disbelief.

In early November five battalions of assault engineers, veterans of urban combat, arrived in the city to deliver the final blow. They attacked shortly after midnight on the 9th and captured one stubborn strongpoint, but after 24 hours only one in five of them was still alive. On the 11th the 6th Army managed one last offensive spasm: German forces reached the river by the Red October factory and brought the crossing under direct fire. Russian troops caught in the middle of the Volga River drowned in the freezing waters. Icebergs now drifted down the river, crushing Soviet boats, which meant that the 62nd Army could not be properly supplied again until it froze completely – several weeks later, on 16 December. But Paulus's forces were in no position to take advantage. Baron von Gablenz, commander of the 38th Division, sent this frank message to his junior officers: 'I am well aware of the state of the division. I know that it has no strength left.... The fighting is cruel and it becomes crueller every day.... The lethargy of the majority of soldiers must be corrected by more active leadership ... those who fall asleep at their posts in the front line must be punished with death.'[54]

While the two punch-drunk armies clung on in the city, plans were afoot out on the steppe. The Soviets had been probing the flanks of the 6th Army and the Axis allied divisions for months. Their attacks had done little to threaten the huge salient occupied by Axis forces, and as a result German generals who expressed concern about the Soviet threat were derided. On 18 November the Chief of the General Staff of the Army, Kurt Zeitzler, attempted to allay fears of a Soviet attack like the one a year before in front of Moscow. He announced, 'The Russians no longer have any reserves worth mentioning and are not capable of launching a large-scale offensive.'[55]

URANUS

A little more than 24 hours later, a gigantic aerial, rocket and artillery barrage shook the southern Russian steppe and minutes later three Soviet army groups, numbering three-quarters of a million men, tore into the flanks of Army Group B.

Two months earlier, on 13 September, Zhukov had outlined to Stalin an astonishingly bold plan to solve the Stalingrad crisis. He could see that the Germans' Army Group B was over-extended, with vulnerable flanks in the open steppe. Zhukov proposed a thrust deep into the German rear. Operation Uranus, as it was called, would cut off the Germans, destroy Army Group B and provide a springboard for an attack towards Rostov to cut off Army Group A. Stalin approved and asked Zhukov how soon he could be ready: 45 days, came the reply. Until then they would rely on Chuikov's army in Stalingrad to force the Germans to concentrate all their attention on the city and ignore their flanks, where over a million men, 13,000 guns and around 900 tanks were secretly moved into position. Trains only travelled at night. During the day, everything stopped moving and was camouflaged. Strict radio silence was observed. Attacking infantrymen did not receive orders until the night before the offensive. Little was written down: all briefings were conducted orally. Even Chuikov was only told less than a day before.

Despite all this secrecy, the Germans realized that something was up. On 31 October their army intelligence reported a large build-up opposite the Romanian 3rd Army. The Luftwaffe too spotted troops massing. On 11 November Richthofen wrote in his diary, 'Opposite the Romanians on the Don the Russians are resolutely carrying on with their preparations for an attack ... their reserves have now been concentrated.... I only hope the Russians don't tear too many large holes in the line.'[56] On 4 November even Hitler had been disturbed by pictures of the bridges across the Don and the enemy build-up. He ordered the 6th Panzer Division and two infantry divisions to be transferred from France as a reserve behind the Axis armies; they would scarcely have time to pack their kit before the Soviet assault crashed into those armies a fortnight later.

All 20 divisions of the 6th Army and the 4th Panzer Army were concentrated in the eastern tip of the giant Army Group B salient, fighting a crippling war of attrition with the Russian 62nd Army in Stalingrad. Their panzer forces were divisions in name only. Thanks to enemy action, wear and tear, lack of fuel and spare parts they were hardly operational. Field mice had nested in their vehicles' engines, gnawing through the wiring. The group's reserve was the 48th Panzer Corps. Impressive on paper, it was composed of the *Wehrmacht's* least battle-ready panzer division, the 22nd,[57] and the

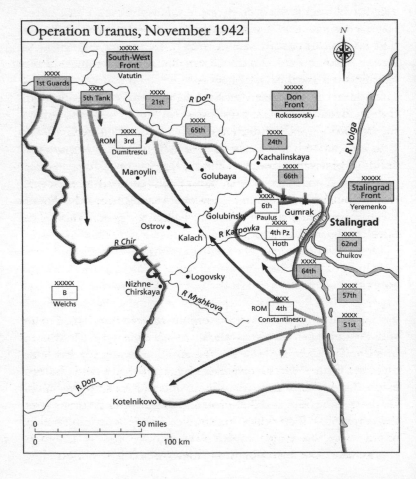

Operation Uranus, November 1942

Romanian armoured division, which was equipped with old Czech tanks from the 1930s. Guarding the flanks of the group were Italians and Romanians. They had been denied proper winter clothing because delivering ammunition to Stalingrad was a higher priority. They had no concrete to build proper bunkers, and were thinly stretched over long sections of the line. The Germans regarded their 37mm anti-tank guns as useless in the face of modern Soviet tanks. It was on these men that the fury of the Red Army descended at 7.20 a.m. on 19 November. Three and a half thousand guns and mortars blasted Romanian positions north of Stalingrad. Every conceivable target was inundated with high-explosive shells. At 8.50 a.m. the Soviets attacked in massed formations of T-34 tanks along a 200-mile (320-km) front. Outnumbered four to one, hungry, freezing and alone, the Romanians collapsed.

The next day, the Soviets tore into the Romanians to the south of the city. Both pincers sped for the town of Kalach, to sever the railway to the west and complete the encirclement of Army Group B. By the 23rd, the Romanians had been annihilated. The steppe was crawling with small groups of them begging to be taken prisoner and fed. The carcasses of their horses and shattered remnants of their equipment littered the snow. By that evening, the Soviet armies from the north and the south had joined up at Kalach. The 6th Army was surrounded.

KESSEL

The majority of the Axis Army Group B was now imprisoned in an area 80 miles (130 km) long and 25–35 miles (40–55 km) in breadth. The Germans called it the *Kessel*, meaning the kettle or cauldron. In it were 20 divisions of the 6th Army and the 4th Panzer Army, two Romanian divisions and a Croatian regiment. In all, there were about 300,000 men, 100 tanks, 1800 artillery pieces and up to 50,000 extremely unfortunate 'Hiwis'– Soviet prisoners of war who had agreed to serve the Axis, usually as labourers or mechanics but increasingly as front-line soldiers. Surrounding

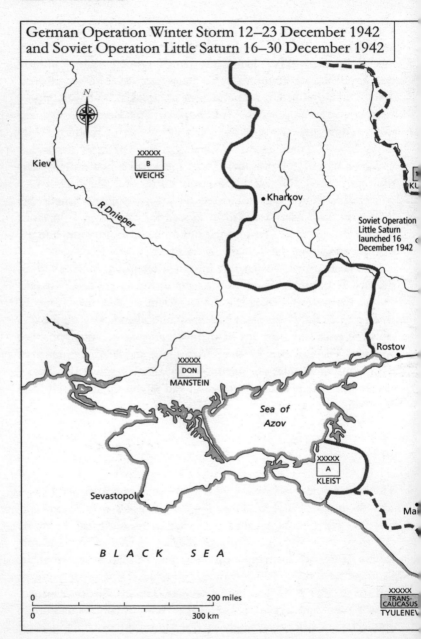

German Operation Winter Storm 12–23 December 1942
and Soviet Operation Little Saturn 16–30 December 1942

N

XXXXX
B
WEICHS

Kiev

R Dnieper

Kharkov

Soviet Operation
Little Saturn
launched 16
December 1942

Rostov

XXXXX
DON
MANSTEIN

Sea of
Azov

Sevastopol

XXXXX
A
KLEIST

Mai

BLACK   SEA

0   200 miles
0   300 km

XXXXX
TRANS-
CAUCASUS
TYULENEV

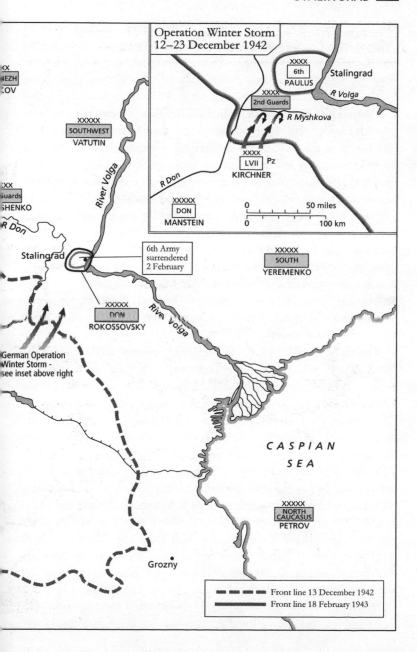

Operation Winter Storm
12–23 December 1942

XXXX
6th
PAULUS

Stalingrad

R Volga

XXXX
2nd Guards

R Myshkova

XXXX
LVII Pz
KIRCHNER

R Don

XXXXX
DON
MANSTEIN

0   50 miles
0   100 km

XX
NEZH
KOV

XXXXX
SOUTHWEST
VATUTIN

River Volga

XX
Guards
SHENKO

R Don

Stalingrad

6th Army
surrendered
2 February

XXXXX
SOUTH
YEREMENKO

XXXXX
DON
ROKOSSOVSKY

River Volga

German Operation
Winter Storm -
see inset above right

CASPIAN
SEA

XXXXX
NORTH
CAUCASUS
PETROV

Grozny

- - - - - Front line 13 December 1942
————— Front line 18 February 1943

this force were 97 Soviet divisions from seven different armies.

Inside the *Kessel*, German officers began preparations for a break-out. General von Seydlitz-Kurzbach, commanding the 51st Corps, wrote to Paulus, 'The 6th Army is faced with a clear alternative: breakthrough to the south-west ... or face annihilation in a few days ... there is no other choice.'[58] In fact, Seydlitz pre-empted the issue by withdrawing one of his divisions from their position in the north-east corner of the pocket. He ordered all non-essential equipment to be destroyed and led by example, burning everything he owned except the one uniform which he was wearing. But Hitler would not countenance withdrawal: 'Too much blood has been shed,'[59] he told Zeitzler. The Führer was also concerned that the exhausted, frost-bitten, starving 6th Army was in no state to break out anyway and that such a plan would end in ignominious defeat. At least a last-man, last-bullet defence in Stalingrad would be suitably glorious. Besides, the head of the Luftwaffe, Air Marshal Hermann Goering, and his chief of staff, Hans Jeschonnek, had told Hitler that it would be possible to keep the 6th Army resupplied by air until a rescue mission could be organized.

The man tasked by Hitler to break the Soviet stranglehold on the 6th Army was one of Germany's finest commanders, *Generalfeldmarschall* Erich von Manstein. He was sent to the Caucasus and given command of Army Group Don, comprising the 6th Army, the 4th Panzer Army, the 3rd Romanian Army and some extra divisions. Immediately, he embarked on plans to break into the *Kessel*.

Meanwhile, the airlift began. The forces in the *Kessel* needed 300 tons of supplies at the very minimum. This meant that 800 Junkers 52 transport planes would be required. But the Luftwaffe only possessed 750, and most of them were flying supplies to Rommel's *Afrika Korps*, which was on the retreat from the Allies in North Africa. A second gaping hole in Goering's assurances was the weather. A major airlift would have been hard enough in the summer, but in the depth of winter it was impossible. On some days flying had to be suspended altogether. On only one day, 7 December, did the Luftwaffe meet the target of 300 tons (over

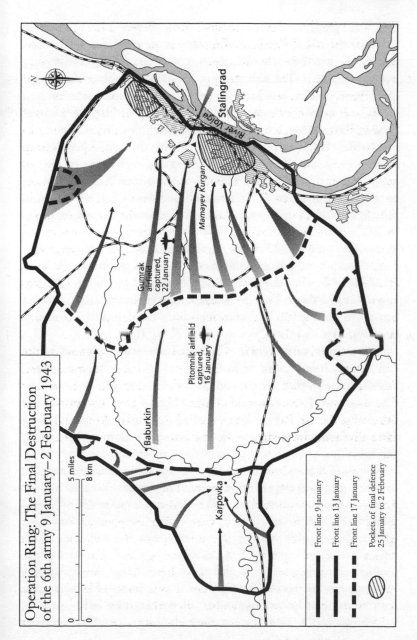

Operation Ring: The Final Destruction
of the 6th army 9 January–2 February 1943

N

River Volga

Stalingrad

Mamayev Kurgan

Gumrak
airfield
captured,
22 January

Pitomnik airfield
captured,
16 January

Baburkin

Karpovka

5 miles
8 km

Front line 9 January
Front line 13 January
Front line 17 January
Pockets of final defence
25 January to 2 February

300,000 kg); its average was 117.6 tons (almost 120,000 kg). In return for this it suffered fearful losses of its own. Enemy fighters waited on their flight routes, anti-aircraft guns lined their journey over Soviet-controlled territory and the cold weather ensured that there were regular accidents. Lacking snow ploughs, the ground crews had to clear runways with shovels: on a bad day they might have to shift up to a foot (30 cm) of snow.

The Axis forces surprised the Soviets with their stubborn defence of the *Kessel*, but they were slowly starving and running out of ammunition. Their last chance lay with the offensive being planned by Manstein, who on 12 December launched Operation Winter Storm. Two divisions from the 57th Panzer Corps hacked their way through 30 miles (50 km) of blizzards and enemy positions. By the 17th they were 25–30 miles (40–50 km) away from the *Kessel*. Hitler had a matter of hours to make up his mind whether to order a break-out by the 6th Army to meet Manstein; neither Paulus nor Manstein had the courage to disobey their Führer and order such a break-out themselves. In the end, Hitler refused to issue the order, claiming that there was insufficient fuel for the 6th Army's tanks. But time was running out: on the 16th Stalin had launched Operation Little Saturn, which aimed to cut off Manstein himself and Army Group A, which was spread throughout the Caucasus. The full force of this attack fell on the Italian 8th Army, who fought stoutly for a few days – but by dawn on the 19th, 200,000 of Mussolini's men were in full retreat. Manstein now had his hands full making sure there was no second encirclement. He would have to fall back and extricate the forces from the Caucasus, and the troops in the *Kessel* would have to fend for themselves.

By Christmas, German troops throughout southern Russia were desperately retreating. There was no longer any hope of relieving Stalingrad. Conditions in the *Kessel* were atrocious and they could only get worse. Between 22 November 1942 and 7 January 1943, 50,000 Germans died, some through enemy action but the majority from exposure and malnutrition. Everything started running out: ammunition, fuel, medical supplies. With the food ration reduced to two ounces (56 grams) of bread and half an ounce (14 grams) of sugar a day, the desperate men dug up dead horses and made soup from their bones. Their winter clothing remained woefully inadequate; their sleep was broken by constant Soviet bombing. Loudspeaker propaganda broadcasts in German told them that if they surrendered they would be fed and their wounds would be treated. But the only sure way for a German to escape from the *Kessel* was to be chosen as a 'specialist' in possession of skills too valuable to lose: 25,000 such men were lucky enough to get out.

THE END OF THE 6TH ARMY

The Soviets gave Paulus the chance to surrender, but in accordance with Hitler's orders he refused. On 10 January Operation Ring began, as a gigantic barrage fired from 10,000 artillery pieces heralded the final assault on the 6th Army. More than a quarter of a million Soviet troops attacked the mere 25,000 Axis combat troops who remained. Somehow, the 6th Army held out for three weeks. At the airfields in the *Kessel*, order broke down. There were riots to get on the planes, any of which could be the last to depart. Men clung to the wings and undercarriages as they took off, before inevitably falling to their deaths. Soviet tanks rolled on to the runway at the *Kessel's* main airstrip, Pitomnik, on 16 January. Another one, Gumrak, fell on the 22nd. Moving into the skeletal remains of Stalingrad itself, the Red Army now had to flush out determined German defenders by splitting the 6th Army in three – just as the Soviets had been sliced apart by the Germans only two months earlier. On the 22nd Hitler signalled Paulus to reiterate his orders: 'Surrender is out of the question. The troops will defend themselves to the last.'[60] If he was going to lose the 6th Army he needed a spectacle that would inspire the soldiers of the *Wehrmacht* for generations to come. On the 26th the Soviet 21st Army linked up with the pathetic survivors of Rodimtsev's 13th Guards, clinging to the north of Mamayev Kurgan. German troops hid in cellars, desperate to escape the terrible weight of Soviet fire; the dead and the living were packed in beside each other.

Despite the Luftwaffe losing 500 planes and 1000 aircrew during the airlift – losses which permanently destroyed their capacity to carry out such operations – they managed one more air drop. On the night of 29–30 January 124 bombers and transport aircraft dropped ammunition and rations. Much of it, however, landed in Soviet hands.

On the 31st Hitler made Paulus a field marshal. No German of this rank had ever surrendered. The message was clear: choose a soldier's death. But Paulus's nerve failed him. The fastidious technocrat who had presided over the biggest and most savage urban battle of all time allowed himself to be taken prisoner. After Soviet forces surrounded his makeshift headquarters in the Univermag department store, a young lieutenant, Fyodor Yelchenko, was invited inside. He stepped over hundreds of shell-shocked, filth-covered Germans to get to Paulus's bedroom. Paulus lay there unshaven. Yelchenko said, 'Well, that finishes it.' Paulus gave him a 'miserable look' and nodded.[61] When Hitler heard the news he flew into a rage, shouting, 'The man should have shot himself just as the old commanders who threw themselves on their swords when they saw their cause was lost.... He could have freed himself from all sorrow and ascended into eternity and national immortality, but he prefers to go to Moscow.... It doesn't make sense.'[62]

Even though he gave himself up, Paulus refused to sign the surrender of the 6th Army and it was left to groups of men to agree ad hoc ceasefires. The last to give in were men of General Karl Strecker's 11th Corps in the factory district, who fought hopelessly for a couple more days. Some could not face surrender. The commander of the 71st Division, General von Hartmann, walked into the open and fired at the Soviet positions with a carbine. A sniper's bullet soon struck him in the head. Others killed themselves with their own pistols.

At 4 p.m. on 2 February 1943 the Soviet guns fell silent. The siege of Stalingrad was over. It had been among the bloodiest battles of all time. It is difficult to calculate exact casualties, but the entire campaign had cost Hitler and his Axis allies around one and a half million killed, wounded, missing and captured. The figure for the

Russians is thought have been up to one million more. The scale of the bloodshed reflected the importance that both sides attached to what was to be the most decisive clash on the Eastern Front in the Second World War. It marked the point at which the Third Reich lost any chance of winning the war. On every level, Stalingrad was a disaster for Hitler. In purely military terms, it was the greatest defeat in German history. Around 50 divisions were annihilated and one air fleet utterly ruined. On 2 February Siegfried's Funeral March from Wagner's *Götterdämmerung* was played repeatedly on German radio. There were three days of national mourning. Strategically, it was just as disastrous. The oil remained in Soviet hands. Hitler's sacrifice of irreplaceable men had achieved absolutely nothing, and now his Axis allies began distancing themselves from his regime. Italy, Hungary and Romania had each lost an entire army at Stalingrad. They refused to send more men to the east, and some countries, such as Hungary and Finland, began to put out feelers for a separate peace with the Allies. Turkey was persuaded not to join the war on the Axis side. Germany would begin the campaigning season of 1943 with far fewer men, guns, tanks and aircraft than the Soviet Union. There was no talk of knocking the Soviet Union out of the war in 1943, merely a grim determination to fight a war of attrition that the Axis could not hope to win. But perhaps the greatest consequence of the Battle of Stalingrad was symbolic. Soviet soldiers, and Allied servicemen and women the world over, began to believe in victory. The myth of the invincible *Wehrmacht* had gone. The Germans came face to face with the possibility of defeat. For Hitler himself it was a bitter humiliation: he could not escape the blame. The responsibility for the tragedy was very largely his. It was the beginning of a rift in the German High Command that would end in plots, purges and a total breakdown in effective leadership.

Stalin made himself a marshal at the end of February and for the next two years rarely appeared out of uniform. Never again did he lose his nerve. Soviet forces inflicted a series of crushing defeats on the *Wehrmacht* and in early May 1945 General Chuikov's 62nd Army captured the Reichstag, the parliament building in Berlin, ending the Second World War in Europe. Stalin replaced

Nazi domination of eastern Europe with a Communist empire that kept Europe divided almost to the end of the twentieth century.

Most of the Germans who survived the battle did not see the end of the war. As well as Paulus and 23 other generals, 90,000 Axis troops were taken prisoner. The generals were well treated, but the men's suffering was to continue. As the snaking column of captives trudged through the snow, the Germans were beaten and robbed. Many died of starvation or exhaustion along the way, and only 15,000 were alive the following spring. After the war, they were made to rebuild the city they had destroyed. Only 5000 of them made it back to Germany in the 1950s, Paulus among them. He worked as a police inspector in Dresden in Communist East Germany until his death in 1957. As for those among the population of Stalingrad who had managed somehow to survive the battle, few could remain alive in the skeletal remains of the city: they were nearly all wiped out by hunger and disease. There was not a building that remained undamaged. The top of Mamayev Kurgan was reckoned to contain between 500 and 1250 splinters of metal per square metre, and the shape of the hill itself had been changed by so much bombing and shelling. It is now crowned by the biggest free-standing statue in the world: the 170-feet-high (50-metre-high) *Rodina-Mat*, the Mother Goddess defending the Homeland. At her feet lie the bodies of 35,000 Soviet veterans. Among them is Chuikov, the only marshal of the Soviet Union not to be buried in the Kremlin. Every day, veterans of the battle make the journey to kiss his grave.

THE IMJIN RIVER

Members of the platoon lay on their stomachs, peering over the rise at the river shimmering in the moonlight. They stared down at the water, waiting. At around midnight a small group of men emerged from the trees and dense vegetation on the far side and stealthily stepped into the shallow water. These figures, armed with a motley assortment of weapons, wore light cotton uniforms and carried rolled-up blankets around their shoulders in which to carry their kit. They were unmistakably the men of the 'People's Volunteer Army', which was, in truth, just another name for President Mao Tse-tung's Chinese Communist army. The platoon, from C Company, 1st Battalion of the Gloucestershire Regiment, waited until the river was packed with thousands of troops and then let rip with everything it possessed. Magnesium parachute flares hung in the air over the Chinese as tracer screamed into the mass of men, who were totally exposed as they waded across the river. Few of the soldiers in the British platoon that night could have explained exactly why they were fighting on the banks of the Imjin River in Korea, but without knowing it they had just fired the opening shots of one of the most heroic, bloody and tragic actions in the history of the British army.

The Korean War is the most unremembered British war in recent times. It followed hot on the heels of the Second World War and in Britain people wanted to rebuild their lives, homes, families and even society itself – not expend blood and precious resources in a land that few had ever heard of and fewer still cared about. Yet there have not been many occasions in British history when the nation has gone to war for more noble reasons. No national interests were at stake and there was no hope of any financial gain, yet the British government spent money it could ill afford committing troops to uphold a principle: that unprovoked aggression should be punished wherever in the world it occurs. It was a great test for the fledgling United Nations to see whether it would follow its predecessor, the League of Nations, into redundancy or whether a new era of international cooperation had truly dawned and the excesses of the 1930s had been banished. All this meant little to the men who fought in the extreme conditions of the Korean peninsula, among a people whom they did not understand and never warmed to. They fought as their forebears had fought in Afghanistan, Burma, South Africa and Iberia, because they had been told to. They fought hard because they didn't want to let down their mates. On the banks of the Imjin River and in the Kapyong valley, British and Commonwealth troops fought as well as at any time in British history and played a disproportionately large part in defeating a Communist offensive that aimed for the total destruction of the UN's forces in the Korean peninsula and of the South Korean state itself.

Like so many of the conflicts of the second half of the twentieth century, the roots of conflict in Korea lay in the messy conclusion to the Second World War. On 9 August 1945 a nuclear weapon was dropped on the Japanese city of Nagasaki. On the same day Stalin's veterans, straight from their destruction of the *Wehrmacht* in the ruins of Berlin, launched a massive offensive against the Japanese empire in Manchuria in north-east China. The Japanese collapsed. America viewed the success of its wartime ally with alarm. It was already clear that huge ideological schisms papered over during the struggle against Hitler would not take long to re-emerge following his demise. The United States was keen that one Asian empire run from Tokyo should not be replaced by an even greater one run from Moscow. The eyes of the State Department fell on the Korean peninsula, Manchuria's neighbour, which had been conquered by the Japanese in the late nineteenth century. It looked like the logical place to draw a line between the Soviet zone of influence to the north and west and the American one to the east and south. Two officials in Washington noticed that the 38th parallel neatly split the peninsula in half. As the Soviet 25th Army entered Korea, the Americans suggested that both nations should occupy half of the peninsula, with the 38th as the temporary barrier. The Soviets agreed. American troops were rushed into Korea and were met by streets thronged with people cheering their liberators.

The American occupation of the South was ham-fisted. Lieutenant General John Hodge, commander of the US forces in Korea, immediately developed a strong dislike for the Koreans. Instructed to treat them as a 'liberated people', he thought them 'the same breed of cats as the Japs'.[1] He briefed his officers to regard them as 'enemies of the United States'.[2] In fact, he found he was better able to do business with his former enemies, the Japanese, many of whom he allowed to stay in their key administrative posts – they were efficient and amenable. The Koreans were bitterly disappointed: the Americans were apparently blocking their wish for independence. The hated national police, a tool of the Japanese occupation which Koreans wanted to be disbanded immediately, was not only retained but also doubled in size. Some 8000 Koreans who had worked for the Japanese were promoted. In 1948, 53 per cent of the officers and 25 per cent of the rank and file among the police were Japanese-trained.

The situation in South Korea was one of growing instability. From the outset, the Japanese occupiers had systematically tried to destroy indigenous Korean culture. By 1945, the country was hugely exploited and its infrastructure run down; it was not promising territory for building a Western-style democracy. Political factions began to raise private armies and banditry was rife. By late 1945, Hodge needed a strongman and there was one obvious candidate, a man unblemished by association with the Japanese but sufficiently anti-Communist to appeal to the US military authorities: that man was in Washington DC. Yi Sung-man had escaped to the United

States early in the century after suffering arrest and torture at the hands of the Japanese in Korea. Once there, he westernized his name to Syngman Rhee. He went on to gain an MA at Harvard and a PhD at Princeton, becoming the first Korean to receive an American doctorate. He had lived in America since 1919 with his Austrian wife, running a self-styled government in exile. He was happy to pay lip service to the democratic ideals of his host country, and he was rabidly anti-Communist. The US State Department knew Syngman Rhee and distrusted him: it refused to issue him with a passport. However, Hodge orchestrated a campaign, involving more than a hint of corruption, whereby a passport was obtained and Syngman Rhee was whisked off to east Asia. At elections held in 1948, the right swept to victory. Squads of right-wing thugs had been active on the streets. On 24 July Rhee became South Korea's first elected leader, and on 14 August the US flag came down in Seoul to be replaced by that of South Korea.

The American occupation had been characterized by ignorance, lack of planning and a benevolent clumsiness. Only one man on Hodge's staff had learned much Korean. Things in the North had been very different. The Soviets brought with them a pack of Korean exiles who had spent years in Moscow, learning the Soviet way of running things and, most importantly, who would do what they were told. One of them was Kim Sung-ju. Born in 1912, Kim had joined the anti-Japanese Communist partisans in the 1930s, when he changed his name to Kim Il Sung after a Robin Hood-type legendary figure who was a champion of the commoners against tyrannical landlords. In 1941 he went to the Soviet Union to train as a Red Army officer. He arrived home in Korea in 1945 and was rapidly appointed to a key position by the Soviets. Behind Kim there was a typically efficient PR machine. The Communists were there to carry out a 'democratic revolution', not to impose an alien creed. The corruption that plagued the South was all but absent in the North. Populist measures such as land reform were immediately forced through; and there were opportunities to participate in people's committees, making the population feel as if they were involved in the running of the state. Dissidents were gradually silenced, and in

▲ General Vasilii Chuikov (centre), the Soviet Army commander, in Stalingrad at his headquarters. Chuikov's tenacity and drive, did much to sustain the determination of the Soviets to cling on to their toehold on the west bank of the Volga.

▲ Friedrich Paulus (left) surrenders to the Soviets in Stalingrad on 31 January 1943. Hitler had just made Paulus a Field Marshal, hoping he would redeem Nazi honour by committing suicide. But Paulus survived and died in Dresden in 1953.

STALINGRAD

▶ A German soldier fights to the bitter end as Stalingrad burns in early 1943. Men were as likely to die from exhaustion, malnutrition and the cold as they were from enemy fire.

▼ A Red Army Assault Group in Stalingrad. Chuikov did much to pioneer new techniques of warfare in urban areas. It quickly became apparent that the most effective way to fight was in small groups.

Union. Republicans criticized him for being far too lenient. Mao's victory in China was seen as a defeat. Senator Joe McCarthy had made his name attacking State Department officials who had supposedly let the Chinese Communists win. So Truman developed a policy, summed up in a critical study by the Joint State Defence study group, NSC-68, which was to become known as the Truman Doctrine. It stated that Moscow was bent on global domination and that the USA should rearm and challenge Communism on its next attempt at annexing a free state. So in June 1950 Truman and his advisers were looking for a fight, and Kim Il Sung had just given them an opportunity.

The newly formed United Nations gave Truman the opportunity to give his anti-Communist action the shiny legitimacy of international endorsement. A meeting of the UN on 25 June condemned the attack and called for the North Koreans to withdraw. The resolution was passed by 9–0. The Soviet delegate, Yakov Malik, had walked out only a couple of weeks before, protesting at the failure of the UN to recognize the result of the Chinese civil war and give China's seat to Mao's Communist government. The rest of the world was genuinely galvanized by Kim's spectacular aggression.

The United Kingdom still considered itself to be a great power. Although the war had cost Britain a quarter of its national wealth and the Labour government was embarked on the gigantic project of building a welfare state, large amounts were still being spent on defence. Prime Minister Clement Atlee personally pushed for the development of Britain's independent nuclear deterrent and insisted that a large proportion of the country's gross national product went on its armed forces. On 27 June the British Cabinet met and decided that 'it was the duty of the UK Govt to do everything in their power, in concert with the other members of the United Nations, to help South Korea resist this aggression'.[6] There was broad support across the political spectrum: even left-wing MPs approved of the idea of concerted international action, under the aegis of the new UN, against aggression. The Far East fleet, consisting of a light carrier and seven other ships, was moved into

Korean waters; but it was felt that sending troops would put an intolerable strain on the overstretched imperial resources.

The nearest US bases to Korea were in Japan, and it would be that garrison that would have to bear the brunt of any initial fighting in the Korean peninsula. But these men were not ready for battle. Peacetime duties had eroded their combat-effectiveness. The four divisions were all severely under strength, numbering at least 6000 less than their full wartime establishment of 18,000. Parcelled out around Japan, they had not trained together in large formations. They were short of tanks and artillery, and had little experience in the vital area of ground–air cooperation. In short, they were not the mighty force that only five years earlier had swept across the Pacific, inflicting defeat after defeat on the highly motivated Japanese forces. Instead, as a major in the 24th Infantry Regiment, Charles Bussey, later said, 'The lifestyle involved a lot of leisure, a lot of involvement with the native women. The officers were involved with buying furniture, buying fancy chinaware for their homes. There was no concern whatever about combat-readiness.'[7] Their commander, and the man responsible for both the string of glorious victories and the subsequent erosion of effectiveness, was General Douglas MacArthur.

MacArthur had retired from the US army in 1937 after a glittering career. He had fought with enormous distinction in France during the First World War and became the youngest divisional commander in the US army. His father had fought during the American Civil War, and they had the distinction of being the first father and son both to win the Congressional Medal of Honor. In 1941 he was recalled to the US army and was commanding an American and Filipino force in Manila when the Japanese invaded, routed his troops and forced him to flee. As he boarded the boat, he had stated grandly, 'I will return.' A legend was born. Return he did, as he masterminded the strategy that brought the Japanese empire to the point of ruin in 1945 by launching one amphibious invasion after another against key Japanese outposts on Pacific islands. He ran his staff like the court of a potentate and, as success followed success, became utterly convinced of his own genius. Since taking

Japan's surrender, he had run the country as a proconsul, having been given essentially a free hand by Truman. He had flirted with the Republican presidential nomination in 1948 and there were some who thought that, like Mark Antony, MacArthur's sojourn in the East had eroded his judgement and exaggerated his massive vanity. However, the majority of Americans were in awe of MacArthur and although the leaders of the administration had their doubts, they dared not question his judgement and would continue to defer to him until disaster threatened to overwhelm their cause.

For the moment, though, the crisis that had engulfed the South Korean army needed immediate resolution. MacArthur visited Korea, and came back in no doubt that only American boots on the ground could stabilize the situation. Soon after he returned to Tokyo, the first elements of the 24th Division were embarking for Korea. The 1st battalion, 21st Infantry Regiment of the 24th Division, arrived in Korea on 1 July 1950. Corporal Robert Fountain of the communications platoon thought, 'When the gooks hear who we are, they'll quit and go back home.'[8] He was to be cruelly disappointed. Instead of quitting, the enemy inflicted a series of stunning defeats on US forces attempting to block their march south.

The North Koreans were superior to the Americans in numbers, equipment, training and morale. Major Charles Bussey was withering about the performance of his own side and full of respect for the enemy. American kit was 'unserviceable to non-existent'. The North Koreans 'were able to climb the mountains to do the things that were necessary to engage the Americans, who were in poor condition, absolutely poor. They were determined, believe me. They were well trained and tremendously motivated.' As for his own side, 'We were not ready to fight a war…. That's the long and short of it.'[9]

The 24th Division came near to total destruction. Sergeant Daniel Cavanaugh was a medic who later wrote, 'We were out-manned, outgunned, outtanked and outflanked.'[10] They were saved by three divisions which arrived from Japan by 15 July. As the 24th withdrew through these other units to recuperate, it was calculated that they had lost 30 per cent of their strength, around 2500 men.

The other divisions were no more able to halt the advance than their hapless comrades in the 24th had been. The North Koreans were suicidally brave when they were going forward, charging straight at American positions. It would take many months of fighting before the Americans and UN troops learned to stand firm against such an onslaught.

By the beginning of August, the time had come for the Americans to stand and fight. They had run out of space and their backs were now to the sea. General Walton Walker, who had served under the legendary General George Patton in Europe during the Second World War, was the rugged Texan in command of the 8th Army in Korea. He made a final withdrawal to the high ground south of the Naktong River and made it clear to his men that they were now fighting for their survival, telling them, 'There will be no retreating.... We must fight until the end. Capture by these people is worse than death itself.'[11]

Walker's perimeter around the vital port of Pusan had to hold until the USA and her UN allies could find more troops and turn the tide in the Korean peninsula. The Americans pushed raw recruits into Korea without even teaching them how to adjust the sights on their rifles. In Britain, 2000 reservists were called back to the colours for service in Korea. The overwhelming response was one of rage. These were veterans of the Second World War, now married and trying to rebuild civilian lives. The majority didn't know where Korea was or why they were fighting there. Meanwhile, a portion of the 27th Brigade was sent to Korea from Hong Kong to provide troops in the short term. Three-quarters of the officers and men were conscripts doing their national service.

Walker's troops manned a perimeter about 130 miles (200 km) long. He had insufficient troops to hold the entire line in strength, and so had to counter-attack with specific elite units every time there was a North Korean thrust. The North Koreans attacked at night to avoid the potent US air strikes. Typically, they would infiltrate a weakly held section of the line and surround units. The UN forces had to hold their nerve and be prepared to fight an enemy on all sides until the morning light brought accurate air and artillery strikes and counter-attacks by one of Walker's 'fire brigade' units.

But, although demoralizing for the men of the 8th Army, the tactics of the North Koreans were bleeding their own side dry. Walker commanded enough artillery and airpower to break up formations of men with great accuracy anywhere on the perimeter. Firepower was trumping numbers. The perimeter would hold. General Walker has not gone down in history as a great commander, but his terrier-like tenacity won the battle of the Pusan perimeter and staved off defeat. It was now up to a man of much greater strategic vision to see if he could deliver a victory.

MACARTHUR'S MASTERSTROKE

General MacArthur had total control of the sea. He was determined to use this advantage and unleash a force that would surround and destroy the North Korean army. Holding him back was his lack of manpower – he couldn't weaken the Pusan perimeter to find troops for a second front. He needed more men.

In the middle of July the commander of the Fleet Marine Force, Pacific, General Lemuel Shepherd, had visited MacArthur and told him of a plan to scrape together a marine division from small detachments on duty in embassies and on ships all round the world. MacArthur had said to him, 'If I had the 1st US Marine Division, I would make a landing here at Inchon and reverse the war.'[12] Later that summer, the 1st Marine Division was a reality, and MacArthur was determined to use it to win the war at one blow. They would land at the port of Inchon, just west of Seoul and hundreds of miles behind enemy lines. When MacArthur unveiled his plan, many were shocked. Inchon had high sea walls and a very narrow entrance, and its 32-foot tidal range (just under 10 metres) was one of the most extreme on the planet. Rear Admiral Doyle, who had been appointed to command the naval force, blurted, 'The best I can say about Inchon is that it is not impossible.' MacArthur responded, theatrically with a tear in his eye, that he 'never thought the day would come, that the navy would be unable to support the army in its operations'. He went on to say that he could 'hear the ticking of the second hand of destiny. We must act now or we will die … we shall land at Inchon and I will crush them.' Doyle stood up and, ashamed at his earlier cynicism, declared emotionally, 'Sir, the navy will get you to Inchon.'[13]

The landings had to take place at high spring tide, so there was a limited window. The date of 15 September was chosen. A massive naval bombardment and aerial assault would attempt to neutralize the harbour defences. Marines would storm ashore in two waves, separated by 11 hours while the tide went out and came back in again. The chances of surprise at Inchon were therefore non-existent. To help solve this problem, diversionary attacks were to be made around the coast.

On 5 September a fleet of 260 ships, made up of US naval vessels and commandeered Japanese freighters, steamed out of Yokohama in Japan. Despite hitting a typhoon which tore tanks from their lashings below decks, the fleet arrived off Inchon in time and a massive naval bombardment began before dawn on the 15th. HMS *Jamaica* had the most spectacular hit of the day when one of its shells hit an ammunition dump ashore, causing an ear-splitting explosion.

Just after dawn, the marines went ashore. Officers had been told to prepare for suicidal resistance, like that put up by the Japanese on Iwo Jima in 1945. They were to push on even if they suffered two-thirds casualties. Ensign George Gilman recalls that, 'My boat was in the first wave and I felt naked as hell.'[14] But in fact, by the time the second wave went ashore at 5.31 p.m., there were only a few dazed soldiers and civilians cowering in the ruins. Above the landing craft, marine and navy planes provided very close support. Private Fred Davidson remembers, 'Those marine Corsairs came flying through the smoke toward the beach not more than thirty feet over our heads! Hot, empty machine-gun shells fell on us. Talk about close air support.'[15] A few firefights flared up, but for the most part the shell-shocked Communists gave themselves up.

Large US navy ships grounded themselves on one of the beaches and from inside them poured the military hardware – tanks,

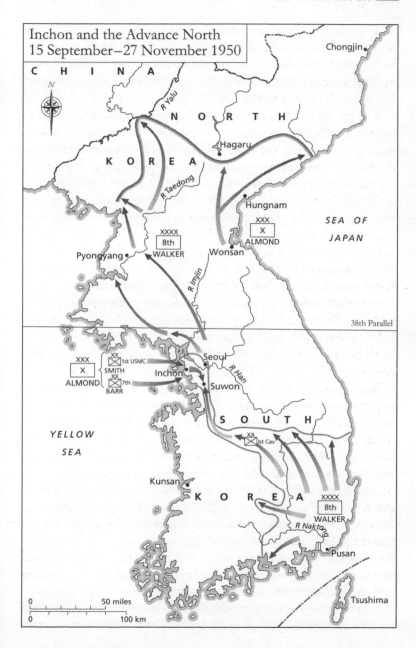

Inchon and the Advance North
15 September–27 November 1950

CHINA

N

NORTH

KOREA

R Yalu

Chongjin

Hagaru

R Taedong

Hungnam

XXX
X
ALMOND

SEA OF
JAPAN

XXXX
8th
WALKER

Pyongyang

Wonsan

R Imjin

38th Parallel

XXX
X
ALMOND

XX
1st USMC
SMITH

Seoul

XX
7th
BARR

Inchon

Suwon

R Han

SOUTH

YELLOW

SEA

XX
1st Cav

KOREA

Kunsan

XXXX
8th
WALKER

R Nakto

Pusan

0   50 miles
0   100 km

Tsushima

artillery pieces and trucks – that would allow the Americans to beat off counter-attacks and push forward towards Seoul. By nightfall, only 20 men had been killed. MacArthur dined on the USS *Mount McKinley* off Inchon, jubilant about the success of an operation which he believed would secure his place in the pantheon of military greats. As the Americans pushed towards Seoul, civilians lined the road, seemingly glad to see them. The harsh nature of Rhee's regime appeared benign compared to the atrocities committed by the Communists during their brief occupation.

MacArthur was so desperate to retake Seoul by the 25th, three months to the day since the start of the war, that he announced it had been liberated even while the marines were still fighting their way to the capitol building. Meanwhile, the US 7th Infantry Division pushed south from Inchon and on 26th September met the US 1st Cavalry Division advancing north from Pusan. It was now the turn of the North Koreans to flee: they had lost upwards of 150,000 men since the invasion. It looked like MacArthur had his victory.

By now the UN forces had grown to include contingents from many countries. The Danes sent a hospital ship, the Thais a battalion of infantry and the Norwegians a field ambulance and mobile hospital. The Turks sent a brigade-sized unit: its commander had been presented with a flag signed in their own blood by the pupils of a high school in Istanbul. The Ethiopians sent an impressive unit from Emperor Haile Selassie's own bodyguard. Another British brigade, the 29th, was en route to Korea. It was a powerful unit with three battalions, a strong force of new Centurion tanks and good artillery support. The 27th Brigade, now veterans of the fight around Pusan, changed its name from the British to the Commonwealth Brigade when an Australian battalion joined it on 27 September. Canadians and New Zealanders were on their way.

MacArthur had no doubts as to how he intended to use his growing force. Kim Il Sung had started the war with an act of unprovoked aggression and his men had committed hideous crimes. North Korea must be punished. Those who advocated staying out of the North for fear of stirring up the Russians or Chinese were drowned out by those, blinded by success, who wanted Kim's regime removed and Korea united. On 27 September MacArthur was given permission to cross the 38th parallel, but with one important provision: that Korea's Communist neighbours did not enter the war. To make that outcome less likely, he was instructed to keep non-Korean troops away from those provinces bordering on the Soviet Union and China.

Pyongyang fell to the UN on 19 October. On the 24th the temperature plunged below zero for the first time. It was the beginning of a horrific winter. The men of the 27th Brigade had been stationed in tropical Hong Kong and lacked any winter clothing or kit; the Americans provided them with blankets, clothing, cookers and sleeping bags. UN forces advanced closer to the Yalu River, the border with China. The British started to worry, and suggested that Chinese and UN troops should jointly patrol a buffer zone south of the Yalu. MacArthur was disgusted and thought it akin to the moral cowardice of appeasement in the 1930s. On 24 October he lifted all sanctions on American troops moving towards the Yalu. Washington made no move to restrain him, even though he had gone way beyond the powers granted to him. All Washington did was ask him to issue a report to allay Chinese fears. MacArthur refused even to do this. He had always hated Chinese Communism but now, flushed with victory, he did not fear it. What did the genius of Inchon care for Mao's peasant levies?

ENTER THE DRAGON

On 25 October a battalion of the ROK 6th Division was ambushed and destroyed. The South Koreans immediately told the Americans that the men who had attacked them spoke Chinese. This and other reports did not bother General Walker, who commented that there 'were a lot of Mexicans in Texas'.[16] However, more and more ROK units were subsequently attacked. On 1 November the tanks of the US 1st Cavalry pushed north through the ROK stragglers to see what all the fuss was about. That night, the Chinese fell upon them.

Infantry descended from the hills with horns blowing and cymbals clashing, and rockets, rifle fire and grenades ripped through columns on the mountainous roads. The British commander of the Commonwealth Brigade was summoned to his American superior and greeted with the news: 'The Chinese are in. World War 3 has started.'[17]

The Chinese had arrived like a bolt from the blue, and once again the Korean War was turned on its head. The West was utterly shocked, but signs of impending Chinese intervention had long been clear. From midsummer 1950, the British consulate in Mukden had noted the presence of People's Liberation Army units training in unusually large numbers. Many had soldiers of Korean descent in their ranks. From Inchon onwards, K.M. Panikkar, the Indian ambassador in Peking, reported to Prime Minister Nehru in Delhi that the Chinese were deeply concerned about the approach of UN forces. Nehru passed this information on to the Foreign Secretary, Ernest Bevin, in Britain. Mao was all too aware that 20 years earlier Korea had been the springboard for a Japanese invasion of China. Now he believed that a rampant American army on his border might well whet Washington's appetite for further assaults on Communism. Given MacArthur's ill-disguised public warmongering, it is not entirely unreasonable that he should have done so.

As far back as 3 October, the Chinese Prime Minister, Chou En-lai, had called Panikkar into his office at 1 a.m. and told him that China wanted a peaceful resolution but would intervene if the 38th parallel was crossed. Washington remained deaf to these warnings. On the 8th the Chinese army, under the assumed name of the Chinese People's Volunteers, crossed the Yalu into North Korea and waited in the mountains for Peking to make its decision. The army was commanded by Peng Te-huai, a former deputy commander of the People's Liberation Army and a close friend of Mao.

For the first three days of November, the Chinese savaged the UN forces, annihilating an ROK division and soundly beating the US 1st Cavalry. Then they disappeared and the fighting stopped. The Chinese wanted to keep the forces of capitalism away from their borders, not to precipitate a general war: these attacks had been a warning. Sadly for the men on the ground, that warning fell on deaf ears. MacArthur was convinced that there were no more than a few Chinese divisions in Korea and that the brief attack had represented the very limit of Chinese capabilities. If anything, the Chinese attack stirred MacArthur to push his advance with renewed vigour. The widely spread American divisions were to advance to the Yalu, while its bridges were bombed even though supplies could now be carried across the ice. After a sumptuous Thanksgiving dinner, the race north continued; for many of the men it was to be the last hot meal for quite a while.

On the night of 25 November, with temperatures well below zero, the Chinese came again. The ROK troops on the right flank of the 8th Army collapsed under this onslaught, and the American 2nd Division now found the Chinese attacking its flank and rear. Administrative units were over-run, and the division was at risk of being surrounded. There was only one course of action available. The mighty US army began what was to be the longest, harshest and most humiliating retreat in its history.

The Americans were shocked by the aggression, skill and physical size of the Chinese soldiers. Most had experienced Chinese people only as the docile, low-paid workers back home. In fact, Mao's men were veterans, many over 6 feet tall (nearly 2 metres). A period of 20 years and more fighting the Japanese and the Chinese Nationalists had perfected their infantry skills and physically prepared them for combat in Korea in a way that occupation duty in Japan had not for the Americans. Their morale was high; Private Szu Chiin-chang remembers how their officers would fire them up. 'Before we engaged the enemy, the Communists always held big meetings to get us worked up.... We swore to triumph in the Communist cause and protect everything the revolution had won for us.... They warned us if we didn't wipe out the enemy in Korea now, one day they would come back to China and we would lose everything.'[18] Chinese troops did not need a huge logistical tail. They moved on foot, carrying a week's supply of rice and ammunition with them. It required approximately 60 lb (27 kg) of fuel, rations and other supplies to keep a UN soldier in the field for one day; the equivalent for a Chinese

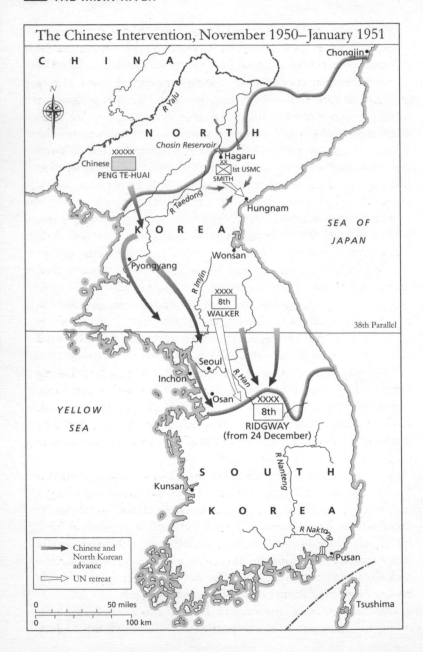

The Chinese Intervention, November 1950–January 1951

CHINA

Chongjin

R Yalu

N

NORTH

Chosin Reservoir

XXXXX
Chinese
PENG TE-HUAI

Hagaru
XX
1st USMC
SMITH

KOREA

R Taedong

Hungnam

SEA OF
JAPAN

Pyongyang

R Imjin

Wonsan

XXXX
8th
WALKER

38th Parallel

Seoul

Inchon

R Han

Osan

XXXX
8th
RIDGWAY
(from 24 December)

YELLOW
SEA

SOUTH

Kunsan

R Nanteng

KOREA

R Naktong

Pusan

Chinese and
North Korean
advance

UN retreat

0 ———— 50 miles
0 ———— 100 km

Tsushima

soldier weighed less than 10 lb (4.5 kg). Unlike the vast convoys of trucks that carried the UN's supplies, everything the Chinese needed was carried by tens of thousands of porters on their shoulders. The troops were expert at camouflage, hiding during the day and moving at night. Private Kuo Fei-wu later recalled, 'We had to give up moving by day because of the danger of being attacked by American warplanes. If they found us they rocketed us and dropped napalm bombs. At night we covered 100 Chinese Li – that's 50 or 60 km – that was what we were trained to do.'[19] They had totally fooled American intelligence as to the number of Chinese troops in Korea: at the start of the attack there were perhaps 250,000 men.

The Chinese army was essentially a vast peasant force with access to a manpower reservoir of millions. However, they had little artillery and no armour. The infantry carried a vast mixture of captured American, Chinese and Russian weapons. They lacked modern communications equipment. Although the cymbals, bugles and gongs they used to coordinate their attacks terrified inexperienced troops, they were no substitute for radios. They relied on speed, surprise and fear, attacking nearly always at night, from all sides, screaming and blowing bugles.[20]

The American 8th Army came close to collapse in its headlong retreat. Pyongyang, with its massive stores of fuel and ammunition, was abandoned on 5 December and the flight south continued. Eleven thousand US troops were left behind in the rush. But over to the east, American units were threatened with an even greater disaster.

On the night of 27 November the Chinese attacked the 1st Marine Division along its entire length. It was strung out along a supply road, from Yudam-ni on the Chosin reservoir for about 30 miles (48 km) to the south. By morning, the marines had been forced into three separate areas, all cut off from each other. Just as Rome had lost its legions to the German leader Arminius in the dark forests of the north, so America was now looking at the possible annihilation of some of its finest combat troops.

On the perimeters, the marines hacked into the solid ground, trying to shore up defensive positions to stave off the nightly attacks. The cold jammed their weapons and caused widespread frostbite. During the day, airpower prevented the Chinese from moving, but at night the screams and bugles heralded wave upon wave of assaulting infantry.

On 1 December the 10,000 marines on the reservoir began their retreat south. The disciplined retreat from Chosin was to salvage honour for the American forces at one of the least impressive moments in US military history. The marines brought their equipment out with them; the column even dragged its cumbersome artillery. Much of the time, Chinese mortars and small-arms fire raked the column. The marines attempted to leave the road and fight the enemy on the higher ground. Wading through waist-high snow, they often managed to clear Chinese riflemen from the lower slopes, providing some respite for the troops on the road. Airpower was the vital ingredient. Napalm, cannon and rockets silenced Chinese artillery and mortar positions: without their comrades in the air wing, many marines doubt they could have made it out. On one day, low cloud prevented air action, and the column hardly moved. The commander of the division, Major General Smith, told the press that the marines were not retreating: 'We are merely advancing in another direction.'[21] One of his subordinates, Colonel Lewis B. Puller, stood on a ration box and shouted, 'I don't give a goddam how many Chinese laundrymen there are between us and Hungnam. There aren't enough in the world to stop a marine regiment going where it wants to go!!'[22]

Nobody could wait for stragglers – the weak would be killed by the Chinese or succumb to the temperatures, which were now 35°C below zero. To stop was to die. But the terrible cold and the air attacks took their toll on the Chinese too, who were suffering even more than the marines below them. Chinese attacks grew less frequent, and both sides now focused on surviving the awful conditions. Marine Company Commander Edwin Simmons 'felt sorry for them. They did not have the equipment we had, they did not have the uniforms we had. Ours were poor enough. We were not really prepared for an arctic winter ... but they were wearing canvas shoes, they had no gloves for the most part, their hands froze, their feet froze, we took a lot of prisoners … their feet would be just blocks of blue ice.'[23] The 1st Marine Division arrived at the port of Hungnam and were evacuated. They had maintained their cohesion, despite suffering 4418 battle casualties and more than 7000 to the cold weather.

Meanwhile, the 8th Army was in headlong retreat, and so-called 'bug out' fever was rife. The withdrawal continued long after contact with the Chinese had been lost. In ten days, they retreated around 120 miles (190 km). The 38th parallel was crossed and still the flight south continued. Experienced NCOs wept at the state of their beloved army. Major Bussey remembers his horror: 'It was … disgusting. All grades.… I never felt so inadequate in my life as to be part of an army that was running helter-skelter, pell-mell.'[24] The newly arrived British 29th Brigade immediately formed the rearguard, with its men wondering why they were retreating so far so fast without even putting up a fight.

Men froze to death on the road, abandoned by their units; civilians were treated brutally. In the midst of the chaos, one death in particular would have a profound effect on the course of the war. On 23 December General Walton Walker was thrown out of his jeep after it hit another vehicle. Shortly afterwards he died of his injuries. It was a turning point for the 8th Army. Walker was the hero of Pusan, but he and his staff had been psychologically broken by Chinese entry into the war. The next commander of the 8th Army felt no responsibility for that and arrived in the job determined to stop the rot.

Lieutenant General Matthew Ridgway had fought through Europe in 1944–5, initially as commander of the 82nd Airborne, and he was widely regarded as one of the best American soldiers of the Second World War. From a job at the Pentagon, he was now propelled into a disastrous situation with little time for preparation. He landed in Japan on Christmas Day. MacArthur told him, 'Do what you think best,'[25] and put him on a plane to Korea.

Ridgway's appointment was a case study in the importance of leadership. Within days, he had ordered his units to get off the road into the hills. He fired regimental and divisional commanders who ran the battle from far in the rear. Units were told to hold their positions, send out patrols and get ready for combat by preparing all-round defensive positions. Procedures for air support were honed until a unit calling for emergency air strikes could expect them within one hour and to within 330 feet (100 metres) of accuracy. He visited as many units as possible, dressed in combat fatigues with grenades fastened to his webbing. The expectation of withdrawal was replaced bit by bit by one of holding ground, toughing it out and pulling back in an orderly fashion if they had to. He was forced to give up more ground, including Seoul itself, but it was a controlled withdrawal that forced the Chinese to pay a terrible price for every mile of their advance. Thanks partly to Ridgway's injection of purpose into the UN forces, by New Year the Chinese advances were halted.

At the beginning of 1951 there were nearly 500,000 Chinese troops in Korea to the UN's 365,000. They had retaken North Korea, captured Seoul and looked to be in a position to take the whole peninsula. Even so, Ridgway felt confident enough to launch a series of very limited probes north. Each attack would have massive air and artillery support. Three operations, Thunderbolt, Killer and Ripper, took the UN forces creeping back up the peninsula. Seoul was recaptured, and his men reached the 38th parallel. Ridgway felt that the only way the UN could now be defeated was if the Soviets entered the war.

For one man, however, the stabilization of Korea was a disappointment. General MacArthur did not want his career to end in a messy stalemate around the 38th parallel – he wanted to take on Asiatic Communism and defeat it decisively. It was impossible for him to accept the limited aims of Washington, which were now simply the protection of South Korea. On 5 April a letter from MacArthur was read out in the House of Representatives. In it he made clear that he disagreed with his political overlords in Washington: 'It seems strangely difficult for some to realise that here in Asia is where the communist conspirators have elected to make their play for global conquest ... if we lose this war to communism in Asia then the fall of Europe is inevitable.'[26] The time had come for the general to go. Truman sacked him, announcing that MacArthur was unable to 'give his wholehearted support to the policies of the United States government'.[27] When he arrived back in Washington, MacArthur spoke to Congress: his audience wept and scrambled to try to touch the great man.[28] Truman, less impressed, called the speech 'one hundred percent bullshit'.[29]

Ridgway was promoted and moved to Tokyo, to be replaced in Korea by 59-year-old James Van Fleet. He had commanded a division in western Europe in the Second World War before running the Joint Military Aid Group in Greece, which had trained the Greek army to defeat a Communist insurgency. Both Van Fleet and Ridgway were convinced that the administration was right in not wanting the Korean situation to escalate into a major war. Van Fleet would face his first test sooner than he might have liked. The Chinese were going to make one last massive attempt to smash through the UN lines and prevent the war stagnating into a war of position that they could not hope to win. It was to be the largest offensive of the Korean War.

THE SPRING OFFENSIVE

Marshal Peng promised Mao that Chinese troops would enter Seoul by May Day. To ensure that this happened, Peng planned to use fresh troops comprising his 3rd, 9th and 19th army groups, in all about 270,000 men. They would advance down the two well-worn, traditional invasion routes into South Korea. One army group would attack across the Imjin River and head for Seoul. Further east, another huge force would attack through Kapyong, down the valley of the Pukhan River and west along the Han valley to Seoul. In between the two main thrusts, secondary attacks would try to outflank and encircle any UN forces that chose to stand and fight.

On account of the high calibre of the two British and Commonwealth brigades, they had been stationed astride the invasion routes, the 29th Brigade on the south side of the Imjin and the 27th Commonwealth Brigade at Kapyong. The UN were expecting something. Aerial intelligence showed huge amounts of supplies heading south and significant troop movement. The Turkish brigade captured a group of Chinese artillery officers, armed with rangefinders and slide rules, who told their captors that they had been supposed to set up an observation post from which they could direct artillery fire for a Chinese assault that night. The Turks quickly reported this news, and all units were told to expect an attack.

Sure enough, the first blows of what was to become known as the Fifth Phase Offensive were to fall on the Turks. They were heavily shelled at 8.30 p.m. on 22 April. Just before midnight, the artillery gave way to small-arms fire and mortar rounds, the tell-tale sign that an infantry assault was on the way. There had been an expectation that the Chinese might try to employ tanks in this offensive but, as Ridgway recorded, 'the enemy resorted to the familiar tactics … night attacks by great numbers of foot soldiers, moving in almost at arms length behind the artillery barrage and hurling grenades without regard to losses. And again the wild bugles and barbaric screams sounded up and down the lines, while enemy infantry, padding silently up dark hillsides in rubber shoes, infiltrated our positions.'[30]

At 2 a.m. the Turks withdrew. Their position was effectively taken by an American unit, and the Turks re-formed in good order behind them. On the right of the Turkish brigade, the American 25th Division had come under heavy attack just after the Turks, and had also been forced back. To their right, the 24th Division as well gave way slightly, and by morning the Chinese had advanced about half a mile (a kilometre or so). American GI Raymond 'Doc' Frazier had 'never seen so many people in my life coming at me at one time. There were literally thousands of 'em.'[31] Both divisions were then instructed to withdraw to a new defensive position called Line Kansas. While these troops retreated in good order, further along the line the Communist troops achieved just the kind of breakthrough that they had hoped for. As so often during the Korean War, it was the badly led, poorly equipped men of the South Korean army who panicked and precipitated a major crisis.

The ROK 6th Division had not prepared their defensive positions well: there were gaps, and not enough barbed wire. Their commander had moved all his reserves forward to just behind the

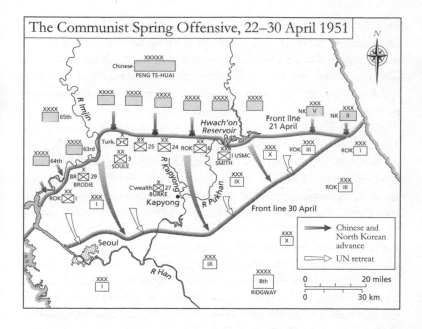

The Communist Spring Offensive, 22–30 April 1951

front line in an attempt to stiffen the resolve of his men, but this well-intentioned move only exacerbated the catastrophe when it came. The Chinese fell on the 6th Division on the night of 22 April. Within minutes, the ROK troops ran. A gaping hole had been torn in the UN line, and the Chinese were in a position easily to outflank the American divisions on either side. The 1st Marine Division, under the redoubtable Smith, was coming under heavy attack, but he was forced to send his reserves to his western flank and form a right-angled line. Luckily for the marines, the Chinese did not realize the extent of their success and so did not try to move round behind the marines, but pushed forward ever deeper into the hole in the UN line.

In their way was the 27th Commonwealth Brigade. The US 5th Cavalry Regiment was ordered to join them and hold off the Chinese. Both units had been in reserve but were now rushed forward and took up positions 4 miles (6 km) north of Kapyong town, getting there just before the Chinese.

The Middlesex Battalion of the 27th Brigade had been packing for home when they were ordered to protect the New Zealand artillery batteries that had been supporting the ROK 6th Division but were now threatened by the Chinese. They were not best pleased to be thrown into battle when they were expecting to leave Korea any day now. The Canadian Battalion, the Princess Patricia's Light Infantry and the 3rd Royal Australian Regiment took up positions further forward, separated by about 3 miles (5 km). One company of Australians were on top of a hill rising like an island out of the valley, while the other companies were spread along the road to the east and the other side of the valley. They had no mines or barbed wire, but luckily they did have the American tanks: 'A' Company of the US 72nd Battalion was composed of 15 Shermans, which proved a huge asset. The road was still blocked with fleeing ROK troops being hotly pursued by Chinese forces. The Chinese blundered into the Australian positions, and received quite a shock. The tanks on the ridge caused havoc, forcing the Communists to try to take the hill. The Australians now showed their calibre, holding off attack after attack with very little supporting artillery – the New Zealand artillery was still withdrawing and would not be ready to provide support until dawn on the 24th. All night the Australians fought a vicious, often hand-to-hand battle. Positions were lost and retaken and the Australian commander, Lieutenant Colonel Ferguson, had difficulty directing the defence because the retreating ROK troops had ripped away the wire for field telephones and radio worked only intermittently. The American tanks attached to the Australians were forced to fire their machine guns at each other in order to clear the Chinese troops that swarmed around their positions. By morning, the tanks had fired 162 rounds of main armament ammunition and 43,000 rounds of machine-gun ammunition.

Ferguson was not certain his unit was going to survive another night. Chinese infiltration meant that the road leading from his position to the Middlesex Battalion further back was now under constant fire. He ordered the Australians to pull back: the tanks ferried men and helped to cover the retreat, while the New Zealand artillery, which was by now in position, fired smoke and high-explosive shells to stop the Chinese overwhelming the Australians. The Chinese followed as closely as the artillery barrage allowed, but the sight of the Middlesex Battalion and the Australians in new positions made them stop. Rather than pressing home the assault, they headed west to where the Canadians sat isolated on top of Hill 677. The Canadians saw the danger and their commander, Lieutenant Colonel Stone, redeployed his four companies so that they faced in every direction. At 10 p.m. on the 24th a large group of Chinese troops approached and the Canadians directed the New Zealand artillery to fire on them, causing terrible damage. Another group of Chinese crept up a gully and launched themselves at B Company. The attacks continued all night and one of the Canadian company positions was taken, but later recaptured by a counter-attack in which even the wounded participated, grabbing their rifles and charging with bayonets fixed. At 2 a.m. on the 25th D Company bore the brunt of another attack. The numbers facing the Canadians were so overwhelming that the company commander called in artillery strikes on his own positions: his men lay in their dugouts and survived as shrapnel tore through the Chinese caught standing in the open.

Since the Canadians were now effectively surrounded, Stone asked for an airdrop of supplies. With extraordinary efficiency, C-119 transport planes from Japan responded just six hours later. The tanks of the 5th Cavalry now counter-attacked up the valley and briefly retook the Australians' old positions, which forced the Chinese back and allowed the Canadians to disengage. The 27th Brigade fell back, but its vigorous defence had stabilized the front. Together with the veteran 1st Marine Division to the east, it had blunted one of the two Chinese thrusts. This had been a textbook operation: they had been prepared to fight the Chinese on all sides, had used artillery effectively and had slowly given up ground to take up strong positions further to the rear. As they withdrew, they took what supplies they could and burnt the rest. Everyone who was there remembers the strange way in which the Kapyong valley smelt of burnt toast for days afterwards. The Canadians, the Australians and the American tank battalion were all awarded the US Presidential Unit Citation. The action was enormously impressive. But today it is largely forgotten because at the same time, further to the west, a struggle was taking place which has become one of the most notorious dramas in British military history.

THE IMJIN

The British 29th Brigade took up position in April 1951 just south of the Imjin River, digging in on a succession of large hills which dominate the route south. Today, the road from the crossing point to Seoul still snakes along the valley floor. On top of one hill sits the ruin of an ancient castle – testament to the importance of this traditional route to Seoul. Standing on the river bank, looking south, one is struck by the huge expanse of terrain which the 29th Brigade occupied. Their commander, Brigadier Thomas Brodie, was unhappy. The section of front given to his brigade was almost 7 miles (12 km) long, and a whole division was needed to secure it properly. Brodie's superior, General Soule, the commander of the 3rd Division, was certain that the advance would continue shortly; in the meantime, the 29th Brigade would have to do the best it could. The distance to be defended meant that the three British battalions and the one Belgian would not be able to provide fire support for each other. Some of the battalions could not even see the others. Even within the battalion, the rifle companies would be as far as a mile (1.6 km) apart. The yawning gaps would be easy for the Chinese troops to infiltrate. The brigade's artillery support was composed of light guns only; the mortars were split to give support to all the units. Little barbed wire and few mines were provided. On top of this, the rocky ground made it extremely difficult to dig trenches; veterans remember the deepest as being only 3 feet (just under a metre) deep. Instead, rocks were heaped up into sangars.[32]

The 1st Battalion the Gloucestershire Regiment held the left flank of the position overlooking a ford through the Imjin. Next to them, inside the curve of the river, were the Northumberland Fusiliers. The Fusiliers were getting ready to celebrate their regimental day, 23 April, when in honour of St George they wore red roses in their headdress. This year, the lack of roses was compensated for by artificial ones made in Japan. Across the river to their front was the Belgian battalion, while further back, on the lower slopes of the largest of the hills, the mighty Kamak-san, were the Royal Ulster Rifles, spread along a north–south road on which the Centurion tanks of the 8th Hussars were also stationed. After the horrific winter they had endured, the men were enjoying the warm Korean spring. The Chinese had been retreating for some weeks and some of the officers worried that the men were getting overconfident. Major Toby Younger, an engineer, was concerned that because the brigade had been going forward for months they weren't in a 'defensive frame of mind'.[33] For example, it was not known for sure where exactly the river was fordable.

Unluckily for the British, the answer to that particular question was: nearly everywhere. Although the Imjin was over 270 yards (250 metres) wide, it was shallow and easy to cross. Since arriving on its banks, the 29th Brigade had been carrying out patrols and reconnaissance across the river. Centurion tanks, possibly the best in the world at the time, would usually cross the river and sweep through no man's land. Occasionally, they met small Chinese forces with whom they would exchange fire before the Chinese fell back. They never came across anything other than light forces. Aerial reconnaissance confirmed that there were no major Chinese forces in the area.

On 22 April that all changed. Early that morning, patrols from the Northumberlands and the Gloucesters reported large numbers of the enemy advancing towards the river. Immediately, the Gloucester's CO, Lieutenant Colonel Fred Carne, headed down to the crossing point and prepared to direct mortar fire at the advancing Communist troops on the far bank. Carne had been in the Gloucestershire regiment for 25 years, a quiet, deeply professional man. When serving in East Africa he had eschewed the pleasures of Nairobi, preferring to spend time in the bush. In the coming days he was always to be found where the action was fiercest, and every veteran remembers the inspirational quality of his leadership.

As night fell and the Fifth Phase Offensive crashed into the UN lines, the ROK 1st Division to the west of the 29th Brigade was hard hit and began to fall back, opening a wide hole to Brodie's left. The 29th Brigade was in a vital portion of the line: not only was it known to be the easiest and most likely invasion route to Seoul, but to his right the rest of the American 3rd Division and other UN forces were to the north-east. If Brodie retired, the centre of the UN line across the peninsula would have been outflanked, possibly with catastrophic consequences. The Belgians on the far side of the river were the first to report enemy contact. They were fairly isolated on the north bank and Brodie decided to get them out. He sent a battle patrol of Ulsters down to the river to evacuate the Belgian troops, but as they crossed the river and reached the far bank they were caught in a hail of fire. The survivors of the ambush retreated to the south bank. The battle of the Imjin River had started in earnest.

On the left of the 29th Brigade, the Gloucesters held up the advancing Chinese: Lieutenant Guy Temple and his platoon lay on a small rise, pouring fire into the enemy as they attempted to cross the river. Temple was a hell-raiser, always in trouble for unautho-rized nightclub visits during peacetime, but ideally suited for this kind of work. Four attempts at crossing were repelled. He recalls seeing the Chinese 'thick in the water…. Somewhere around about 2000 men…. It was an astonishing target. That's how we saw it. And we did use all our ammunition.'[34] When it ran out, Temple was forced to take his men back to the C Company perimeter on a hill a mile or two to the rear.

The Chinese had discovered another ford about a mile (1.6 km) below the crossing held by the Gloucesters, and through the night they streamed south across the river and began to probe the Gloucesters' defences. The Communist forces quickly realized that the companies were widely spaced, and focused on one at a time. Men in other companies listened to ferocious, isolated fights on nearby hills and wondered when it would be their turn, some of them frustrated that they couldn't do much to help their comrades

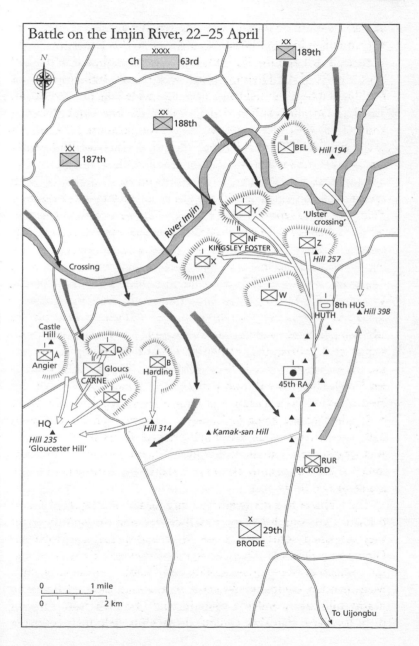

Battle on the Imjin River, 22–25 April

N

Ch | 63rd (XXXX)

189th (XX)

188th (XX)

187th (XX)

River Imjin

Crossing

BEL (II) *Hill 194*

Y (I)

NF (II)
KINGSLEY FOSTER

X (I)

'Ulster crossing'

Z (I)
Hill 257

W (I)

8th HUS
HUTH

Hill 398

Castle Hill

A (I)
Angier

D (I)

Gloucs
CARNE

B (I)
Harding

C (I)

45th RA

HQ
Hill 235
'Gloucester Hill'

Hill 314

▲ *Kamak-san Hill*

RUR (II)
RICKORD

29th (X)
BRODIE

0 — 1 mile
0 — 2 km

To Uijongbu

in other companies. The British fought the enemy off as best they could with their Vickers machine guns and 3-inch (7.6-cm) mortars. Two Gloucester companies were savaged by countless Chinese attacks: with shrieks and bugles blasting, they came forward with a suicidal lack of concern for casualties. Nineteen-year-old National Serviceman David Green wrote in his memoirs, 'The bastards were coming and there was little we could do to stop that flood, except take as many with us as we could.' He fought all night, trying to conserve ammunition by firing only at very good targets. He had to be careful, however: 'There's always a danger in close combat of hitting one's own mates. With the Chinks crawling all over the spur, stuff was flying everywhere. I could hear them chanting "*Doladola*," out of breath and chattering.'[35] Lieutenant Whatmore from D Company of the Gloucesters told his company sergeant major on the field telephone, 'They are right among us, but we are coping.' At dawn he realized that he and his men had been firing their weapons so much that 'they were hot and uncomfortable to handle'.[36]

At first light all the units tried to reorganize. The Ulsters had put up stiff resistance. Mervyn McCord recounted, 'You knew if it wasn't them it was you.... It was either they killed us or we killed them.... There were lots and lots and lots of them.'[37] His comrade, Private John Dyer, had 'never seen so many troops in my life. The hillside was literally covered in them ... then we realised that we were into trouble. I mean, we wouldn't be human if we hadn't got scared. I mean, a mass of people rushing at you, bayonets fixed, grenades being thrown, shouting, screaming. Because they used it as a fear tactic, you see.'[38] The Northumberland Fusiliers found to their horror that Chinese troops had infiltrated between their positions and captured some high ground overlooking them: they were forced to fall back. Harry Gledden of the Fusiliers never forgot that night, 'A load of old bugles blowing. The Chinese screaming their heads off. Fireworks going off ... it was pandemonium really.'[39] Centurion tanks were sent to help them withdraw and the Ulsters were pushed forward to try to keep the vital road to the south clear. By this time, the Chinese had thoroughly infiltrated the line: even the Brigade rear echelons and artillery were coming under small-arms fire.

The Gloucesters were having a tough time over to the left. Throughout the night, A Company on 'Castle Hill', named for the ruin on the top, had faced attack after attack. Lieutenant Philip Curtis led a counter-attack to retake the summit. He had been wounded during his charge, but kept going and used grenades to kill the Chinese machine-gun crew; seconds later, he died from his wounds. He won a posthumous Victoria Cross. Later, company commander Pat Angier spoke to Carne on the radio. 'I'm afraid we've lost the castle site,' he said. 'I want to know whether I am to stay here indefinitely or not.' Carne told him to hold his positions at all costs. Angier signed off, 'Don't worry about us, we'll be alright.'[40] Fifteen minutes later he was killed. He was one of the last men whom there was time to bury. His batman wept. There was one final radio call from the hill: 'We've had it. Cheerio.'[41]

The Chinese, however, were suffering even worse casualties. Hwang Chen was a medical officer who years later described what it was like to be on the receiving end of UN artillery: 'Shells rained down. In front of me a whole squad was blown to pieces and the bodies of the dead and wounded scattered along the track.... I got through, but when I think about it now I feel terribly, terribly frightened.'[42] The Chinese infantry were paying a dreadful price for each yard gained on the Imjin.

The Fusiliers tried to make up for their precipitate withdrawal from their positions by counter-attacking up one of the hills from which the Chinese were now firing on them. W Company of the Fusiliers charged up the slope and saw the Chinese fleeing. However, another group of defenders stood up and counter-attacked: the Fusiliers fled down the hill. Bullets whipped into the retreating men, and half of those who had attacked failed to return. The action was not entirely futile, though, because it allowed the Belgians to withdraw and redeploy just to the rear of the Northumberlands.

The shadows began to lengthen and the warm, sunny afternoon turned to evening. Isolated on their hilltops, the men of the

Gloucestershire Battalion felt a long way from home. During the day, the Chinese had lain fairly low and tried to reorganize and resupply without attracting American air strikes. But after darkness fell it would be a different matter. The Reverend Sam Davis remembers thinking, 'The Chinese would probably start a night attack and we would be very lucky to survive that.'[43] In the daytime they could call on very accurate artillery to blunt the Chinese onslaught, whereas at night it was hard to spot an attack until it was virtually on the perimeter. Carne realized that his outlying companies would not survive another night, so he withdrew the shattered remnants of A Company and D Company to his own position on Hill 235 which would become known as Gloucester Hill. The hill had a gentle gradient, now stripped bare of nearly all its trees and shrubs and largely featureless except in a few places where it was bisected by jagged ravines. David Green remembers 'trying to dig myself a dugout, having only my bayonet with which to do so, all the picks and shovels having been left behind. It was soon quite obvious that I was wasting my time.'[44] C Company joined them on Gloucester Hill, but B Company was under too much sustained Chinese pressure to withdraw. All night, B Company fought off repeated attacks, and only joined the rest of the battalion at dawn.

That night, the Chinese came screaming out of the dark again. Guy Temple remembered the bugles in particular. They were 'not strident … like European bugles are. I wouldn't say they're melodious either. They're haunting … sad.'[45] The Gloucesters suffered terribly, and in turn inflicted huge numbers of casualties on the Chinese. Machine guns grew so hot from firing belt after belt of ammunition that they started to seize up or become too hot to hold. There was hand-to-hand fighting. Sergeant F.E. Carter was manning his Bren gun and fired hundreds of rounds. He recalls, 'Once more they overran our position. I can remember ducking as they ran by our trench on to Company HQ, only to be driven back once again by our section higher up the hill.' Trenches were captured and recaptured as small groups of men fought with bayonets and knives. Carter's mate, Spud, had spent the night 'throwing grenades as fast as he could pick them up', until by dawn 'he was lying face down in

the bottom of the trench; he never moved when I shouted to him'.[46]
On the morning of the 24th there were probably only 400 effective
combat troops left out of the 700 there had been two days earlier. B
and C Companies had to be merged into one weak company. In the
dawn light they could see hundreds, if not thousands, of Chinese in
the valleys below, swarming to the rear. They made an easy target
and horrific casualties were inflicted on them by British artillerymen, their shots carefully coordinated by spotters on Gloucester
Hill.

Uniquely in the British army, the Gloucestershire Regiment wear
two cap badges. As well as the normal badge on the front of their
berets they have another in the form of a sphinx worn at the back of
the head. It commemorates the heroic stand of their forebears, the
28th Foot Regiment, at the Battle of Alexandria in 1801, when they
were fighting the French infantry to their front and were then
attacked from behind by French cavalry. Rather than panicking, the
colonel ordered the rear rank to about face and deal with the new
threat. Despite being 150 years old, this proud tradition gave a real
boost to the beleaguered Gloucesters: from Carne down, nobody
doubted that they could stay on that hill until they were reinforced.[47]

An attempt to break through to them was made. A hastily assembled force, including ten British Centurion tanks, advanced up the
track towards Gloucester Hill, while Filipino infantry attempted to
clear the slopes on either side. The day before such a rescue mission
might have worked, but now the hills were alive with Chinese
troops who had pushed beyond the Gloucesters. The operation
had to be abandoned when one of the Filipino light tanks which
were leading the column was knocked out by a mortar or a
mine and blocked the road. The column withdrew. They were 2000
yards (1800 metres) short of Gloucester Hill. It was Brodie who
ordered the withdrawal, possibly disobeying Soule, who wanted
them to stay and resume their advance in the morning. But even
if they had managed to break through to the Gloucesters, it is
entirely possible that they would have been unable to break out
again.

Brigadier Brodie was very anxious. Having borne the brunt of an attack by two Chinese divisions, he had requested a withdrawal, but his American commander had ordered him to stay. The 29th Brigade was holding a vital section of line. American units were withdrawing on their right, and if the 29th gave way the Americans could well be attacked from the flank and rear as they pulled back. Many of the survivors of the brigade feel that Brodie and his American superiors failed to communicate as effectively as men from the same nation and cultural background would have done. Brodie famously told Soule that things were 'a bit sticky'.[48] This classic piece of British understatement was not fully appreciated by Soule as he attempted to extricate his entire division from massive enemy attacks, and resources were not committed in proportion to the threat that the 29th Brigade faced. Perhaps Brodie didn't want to be seen to let the Americans down. Anthony Farrar Hockley, at the time a captain in the Gloucesters, remained angry until his death in 2006 that the brigade didn't withdraw to prepared defensive positions that they had dug and wired only weeks before. Brodie could well have felt that to insist on withdrawing or to ask for extra support might reflect badly on the British. But the fact was that the 29th Brigade was not up to the job of stopping two crack Chinese divisions. The light artillery pieces of the 45th Field Regiment were not enough. Unfortunately, the Gloucesters' American artillery liaison officer had been withdrawn just before the battle, and they had no way of calling in the American medium and heavy guns. In the same way, the air strikes that had proved so decisive in the war thus far were in short supply in the battle on the Imjin. Either the Americans were unwilling to use precious resources on foreign troops when their own needed help, or the 29th Brigade wasn't making its predicament clear. When air strikes did arrive, they were lethally effective. David Green and his fellow Gloucesters watched in awe as Mustangs gave a 'brilliant display of precision strafing no more than 50 yards from us'. But when the napalm started to fall, 'Our admiration changed to disgust and pity, if you can believe it, for our Chinese counterparts.'[49]

THE IMJIN RIVER

Despite the blithe confidence of the men that someone would come and get them out, the battle continued with dwindling ammunition and no sign of reinforcements. David Green remembers an attempt to airdrop supplies to them. 'At last we saw the Dakotas in the far distance, headed our way ... the parachutes began to tumble out. To our anger and great disappointment, they drifted like dandelion seeds in the wind and fell outside our perimeter.'[50] The Northumberlands were forced to throw tins of cheese at the Chinese, hoping that they would be mistaken for grenades. The men were exhausted, unable to sleep at night because of the continuous assaults, while during the day they were pounded by mortars and pinned down by sniper fire from the higher slopes.

Finally, on the night of 24–25 April, Brodie got permission to withdraw. The commander of the Royal Ulster Rifles was furious – his men had repulsed all attacks and leaving the high ground would place them at greater risk than they faced at present. He was ill informed about the rest of the brigade, however: the Fusiliers were at the end of their strength and the Gloucesters would experience another night of vicious fighting, often hand-to-hand. Carne himself led counter-attack after counter-attack, but when Anthony Farrar Hockley asked what he had been up to he replied vaguely, 'Oh, just shooting away some Chinese.'[51]

At 8 a.m. on the morning of the 25th the Fusiliers began their retreat; the Chinese looked down on them and pressed home their attacks with increased vigour. Deprived of sleep for up to 72 hours, the men stumbled in a trance down the road to the south. Some of the Ulsters held a crucial defile through which they passed to relative safety. The rest of the Ulsters and the Belgians leap-frogged down the hill – one unit holding, the next withdrawing and setting up a position further back, and so on. This is one of the hardest manoeuvres in warfare, and slowly the men lost their cohesion and groups of infantry made off down the hill towards the track to the rear. It was now that the tank, which had had a very quiet war so far, finally came into its own. British Centurions sprayed the hillside with their machine guns and main armament; others ferried the wounded and exhausted fugitives back down the road. Eventually, the Chinese rushed on to the road and threw themselves on to the hulls of the tanks; they turned their guns on their fellow tanks to try to clear the Chinese off, and one tank commander drove through a Korean house to try to dislodge a Chinese soldier who was trying to get into his turret hatch. The colonel of the Fusiliers was killed as he retreated in his jeep; he had ignored a warning that the track was being swept by enemy fire, which was attracted by vehicles in particular. It was a race between the British on the road and the Chinese as they moved across country and fired down upon them. A US force had taken a blocking position across the road, and as the last of the Centurions passed through it word was passed that, 'Everybody's come down who's coming.'[52] The road behind them was strewn with bodies, smashed equipment and a few tanks, wrecked by their crews so that they would be of no use to their enemies.

Another brief attempt was made that morning to rescue the Gloucesters. The US 65th Infantry Regiment moved into the defile that had halted the rescue mission the day before, but Chinese fire and the discovery that only the lightest tanks could fit up the road meant that it had to be called off. The last hope for the beleaguered battalion was gone. The Gloucesters were finally told that there was no chance of relief. Carne informed Brodie by radio, 'What I must make clear to you is that my command is no longer an effective fighting force.' However, 'If it is required that we stay here … we shall continue to hold.' He asked what had happened to the armoured column. The response was, 'It isn't coming.'[53] The unflappable Carne now faced a decision: should he stay, surrender or attempt to break out? As he sucked on his pipe and offered words of encouragement to his men, his adjutant, Captain Farrar Hockley, ordered the drum major to respond to the endless Chinese bugling with his own. He was to play every call he knew 'except retreat'.[54] The drum major stood to attention and played 'Reveille', 'Cookhouse', 'Defaulters', and 'Officers Dress for Dinner'. No one who was there ever forgot it.

The final blow came at 9.30 a.m., when Carne was informed that the other battalions had now withdrawn and the Chinese were so far behind them that they threatened the artillery. The 45th Field Regiment was going to have to pull out its guns. The importance of the artillery is brought into sharp relief by the fact that its removal made Carne's decision for him. It was absolutely impossible to survive where they were without the British guns holding off the enemy. The night before, the Gloucesters had called in fire on their own positions. The men had stayed low while shells exploded around them, sending showers of shrapnel upwards and outwards to kill the attacking Chinese.

Carne ordered his company commanders to lead their men back to the British lines. The wounded would have to stay where they were; the chaplain and some medical staff stayed behind with them. As the companies prepared to leave the hill, the last ammunition was parcelled out: each man had no more than two or three rounds left for his rifle. Captain Harvey led 90 men of D Company north towards the river, then turned and headed back to the UN lines. After brushes with the Chinese, the survivors found some American tanks, which at first opened fire on them and inflicted some casualties. When they identified themselves, he and his remaining 39 men were taken back to the UN lines. They were the only survivors of the Gloucestershire Battalion to get there. A, B and C companies headed directly to the south, but ran straight into a machine-gun position. It fell to the tough and ambitious Captain Farrar Hockley to sacrifice professional pride and shout for his men to stop and lay down their arms: 'It was a very shameful moment, surrendering. I hated doing it. Surrendering seemed to go against everything that I thought soldiering should be about.' Carne evaded capture for 24 hours, but was eventually brought in. For some men it was an awful repetition – they had spent the majority of the Second World War as German prisoners, and now a long stint in a Chinese prison faced them. Thirty of the Gloucesters would not survive captivity.

It was a disaster. There were 1000 29th Brigade casualties, around a quarter of their front-line strength. The Gloucesters lost approximately 70 killed and 200 wounded, 530 men entered captivity. In return, the brigade had inflicted terrible slaughter on the attacking Chinese: 10,000 is the figure given, although it is only a very rough estimate based on observation.

Van Fleet and Ridgway were deeply disappointed to lose the Gloucesters. In public they heaped praise on them, Van Fleet called their stand 'the most outstanding example of unit bravery in modern warfare'.[55] He later said that the loss of the Gloucesters had been necessary to save the whole 8th Army. They even received a Presidential Unit Citation.[56] But in private there was deep concern. Van Fleet ordered that from now on all units should be kept within supporting distance, and they were not allowed to be cut off. Ridgway wrote to him on 9 May: 'I cannot but feel a certain disquiet that down through the chain of command the full responsibility for realising the danger to which this unit was exposed then for extricating it when that danger became grave was not recognised nor implemented.... I have the feeling ... that neither the Division, or the Corps commander was fully aware by direct personal presence as near the critical spot as he could have gotten of what the actual situation was.'[57]

In his book *The War in Korea* Ridgway wrote that 'the brigade held its vital positions for three days, thus enabling I Corps to complete its withdrawal successfully'.[58] There is no question that, even taking into account a certain amount of exaggeration, the action fought on the Imjin dramatically slowed down the Chinese offensive and allowed the rest of the 8th Army to 'roll with the punch'. Any chance that the Chinese had of taking Seoul was crushed. They had sustained horrific casualties, and their timetable had been completely thrown. When they did resume the advance, they found that the UN had withdrawn to a line known as 'Golden', just north of Seoul, which had been constructed by Korean workers over the previous weeks. The 25th Division's sector of it alone had 786 crew-served weapons such as heavy machine guns, and was protected by 74,000 yards (nearly 68,000 metres) of double apron tactical wire fence, 510,000 sandbags and 25,000 logs. The Chinese troops carried food for only five days, and with so much time and effort having been taken up fighting the 29th Brigade on the Imjin the spent forces had no chance of smashing through this fortified line.

Nevertheless, over the next few days, the Chinese crawled forward, hammered by massive artillery and air attacks, and made an attempt on Seoul; but it was beaten back with heavy losses. They tried to cross the Han River in small boats, but aircraft, artillery and naval fire decimated them and the survivors struggled ashore to be met by a South Korean marine battalion which showed no mercy. Fought to a standstill, they had no choice but to withdraw; their war-winning offensive had bought them only 25 miles (40 km) of territory. One last offensive was tried in the east of the peninsula, where on 16 May the ROK were routed and a wedge driven into the UN lines. But this time there was no shortage of American artillery: Van Fleet called it his 'Day of Fire'. It could perhaps be seen as a direct response to the UN's losses on the Imjin: 'I want to stress.... We must expend steel and fire, not men. I want to stop the Chinaman here and hurt him. I welcome his attack and want to be strong enough in position and fire power to defeat him. I want so many artillery holes that a man can step from one to another. This is not an overstatement; I mean it.'[59]

The Chinese attack finally ground to a halt. The UN had lost around 25,000 men in decisively defeating both attacks of the Fifth Phase Offensive, the Communists an estimated 85,000. Its lessons were immediately obvious: the Chinese could no longer expect to arrive on the battlefield and watch the fleeing backs of their enemies; the UN had mastered the tactics needed to inflict massive casualties. Marshal Peng reported to his political masters that it would be months before his forces recovered from their losses. Never again did the Chinese attempt to win the war with a spectacular breakthrough on the battlefield. The fighting would go on until 1953, but the defeat of the Fifth Phase Offensive taught Mao that a negotiated solution was inevitable. He approached the USSR to broker a deal. On 23 June Jacob Malik, the Soviet ambassador to the UN, implied in a radio interview that the Communists would accept negotiations. Even so, the war would rumble on. The men in the hills would, sweat, freeze, toil and die while negotiators wrangled over prisoner repatriations and protocol. Three million people of all nationalities died during the course of the fighting making it arguably the bloodiest war of the twentieth century after the two World Wars. Eventually, a truce was agreed and both sides agreed to withdraw 1½ miles (2 km) from the front line. But this was never followed by a treaty, and as a result the two Koreas are still in a state of war.

Today the border is the most heavily armed in the world. North Korea remains frozen in the Cold War. Led by Kim Il Sung's son, Kim Jong Il, it is one of the world's last Stalinist dictatorships. The country's pursuit of nuclear weapons, which included the detonation of a nuclear device in October 2006, has made it a virtually universal pariah. International agencies estimate that up to 2 million North Koreans have died since the mid-1990s because of acute food shortages caused by poor harvests and economic mismanagement. This totalitarian state is kept afloat by China, which supplies it with energy and just enough food, still preferring a friendly despot on its borders to an economically dynamic and democratic united Korea. South Korea has shaken off the yoke of Rhee and his successors. Its bustling streets and vocal press remind a visitor of London, Tokyo or New York. Yet just a few miles from Seoul the third and fourth largest armies in the world eye each other nervously over no man's land. This last relic of the Second World War and the Cold War may yet come to haunt the twenty-first century.

THE TET OFFENSIVE

At 2.47 a.m. on 31 January 1968 a taxicab and a Peugeot pick-up truck drove through the streets of South Vietnam's capital, Saigon, on a mission that would change the course of the Vietnam War. The vehicles were carrying 19 Vietnamese Communist guerrillas and an armoury of weapons and explosives assembled in a garage over the past few days. It had not been easy: the Vietcong, as the guerrillas were known, had smuggled the guns and the C4 plastic explosive from their underground hideouts into the city, concealed under vegetables in a cart.

The team of combat engineers from the VC's 'C-10' unit were only a tiny fraction of the force of tens of thousands of Vietcong ordered into battle in South Vietnam's cities that night. But their target was the most important of all: they were out to strike a blow at the symbolic heart of America's presence in Vietnam. Their attack on the United States embassy was part of a massive military operation that would become known as the Tet Offensive. The Vietcong hoped to cause such damage and chaos throughout the cities and towns of South Vietnam that its government would fall and its American allies would be driven out of the country once and for all.

It was the second day of Tet, the Lunar New Year holiday in Vietnam, a time for rowdy celebration. By tradition there was also a truce in the war that had been racking the country without any sign of resolution for several years. As savage and bloody as most

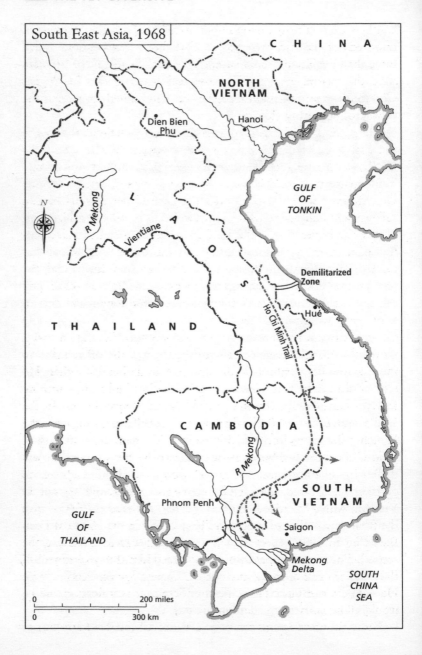

South East Asia, 1968

conflicts are that turn a nation upon itself, it was costing the lives of hundreds of thousands of people. But this war was about much more than the blood of soldiers and civilians: the people of Vietnam were the victims of a fight to the end between two ideologies, Communism and Capitalism. Each was determined to prevent the other from claiming victory.

The scale of the bloodshed and suffering was heightened by the military resources that the two superpowers, the USA and the USSR, poured into the conflict: both believed the outcome would fundamentally affect the world balance of power, but it was the United States which was to suffer the greatest defeat – its biggest military and political setback of the twentieth century. At the height of this war, at the time of the Tet Offensive, America had half a million of its men fighting in Vietnam: it was to lose a tenth of that number killed in action during the whole war. And, in the end, the rest of the world and most of America were left shocked and ashamed at the human and material cost of the longest conflict of the twentieth century.

On the one side was the government of South Vietnam, a shaky, virulently anti-Communist military regime. On the other side was the Communist north: its leader, the veteran nationalist fighter Ho Chi Minh, was halfway to achieving his lifetime ambition – uniting the two halves of his country under a Marxist government. In the 1940s and early 1950s he had led a guerrilla army against the French colonial regime, which governed Vietnam and the rest of Indo-China. Uncle Ho, as he was known by his supporters, was driven by determination not just to throw out the French but to replace the age-old semi-feudal economic and social system in Vietnam with a Marxist revolution. He had achieved the first – with the final destruction of French military power at the Battle of Dien Bien Phu in 1954 – and he was well on his way to achieving the second. The international community ceded him the government of the northern half of the country in the Geneva agreements of 1955. He was now committed to achieving Vietnamese unification and he would allow nothing to stand in his way.

His main obstacle was the determination of the southern part of

Vietnam to pursue a different political path from that of its northern neighbour. Ho Chi Minh was a national hero who had thrown out the European colonialists, and there were Communists in the south who wanted the country united under a Marxist government. But there was a powerful anti-Communist constituency in South Vietnam too. Buddhists and Catholic Christians, who rejected Communism and were committed to a more liberalized Western economic agenda, were determined to thwart Ho's ambition. But the government of the south was fragile, with limited popular support; it had not been tested in full and free democratic elections, and it faced an increasingly effective rebellion by Communist insurgents supported by North Vietnam. After the collapse of French rule, the southern regime looked to America, as champion of the anti-Communist world, to support it against the threat from the north. And the United States was willing to help.

President Kennedy was in the White House at the critical time when the rebellion of the South Vietnamese Communists began to bring real pressure on the Saigon government. He had inherited from his predecessors a profound suspicion of the ambitions of the two great Communist powers, the USSR and China.[1] He believed that they were out to undermine regimes friendly to the USA in Asia: if a stand was not made in one threatened country, and it fell to Communism, the rot could spread from one state to another. Friendly pro-Western governments could fall like dominoes.[2] This concern was fuelled by a particularly bitter encounter with the Soviet leader Nikita Khrushchev at the Vienna summit of 1961. Kennedy came out of the meeting and said to the *New York Times*'s James Reston, 'Now we have a problem in trying to make our power credible and Vietnam looks like the place.'[3]

THE BALANCE OF FORCES

Kennedy put military 'advisers' into South Vietnam and embarked on a policy of arming and assisting the Saigon government; by 1965 this aid had escalated into a full-scale commitment to send in fighting troops. The problem was that the South Vietnamese regime was little more than a dictatorship. It had dubious internal or international legitimacy, and it was not long before a growing number of Americans began to question the wisdom of President Kennedy (1961–3) and his successor President Johnson (1963–8). Many of the critics applauded the principle of drawing a line against Communist expansion in Asia, but they were appalled at the quality of the regime the USA was supporting and the growing death toll among American troops, not to mention innocent Vietnamese civilians. The nagging worry gathered momentum as the 1960s went on: America appeared to be engaged in a war whose political purpose did not justify the bloodshed and suffering it caused. This made it all the more urgent for the administration to bring the war to a victorious conclusion as rapidly as possible.

So Washington piled in the troops and by the summer of 1967 there were over half a million American soldiers, sailors and airmen committed to the struggle. They were equipped with the most powerful weapons systems in the world – together with 2500 warplanes, 3000 helicopters and 3500 armoured vehicles. In terms of military strength, the advantage was massively with the Americans and South Vietnamese; the latter had another half million men under arms as well as armoured forces and an air force which, although much of it was still poorly trained, had more than enough firepower to crush the Vietcong. The US forces operated mainly from huge bases strung along the coast from the Mekong Delta up to the DMZ – the demilitarized zone – which had been established between the two halves of Vietnam at the Geneva Conference of 1955. Their task was to identify and track down the Communist rebels – the Vietcong: they would launch 'search and destroy' missions, wipe out the 'VC' or 'Charlie Cong', and enable the villages and countryside to be pacified and effectively governed by the Saigon regime.

Vietnam's geography might appear, at first sight, to favour the Americans and their South Vietnamese allies. The country is 1000 miles (1600 km) long from its mountainous northern border with China to the vast rice-growing expanse of the Delta in the south. The border between the two halves was a narrow neck – only around 50 miles (80 km) from west to east – and American troops guarded the southern side of the DMZ from fortified strongholds called firebases. All this made it very difficult for the North Vietnamese to supply and reinforce their Vietcong allies using routes within Vietnam itself. So they developed another channel of supply – the so-called Ho Chi Minh trail, a network of tracks and paths that stretched down through the jungles of supposedly neutral Laos and Cambodia next door. The Vietcong used everything from trucks to backpacks to carry vital supplies hundreds of miles. It was an extraordinary human and logistical achievement, and American bombers did their best to disrupt it. Just one B52 high-level heavy bomber could drop its load of up to 100 750-lb (340-kg) bombs and create a moonscape of destruction a mile long and a quarter of a mile wide (nearly 2 km by half a kilometre). The cost was astronomical – but the effects disappointing. The rebels' supply line defied all attempts to destroy it. It has been calculated that on average it took the US air force 100 tons of bombs to kill just one infiltrator: the annual cost of the bombing was some £2 billion. This prompted Dr Henry Kissinger (US Secretary of State in the early 1970s), for one, to write that he believed an essential condition for US victory in Vietnam was intervention on the ground to block the Ho Chi Minh trail. But the USA and its allies were reluctant to escalate the conflict by sending their forces across the border. And with a resilience that has seldom been equalled in the history of warfare the North Vietnamese supply line quickly re-established itself after each bombing raid. By 1967, a massive 90,000 North Vietnamese reinforcements a year were being funnelled down the trail to aid the hard-pressed rebels in the south.

The US had the pick of its forces in Vietnam: marines, airborne infantry and the helicopter-borne air cavalry, who could swoop like Valkyries on any suspected pocket of Vietcong in a matter of minutes. They had the M48 tank, artillery, napalm, the F4 Phantom fighter-bomber and the giant B52 bomber – equipment and munitions that were state-of-the-art. The Communists had perhaps the world's best-ever personal weapon, the AK47 light machine gun, but precious little else except their own extraordinary tenacity and ingenuity. Guerrilla training nurtured by decades of fighting the French and other modern conventional armies had turned them into a lethal and elusive enemy. Their units, large and small, could transform themselves into groups of innocent-looking civilians in seconds. They could disappear by day into the jungle, into friendly villages, into the network of tunnels that they dug under the countryside; at night they could reappear and reoccupy the areas they had lost to American search-and-destroy operations during the daytime. But they were a long way short of victory in the war.

By 1967 massive American firepower was taking its toll on the Vietcong and the North Vietnamese Army. They were suffering more casualties than the Americans and the South Vietnamese government troops. Much of the countryside may have been largely outside the control of the Saigon government, but the towns and cities of South Vietnam were on the whole secure. There was no prospect of a victory for the north while the Americans remained committed to backing the South Vietnamese generals and their forces. The US command, for its part, under the upbeat General Westmoreland, believed the war could be won. He had constantly extracted troop reinforcements from President Johnson, claiming that victory was within reach.

That summer, Ho Chi Minh's military chief, General Giap, conceived a plan which he believed could hasten the end of the war and final reunification of the country under the Communist regime in Hanoi. He masterminded a plan called General Offensive General Uprising: a countrywide assault, not on the countryside but on the towns and cities of South Vietnam. The offensive would deal a massive shock to the South Vietnamese armed forces and prompt the population to rise against the Saigon regime. It would take place at Tet – the Lunar New Year holiday in January. The North Vietnamese strategy was two-pronged. They would prepare simultaneous assaults on the urban areas of South Vietnam, secretly mobilizing all the resources of the network of Vietcong communications and supply channels to smuggle everything that was needed into the cities. But immediately preceding that they would carry out a major ground attack on a fixed American military base far from the cities.

The place Giap chose to make the focus of this first part of the offensive was an American combat base called Khe Sanh, deep in the countryside. About the broad lines of the plan there is no dispute. What is less clear is its precise scope. It is not clear even 40 years later whether the assault on Khe Sanh was intended wholly as a diversionary tactic to draw US attention and resources away from the cities or a forthright attempt to destroy American forces in an open conventional battle.[4] Perhaps it was designed to do both. At all events, it was to succeed partially in the first but to fail in the second.

THE SIEGE OF KHE SANH

In January 1968, American patrols and electronic sensors at the marine base at Khe Sanh began picking up signs that two North Vietnamese divisions, comprising some 20,000 men, were establishing themselves in hilly country around the stronghold. Khe Sanh was a well-fortified base with an airstrip, which is still visible today amid the scrub of a remote valley a few miles south of the DMZ. It had been constructed several months earlier to plant an American military presence in the northernmost province of South Vietnam, near the Ho Chi Minh trail just over the border in Laos. Colonel David Lownds had a force of marines dug in at the base itself and in a number of the surrounding hills, each of them designated in the usual military style by a number simply marking its height in feet. Lownds had outposts on some high ground, such as Hill 861 and Hill 881, as far as three miles away from the base.

On 20 January his marines intercepted a patrol and captured a man who said the attack would begin that night. 'Do you believe this guy?' Lownds asked his intelligence team. When they replied that they did not know, he said, 'Let's act as if we believe him.'

First Lieutenant Nick Romanetz remembers a command reaching his trench that every marine should wear his helmet and flak jacket and carry his weapon and gas mask at all times. 'Until this point, the only time we wore a flak jacket or helmet was when we

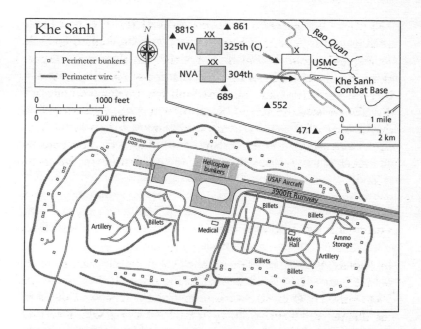

went on patrols or work parties outside the wire, or when we were standing to or standing down. When this word came down, it really had a lot of guys chuckling. Everybody was saying, "Hey, who are these guys kidding? This is Khe Sanh. It's the quietest place."'5

But Colonel Lownds's prisoner was right. In the small hours of 21 January an assault began which was to go on without let-up for the best part of three months. Lownds rapidly built up Khe Sanh's garrison to a total of 6000, but fire from small arms and Communist artillery exposed them to a pulverizing bombardment and constant probing attacks from well-trained infantry: one of the attacking divisions had led the victorious assault on the French at Dien Bien Phu.

Survivors of the siege of Khe Sanh recall the shrieks of the incoming shells, the mind-numbing noise of the explosions, and the nights they hunched terrified in the bunkers they had dug rapidly after the first attack. One young marine, Frank Jones, thought he was having a heart attack. 'I was hyperventilating and had chest pains. I was very scared. I was twenty-three years old, and I was scared almost to death.... They just kept pounding us. The dust and dirt was falling in. It seemed like everything became very pronounced – I could really smell the odor of the sandbags and the dust, the sounds were magnified, the colors were brighter. I sat with my back to a pillar, looking at the entry way tunnel into the bunker. I had my six-shot revolver and was thinking I would stack up anyone who came through the tunnel in front of me. We kept hearing the lieutenant in Khe Sanh village calling for artillery to be fired on top of his own position. It was like listening to a movie. I couldn't believe it was happening, that they were over-running us, that they were going to take us down. I started thinking that we were all going to be killed.'[6] Another marine recalled that, when the shelling was at its worst, he jammed himself tightly into his bunker with his face almost touching its ceiling and reflected that if he got a direct hit he was already in his coffin.

From the moment the attacks began, the defenders of the base and its protective hills dug themselves deep into bunkers and set an elaborate network of lethal traps in the ground immediately in front of their trenches. They put out at least three rows of concertina wire – with razor blades attached. In front of that they put big 55-gallon (250-litre) drums, cut in half and filled with a napalm-like mixture which would ignite when the attacking enemy triggered off claymore mines stuck in the soil around the barrels. Beyond that, the marines stretched what they called Tanglefoot – a labyrinth of wire in one-foot squares with the strands criss-crossing and fixed in the ground with stakes. Beyond that, again they planted mines, with more wire in between them.

Each morning, when there was a pause in the barrage, soldiers peeked fearfully out at the scene of devastation: dead bodies, shattered buildings and trees, burning vehicles, the runway pitted with craters. Within days, the scene at Khe Sanh was being described by marines as a 'moonscape'. Virtually nothing was left standing. And still the shells kept coming in, and they were never free of the fear of being attacked across the wire. Nick Romanetz recalls how he would have his whole platoon woken up each morning at 5 or

5.30 a.m. and – after a shave and breakfast – he would organize a team to check the state of their defences.

'There was a fear that the enemy would sneak in at night and cut the wire and put it back together so that, if the ground attacks ever came, they would be able to get through. Besides, the wire was always getting chopped up from the incoming. So, on a daily basis, we had to send a three- or four-man team out to check the wire. This was no big deal until we started to get snipers three or four hundred yards in front of the wire. As it turned out, we had to get up while there was still fog and shimmy and shake the wire to see what was going on. Then, as the fog started to lift, we had to hope we could get back in. Eventually, a couple of marines did get shot by the snipers.'[7]

Conditions in the trenches became worse as the siege went on. Men would wake to find rats crawling over them. Some grabbed pistols and shot at them. One soldier who refused to sleep with his face covered had a chunk bitten out of his cheek. And the danger of death was always just seconds away. Marine Anthony Astaccio recalled: 'We had a man who caught an artillery round. A shell came into this man's trench and what they had to send home of him would probably fit inside a handkerchief.'[8]

The siege of Khe Sanh had precisely the effect on General Westmoreland that General Giap had hoped for. US intelligence had for some time been picking up reports that a major Communist offensive was planned. Some had even identified the towns and cities of South Vietnam as the main target of the planned offensive, but Westmoreland was preoccupied with what he saw as a threat to the northern sector nearest the DMZ. Over the winter months of 1967–8, he diverted ever-increasing supplies of men and ammunition to the northern provinces in order to bolster bases like Khe Sanh. He welcomed the prospect of an attack in the countryside: his strategy was to catch the Communists whenever and wherever they concentrated their strength, and when he heard of the force that had gathered around Khe Sanh he believed he now had the chance of fighting the kind of pitched battle he wanted.

Once Westmoreland's forces could identify and pin down their enemy in open country, they had one matchless advantage on their side: airpower. The US air force provided air support to Khe Sanh's beleaguered garrison on a breathtaking scale. When the North Vietnamese cut the road to the base, the USAF created an air bridge and its bombers and strike aircraft dropped some 5000 tons of munitions every day. Over the three months of the siege of Khe Sanh, the air force dropped explosive equivalent to five of the atomic bombs dropped on Hiroshima. B52 bombers diverted from the Ho Chi Minh trail created swathes of destruction in the wooded valleys: the North Vietnamese took thousands of casualties, but still they kept coming. The US aircrews suffered too. Supplying the reinforced garrison of some 6000 marines and South Vietnamese rangers became something close to a suicide run for the pilots of the transport planes and helicopters.

The main supply aircraft were C130 Hercules cargo-carrying planes which ferried in supplies through a hail of hostile fire. They would land, taxi slowly along the runway as they dumped supplies out of their aft-end loading ramps, and then take off again without stopping. Sometimes they would disgorge reinforcements, who would drop off the moving aircraft ramps and sprint for what cover they could find at the side of the airstrip. One unlucky C130 took a direct hit on the runway and blew up instantly. Helicopters which landed to unload supplies had around 30 seconds on the ground before they were forced to take off again as enemy fire homed in on them.

The siege of Khe Sanh may have presented Westmoreland with what he saw as an opportunity, but it also posed a threat: it became a bloody and expensive burden on the American High Command. President Johnson himself grew obsessed with Khe Sanh. Two weeks into the siege, he had a relief model of the combat base and its surroundings built in the White House and followed every detail of the battle, which he was determined the United States would win. He was mesmerized by the superficial similarities between Khe Sanh and the French mountain base at Dien Bien Phu, whose capture by the Vietnamese in 1954 had spelled the end of the French empire in Indo-China. In his broad Texan accent, Johnson swore to his advisers that this would not be his 'Dinbinphoo'. He was even urged by his commander-in-chief in Vietnam to expand the range of weapons deployed if there was a massive attack across the demilitarized zone.

Westmoreland told him: 'I visualize that either tactical nuclear weapons or chemical agents would be active candidates for employment.'[9]

There was no doubting the success of General Giap in forcing the Americans to focus time, attention and resources on the threat to Khe Sanh. In fact, one half of the US army's mobile reserve was moved to within striking distance of the base. But some reckon that Khe Sanh also represented a failure for the North Vietnamese. One of America's top CIA operatives at the time, George Allen, was one of those who believed that the siege had a double purpose: to draw eyes away from the cities, but also to attempt to secure a major victory in the field and demonstrate that America faced more than a tiresome guerrilla war in Vietnam.[10] This the siege failed to achieve. Westmoreland was able to concentrate so much firepower and so much airlift capacity on keeping Khe Sanh's lifeline open that he managed to deny the North Vietnamese a spectacular prize – the surrender of a major US firebase.[11] But the attack on Khe Sanh would have succeeded in its first purpose – to create a successful distraction from the planned assault on the cities – if it had not been for one perceptive general under Westmoreland's command.

SAIGON

Major General Frederick Weyand led the American field forces in the zone around the capital, Saigon. He, like all Westmoreland's generals, had for some time been practising his commander-in-chief's strategy of deploying his forces far out in the countryside near Vietnam's western border. As many as 39 of his 53 combat battalions were operating there, hunting down the Vietcong. But Weyand's interpretation of the intelligence warnings of an offensive was that it would come in the cities rather than in the countryside. He telephoned General Westmoreland and persuaded him to allow a substantial number of men to return from the border area to the cities. Although Westmoreland was absorbed by the threat in the north, he was alarmed enough to suggest that the ceasefire and military leave planned for the Tet holiday at the end of January be cancelled. But South Vietnam's President Thieu, a soldier himself, was not going to cancel the traditional 48-hour ceasefire or cancel any leave for his South Vietnamese troops: Tet was the biggest holiday of the year. He did, however, agree to limit it to 36 hours, from the evening of 29 January to the morning of the 31st.

Weyand was right to suspect that something big was afoot. Over the past months, the Vietcong and their North Vietnamese allies had been painstakingly preparing for an assault on every town or city of any size in South Vietnam. A vast network of underground tunnels, most of them so narrow that only the leanest man or woman could wriggle through, allowed the Vietcong to hide themselves and their weapons within easy reach of Saigon. The Cu Chi tunnel complex is today one of Vietnam's top tourist sites.[12] One of the Vietcong's training team, Duong Sang, later revealed how vital the role of the tunnels was.

'We used Cu Chi as a training base and staging area. We enlisted recruits in Saigon and trained them here, in the tunnels. We raised their political consciousness and taught them tactical skills preparing them for big assignments such as attacking large enemy hotels. They learned to use automobiles and Honda motorcycles – firing hand guns to hit the enemy with a single shot. In the city, we had people who specialized in forging documents. Whenever the enemy produced any kind of document, we were always able to acquire a copy and produce an exact replica, right in the heart of Saigon itself.'[13]

One of the tunnel complexes ran beneath a US base, but was never discovered. But the Americans did find some of the tunnels and were constantly trying to destroy them. Some particularly agile troops, who became known as 'tunnel rats', were tasked with ferreting the Vietcong out of their underground hideaways, and there were a number of clashes. Tran Thi Gung, 22 at the time of the Tet offensive, was the only woman in one unit which had the job of

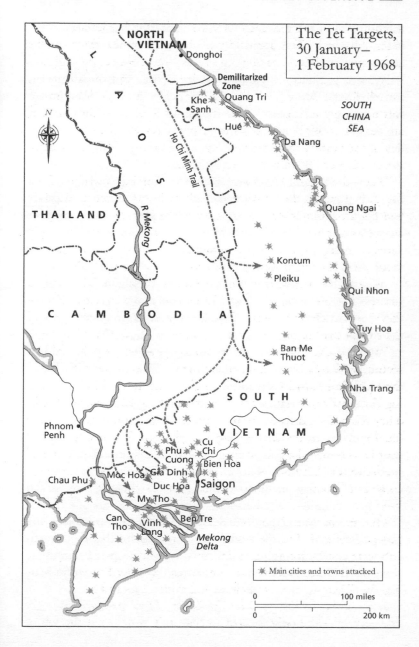

The Tet Targets,
30 January–
1 February 1968

NORTH VIETNAM

Donghoi

Demilitarized Zone

Khe Sanh

Quang Tri

Hué

Da Nang

SOUTH CHINA SEA

Ho Chi Minh Trail

L A O S

Quang Ngai

THAILAND

Kontum

Pleiku

Qui Nhon

C A M B O D I A

Tuy Hoa

R. Mekong

Ban Me Thuot

Nha Trang

Phnom Penh

S O U T H

V I E T N A M

Cu Chi

Phu Cuong

Bien Hoa

Chau Phu

Moc Hoa

Gia Dinh

Duc Hoa

Saigon

My Tho

Can Tho

Vinh Long

Ben Tre

Mekong Delta

✳ Main cities and towns attacked

0   100 miles

0   200 km

N

defending the Cu Chi tunnels. On one occasion she and her comrades shot and killed some US troops who came close to their hiding places.

'We had to wait for them to come very close. As soon as I started to fire, I killed an American.... After a few minutes they pulled back, taking the bodies of their friends with them.... In that first battle against the Americans I shot so many GIs I was awarded a decoration with the title "Valiant Destroyer of American Infantryman".

'Their shells and bombs were extremely powerful and sometimes they killed people in the tunnels, but it didn't happen as often as you might think. The Cu Chi tunnels had such small openings it was very rare for a bomb to land right in a tunnel. As Uncle Ho said, "A stork can't shit into a bottle", so with our tunnels we shouldn't be scared of American bombers.

'When GIs discovered tunnel openings they dynamited them, but the tunnels were too deep and had so many twists and turns they couldn't do too much damage. It was like an underground maze. Most of the tunnels were just wide enough to crawl through and so cramped. There were only some places where you could sit up, never mind stand. Most of the time we lived in the dark.'[14]

One young South Vietnamese, Tran Van Tan, moved down from Da Nang to work undercover for the Vietcong in Saigon. 'At the time of the Tet offensive, I was a textile worker. That was my legal cover, but my real work, day and night, was as a secret agent. For your own protection you weren't allowed to reveal your revolutionary activities to anyone else, even your own parents.

'During the day in the textile mill, I tried to recruit workers to join the revolution. But I had to be very careful and selective.... Since everyone was being drafted by the Saigon military, one of my first goals was to persuade workers that fighting for the puppet government meant shooting and killing your own people. If I couldn't persuade them to work for the revolution, maybe I could at least convince them to dodge the draft.'[15]

31 JANUARY 1968

The date for General Offensive General Uprising was set for the small hours of 31 January 1968 – at the height of the Tet holiday celebrations, when the South Vietnamese forces believed the truce would be in effect.

But then – whether by mistake or by design – the night before the planned offensive Vietcong attacks were launched on several towns in the central highlands. Raids took place at Ban Me Thuot, Pleiku and Kontum. Because the targets were limited to a small area of Vietnam, the Americans and South Vietnamese were able to concentrate their forces and crush the assault decisively. A quick assessment of the situation led some Americans to believe that the offensive predicted by US intelligence sources had now taken place. Others were more canny: it was always possible that some local commander had somehow fumbled his dates, and it could be that worse was to come. General Westmoreland was taking no chances: at 11.25 a.m. on 30 January all US forces around Saigon were put on full alert.

The Tet festivities went on late into the night of the 30th in all the towns and cities of South Vietnam, when the country's armed forces believed that the truce would be in effect. Fireworks were still going off everywhere after midnight, and the streets were alive with high-spirited revellers making a lot of noise. The celebrations – and the truce – were a welcome respite from the anxiety of the war that never seemed to end. It appeared quite natural to the guard at Saigon's radio station when some jeeps drove up just before 3 a.m. and an officer in riot police uniform approached, saying he had arrived with reinforcements. As the guard talked to the man, who was in fact a Vietcong guerrilla, the man pulled a gun and shot him dead. A machine-gunner provided covering fire from a nearby building and took a heavy toll of a unit of South Vietnamese paratroopers who had been sleeping on the roof. The small team of Vietcong, who then occupied the building, had with them a tape of Ho Chi Minh encouraging the people to rise in rebellion against the South Vietnamese government and its US protectors. The radio specialist who carried the tape had detailed plans of the radio station and duplicate keys supplied by one of the Vietcong agents who had infiltrated nearly every important government organization. Almost at the same moment, attacks were made on a range of vital installations in the capital: the naval dockyard, Tan Son Nhut airbase, the Phu Tho racetrack and President Thieu's Independence Palace in the heart of Saigon. Fourteen Vietcong sappers were assigned to the attack on the palace, and succeeded in exploding a large device by the staff entrance. A whole Vietcong battalion seized the racetrack

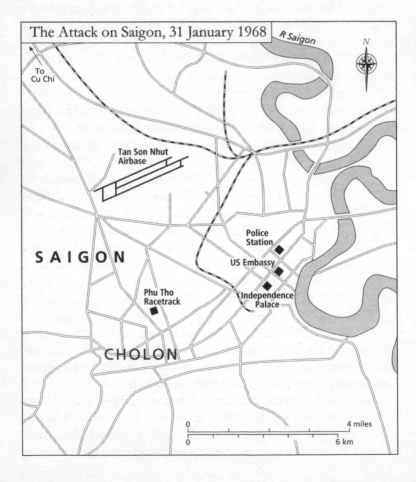

The Attack on Saigon, 31 January 1968

and several positions in the Chinese quarter of Cholon. The race-track was an obvious place for the guerrillas to set up their headquarters; it would also deprive the Americans of a useful landing zone for helicopters near the centre of the city.

Tran Van Tan found himself busy guiding teams of what he called 'revolutionary troops' to their targets in Saigon. 'On the second day of Tet ... a knock at the door woke me up. It was a Liberation Army commander. He asked for a glass of water. That was the code of recognition. Then he asked me for directions to the Nguyen Van Cu police station where I thought enemy units might be located. I told him everything I knew. Not too long after that, I heard the sound of American tanks coming into the area. People were fleeing the neighbourhood and I saw a swarm of choppers circling overhead.... Later I went to the scene of the battle and saw several burned out American tanks.'[16]

In his tactical operations headquarters, General Weyand, whose foresight had earlier caused reinforcements to be sent back into the Saigon area, watched his electronic map of South Vietnam light up like a 'pinball machine'. Communist raids were reported in 100 towns and cities throughout the country. And the Vietcong did not spare American bases either. One GI, Scott Higgins, remembers waking in the early hours at the huge US base at Bien Hoa. 'I will never forget it. It was a complete surprise. I was asleep. I wasn't on duty.... It was 3 a.m. I jumped out of bed, grabbed my flak jacket and my underwear, grabbed my .454 and my helmet, which I put on, and ran out the door. What woke me were these 22-mm rockets that started to come in. *Whoosh, crack*. That scared the living hell out of me. You could smell the graphite.'[17]

No one had anticipated fighting on a scale like this. More than 80,000 guerrillas and regular North Vietnamese troops (NVA) were involved in a synchronized offensive. It was potentially catastrophic for the Saigon government and its American allies.

The attack which was ultimately to have the greatest effect on the history of this war began at 2.47 a.m. when a taxi accompanied by a truckload of Vietcong drove past the main gate of the American embassy compound in Saigon, raking it with machine-gun fire. Two of the guards sounded the alert and slammed the gate. But within moments, the guerrillas, a group of 19 combat engineers, planted a charge of explosive at the foot of the embassy wall and blew a 3-foot (1-metre) hole in it. When they charged through, the American guards immediately shot dead the two Vietcong commanders; but the rest of the raiders poured through the hole into the compound, blazing away with AK47s at the two guards. One of the guards just had time to shout for help into his radio set before he and his colleague were killed by enemy fire. Two other guards were shot dead when they drove up in their jeep. The raiders then planted more charges by the entrance to the embassy building itself, which was now only protected by a couple of lightly armed guards. One of them tried firing at the advancing Vietcong with a shotgun, but it jammed. The ambassador, Ellsworth Bunker, was helicoptered away from his nearby residence to a safer location. The embassy now appeared to be wide open to being stormed by the Vietcong.

The American command's initial reaction to the attack on their embassy was that it was a 'piddling platoon action' not worthy of a major response. These military men did not immediately grasp the dire symbolism of a Vietcong presence on what was sovereign American soil, and felt there were other targets which had greater priority. An aide to General Westmoreland, Captain Charles Sampson, telephoned Marine Sergeant Ronald Harper, who was sheltering as best as he could in the embassy's reception area, and asked him: 'What's the trouble, Sergeant?'

'The VC are right outside the door.'

'You're not scared or anything, are you, Sergeant?'

'You bet your ass I am!' replied Harper.

It was not until 4.30 a.m. that General Westmoreland responded to the threat to the embassy by ordering armoured vehicles and helicopters to speed to the rescue of its beleaguered guards.

The two elements of the Tet Offensive in Saigon that threatened to have the most catastrophic political effects, the assault on the embassy and the storming of the radio station, now stalled. The superbly laid plan to capture and use the radio station was foiled by the foresight of the South Vietnamese colonel in charge of its security. In the event of an attack on the station, he had arranged for a code to be triggered instantly to order electric power to be cut off from the transmitter. His precautions paid off. Although the Vietcong occupied the station for six hours, they were unable to broadcast Ho's message: no call went out from the radio station for a general popular uprising.

President Thieu survived the attack on his palace, which was the best-defended location in the city. Its South Vietnamese guards – assisted by two tanks – were soon able to corral the attackers in a nearby building. They held out for 15 hours, and though they made a heroic last stand all but two of those who had assaulted the palace were killed.

The Vietcong attack on the US embassy also ended without success. Deprived of their leaders, the guerrillas milled around in the compound and failed to seize the chance to storm the embassy building, which was almost defenceless. They drove off the first attempt to reinforce the guards by firing at the helicopter which was bringing them, and the Americans decided to wait until daylight before trying again. It was well after dawn when the surviving Vietcong, who had failed to capitalize on their early success, were finally killed.

But long before this moment, another group of people had been alerted to the attack on the embassy. Press and television reporters from around the world happened to be staying at hotels not far from the US embassy, and word quickly got around that it was under attack. Journalists raced to the embassy compound, to be met with firing and confusion. What they were to write in the next few minutes and for several hours afterwards was to play a major part in changing the course of the Vietnam War. They knew instinctively that the chaos in the embassy was a bigger news story than anything else that was happening in the country at that moment. It was the most symbolic location in the whole of Vietnam, right in the heart of downtown Saigon, and here it was being stormed by Communist rebels. At 7.25 a.m. Saigon time, when it was 6.25 p.m. in New York and the main editions of America's big newspapers were finally setting their front pages, the Associated Press were reporting that part of the Saigon embassy had been invaded. It was prime time for television news as well, and their reporters were in the embassy garden watching the battle. The Vietcong may not have succeeded in seizing the embassy, but they had snatched the international headlines.

Colonel George Jacobson, a special military assistant to the ambassador, had spent the night trapped by the fighting in his second-floor apartment at a house in the embassy garden. He managed to telephone for help and reported that one of the armed rebels was on the first floor of his house. A marine promptly ran across the grass and threw up a .45 pistol to Jacobson, and as the Vietcong fighter burst into his room spraying bullets from his AK47, Jacobson leaped out from behind a recess and shot him dead.

It had been a close-run thing. The Vietcong, deprived of their officers in the first minute of the attack, had failed to develop their successful initial assault into the capture of the embassy building. They never got through the main door into the lobby, where Ronald Harper was preparing to fight for his life. But the television and newspaper reports and pictures of the dead bodies in the embassy garden sent shockwaves around America. And General Westmoreland did not improve the situation by appearing later that morning in the embassy porch and announcing that the 'enemy's well-laid plans had gone afoul'. There he was, proclaiming that all was well, when the enemy had caused death and destruction in scores of towns and cities all over the country and in the compound of the United States embassy itself. This was the commander-in-chief who had announced to the press only two months earlier that he 'had never been more encouraged by the progress being made in Vietnam' in the four years since he had been in the country.

Barry Zorthian was the leading US spokesman in Vietnam, and he was with Westmoreland at the embassy that day. 'I urged him to talk to the press and put the whole event into context.... He was heavily criticized for claiming success in repelling the VC at the embassy and saying everything was under control. But he was talking to his troops, not to the world.... When you hear his words in the face of headlines about VC attacks in forty different places, penetrating the embassy compound and fighting in the heart of Saigon, it almost seemed fatuous to be complimenting his troops on their victory.'[18]

Yet, within 12 hours of the beginning of the offensive, in South Vietnam's towns and cities most of the attacks had been blunted and the Vietcong assault squads either killed or captured.

HUÉ

There was only one city where the violence continued. For three whole weeks after the rest of the Tet Offensive had burned itself out, the ancient imperial Vietnamese capital of Hué was racked by some of the most savage fighting of the Vietnam War. Previously untouched by war, the city of Hué was one of the most venerated places in the country and had deep iconic importance for both North and South Vietnam. Hué was a centre of religion, learning and culture: both Ho Chi Minh and General Giap had been educated there. It was in this pivotal city – halfway up the coastline of Vietnam – that the Communists decided to strike the largest of all the blows they struck during the Tet Offensive.

At almost the same instant that Saigon was attacked, two North Vietnamese battalions, the 800th and the 802nd, broke through several entrances on the west side of the great citadel of Hué and seized strategic points all over the old city. Within two hours Communist forces had secured the entire city and were embarking on a systematic search for some 5000 people whom they had black-listed before their attack. Almost all the key business and professional men and women in Hué were rounded up and executed. Around 3000 in all were massacred and buried in mass graves. Two US diplomats were among the dead, as were several foreign doctors and priests.

Nguyen Qui Duc was the ten-year-old son of the South Vietnamese deputy provincial governor. He remembers his father looking out of the window, seeing people in uniform and believing they were compound guards. But they were North Vietnamese soldiers. 'When the soldiers came into the house my mother screamed.

We were completely terrified. It was the first time we'd seen the enemy. The most frightening and shocking thing was realizing they were regular North Vietnamese army soldiers who had come down the Ho Chi Minh trail and spoke with very strong northern accents. They were described to us as atrocious, horrific people.... We were given a lecture by one of the soldiers. As scared as I was I had the impression that he was a very persuasive and eloquent man. I don't remember his words, but there was passion in his speech and I was moved by the way he talked about the nation.' Duc says he couldn't help admiring his enemy as well as fearing him.[19]

Hué is really two cities on either side of the Perfume River. To the north, the old Vietnamese imperial city was constructed on the lines of the French fortresses built by Louis XIV's military engineer Vauban in the eighteenth century. A gigantic 200-year-old citadel, crisscrossed by small streets, it has the Imperial Palace as its centrepiece. The Communists soon secured all of it except for a small South Vietnamese military enclave in the north-east corner. Fortunately for the South Vietnamese, the brigadier in command, Ngo Quang Truong, had received reports of the attacks by the Communists a day earlier, and had placed his troops on alert. On the south side of the river was the new city: here too the Communists were soon in control of the whole area except the US military headquarters, the MACV complex (the Military Assistance Command Vietnam), which was held by a handful of US troops. The American High Command rapidly concluded that it could not allow Hué to remain in Communist hands. If they became entrenched in this key city, Ho Chi Minh would be able to claim a spectacular propaganda victory.

The US marine battalion at Phu Bai, a few miles south of Hué, was ordered to reoccupy the city. What followed was to become one of the epic sagas in US Marine Corps history: a vicious, unrelenting, house-to-house battle that led eventually to the destruction of much of Hué.

At first the marines in Task Force X-ray under Brigadier General Foster Lahue had a problem. They were very slow to react, and when they did they failed to use enough force. Lahue had just two marine regiments available because many of his men were away

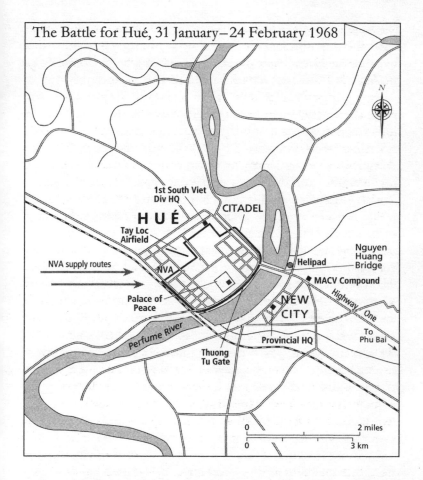

The Battle for Hué, 31 January–24 February 1968

trying to protect rural areas. At 8.30 a.m. on the 31st he released A Company of the 1st/5th Marines to go up Highway One towards the old city and relieve the MACV complex on the south side of the river first. But Lahue was sending a company of around 150 men to counter-attack against several thousand enemy fighters.

The small garrison at the MACV fought valiantly to hold off the North Vietnamese until the relief force arrived. One soldier climbed a 20-foot (6-metre) wooden tower and manned the machine gun there until he had killed 40 assaulting North Vietnamese soldiers.

The reinforcements from Phu Bai got bogged down in fighting well before they reached the MACV. On the way in, they joined up with four M48 tanks and were eventually reinforced by G Company of the 2nd/5th Marines. It took them until 3 p.m. to reach the MACV.

Marine Sergeant Alfredo Gonzalez, a 21-year-old from Texas, was one of those who fought his way into the city. A North Vietnamese machine gun opened up on the advancing marines on the road in and, while his squad sheltered behind the escorting tanks, Gonzales scrambled into a ditch by the road and crawled forward towards the machine-gun post, hurling grenades at it. The firing stopped. Gonzalez was killed in Hué just a few days later.[20]

The marines were already meeting tough opposition, but they would now see just how fearsome the task ahead of them was. Just after 4 p.m., US HQ ordered the marines to drive over the Nguyen Hoang girder bridge to relieve the South Vietnamese army compound in the north-east of the citadel. One colonel, called Gravel, was now given command of the two companies; he had a premonition that he was being asked to take too much of a risk, and complained that the opposition was too great for his small force to tackle alone. But he was ordered to proceed nevertheless. Halfway across the bridge he and his men came under devastating fire from straight ahead – the walls of the old citadel. Ten marines died instantly. But they battled on across the bridge and struggled to get into the citadel. There were VC and NVA everywhere: street-fighting turned into house-to-house fighting, and that took a heavy toll.

It was not the kind of fighting the marines were trained for: this was urban combat and they took many casualties. They were also under heavy constraints imposed by the South Vietnamese. The imperial city was not to be bombarded by heavy artillery or air strikes, and so they were denied the kind of support they were used to. Officers and warrant officers were dangerously exposed. When a group of marines broke through a hole in a wall, the leaders of the assaulting force would often be killed. The concentration of Communist fire became greatest when they turned into the short street that led up to the Thuong Tu gate. The scene remains the same today: a shop-lined street with a few large trees which afforded the marines some shelter, and straight ahead the massive fortified gate in the citadel's 100-foot-thick (30 metres) wall. Above and beside the gate were huge protective battlements that provided perfect cover for the North Vietnamese. The marines were outnumbered and outgunned. By the evening they were back – those who had survived the weight of fire from inside the citadel – on the south side of the bridge. The North Vietnamese had more than 6000 men in Hué: it was going to take a lot more than two companies of 200 US marines to force them out.

The Americans decided to clear the New City on the south bank of the river first. It was smaller, and there were no great battlements to surmount – just the five or six blocks that lay between the MACV complex and the provincial headquarters half a mile (a kilometre) to the west, which the Communist forces had made their south bank stronghold. It was to take the marines ten days to complete this operation.

On 3 February the marines moved off westward in two columns, each led by an M48 tank. Every building had to be painstakingly cleared, using 90mm tank fire, 106mm recoil-less rifles, 81mm mortars and CS gas. The marines raked one house after another with fire and then stormed in to clear the rooms with rifles and grenades, or sometimes with gas. In the chaos of the close-quarter fighting many were killed and wounded; they also ran the risk of shooting each other.

One US officer, Captain Myron Harrington, described how painfully slowly they moved down the streets. 'We tried our best to avoid malicious damage…. But when we had to shoot at a house, we shot at a house. When we had to destroy a house, we destroyed it. But we didn't go in there with the express purpose that this is a wonderful opportunity to show how great our weapons are and how much destructive power they possess. As a result of their [the VC] being so entrenched, it required us to bring maximum fire power at our disposal to eliminate them.'

Harrington went on to describe the severe strain he and his men suffered. 'Throughout all of this, you constantly had this fear. Not so much that you were going to die, because I think to a certain degree that was a given. This was combined with the semi-darkness type of environment that we were fighting in because of the low overcast. The fact that we didn't see the sun gave it a very eerie, spooky look. You had this utter devastation all around you. You had this horrible smell. I mean you just cannot describe the smell of death especially when you're looking at it a couple of weeks along. It's horrible. It was there when you ate your rations. It was almost like you were eating death. You couldn't escape it.'[21]

Slowly but surely, sheer weight of firepower carried the marines through the built-up area and into the suburbs beyond. By 14 February, most of the New City was in American hands. Meanwhile, in the old citadel, Brigadier Truong and his South Vietnamese force had retained control of their HQ complex in the north-east corner. But Communist demolition experts had destroyed the bridge across the river, and the South Vietnamese had to wait until 11 February for marine reinforcements. A company of around 200 men was sent in, but many of them had to turn back when the pilot of their heli-copter was wounded by ground fire. The rest of the company and two further companies made the journey by landing craft a day later. They had a hazardous river journey skirting an island where Communist snipers had taken up positions and were under fire until they reached the north-east corner of the citadel. There they disembarked and linked up with Truong's South Vietnamese troops.

The marines then began the nightmarish task of clearing blocks of houses on the east side of the citadel. The North Vietnamese were holed up in houses along the great fortified wall that ran around it. They had put snipers in the lofts and windows: each position was well camouflaged, and they were very skilful about supporting each other with covering fire. The NVA had more than small arms: they had B40 rockets as well. In this scenario, being fired at constantly, the Americans were lucky to clear 600 feet (200 metres) of buildings and fortifications a day. After a week, many of the ten rifle platoons were led not by their officers but by sergeants who had taken over when their commanders were killed or wounded. Two platoons were led by corporals

Sergeant Steve Berntson was one of the marines who found himself caught up in this desperate battle for the citadel. At one stage, with enemy fire spraying all round him, he raced forward and rescued a badly wounded comrade. He was fighting a house-to-house battle up one of the streets, with armoured vehicles giving his platoon valuable fire support. But then, as he watched, a rocket struck a US tank and it had to retire, leaving his men dangerously exposed. Another rocket exploded only 4 feet (just over a metre) away from him. When he came to, he found himself lying on his stomach, several feet from where he had taken the blast. He tried to get up, but he couldn't move. He looked down and saw a big fragment of shrapnel sticking out of his arm, just below the shoulder. But he survived after being evacuated by helicopter. [22]

The troops remember the struggle for both parts of Hué as some of the hardest fighting in Marine Corps history. In that first week in the Old City, 47 marines were killed and 240 wounded. Many of the wounded insisted on returning to the fray. Most of the marines had no experience of street fighting, and when replacements began arriving direct from training in the United States they were hopelessly ill equipped to deal with the task and took heavy casualties. Even with the lifting of restrictions on air strikes, heavy weapon firing and artillery, the infantry advance slowed to as little as 300 feet (less than 100 metres) a day. The tanks and armoured vehicles found it almost impossible to manoeuvre in the narrow streets. On 16 February the force commander requested permission to withdraw his men; it was refused. A day later, one company was almost out of ammunition. And still the pace of advance was pitiably slow – the marines did not reach the Imperial Palace itself, the final stronghold of the Communist invading force, until 21 February, when, its defenders severely depleted by massive bombardment, its walls were at last penetrated. But on the threshold of victory the exhausted marines had to stand by and watch the South Vietnamese stage the final assault, because it was thought politically appropriate that the troops of the Saigon regime should perform the final act of liberation to end the Tet Offensive. Late on 24 February troops of the Republic of South Vietnam pulled down the VC flag from the top of the southern wall of Hué's citadel.

THE COST

The reconquest of Hué was the longest sustained infantry battle of the Vietnam War so far. In 25 days of fighting 384 South Vietnamese were killed and 1800 wounded. The Americans lost 142 killed and more than 850 wounded. They claimed over 5000 North Vietnamese and Vietcong killed or wounded and 90 captured. Between 60 and 80 per cent of Hué was destroyed or severely damaged; 24,000 homes were uninhabitable; 80,000 out of 150,000 residents were made homeless. Three weeks of savage warfare had almost destroyed Vietnam's most venerated city: only the robust work of the eighteenth-century builders had saved the citadel from being obliterated.

The Tet Offensive was finally over. To the American generals on the ground it looked like a victory. To the North Vietnamese, at first sight, it seemed like defeat. The Vietcong had lost between a third and a half of the force of some 80,000 which had attacked at the end of January. The Communists had failed, as Hanoi's General Tran Van Do remarked later, to provoke the general uprising they had aimed for in South Vietnam.[23] The Vietcong lost a lot of key people at village and town level – the core of the jungle-fighters who had spearheaded the offensive. General Westmoreland's conclusion was that, given quick reinforcement, he would have the opportunity to deliver his enemies a crushing blow. He requested another 206,000 troops.

But there was another view among people on the ground in South Vietnam, and it was far less optimistic in its assessment of the outcome. Tet had exposed the fragility of the government's control of the countryside of South Vietnam, and the vulnerability of its cities. The large number of casualties the South Vietnamese had suffered had shaken their strength and their morale. The government's plans to pacify the countryside were badly damaged. One of the American officials administering the pacification programme, Richard Hunt, wrote later that the withdrawal of soldiers and other pacification workers in the countryside 'contributed to a drop in territorial security'. He cited a government survey which estimated that by February 1968 the Saigon government had lost another 7 per cent of the rural population to Vietcong control. Villagers became more vulnerable to Vietcong taxation, conscription and terror.[24] Alain Endhoven, one of the assistant secretaries of state at the Pentagon, wrote a memo to the new Defence Secretary, Clark Clifford, saying that the Tet Offensive had killed pacification 'once and for all'.[25]

There was, in short, massive disagreement at the highest level in Washington about the implications of Tet. And it was to take just one month from the marines' victory at Hué for the debate to be resolved in a way that was to have a decisive impact on the outcome of the Vietnam War.

If there was one action that forced a rapid conclusion to the debate, it was the Pentagon's request – applauded by General Westmoreland – for another 206,000 troops to be sent to Vietnam. The news of this request rapidly leaked to the press and landed President Johnson's administration with the need to make a strategic decision about the future conduct of the war. And it was a decision they had to make in an atmosphere of growing popular disapproval at the cost of the Vietnam War and the suffering it was causing.

This was the first real televised war in history, and the pictures the American people saw of the Tet Offensive provided a stark contrast to the upbeat views of the generals. From the moment they saw the garden of the US embassy in Saigon strewn with bodies on the first day of the action, television viewers were given compelling evidence that the Vietnam War was far from over. Moreover, they were also presented with pictures of the damage and suffering which the Tet Offensive, and the US and South Vietnamese response to it, were causing in Vietnam. They saw the ruins of Hué and of many other towns and cities all over the country. They saw film of a South Vietnamese general putting his pistol to the head of a Vietcong captive and shooting him dead. They heard an American major telling one reporter that in order to save one city in the Mekong Delta, Ben Tre, they 'had to destroy it'.[26] Many people asked themselves if this was the kind of war America should be fighting; and if they were winning it, why were the generals asking to raise the number of troops by more than a third? A Gallup poll registered a substantial drop-off in approval of the Vietnam War between February and March 1968: one in five Americans switched from supporting the war to opposing it.[27]

Most serious of all for the administration was the line that many of the most respected commentators were taking. The *Wall Street Journal* for 23 February said: 'We think the American people should be getting ready to accept, if they haven't already, the prospect that the whole Vietnam effort may be doomed, that it may be falling apart beneath our feet.'[28]

Walter Cronkite, the CBS anchorman, was the most respected television journalist in America. He had approved the broad principle of the war in the past. But on his return from a visit to Vietnam he went on the air on 27 February and spoke these words: 'Who won and who lost in the great Tet Offensive against the cities? I'm not sure.... To say that we are mired in stalemate seems the only realistic yet unsatisfactory conclusion.... On the off chance that the military and political analysts are right, in the next months we must test the enemy's intentions in case this is indeed his last gasp before negotiations. But it is increasingly clear to this reporter that the only rational way then will be to negotiate, not as victors but as an honourable people who lived up to their pledge to defend democracy and did the best they could.'[29]

Within the American administration there was consternation that public opinion was turning against the war. 'If I've lost Cronkite,' said Johnson, 'I've lost America.' The new Defence Secretary, Clark Clifford, set in motion a whole set of in-depth briefings for himself and the President about the state of the war. Johnson was taken aback at the degree to which so many of Washington's elder statesmen now felt that America should be winding down the war rather than reinforcing it. Clifford himself told the President, 'We are not sure that under the circumstances that exist at the moment that a conventional military victory, as commonly defined, can be had.'[30] And the President, who faced re-election in November 1968, sensed the political ground shifting beneath him when Bobby Kennedy announced that he would put his name forward to run against Johnson in the contest for the leadership of the Democratic Party.

On 31 March, Johnson astonished his own colleagues and the American people by making the ultimate political sacrifice. He went on television to announce a reduction in the bombing of North Vietnam, and ended his address with the words: 'I do not believe that I should devote an hour or a day of my time to any personal partisan causes or to any duties other than the awesome duties of this office – the Presidency of your country. Accordingly I shall not seek, and I will not accept, the nomination of my party for another term as your President.' The Tet Offensive had claimed its loftiest victim.

General Westmoreland did not get the extra troops he wanted. His request for reinforcements was massively reduced and he himself was recalled to Washington. The White House now shifted the burden of the war more and more on to South Vietnam. Johnson, and Richard Nixon after him, pursued a policy of 'Vietnamization', providing the Saigon regime with generous shipments of arms while reducing American manpower on the ground. It was a policy that ended in failure in April 1975, when North Vietnamese and Vietcong troops over-ran Saigon, renamed it Ho Chi Minh City and reunited the country under Communist rule. The Tet Offensive made a decisive contribution to that final outcome by critically weakening America's will to soldier on.

We shall never know whether a robust American response to Tet, with massive reinforcements and a forthright escalation of military effort for the next few months, would have proved the last straw for the Communists. North Vietnamese sources have revealed how hard-pressed they were after their offensive failed to secure its military objectives. But somehow, the Hanoi regime managed to find the resources of manpower and national morale to drive through to final victory in 1975 – seven years after the Tet Offensive. The irony of it all is that America's failure in Vietnam did not lead to Communism advancing into any other country in Asia, and Vietnam itself is rapidly developing into a tiger economy to rival any of its capitalist competitors in Asia.

YOM KIPPUR

At two o'clock in the afternoon of 6 October 1973, the handful of Israeli front-line troops on the Suez Canal in occupied Egypt and on the Golan Heights in occupied Syria were suddenly engulfed in a war that caught them by surprise. Just 450 men in the Israeli forts on the Canal's east bank faced an assault across the water by 100,000 Egyptian troops. Some 350 miles (560 km) away to the north-east, on the Golan, a massed array of 1400 Syrian tanks threw itself at a defending Israeli tank force of just 180. The attacks by Egypt and Syria were simultaneous and meticulously coordinated with an artillery barrage and air strikes by the two Arab air forces. The joint offensive was a masterpiece of secret planning and strategic deception which few believed the Arabs were capable of. Within hours, the two Arab countries, which had lost great swathes of their territory to Israel in the Six-Day War only six years earlier, appeared well on their way to winning their land back. Many Israelis believed their country was facing the most dangerous threat to its existence since its birth 25 years earlier.

Lieutenant Micha Kostiga was in one of the Canal forts which came under an opening barrage that badly wounded his commander. At 21 years old, he found himself giving the orders in what was to become a desperate and futile struggle to hold the line of the Canal. He heard an Egyptian officer shouting at his men, who had just crossed the Canal in small boats, to storm the fort. Kostiga leaped up from his trench and fired off every round of his Uzi ub-machine gun at the Egyptians. They ran for it, but more boats were heading for the fort and it would not be long before Kostiga, his injured commander and his comrades were surrounded.[1]

On the Golan, the front line was equally thin and the plight of the outposts no less grave. Another young lieutenant, Yossi Gur, had arrived only a day earlier. He had relieved the regular commander, who had been allowed home for the holiday of Yom Kippur, the most sacred date in the Jewish calendar. He and the 14 men under his command were subjected to a massive opening artillery barrage that had them scurrying for their bunkers. Squinting through a periscope, Gur saw two columns of Syrian tanks approaching. They were headed for the Israeli anti-tank ditch which ran just behind his position on the border. All Gur could do was to call urgently for the three Israeli tanks that were supposed to be supporting his position, but they were several miles away and would take some time to arrive.

Israel faced the prospect of defeat. In the next few days, the two Arab armies were to have their best-ever opportunity of avenging the series of catastrophes they had suffered at the hands of the Jewish state. In the end, Israel was to stage a remarkable recovery and turn defeat into victory, but the psychological trauma of the surprise attack on the day of Yom Kippur in 1973, and the boost it gave to Arab morale, were to transform the map of the Middle East.

THE DEEPENING CONFLICT, 1948–73

Ever since Israel carved out its slender slice of territory in Palestine and established its independence in 1948, it had been at war with the entire Arab world. The Arabs were the losers in the war with the Jews in 1947–8, and in June 1967 Israel responded to what it saw as a series of unacceptable threats to its existence by overwhelming its Arab neighbours in a six-day whirlwind of destruction. Israel became a Middle East superpower as the territory under its control expanded fivefold. President Nasser's Egypt lost the Sinai peninsula and had to face an Israeli front line on the eastern bank of the Suez Canal, only 60 miles (just under 100 km) from Cairo. King

Hussein's kingdom of Jordan lost the West Bank territories that his grandfather, Abdullah, had managed to deny to the Jews in 1948. The Syria of Hafez el Assad lost the entire Golan Heights escarpment that looked down on the Sea of Galilee.

Israel announced it would withdraw from the newly occupied territories only if the Arabs gave the Jewish state full recognition and agreed to borders that would give Israel security. But the Arabs refused to contemplate recognition and peace unless the Israelis made it clear that they would withdraw from every bit of captured land. All international attempts at mediation were fruitless. A state of suspended warfare persisted, with occasional outbursts of open fighting – particularly along the Suez Canal. The Middle East became an increasingly explosive front line in the Cold War, with the Soviet Union lined up behind the Arabs and the Americans supporting the Israelis. Both supplied their clients with enough tanks, guns and aircraft to make the Arab–Israeli conflict arguably the most dangerous threat to peace anywhere in the world.

But by the summer of 1973 the world was beginning to get used to the idea that the Middle East, though tense, would settle down into a semi-permanent state of 'no peace, no war'. Both the Russians and the Americans felt they had nothing to gain and a lot to lose if there was open conflict. The Americans had hopes that the new and more pragmatic Egyptian leader, Anwar Sadat, would have less appetite for war. He had opened a promising dialogue with the US Secretary of State, Henry Kissinger, and he had even dismissed the flock of Soviet military advisers whose presence had been particularly effective in building up an Egyptian air defence missile screen after the Six-Day War of 1967. The Israelis for their part, after the devastating blow they had dealt the Arabs in 1967, had established what they hoped would be impregnable defensive positions along the Suez Canal and on the line of hills that marked the eastern edge of the Israeli-occupied Golan Heights. Most senior Israeli strategists believed, as did most of the world's experts and military planners, that the Arabs simply did not have the will or the capacity to stage a major attack on Israel. Anyway, the Israelis were confident that they would have ample warning of any Arab assault. Their Prime

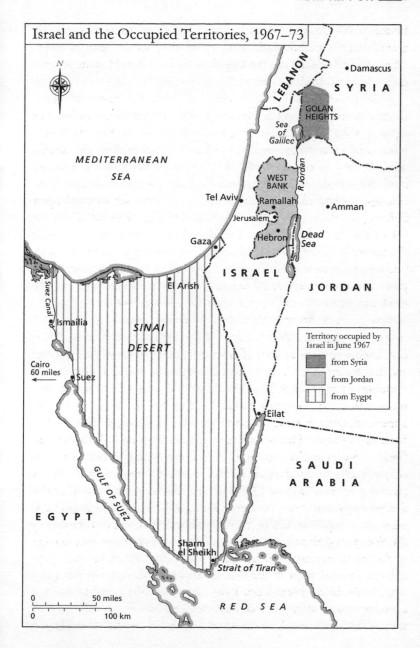

Israel and the Occupied Territories, 1967–73

Territory occupied by
Israel in June 1967

from Syria

from Jordan

from Eygpt

Minister, Golda Meir, a fortress of a woman who was a 74-year-old grandmother, had insisted that Israel had the military clout to defend itself against any onslaught without having to resort to the kind of pre-emptive attack that had routed the Arabs six years earlier.

All this played into the hands of Egypt's President Sadat, who was now to surprise the world with a bold combination of military and diplomatic ingenuity intended to offset the humiliation the country had suffered in the Six-Day War. He was convinced that the only way to drive the Israelis into meaningful negotiations was to deliver them a massive military blow. It had to be from at least two directions (east and west) simultaneously and it had to be a total surprise. He appointed a popular and imaginative paratroop general, Saad el Shazli, as his chief of staff and tasked him with the job of achieving a successful crossing of the Suez Canal. And he agreed a joint plan with Syria's President Assad that would see an all-out drive by Syrian tanks to shatter Israeli defences on the Golan Heights at the same moment and threaten Israel's northern heartland. Both leaders knew they lacked the power to destroy Israel.[2] But they hoped to sustain an advance into Israeli territory long enough to propel their enemy into making serious concessions. For both of them, the realistic strategic goal was not the annihilation of Israel but the recapture of the territory they had lost in 1967.

On 21 August Shazli met the Syrian military high command in Alexandria and they agreed on their tactical plans – with only the date for the coordinated offensive left open. The Egyptian plan was to cross the Suez Canal in rubber boats. Spearhead troops would plant rope ladders at the top of the towering sand ramparts the Israelis had built on the east bank. Egyptian troops would then swarm up and overwhelm the Israeli strongpoints. Water cannon would blast gaps in the sand obstacles to allow follow-up troops and vehicles to storm through and establish bridgeheads beyond the Canal bank. Egyptian infantrymen armed with portable Sagger and lighter RPG7 anti-tank missiles would move forward to resist the expected counter-attack by Israeli tanks. The Israeli air force would be held at bay by batteries of SAM 2, 3 and 6 Soviet-supplied surface-to-air missiles, and mobile anti-aircraft guns fired from the west bank.

The essential prelude to this attack was a deception plan that had to be deft enough to fool Israel's formidable military intelligence machine. Shazli's staff announced plans for a routine exercise – Exercise Tahrir (Liberation) – to start at the beginning of October. It would involve the movement of large numbers of troops up to the Canal. Shazli told his brigade commanders to move up in strength by day and then to *appear* to move back westward by night, with a great show of lights and much noise. In reality, only a fraction of each brigade would withdraw, leaving most of its men to take up their assault positions on the Canal bank. Sadat's government even made a show of standing down 20,000 reservists on 4 October. Right up to the moment of the attack, special detachments would swim and sunbathe – even fish on the Canal bank – to give an impression of lazy normality.

On the Syrian front, surprise would ensure a superiority of something like 8 to 1 for the Syrian tank forces that would drive through Israel's forward defences and then exploit any breakthrough. If the Syrian tanks could maintain their momentum, they could hope to be at the bridges over the River Jordan within 24 hours.

On 22 September Sadat flew to Damascus to meet Assad. They agreed to attack together on 6 October: it would be Israel's holiest day of the year, Yom Kippur.

The Israelis prided themselves on the quality of their military intelligence. The man in charge, General Eli Zeira, had already persuaded the government of his worth in the spring of 1973. He had, correctly, assured Israel's two key men – Defence Minister Moshe Dayan, with his famous black eye-patch, hero of the 1967 war, and chief of staff General David 'Dado' Elazar, who had masterminded the seizure of the Golan Heights – that an Egyptian exercise that spring was not the first stage of an offensive, thus avoiding the costly mobilization of Israel's reserves. Six months later, in early October, he told them the same story, and this time he was wrong.

In that fatal month Israel's shortcomings in the field of intelligence were matched by another grave weakness – the level of its standing forces. Unlike Syria and Egypt, Israel did not have the manpower and resources to maintain a huge army in the front line. Israel's regular army was small. Except at moments of high alert, Israel had only around 80 tanks on the Golan and a handful of some 200 infantry in the front-line bunkers. There were only 90 tanks and 450 infantrymen on the Suez Canal bank, with another 200 tanks in reserve several miles back. Between them, these meagre forces would face 150,000 Arab troops and more than 3000 tanks.

But the Israelis had a well-honed mobilization process that could reinforce the front line within 24 hours. The army alone could count on 375,000 men at full strength. Most of them were reservists, but many had seen action and all were trained to join their units instantly when the alarm was raised. If Israel's positions were in danger, its generals would rely on military intelligence to give them enough warning to bring their forces up to full strength. But the generals were deeply divided. At the very beginning of October 1973, both Dayan and Elazar accepted Zeira's assessment that there would not be a war. But General Israel Tal, head of the Armoured Corps, was warning of an imminent attack on the Golan. He pointed out that Syrian bridging tanks had been brought forward, almost certainly to prepare the ground for an armoured thrust across the Israeli anti-tank ditches. A few days earlier, Dayan had taken Elazar and Zeira up to the Golan. As they were scanning the no-man's land in front of them, an Israeli tank officer pointed to the build-up of Syrian tanks ahead of them and said, 'War is certain.'

'No,' retorted Zeira. 'There will not be another war for ten years.'

On the Suez Canal, an Israeli signalman, Avi Yaffe, noticed a stirring on the Egyptian side in the first week of October. 'We started to observe Egyptian officers standing on ramps across from us, holding maps, pointing at different things in our direction. Later we learned it was the Egyptian chief of staff, and they were planning their moves. We, of course, reported what we saw, but the higher ranks were not impressed.'[3] Israeli intelligence had long been of the view that the Arabs would not fight Israel again until they had rebuilt their air forces, a process which it believed would take at least ten years.

What had prompted Dayan to go up to the Golan was a secret meeting that King Hussein of Jordan had held, on his request, with Golda Meir in late September. Hussein had held many secret talks with the Israelis. He had made the mistake of getting involved in the Six-Day War of 1967 that had lost him the West Bank, and was determined not to be involved in another. The King told Mrs Meir he had a 'very very sensitive source in Syria' and that he now understood the Syrians to be in a 'pre-jump-off position' for war.[4] But Golda did not believe the King meant to warn her that the Syrians were definitely going to war. By contrast, her personal assistant, Lou Kedar, who was present at the meeting, later said she could not believe that Golda had not taken Hussein's words to her as a serious warning.[5]

While the Egyptians and Syrians were spending the first days of October successfully allaying most Israelis' suspicions, an important step was taken in Moscow on the 4th. The Soviet Foreign Minister, Andrei Gromyko, told his top officials that he had been informed that Egypt and Syria would attack Israel two days later.[6] The families of Russian advisers were immediately told to stand by for an emergency airlift out of the two Arab countries, and by that evening the Israelis had picked up the first signs of it. The following morning, Zeira was asked what he made of the airlift. He said the Russians had probably misinterpreted what was going on in Syria and Egypt as preparation for war; he still insisted that he himself did not expect war.[7] But Elazar was worried enough to order another 100 tanks to the Golan. Egyptian soldiers had been ordered to break their Ramadan fast, which they would never do during a mere exercise, and bulldozers were cutting holes in the Egyptian ramparts to allow vehicles access to the Canal bank. But that evening, 5 October, the Israelis sent a message to Henry Kissinger saying, 'Our assessment is that the alert measures being taken by Egypt and Syria are in part connected with manoeuvres and in part due to fears of aggression by Israel.' Kissinger says he was also receiving the same sort of advice from the CIA. 'Our definition of rationality', he says, 'did not take seriously the notion of [the Arabs] starting an unwinnable war to restore self-respect.'[8] Within

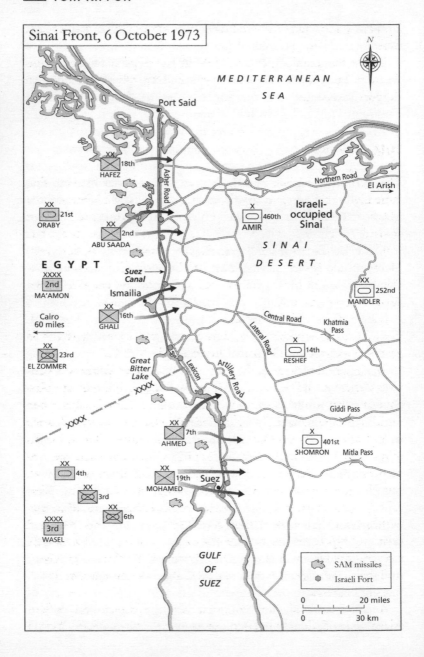

Sinai Front, 6 October 1973

24 hours, the world would know how wrong those assessments were.

By late that night, Egypt had 100,000 troops poised for action on the west bank of the canal, and Syria had 45,000 men waiting to support an assault by 1400 tanks.

YOM KIPPUR

The director of Mossad, Israel's secret service, was in London that same night on a mission to contact a man codenamed 'The Source'. Much of his information had been accurate before, and he now advised Israel's top spymaster, Zvi Zamir, that Egypt and Syria would indeed attack. Zamir rang Elazar, waking him, at 4.30 a.m. Elazar promptly rang the head of Israel's air force, General Benny Peled, and asked him if he was ready to take pre-emptive action against Egypt and Syria.

'I'm ready,' answered Peled.

'Roll it: I'll get permission,' said Elazar, fully expecting that he'd get the go-ahead from Prime Minister Golda Meir.[9]

When he met Dayan at 5.50 a.m. on 6 October, Elazar was convinced there would be war. But Dayan counselled him against doing anything that would allow the outside world to claim that Israel had initiated the hostilities. He even forbade Elazar to order full-scale mobilization of the reserves. Elazar was for alerting 200,000: Dayan told him to keep it to less than 30,000. Two hours later, the two men met Golda Meir: she upped Elazar's mobilization to 100,000, but she too vetoed any pre-emptive strike. At 12.30 p.m. Meir called a cabinet meeting and told her ministers there would be war within hours. They were dumbfounded: over the years they had come to expect to get at least two days' notice, so that Israel's reserves could be at the front. On 6 October 1973 Israel was about to fight a war under the most unfavourable circumstances in its 25 years of existence.

At 6.30 a.m. Washington time, Henry Kissinger was sound asleep when 'Suddenly Jo Sisco, Assistant Secretary of State, barged into my bedroom. As I forced myself awake, I heard Sisco's gravelly voice all but shouting that Israel and two Arab countries were about to go to war.' Kissinger says he was flattered at Sisco's suggestion that he, Kissinger, could rescue the situation before shooting began. 'Unfortunately, it turned out to be exaggerated.' Ten minutes later, Kissinger was calling the Soviet ambassador in Washington, Anatoly Dobrynin, to tell him that Israel was not planning an attack. Three hours later, Dobrynin rang back, claiming that Israel had provoked the attack by starting a naval battle. 'You and I know that's boloney,' retorted Kissinger. The Secretary of State was quietly confident that Israel would soon throw the Egyptians back and he had the satisfaction of knowing that, unlike the Russians, he was in touch with both sides. He had already talked to the Egyptian Foreign Minister, Mohamed el-Zayyat.[10]

On the Suez Canal, at 1.55 p.m. that day, Egyptian guns opened with a huge barrage of 10,000 shells. Fifteen minutes into this bombardment of the Israeli bank, 4000 Egyptian commandos paddled or motored across the water in 700 rubber boats. Loudspeakers chanted, 'Allahu Akbar' – God is great. As planned, the most agile of the troops shinned up the Israeli sand ramparts and secured rope ladders at the top. General Youssef Afifi, commander of the 19th Infantry Brigade, recalled some of his men finding rope ladders too difficult to climb: 'They abandoned their portable ladders and climbed on each other, forming a human ladder to scale the ramparts.'[11]

At the same time, Egyptian engineers equipped with high-pressure hoses powered by diesel pumps approached the bank: then they released great jets of canal water at the barrier of sand to make gaps for their armour to move through. According to the Egyptians, Israeli plans to squirt oil on to the Canal and then ignite it were foiled by their frogmen, who had crossed the night before and cemented up the oil outlets. They claimed their first prisoner of war was an Israeli engineer who was seized trying to repair the jets as the commandos reached the east bank.[12] Behind them, the main body of soldiers scrambled up the sand ramparts.

Egyptian Lieutenant Awad Allam saw it all: 'The units started

▲ Khe Sanh, South Vietnam. US marines lie prone on the ground among sand-bagged bunkers as they take cover from Communist mortar fire. The remote base was besieged by two North Vietnamese divisions in January 1968 as a prelude to the Tet Offensive.

▶ An American soldier prepares to enter a Vietcong tunnel during the lifting of the siege of Khe Sanh on 7 April 1968. The labyrinthine tunnels constructed by the Communist insurgents in South Vietnam provided them with almost impenetrable hide-outs.

THE TET OFFENSIVE

▶ 1 February 1968, Saigon. South Vietnamese police chief, Brigadier General Nguyen Ngoc, executes a Vietcong captive during the clear-up after the Tet Offensive. This picture of a such a brutal piece of summary justice did much to undermine US public support for the Vietnam War.

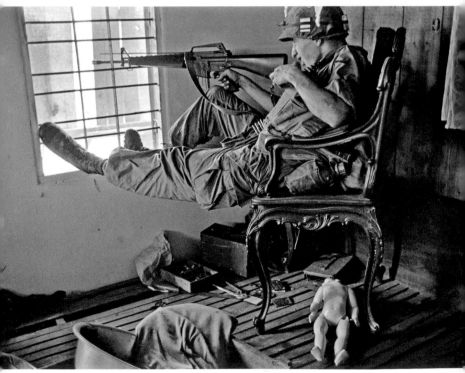

▲ An American GI finds himself a comfortable vantage point during one of the operations in 1968 to clear the Vietcong from the suburbs of Saigon.

◄ 31 January 1968, Saigon. South Vietnamese soldiers drag the body of a dead Vietcong guerrilla away from a government building during the Tet Offensive. Saigon was just one of scores of towns and cities hit by the Vietcong attacks.

► American Military Police secure the garden of the US Embassy in Saigon the morning after the attack. On the ground lie the bodies of two of the Vietcong guerrillas who stormed the embassy garden but failed to penetrate the offices. Although the Vietcong's mission failed, the political effect of targeting this symbol of American power was to prove seismic.

◄ The Tet Offensive in Hué, January–February 1968. US marines inside the citadel rescue the body of a dead comrade. It took the marines three weeks to restore order in Hué.

◄ Hué, South Vietnam, January–February 1968. US troops conduct searches of houses in the old imperial capital of Vietnam during the fighting with North Vietnamese forces, who overran the city during the Tet Offensive. Thousands of civilians in Hué were killed and over 100,000 fled from some of the fiercest fighting seen during the Vietnam War.

▲ The citadel in Hué today – one of Vietnam's top tourist spots. In 1968 North Vietnamese troops seized these massive walls and watchtowers and made them their stronghold. US marines had to fight one of the toughest battles in their history to dislodge them.

▲ An Israeli tank crew on the Golan Heights, 13 October 1973. Many Israeli troops had to fight for three days and nights without sleep until reinforcements began to drive back the Syrian attack.

▲ Fardan, Egypt, October 1973. Egyptian troops and tanks cross the Suez Canal on one of several bridges they constructed after their successful surprise crossing during the Jewish holiday of Yom Kippur. The crossing was a military triumph, but it was followed by a series of mistakes that led to near disaster.

■▬ YOM KIPPUR

▶ A wounded Israeli soldier on the Golan Heights. Israel's comparatively small population paid a terrible price for its lack of preparedness in October 1973: nearly 2700 killed and over 7200 wounded.

▼ The Golan Heights, 7 October 1973. An Israeli armoured brigade makes its way up from the Galilee at dawn on day two of the October War. Its task: to relieve the hard-pressed Israeli forces who have been under attack from Syrian tanks for 18 hours.

◄ Egypt, October 1973. An Egyptian soldier holds up a portrait of President Sadat during the Egyptian advance into Sinai. Whatever failures of military judgement Sadat may have made later in the war, the planning and the achievements of its first days did much to restore Arab pride.

▲ Golan Heights, 11 October 1973. Five days into the October War, Israeli soldiers fire a 175mm self-propelled field gun against Syrian forces on the Golan Heights. Israeli soldiers, heavily outnumbered, had fought desperately to repel a Syrian offensive that threatened to reach the Galilee.

▲ Egyptian forces occupy one of Israel's Bar Lev line forts on the east bank of the Canal. The tiny Israeli garrisons totalled only 450 men. More than 100,000 Egyptians crossed the Canal on Day One.

▶ General Ariel Sharon (left) and Defence Minister Moshe Dayan (centre) at the spot where Israeli troops – largely under Sharon's command – forced a bold crossing of the Suez Canal on 15 October 1973.

moving according to the schedule. The engineers first ... the infantry crossed by the thousands, they didn't wait for the bridges, they just used rubber boats. I was very close to the crossing point. I saw Israeli airplanes trying to come and [Egyptian] SAMs going up ... it was very effective.... We crossed, during the day, and actually I was sitting on a big truck loaded with fuel in jerry cans ... and I came out of the cabin and sat on top of the truck and I even took my helmet off because I really didn't see the Bar Lev [Israelis] as scary as they were talking about. I felt comfortable.'[13]

One Israeli officer, Motti Ashkenazi, described the frantic struggle in the front-line Canal forts. 'The devastation was extensive.... I jumped out of the ditch and ran to a sand mound where the smoke appeared a bit thinner. I saw an alarming sight. Tank after tank, one armoured personnel carrier after another, the Egyptian attack force poured off the ramparts and joined the front-line forces, with infantry commando forces positioning themselves behind each vehicle.'

Somehow, Ashkenazi zigzagged across some open ground to commandeer two nearby Israeli tanks.

'"Are you the commander?" I yelled. He yelled back that he was. "Start moving and tell the other tank to follow!"' He managed to guide the tanks through the smoke to where they could take aim at the Egyptian formation. 'One after another, flaming torches were lit, tank turrets flew up into the air and what had resembled an orderly parade ground turned into an inferno of burning men running about, screaming for help, getting run over by the tanks and personnel carriers trying to manoeuvre backwards, to get away.'[14]

Twenty-three thousand Egyptian troops crossed within two hours; there were only 450 Israelis to resist them on the whole 100-mile (160-km) length of the Canal. In the words of one divisional commander, General Hassan Abu Seida, the fact that Egyptians were moving forward in the attack for the first time after so many retreats and defeats had an 'indescribably liberalizing effect' on morale. 'We orientals', he said, 'are emotional people: therefore victory in the first few minutes was immensely important.' He himself crossed the Canal just half an hour after the first commandos, and was received by his exultant troops the other side.[15]

Ninety Israeli tanks raced up from behind to counter-attack: but the Egyptian infantry had crossed the Canal with an anti-tank guided weapon the Israelis were not used to. The Sagger had a 3200-yard (3000-metre) range, and as long as the firer had the daylight to illuminate the target through the launcher's sights it stood a good chance of knocking out an enemy tank. Infantry armed with Saggers and light rocket-propelled grenades were destroying Israel's vaunted ability to crush an enemy with a fast-moving armoured response. Moreover, the Israeli air force, which had caused utter havoc with Arab defences in the Six-Day War, found itself almost powerless to give close support to its men on the Canal because Egyptian missile sites on the west bank were providing their assault force with effective protection against air attack. General Ali Fahmi, Egypt's air defence chief, said after the war, 'When the first Israeli Phantom jet was shot down, the spell that had been woven round Israel's air supremacy was broken.'[16]

The men in Israel's Canal forts were not elite paratroopers but reservists from the Jerusalem Brigade. They fought valiantly, but they were hopelessly outnumbered and by the end of that first day they were virtually wiped out. Ten hours after the first troops crossed the Canal, the Egyptians had thrown 12 bridges across it and blown 60 openings in the Israeli ramparts. The Egyptians were as much as 2 miles (3 km) deep into the Sinai peninsula, and by the following morning the Israelis had lost 180 of the 290 tanks they had in the whole peninsula. The Egyptians, who had expected thousands of their men to be killed in the crossing, had lost just 200. Things were so bad for the Israelis that they decided to make no further attempts to rescue any survivors in the Canal forts. Israel's plight was not helped by the conduct of the man in charge of southern command, General Gonen, who refused to move to his forward headquarters until the battle was well advanced and was rude and overbearing when he did get there. It was clear to anyone at the end of that first day that Israel's predicament in Sinai was acute.

THE GOLAN HEIGHTS

In the north, on the Golan, the first hours of the Syrian advance threatened to do even more damage to Israel's defences than the Egyptians had done in the south. Facing an onslaught of 1400 Syrian tanks, the Israelis had just 180. Without the reinforcements – the 7th Armoured Brigade under Colonel Avigdor Ben Gal had been sent racing up there the previous day – the Israelis would have had only 77 tanks on the Golan. The Syrian plan was to fight their way forward to where they could fill in or bridge the Israeli tank ditches; then they would storm through and press on down the western slopes of the Golan Heights to the River Jordan, where they would be joined by Syrian commandos dropped by parachute.

'One of my tanks fired and I could see a flash where the shell hit, then a Syrian tank that had tried to get up to us. He wasn't hit and we were short of star shells. But we went on trying to spot them by moonlight,' wrote the commander of one Israeli tank battalion, Avigdor Kahalani, in a diary which described every minute of that first day. He remembers firing at a tank that suddenly burst into view only 150 feet (50 metres) away. 'With a boom the shell was gone, its flash dazzling my eyes…. A horrible thought that maybe I had been wrong was dispelled as I saw the flash eliminator on his gun. Only T55s had those….' Then another Syrian tank appeared. 'I bent down and swung the gun traverse towards the moving enemy. "Gunner be ready to fire." A sudden flash from a tank next to mine, and the intruder burst into flames…. The two Syrians were blazing like torches against the night sky. They didn't know where they were. A soldier covered in flames ran like crazy from one of the tanks into the rocks and started to roll on the ground in a desperate attempt to kill the fire.'[17]

The Israeli tanks, few as they were, were well protected and tactically well placed, covering the Syrian line of advance. They took a terrible toll of their assaulting enemy. The battle was an unremitting struggle of tank against tank, and the Israeli gunners were more accurate and faster to reload than the Syrians. As the Syrian tanks funnelled into the crossing points over the anti-tank ditches, the

Israelis fired armour-piercing rounds over ranges of up to 2200 yards (2000 metres), and there were soon several score of blazing Syrian tanks obstructing the ones trying to advance behind them. An Israeli tank commander, Yug Yuva, described the fierce battle that left him utterly exhausted after two nights without sleep.

'We saw 30 Syrian tanks facing us. The duel began instantly. It's a strange feeling to see people who crossed into our territory to destroy us, turn into burning targets, over 2000 meters from us. We saw their crew run in every direction. But another wave of tanks

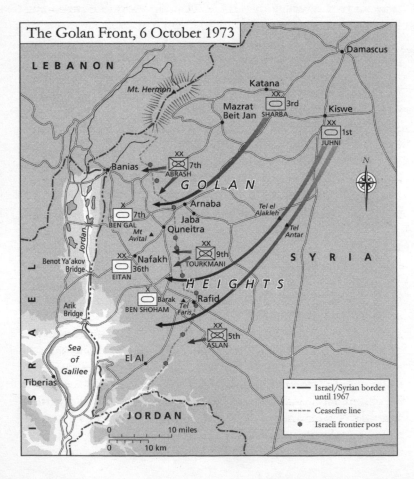

The Golan Front, 6 October 1973

turned up: We counted about 60. Our position was a bit higher. We drove close, to about 1500 meters and within minutes turned many of them into torches. We repaid them....'[18] But if the Israeli positions in the north of the Golan were holding, they had left themselves dangerously exposed on the southern flank. The Syrians were quick to spot the weakness and drove through the front-line strongpoints in overwhelming numbers. Lieutenant Menahem Ansbacher and his platoon fought all night until they were over-run: his final radio message said: 'This is Menahem: the Syrians are at the entrance to the bunker. This is the end. Say goodbye to the guys. We won't be seeing each other again.'[19]

The Syrian 5th Division, which attacked here, was far more effective than its two counterparts to the north. There the Syrians had left their bridging equipment in the rear, depriving the first armoured attack of much of its momentum. But in the south the Syrians quickly bridged the ditches and drove past and beyond the Israeli strongpoints, which they could then subdue one by one. Small Israeli tank detachments like Lieutenant Zvika Greengold's tried to race to the rescue of the front-line troops. Greengold, with just two tanks firing from behind cover, successfully destroyed a number of Syrian tanks. He was left on his own when the other tank was crippled by Syrian fire, but was then reinforced by seven Israeli tanks that had driven frantically up to the rescue from the Jordan valley. But then Greengold's own tank was knocked out. He leaped out of it with his clothes in flames, managed to smother them and then took command of another Israeli tank. His was just one of several Israeli battles against superior numbers that dented but failed to stem the Syrian onslaught. President Assad's tanks now had the southern Golan at their mercy. They pressed on beyond Hushniya, only a short drive from the still undefended Jordan bridges. At 1 a.m. Israel's commander in the north, General Hofi, demonstrated the level of his anxiety by pulling back his command post, much of his ammunition and piles of documents to the west side of the Jordan. If Syria crossed the Jordan before Israel was fully mobilized the outlook for the Jewish state would be bleak.

The Syrians were achieving the kind of sweeping success in the southern Golan that Israel's forces had won in 1967. Then, Israel had had air supremacy: now Israel's aircraft were a prey to Syria's missiles and its ground defences were outnumbered and surprised. One of the most striking early successes by the Syrian forces was the capture of the strategically vital outpost on the top of Mount Hermon at the extreme northern limit of the Golan front. The post was under reconstruction by the Israelis and only lightly held. Syrian Special Forces swooped in by helicopter, supported by a ground assault, and seized the summit: they killed 13 Israelis and took 31 prisoners. The most commanding viewpoint on the entire Golan front and some of Israel's most sophisticated sensors that had been positioned there were now in Syrian hands.

It looked as if the Syrians were unstoppable. But then, suddenly, with one flank of Israel's defence line shattered, they suspended their advance. Ten miles (16 km) short of the Jordan bridges, they were ordered to wait until the two Syrian divisions in the northern Golan had achieved a similar breakthrough. The decision was taken at top level in Damascus, where the high command probably feared that any further advance by the successful force in the southern Golan, unaccompanied by a breakthrough in the north, would leave its flanks dangerously exposed. This strategy may have been based on sound military principles, but it presented Israel with a vital breathing space.

So on 7 October the Syrians remained stationary in the southern Golan while their tanks renewed their attempt to break through in the north. Dayan flew up to Northern Command HQ and was told by Hofi that Israel might have to relinquish this region. Dayan immediately telephoned the Israeli air force commander, General Benny Peled, and ordered him to divert the planes he was using to strike Syrian missile sites to direct support of the troops defending the Golan. 'The third temple is in danger,' said Dayan. The Jews had suffered the destruction of two temples in the past at the hands of the Babylonians and then the Romans. Dayan was voicing the fears of many Israelis on the morning after Yom Kippur that the Arabs now threatened the very existence of their state.

Peled's aircraft were meeting strong resistance from both Arab

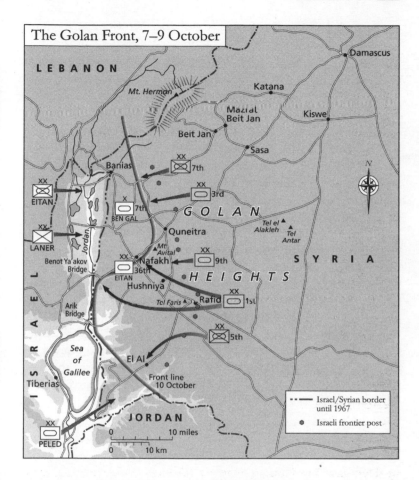

The Golan Front, 7–9 October

armies: anti-aircraft fire and sophisticated Russian-supplied missiles accounted for 35 Israeli planes in the first two days of the war. Postwar evaluation of Israel's air strategy suggested that it was hasty and confused; it failed to concentrate all its efforts on one central task – destroying the missile sites first of one of the Arab attackers, and then of the other.

Colonel Ben Gal's force at the northern end of the Golan had now disabled up to 90 Syrian tanks and was just managing to hold the line. A group of Israeli reservist tank crews – aware of the need to make all haste to the Golan – put together a rescue force of Centurion and Sherman tanks in the Jordan valley and gunned their engines up the road that led towards the most threatening Syrian units on the top of the Heights. Many of the Shermans only had 75mm guns that would probably not even penetrate Syrian armour. But they struggled up the hill: anything to slow the rate of the Syrian advance. By midday, the Syrians looked close to a break-through in the centre of the Golan: they were approaching Israel's headquarters on the Heights, the base at Nafakh. The irrepressible Greengold found himself fighting there on that Sunday, and only retired when he was carted off wounded to hospital. He was to receive Israel's highest award for gallantry.

By the afternoon of the 7th – 24 hours into the war – Hofi was reporting to Dayan that he doubted the Golan could be held. Dayan judged Hofi to be so exhausted that he despatched a former chief of staff, General Haim Bar Lev, to the north where he imme-diately revoked Hofi's order to Brigadier Moussa Peled to hold back his rapidly assembled division of tanks in a defence line on the River Jordan. In this, Bar Lev was partly swayed by Peled himself, who said, 'I don't believe in defence; I believe in attack,' and offered to drive his tanks up the road that led directly to the point of the fur-thest Syrian advance at the southern end of the Golan. 'Agreed,' said Bar Lev. 'You're Israel's last hope.'[20]

THE CANAL FRONT, 7–9 OCTOBER

Meanwhile, on the Suez Canal, the Egyptian crossing operation had been an unqualified success. By midday on 7 October, 100,000 Egyptian troops and 1000 tanks were across with over 10,000 other vehicles. The few Israeli tanks that were immediately available made little headway against the Egyptian anti-tank missiles. An Egyptian sergeant, Abdel Moneim Masri, was a Sagger operator whose unit had advanced 2 miles (3 km) beyond the Canal. He and his team of infantrymen, armed with these missiles – which the Egyptians knew by their Russian name, Molotkas – spotted a number of Israeli tanks that briefly appeared on top of some sand dunes to open fire.

'We three who had the Molotkas knew that we would draw the fire of the tank guns upon us, but it couldn't be helped: we had to carry out our orders and fire at the tanks.' Masri was the marksman who had to guide the missile. A tank appeared again on the hill. Masri fired his weapon, which paid out a fine thread of wire behind it to transmit guidance instructions to the missile. He used a joystick to direct the missile, which to him was a spot of light, straight at the target. He recalls a 'roaring explosion' as the tank blew up, and nobody climbed out of it. Over the next few days, Masri destroyed several more Israeli tanks and was later awarded the Star of Sinai for bravery: he was given a pension of twenty Egyptian pounds a month and free public transport for life.[21]

The Egyptians' success had provoked a bitter row among the top brass at Israel's southern command headquarters in Sinai. One of Israel's most experienced fighters, General Ariel 'Arik' Sharon, a great bruiser of a soldier, who had conducted fearsome attacks on the Arabs in the Sinai during the Six-Day War and on Palestinians in the West Bank, was hauled back from retirement (he was still only in his mid-forties) to command his reserve tank division. Another tank division was led by General Avraham 'Bren' Adan, who had commanded Israel's Armoured Corps and was now about to retire. Both were formidable tacticians, but Sharon was the more vocal and outspoken. He had no respect for authority and had already formed the lowest opinion of the man in command in the Sinai, General Gonen. The moment Sharon arrived in the Sinai he piled into Gonen, demanding that he sanction an immediate counter-attack on the Egyptians before they could establish themselves properly on the east bank. Gonen insisted that would have to wait until the next day and was supported by the chief of staff, General Elazar, who flew down to the Sinai that afternoon. Elazar agreed to a counter-attack, but one that drove south, parallel to the Canal and not towards it: he believed it was imperative to keep his men well back from the Canal. When Sharon actually suggested leading his division west in an attempt to *cross* the Canal, Elazar vetoed it outright. The unfortunate Gonen was left juggling plans for the next day's counter-attack in a way that infuriated everyone.

As the third day of the war, 8 October, dawned in Washington, Kissinger was getting encouraging news from the Israeli ambassador, Simha Dinitz. By lunchtime, Dinitz was able to inform the Secretary of State that Israel had progressed from containing the Arab advances on the two fronts to staging major counter-attacks on them. There was even talk of an Israeli presence the other side of the Canal. But that night Dinitz's tone changed dramatically: in two telephone calls he asked if Kissinger was ready to mount a massive resupply of arms and equipment for the Israeli armed forces. Clearly something had gone wrong. Kissinger asked the ambassador to call on him the following morning.

Dinitz's sudden burst of anxiety came at the end of a day that had started with high hopes of a successful counter-attack, but ended with severe setbacks for Israel on the Suez front. Elazar had left Gonen with orders to restrict any counter-attack to at least 2 miles (3 km) east of the Canal. The strength that the Egyptians had now concentrated on the east bank of the Canal, and the cover from air attack that was provided by their missiles on the west bank, meant that any counter-attack would be hazardous. Elazar wanted his comparatively small forces to focus on any Egyptian attempt to advance east of the Canal. Sharon, for his part, bombarded Gonen with demands that he and Adan should be allowed to lead both their divisions together in a major attack on the Egyptians. But Gonen insisted on sending Adan north and Sharon south, and his orders to Adan swayed dizzily throughout the day: first he was tasked to sweep one way, then another. Sharon was given the same jumble of orders and counter-orders at the southern end of the Canal.

Adan's division ran into fierce Egyptian resistance: one group of around 20 tanks got within 3000 feet (less than 1000 metres) of the Canal, to be met by withering anti-tank fire from Sagger missiles and rocket-propelled grenades. The Egyptian infantry had spent months mastering these Soviet-supplied weapons and the front-line troops had been trained and drilled to tackle the inevitable Israeli counter-attacks. Tanks when advancing are dangerously exposed to a well dug-in defensive force equipped with anti-tank weapons. When the attackers do not have control of the skies, the amount of support available to their side's advancing ground troops is severely restricted. One young Israeli pilot, Joel Aronoff, who had flown US Phantoms in Vietnam and was now flying a newly supplied Phantom in the Israeli air force, described how the ground fire over the Canal was greater than anything he had seen in Vietnam. The Israelis suddenly found themselves confronted with a battlefield that denied them the scope for manoeuvre to which they had been accustomed in previous wars against the Arabs. The effect was disastrous. Adan's division suffered several reverses in the north. After one attack by 21 tanks of Colonel Haim Adini's battalion, 14 were soon wrecked or too damaged to fight. Another battalion attempted to break through to rescue the exhausted defenders of an Israeli fort on the Canal bank: 18 tanks assaulted, but only 4 survived the attack.

At 2 p.m. Gonen reversed his order to Sharon and told him to reinforce Adan. But by the end of the day, Israel's counter-attack had failed. Up to 100 of their tanks had been destroyed or disabled. The Egyptians had clearly won the day. Most of the Israelis in the Canal forts had been either killed or captured. By this time, Avi Yaffe's fort at Purkan was ruined: 'We could only crawl outside. I decided to try and reconnect the phone line. I knew there was a line outside about 100 metres away. I crawled out while my friends covered me with fire; I found the line and connected it. Our intelligence officer … called his commanders to report our situation. The secretary who took the call told him the commander he wished to talk to was busy…. We were shocked. The final realization that everybody just gave up on us came to me after this phone conversation.'[22] Yaffe and his mates were lucky: they later managed a miraculous escape under cover of darkness, sneaking out and finding their way back through the Egyptian lines.

No wonder the Israelis called 8 October 'Black Monday'. Egypt now had two armies and their tank forces securely established on the east bank of the Suez Canal, and its anti-tank weapons and surface-to-air missiles effectively gave Egypt control of a 10-mile-wide (16 km) strip of Sinai along the entire length of the Canal. Syria had won back the best part of half the Golan. The two Arab countries were deep inside what had been Israeli territory; the interesting difference was that Syria's Assad now demanded a ceasefire to benefit from the gains he had made, whereas Egypt's Sadat rejected all talk of ceasefire, convinced he could gain more territory. Morale among Egyptian soldiers was now higher than at any time in living memory. One of them, Mohammed Hassan, told a reporter, 'We have long heard of the might of Israeli soldiers. What we have seen in the past 3 days were not soldiers, but fleeing mice.'[23] Elazar blamed Gonen for the reverses in the Sinai: he had confused his divisional commanders and taken risks he had explicitly been told to avoid. Gonen was ordered to make no more attempts to reach the Canal. Sharon and Adan were apoplectic at what they saw as Gonen's blatant incompetence. Sharon had wasted a day being sent south and then recalled. Adan had been given conflicting sets of orders that made a nonsense of his attempted counter-attack. Israel's southern commanders were in utter disarray, and Elazar and Dayan flew south to Gonen's headquarters to knock their heads together. They were told bluntly to stay on the defensive while Israel mustered its full strength. A Canal crossing was ruled out for the moment, but bridging equipment was to be assembled in case an opening presented itself. For the moment, the imperative was to hold on in the Sinai while the army addressed the even more critical situation on the Golan.

Elazar's decision to switch the emphasis of Israel's defensive action to saving the Golan was wise: Israeli forces in Sinai had hundreds of miles of desert to provide them with defensive depth. Up on the Golan, only a few miles separated the Syrian attackers from looking down on Galilee, which was dotted with Israeli towns and villages and farms. An Israeli attempt to recover the vital observation post they had lost on the top of Mount Hermon had failed. But elsewhere on the Golan, frantic counter-moves by the Israelis – aided by the failure of the Syrians to exploit their breakthrough in the southern Golan – began to stabilize the position.

Moussa Peled's reserve armoured division, pressing up the road from the south-west corner of the Golan, made good progress. Every mile his men moved put the vulnerable Jordan bridges and Israel's heartland beyond them just that little bit further away from the Syrian guns. In the centre, pressure on the headquarters at Nafakh eased a little as Israeli counter-attacks began to unsettle the Syrians.

On the morning of 9 October the increasingly anxious Israeli ambassador, Simha Dinitz, called on Henry Kissinger in Washington as arranged; he brought with him his military adviser, General Mordechai 'Motti' Gur, who had led Israel's attack on Arab Jerusalem in 1967. They painted a black picture of Israel's prospects in an attempt to prompt the Americans into agreeing to an emergency airlift of military supplies to them. But the facts on the ground did much to justify their concern. In just three days of fighting, Israel had lost 500 tanks and 49 aircraft, including 18 of its top-of-the-range F4 Phantoms.[24] Israel's losses were as heavy as Egypt's. The difference was that Israel could not sustain a war of attrition on that scale. Kissinger was convinced that Israel's survival was America's bottom line: 'I never doubted', he wrote, 'that a defeat of Israel by Soviet arms would be a geopolitical disaster for the USA.'[25] He ordered that the Israelis should have full access to all US intelligence, and urged the Pentagon to supply Israel with brand-new F4s. At 4.45 p.m. Washington time he reported to President Nixon that Israel was in danger of losing. Nixon instantly responded: 'Israel must not be allowed to lose.' That night, Kissinger was able to assure Dinitz that America would make good all Israel's losses. If necessary, he told him, the USA would use its own planes to fly the equipment out to Israel. By 14 October, massive C5 Galaxies were carrying vital supplies and munitions to Israel, refuelling at the only airport that any European country would make available to them – Portugal's airbase at Lajes in the Azores.

ISRAEL FIGHTS BACK, 9–14 OCTOBER

In Israel there was a cabinet meeting at 7.30 a.m. that Tuesday, 9 October, at which Dayan took a bleak view of Israel's prospects and all the ministers agreed that the most critical threat lay in the north – from Syria. The Syrians were still piling reinforcements into the Golan and launching Soviet-supplied Frog missiles, which were now striking deep inside Israel. The Israeli air force was ordered to strike at the heart of Syria. As a result, two Syrian power stations were disabled and a wing of the Ministry of Defence in Damascus was damaged; but there was no immediate sign that Syria's war effort was weakened by this strategic bombing.

On the Golan itself, General Moussa Peled's division pushed on north-east up the road that led from the Jordan valley, and his tanks were soon engaged in a fierce battle with the Syrian tanks that had penetrated furthest into the Golan. Fifty-five Syrian tanks were destroyed and Peled's division was reduced to 70; but frantic Israeli repair efforts had 200 operational by the following morning. With Peled's force stemming the Syrian advance in the south of the Golan, the decisive confrontation was to be in the north, where the Syrians piled in more and more armour. President Assad himself took his place in a command bunker to direct what he no doubt hoped would be the decisive breakthrough. His brother Rifat Assad led an elite tank detachment from the presidential guard into the fray.

The Israeli defenders in that northern sector – still centred on Colonel Ben Gal and his men, who had had little or no sleep now for three nights – fought desperately to hold the line. Every minute they could hold on allowed the Israelis to bring further badly needed reinforcements up from behind as mobilization reached full pitch. One Israeli battalion commander, Colonel Yossi Ben Hanan, had been honeymooning in the Himalayas on 6 October when he heard the news on the BBC. By the 9th, he was back and had managed to assemble 13 tanks and rush them up to reinforce Ben Gal. By Tuesday afternoon, superior Israeli gunnery was beginning to turn the battle around, and by the afternoon, Ben Gal was reporting that the Syrians were on the retreat. The exhausted colonel was promptly told to prepare to counter-attack into Syria the following day.

On the Suez Canal, things began to look a little brighter for the Israelis too. The open disagreements between the cantankerous commanders remained as fierce as ever. Sharon, making clear his resentment of Elazar's orders that Israel should for the moment remain on the defensive in Sinai, urged his commanders to press forward and explore prospects for fighting their way across the Canal. Gonen repeatedly ordered him to desist, but by the evening of the 9th, Sharon was reporting back that one of his commanders had found the shore of the Great Bitter Lake deserted. It appeared that the Egyptians had left a gap between their two main forces – the 2nd Army in the north and the 3rd Army in the south. Furthermore, that gap appeared to include a short strip on the Suez Canal itself, at a place called Deversoir, roughly two-thirds of the way down from Port Said in the north. Sharon urged Gonen to let him go for the gap. When Gonen reported this to Elazar, the chief of staff shouted back over the radio: 'Get him out of there! I told him not to cross – *not* to cross.' Sharon continued to argue with Gonen, so Elazar and Dayan agreed to take drastic measures to resolve the leadership crisis in their southern command headquarters. General Bar Lev, the former chief of staff who had already been sent north to restore the situation on the Golan, was now asked to fly south and take over effective command from Gonen. Gonen would remain, but the orders would come from Bar Lev. Sharon, nothing daunted, immediately redirected his vocal campaign for a Canal crossing to Bar Lev.

In Washington, Henry Kissinger was virtually heading up the US administration's conduct of the crisis, as President Nixon was now heavily weighed down by the Watergate crisis. By 10 October, it was becoming clear to Kissinger that he had a potential diplomatic disaster on his hands. He guessed, rightly, that the Soviet Union was pressing Syria and Egypt to agree to a ceasefire. A ceasefire in place would put the two Arab states well inside territory they had recaptured from Israel, and would give them powerful leverage in any peace talks that followed. Egypt's President Sadat later revealed that as early as the evening of 6 October, the first day of the war, the Russians were urging a ceasefire on him. Arab demands for a ceasefire at that stage might have mobilized worldwide support, but Sadat and his Syrian allies had the bit between their teeth and were in no mood to order a halt. Sadat even insisted that there could be no ceasefire without Israel agreeing to withdraw from all the land it had occupied in 1967. This Arab over-confidence rescued Kissinger from the embarrassment of having to oppose a ceasefire, which would have put Israel and its US ally at a huge disadvantage. He was thus able to urge Israel to make every effort to restore its position on the ground before the Arabs changed their minds and called for a ceasefire. Kissinger also took the opportunity of sending a message to try to persuade Jordan's King Hussein to stay out of the war. He got no reply.

Events on the ground now moved very rapidly. By the end of Wednesday, 10 October, the situation on the Golan was utterly transformed. All morning the Israelis watched the Syrians retreat from the areas they had occupied, and by nightfall the Syrians had left 800 destroyed or damaged tanks behind. The scenes of carnage and destruction where the two sides' tank forces had met left an indelible memory on all those who witnessed them. Hundreds of tanks and the charred remains of the human beings who had been bent on killing each other lay everywhere. The Israelis had lost precious lives, but the Syrians had lost more, and, worse than that, they had lost the will to push forward. Golda Meir now pressed urgently for an Israeli counter-attack into Syria proper and, aware that a ceasefire would still put Israel at a disadvantage, ordered her forces to penetrate even deeper than the conquests of June 1967. Israel, she insisted, had to have some extra territory in the Golan to trade for possible losses in the Sinai. And the counter-attack, she said, should start the following day.

Golda Meir's vigorous riposte was rewarded with instant success. All day on Thursday, 11 October the Syrians retreated, hard-pressed by the Israelis. By evening, the Israelis, who had to struggle with some fierce Syrian resistance, were nearly 7 miles (11 km) into new territory and 22 miles (35 km) from Damascus. They had

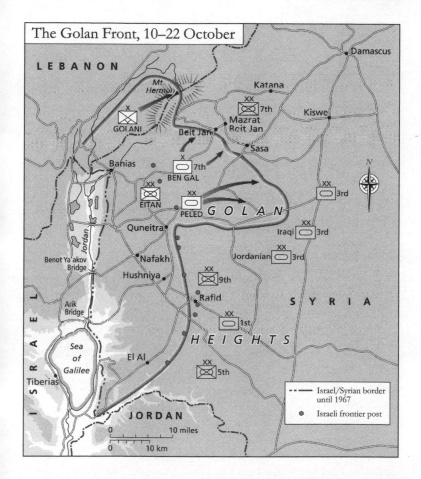

The Golan Front, 10–22 October

Damascus airport within range of their artillery. There they decided to stop. The battle on the Golan went on for several more days, but even reinforcements from Iraq and Jordan failed to claw back any of the territory lost to the Israelis. The critical battle would now be fought not on the Golan but in the western Sinai. Elazar, who was faint with exhaustion by late that night, could afford to transfer the weight of Israel's military effort to the Egyptian front. And it was not long before Sharon's idea of crossing the Canal began to attract more support

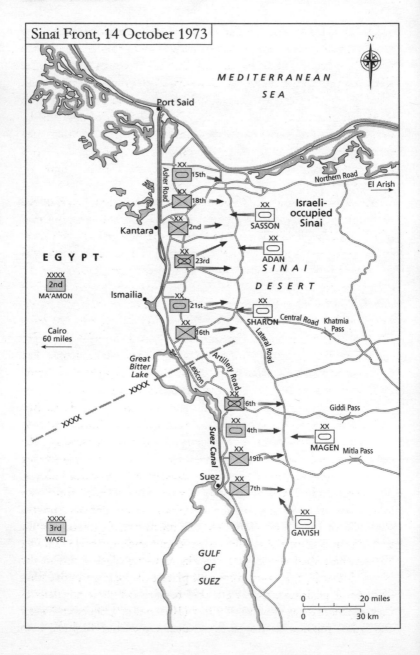

Sinai Front, 14 October 1973

On 12–13 October the Israelis in Sinai were facing an enemy rapidly gaining in strength. Sadat made it clear that he would not accept a ceasefire while Egypt was on the move forward. All the signs suggested that the Egyptians were planning a major tank offensive in an attempt to break out into the Sinai desert and push the Israelis decisively back from the Canal. It had been part of the overall Egyptian plan to win a limited area in Sinai. Sadat now pressed for it to go forward in response to pleas from Syria's President Assad for Egypt to do anything that would relieve the pressure on him.

At 6 a.m. on Sunday, 14 October, the biggest tank battle of the war began. The Egyptians set out to shatter the Israeli front line that had now pulled back to around 20 miles (32 km) east of the Canal. In the northern sector of the front, Egyptian T62 tanks supported by infantry with anti-tank weapons thrust east from Kantara. In the central sector around Ismailia Egyptian armour which had just crossed the Canal struck out towards Sharon's division. In the south, the Egyptian objectives were the Mitla and Giddi passes – 20 miles (32 km) east of the Canal – which commanded the roads into central Sinai. First Egyptian artillery pounded the Israeli lines, and then the Egyptian armour advanced. Soon 2000 Egyptian and Israeli tanks were locked in battle for control of the Sinai.

This time it was the Israelis who had the advantage. Elazar had had a week to move every tank he could spare into Sinai, and now had some 750 of them well dug in in defensive positions. The Egyptians were the ones whose tanks were fully exposed, bouncing and lurching across the desert. They presented mobile but vulnerable targets to the Israeli tanks lying in wait. The Israeli air force – no longer within easy range of the Egyptian missile defences on the west side of the Canal – attacked the advancing Egyptian armour from the air. Colonel Amnon Reshef, commanding a brigade under Sharon, described the Egyptian tanks as like a 'flash flood in the Negev [desert]'. His tanks were well placed on high ground. Firing from fixed positions, they were able to pick off their attackers as they approached as close as 300 feet (100 metres). Egyptian Sagger and other missiles destroyed five Israeli tanks, but Reshef's men wrecked 93 of the attackers. A total of 264 Egyptian tanks were lost that day, and after a visit to the Canal, General Shazli sent a message back to Sadat, saying it was 'our most calamitous day'.[26] He himself had been in favour of keeping Egypt's tanks firmly back within the umbrella provided by its missiles on the Canal. He thought the ambitious plan to break out into the Sinai risked handing the advantage to Israel, whose pilots and tank gunners had free range in the open desert.

Egypt's attempted breakout had turned into a disaster and Israel's armed forces now began to receive the injection of life blood that would help turn the tide of the war. That night, the first C5 Galaxy aircraft landed to begin the US airlift that would fly in an average of 1000 tons of vital military supplies each day. Some of the equipment was in battle within hours: Israel's air force was soon using Maverick and Shrike missiles to give its fighter-bombers a new lethal accuracy. One anti-tank officer, Shaul Shay, recalls using TOW (Tube-launched, Optically tracked, Wire-guided) anti-tank missiles soon after unloading them from the cargo aircraft that had brought them from America.[27]

ISRAEL'S COUNTER-CROSSING

The Egyptian attempt to drive east from the Canal had been blunted, and the time had come for an Israeli counter-thrust. It was to be one of the boldest and riskiest military enterprises ever undertaken. Instead of attacking the Egyptians head on and pushing them back across the Canal, the Israelis would funnel a powerful force through a gap in the Egyptian lines and land it the other side of the Canal. It would then fan out behind the Egyptian lines on the west bank, envelop them and cause chaos in their rear. Israeli commanders were reassured by the fact that the vital reserve divisions of Egyptian armour which had originally been on the west bank of the Canal had been transferred to the east bank and committed to the fruitless attempt to reach the Sinai passes. If the Israelis could force a crossing of the Canal, the west bank was wide open.

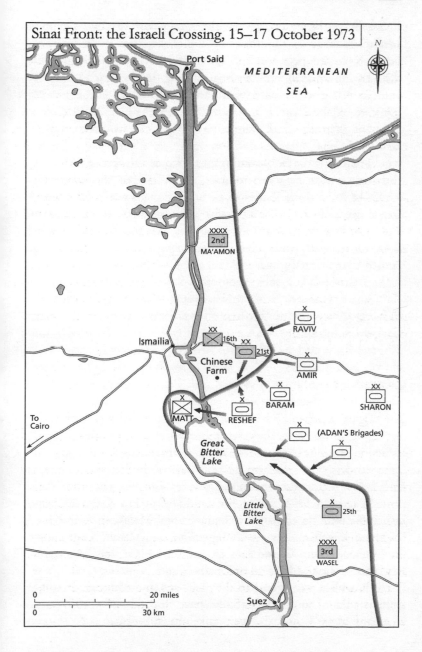

Sinai Front: the Israeli Crossing, 15–17 October 1973

N

Port Said

MEDITERRANEAN

SEA

XXXX
2nd
MA'AMON

X
RAVIV

XX 16th
Ismailia

XX 21st

Chinese
Farm

X
AMIR

X
RESHEF

X
BARAM

XX
SHARON

X
MATT

To
Cairo

X
(ADAN'S Brigades)

X

Great
Bitter
Lake

Little
Bitter
Lake

X 25th

XXXX
3rd
WASEL

0 ____ 20 miles
0 ____ 30 km

Suez

Israeli eyes were focused on the spot where the two Egyptian armies had failed to join up, at the top of the Great Bitter Lake. Six hundred paratroopers under Colonel Danny Matt would slip across the Canal in inflatable rubber boats during the night of 15 October and establish a secure base on the western bank. Then the crossing point would be rapidly bridged by Israeli engineers, and tens of thousand of troops and their armoured vehicles would be hurried across the Canal. Sharon's division was to cross first. Adan's division would follow through, break out into open desert west of the Canal, then turn and drive south to seize Suez City. But there were two vital jobs to be done if the Israeli breakthrough was to succeed. A large Egyptian force at a place called Chinese Farm on the east bank would have to be neutralized: it was too near the planned crossing point for comfort. And Israeli bridging equipment would have to be rushed to the Canal to get the tanks across.

At 5 p.m. Israeli artillery bombarded the Egyptians all along the line. The Israelis sent in to attack Chinese Farm ran into Egyptian defences some three times their strength and a fierce battle began that was to last all night. One group of Israelis penetrated right into Chinese Farm and straight into the core of a main Egyptian divisional headquarters. There was a massive fire-fight. Israel's commander in the battle was Amon Reshef: 'An attacking force should outnumber the defenders at least 3–1. In the Chinese Farm, my brigade attacked a division and a half – in other words, the odds were 5–1 in the defenders' favor instead of 3–1 in ours. It was a brutal fight. The Egyptians staged counterattacks all night. My commanders were performing miracles controlling their units in that hell.'[28] The two sides fought at very close quarters in the dark. One Egyptian soldier climbed on a tank he took to be Egyptian and asked the Israeli commander, Captain Rami Matan, in Arabic for a cigarette. 'He thought we were Egyptian,' said Matan. 'I bent down and pulled the pin from a grenade and tossed it at him. The enemy was totally confused. We were confused too, but less so.'[29]

Meanwhile, the Israeli crossing was seriously delayed. By the 8 p.m. deadline Danny Matt and his paratroopers still hadn't received their rubber boats at the Canal bank because they had been held up by a huge jam of military vehicles on the narrow roads. When the boats finally did arrive, they took one and a half hours to inflate. Matt piled his men in – 22 soldiers to each boat designed to carry just 12. His first platoon commander across the Canal, Lieutenant Eli Cohen, blew a hole in some barbed wire and, without any sign of Egyptian opposition, established the first Israeli foothold west of the Canal. Matt's force quickly established a perimeter and radioed back the codeword for success: 'Acapulco'. It was a sign that the way was clear for the Canal to be bridged. But the gridlock on the approach to the crossing point meant that neither the special metal bridge nor the British-made floating iron cubes that could be joined up to make an alternative bridge had arrived. In desperation, the Israelis turned to their third option – large rafts called Gilowas. It was 6.30 a.m. on the morning of the 16th before they were assembled into huge floats that could begin to transfer the tanks across.

Sharon watched the first tanks float across the Canal. More than 20 of his own tanks crossed first, to press forward and destroy Egyptian missile bases on the west side. But because the crossing point was still so fragile, Sharon was ordered by Bar Lev to use the rest of his division to secure the bridging operation, while Adan's division passed through, crossed the Canal and fanned out into the desert beyond. Sharon had to bite his lip and bear it. Moreover, he was ordered not to allow any major tank force over the Canal until the crossing was absolutely secure. He believed the Israeli high command was mad not to exploit the breach more rapidly, and told them so.

Sadat's first known reaction to the crossing was when he told Alexei Kosygin, the visiting Soviet Prime Minister, that day that what was happening on the Canal was 'an insignificant event'. Shazli, the Egyptian chief of staff, remembers the meeting that evening at which Sadat and his high command planned their reaction to the Israeli crossing. Shazli urged a pullback of at least two divisions to the west side to counter the Israeli thrust. Sadat vigorously opposed him: 'Why do you always propose withdrawing our troops from the east bank,' he shouted. 'You ought to be court-martialled.... I do not want to hear another word.'[30]

The Egyptians may have been slow to react to the crossing, but at Chinese Farm the fighting raged on. The Israelis had to try to stop the Egyptians edging south down the Canal and slamming shut the narrow gap that Israel had driven between the two Egyptian armies. Reshef's brigade lost 56 of its 97 tanks: 128 soldiers died in the battle. Aharon Bar was one of the wounded. 'We found that we were facing huge masses of missile-carrying infantry ... we got into a hollow, behind a crest. From time to time we tried to get out, but the missile fire against us was too heavy. Then we got an order to attack. I felt something I had never felt before in my life. I didn't understand what was happening to me, but I knew something was very serious.... The tank was full of gas.... A missile had hit the tank low down. I opened the driver's hatch and got out: only then did I realize there was an empty space below my left knee. I stood on one foot, holding onto the tank.'[31]

It was not until the morning of Wednesday, 17 October that the Egyptians seriously targeted the Israeli crossing point and began striking it from the air. Sharon, up in the front line and impatient to lead his men across, received a gash on the forehead and soon found himself in a blazing row with his bosses. At noon Defence Minister Moshe Dayan, chief of staff David Elazar and the new southern commander, Haim Bar Lev, gathered with their front-line leaders in Adan's command post behind the east bank of the Canal. Sharon, expecting to be congratulated for forcing the crossing, won no handshakes from anyone. Indeed, Bar Lev scythed into him, saying, 'Any resemblance between what you've done and what you've promised is purely coincidental.' He was referring to the fact that the crossing was still not secure. Sharon later wrote that he had to restrain himself from slapping Bar Lev's face: 'I don't know how I kept myself from hitting him.' Sharon spent most of the meeting urging a mass crossing of the Canal by his and Adan's tanks, but to his fury Elazar took the view that Adan's force should take the lead and leave Sharon's men securing the crossing. While the commanders argued, Adan's force had been busy: they had destroyed an Egyptian brigade that had advanced unwittingly up the east bank of the Great Bitter Lake towards the Israeli crossing point. Dayan crossed the Canal to stand on African soil, and reported back to Golda Meir that 100 soldiers were across so far and the next day the whole of Israel would be there.

Front-line Egyptian officers like First Lieutenant Salama Elsayed, with the 3rd Army, had begun to notice that something was wrong. 'Usually we saw lights at night going from west to east. That night we saw a lot of lights going from the east to the west. We woke up at 5 a.m. in the morning and saw the Israeli flag on the west side ... all of a sudden we saw the Star of David flag on the west side. And Israelis talking to us in our language, telling us we were surrounded. This was the hardest to digest, the fact we're surrounded from the east, surrounded from the north, surrounded from the west. Like a sandwich.'[32] Remarkably, even later that day, when Kosygin again met Sadat, clear reports of the Israeli crossing still didn't move the Egyptian president from his determination to continue rejecting any ceasefire.

Finally, late that evening – after what seemed to Sharon an eternity from the moment the paratroopers had first secured a foothold on the west bank of the Canal – Adan's division crossed, with the loss of two tanks when their raft capsized, and established itself on the opposite bank. Sharon was ordered to stay put and guard the crossing. Again he complained to Israel's high command: Egypt would quickly collapse if they would let him too cross the Canal and range freely on the west bank. Bar Lev urged Elazar to sack Sharon, but Elazar reckoned Sharon was too popular and too valuable to lose.

On the morning of the 18th the Israelis boldly exploited their crossing of the Canal. Adan sent two of his brigades to storm their way down the west bank to Suez and attempt to cut off the entire Egyptian 3rd Army, who, confident that their rear was secure, were established on the east bank. Sharon was finally authorized to take one of his brigades across and exploit any opening he could find on the west bank northwards towards Ismailia. But Sharon wanted more men across: that evening he was telling Gonen over the radio that he was going to take two brigades north. Elazar immediately seized the microphone from Gonen, and shouted: 'Sharon, this is

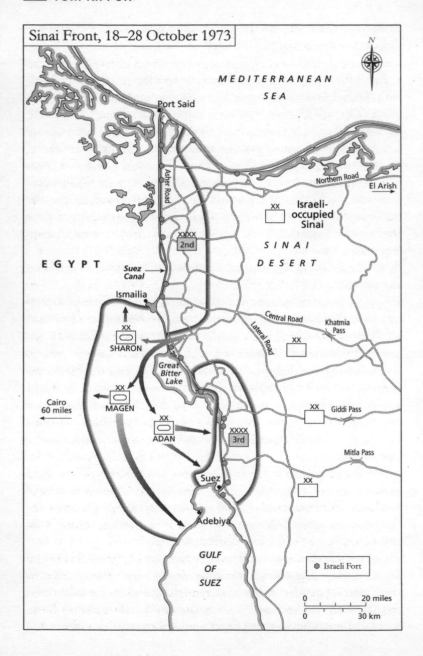

Sinai Front, 18–28 October 1973

Dado [his nickname]. Your plan is totally unacceptable: I want you to hold the bridgehead.'

Late that night, Henry Kissinger received a message from the Russian President, Leonid Brezhnev. It was the Secretary of State's first indication that Sadat was no longer confident of a sweeping victory. The USSR, said Brezhnev, was ready to go to the UN with a ceasefire proposal. The trouble was that the Soviet draft demanded an Israeli withdrawal to the old lines prior to the Six-Day War of 1967. Kissinger knew the Israelis would not accept it and decided to play for time. But the pressure was on: the Arabs were threatening a cutback in oil output of 5 per cent each month, beginning immediately. Fuel prices would rocket. Alarm bells began ringing around the world – particularly in Europe. Pressure to curb the Israelis intensified.

By the morning of 18 October, there were 300 Israeli tanks on the west bank of the Suez Canal. Adan's brigades were well on their way to Suez, meeting occasional bouts of opposition from groups of infantry armed with Sagger anti-tank missiles. There were tank battles, too. A few days into the battle on the west bank, Eitan Haber, the military correspondent of the Israeli newspaper *Yedioth Aharonoth*, reported: 'It sounds as if several regiments of tanks are here in the desert. The Egyptian tanks try to advance and one approaches within almost 1 km away from us. The tank beside me aims at it and fires. The turret opens and a burning man emerges, looking like a living torch. He runs wildly towards our tanks. In the heat and the noise of the battle, one cannot hear his screams. He runs for about 200 yards before finally collapsing on the sand between the two lines of tanks in no-man's land. There is no way to help him. But if we reach him after the battle, after we destroy the Egyptian force, we shall take him with us to the field hospital for treatment. Now he has to suffer on the sand.'[33]

Sharon was pressing north towards Ismailia, and the effect of this Israeli masterstroke was breathtaking. Faced only a week earlier by two massive Egyptian armies apparently successfully established on the east bank of the Canal and threatening Israel's hold on Sinai, Israel had now almost surrounded one of these armies and was fast undermining the other. The triumph of the Egyptian high command had turned to utter dismay. Sadat and his top generals were so paralysed by the fate of their 3rd Army that they failed to agree on any coherent plan to rescue it. Sadat would not contemplate its withdrawal back to the west bank of the Canal. Shazli, who was dismissed after the war, later blamed the President for insisting on a strategy that was 'tantamount to suicide', and accused him of 'throwing away the greatest army Egypt had ever assembled'.[34]

At 11 a.m. Washington time Kissinger was invited by Brezhnev to fly to Moscow and talk peace. The Secretary of State accepted with delight. He now enjoyed a unique moment of power and personal opportunity: his own rapport with the leaders on all sides, and the key grip that Washington alone held on the Israelis through its life-saving airlift of vital arms and ammunition, gave the United States a deciding hand in Middle East diplomacy that was to endure from then on. Late that night in Moscow, he and Brezhnev heard from the Egyptians that Sadat was now ready for a ceasefire. He was no longer insisting it should be linked to immediate Israeli withdrawal. Kissinger had no trouble accepting it.

After a day in Moscow, Kissinger was invited by an anxious Israeli Prime Minister to return to Washington via Tel Aviv. He duly diverted, and on 22 October was ushered into the Israeli 'Guest House' in Herzliyya to meet Golda Meir and her cabinet. He found them in no doubt of the military triumph they had achieved, but sobered and concerned at the scale of Israeli casualties and the difficult prospects in front of them. 'The Israelis knew they had won … but they had lost the aura of invincibility … the Arab armies were not destroyed. The Arab nations had not won but no longer need they quail before Israeli might…. [Israel] was entering an uncertain and lonely future, dependent on a shrinking circle of friends. What made the prospect more tormenting was the consciousness that complacency had contributed to the outcome.'[35]

But the war of Yom Kippur was not over yet. In its last moments it was to bring the superpowers to their most tense nuclear confrontation since the Cuban missile crisis of 1962. The ceasefire that was supposed to be in place by 5 p.m. Cairo time on 22 October was still not in effect two days later. Both sides blamed the other, but Kissinger was in no doubt that the Israelis were the main culprits, determined to press home their advantage and if possible seal off the Egyptian 3rd Army altogether. Kissinger believed it to be essential that any ceasefire would have to allow the Egyptians some kind of supply route to their troops beleaguered on the east side of the Canal.

By the morning of 24 October, the desperation of the Egyptians at the plight of their army and of the Russians at the humiliation suffered by their Arab ally led to a full-scale international crisis. Sadat called for US and Soviet forces to fly to Egypt and enforce a ceasefire. The Americans said they would not send troops and would not tolerate any Soviet deployment. At 9.35 that night in Washington, Soviet ambassador Dobrynin called Kissinger and said, 'If you find it impossible to act jointly with us in this matter, we should be faced with the necessity urgently to consider the question of taking steps unilaterally.' America faced the threat of Soviet troops flying to Egypt to help force the Israelis back. Kissinger judged that the USA had to warn the Soviet Union that this move would be unacceptable. President Nixon, now deeply mired in the Watergate affair, does not appear to have been involved in the decision. Kissinger says that Nixon's chief of staff, Al Haig, told him not to disturb the President. What we do know is that at 10.40 p.m. Washington time on 24 October, Kissinger got the agreement of the National Security Council to raise US nuclear forces to alert status Def Con (Defence Condition) 3. Normal peacetime status is Def Con 4 or 5. And in order to drive the point home, the US 82nd Airborne Division was alerted and the aircraft carrier USS *Franklin D Roosevelt* was ordered to speed into the Mediterranean.[36]

There was a risk, as there was during the Cuba crisis, that nuclear escalation on one side would lead to a hostile response from the other, and that events could spiral out of control. But Brezhnev took the critical decision not to raise the stakes. He dropped all talk of Soviet troops going to Egypt.[37]

The American action had been effective. The following morning, the 25th, both Egypt and the Soviet Union were talking about the need not for US and Soviet troops but for some kind of force of 'observers' to police any settlement in the Middle East. The crisis had almost evaporated. The problem was that Israel seemed determined to achieve the complete humiliation of the Egyptian 3rd Army. Kissinger anxiously urged the Israelis to lay off, and in the nick of time, on 27 October, Sadat made an offer the Israelis felt they could not resist. He agreed to send a top Egyptian military team to hold the first direct peace talks with Israel for 25 years. The Israelis, their encirclement of the 3rd Army complete, had now ceased advancing, and within a day the two sides were negotiating in a tent pitched at a point known as Kilometre 101 on the west bank of the Canal.

WHO WAS THE VICTOR?

The military talks paved the way for serious negotiations between the Arabs and Israelis, not yet about peace, but about a separation of forces. And in the end, after a two-month *tour de force*, Kissinger delivered separation agreements between the two Arab countries and Israel. It was a period of shuttle diplomacy between Jerusalem, Cairo and Damascus that only America had the muscle to orchestrate. The final disengagement pacts left Egypt in the positions it had gained in battle on the east bank of the Canal, and even Syria retained a small fragment of the Golan that it had recently tried to seize back. The overwhelming response of most Arabs was to turn a blind eye to the reverses of the last days of the conflict.[38] Lieutenant Awad Allam, one Egyptian who fought his way right through the war, talked of his 'excitement' at its outcome: 'It was a good feeling; people started to talk with pride and walk with pride and they know that we did fight a real fight and we had hope in the future ... we knew we were going to have a better life and a better country.'[39]

But the real fruit of the new-found confidence and pride that the crossing of the Canal had given Egypt and its President was the great breakthrough of 1977. In November of that year Anwar Sadat suddenly announced that he would go to Jerusalem, even into the Israeli parliament, the Knesset, itself, to achieve peace. It was an initiative that would lead to the Camp David agreement of 1978, the first time any of Israel's Arab neighbours had agreed to put their signatures to a peace treaty. Egypt gave Israel the recognition it wanted. The Israelis, in return, withdrew from the whole of Sinai in 1982.

The October War of 1973 took a heavy toll of both sides. Egypt and Syria are estimated to have suffered up to 55,000 dead and wounded. Israel suffered around 10,000 casualties, of whom nearly 2700 were killed and over 7200 wounded. To a country as small as Israel this level of loss was a huge shock: in the Six-Day War in 1967 they had lost just 760 dead. The other major shock for the Israelis was how deeply they had had to depend on the USA: without rapid replacement of aircraft, tanks, ammunition and missiles, flown in day in, day out by a massive American airlift, Israel would have been hard put to survive. But the trauma in Israel was far greater than that. The failure of intelligence, of leadership and of military strategy that so nearly led to Israel's defeat claimed many famous victims. A commission of inquiry after the war condemned outright chief of staff Elazar and intelligence chief Zeira. Moshe Dayan and Golda Meir were cleared, but both left office within a year. Adan emerged a quiet hero, but never enjoyed the star status of Ariel Sharon, who is identified in most minds with the prime role in the planning and execution of the breakthrough on the Suez Canal. Sharon's insubordination, his boisterous rows with his superiors and his constant impatience to exploit the crossing earned him huge popularity with his troops, and he went on to be Minister of Defence and Prime Minister in right-wing Israeli governments until ill health forced his retirement from politics in early 2006.

As for war matériel, the Arabs lost some 2250 tanks and the Israelis over 500. The Arabs are estimated to have lost over 400 aircraft and the Israelis 100. The Egyptians' Soviet anti-aircraft missiles, and the accuracy and flexibility of their Sagger anti-tank missiles from the same source, worried the Israelis, but it was the tank that ruled the battlefield and played the decisive role. And for all the courage and coordination of the Arab offensives, it was the superior training and initiative of the Israelis, and in particular of their tank drivers and gunners, that helped turn defeat into victory.

THE FALKLANDS

In the early hours of 2 April 1982, the trim English gardens of Government House in the Falkland Islands became a battleground. The house and its ample conservatory stood, as it still stands today, surrounded by lawns and flowerbeds on the waterfront in Stanley, the capital. A force of 2000 Argentine commandoes had landed on beaches north and south of Stanley, and at 6.15 a.m. they surrounded the building that, way down in the South Atlantic, was one of the remotest outposts of British rule. The 69 Royal Marines garrisoning the islands had done what they could to resist the landings on the beaches, but they were now to make their main stand defending the Governor, Rex Hunt. Hunt had been warned the day before that an Argentine invasion force was on its way: 'It looks as if the buggers mean it,' he told his Royal Marine commander, Major Mike Norman. But he still hoped that this, the most serious challenge to British rule on the islands in a century and a half, could be little more than a demonstration: he told his aides he expected the Argentines would land, raise their flag and then depart after a glass of sherry at Government House.

It was not like that at all. For a whole two and a quarter hours that morning Hunt and the handful of marines guarding his house came under persistent fire. The Argentines attacked with armoured cars and heavy machine guns. Mike Norman remembers the fear that he and his men shared when they knew how massively they were outnumbered. 'I was lying there shaking from head to foot like a piece of jelly…. In those situations you have to give yourself a talking to. I said to myself "You knew it was going to come to this.

You told the lads it was going to come to this. Now get a grip, because if anybody climbs over that wall now, you are not going to be able to hit the wall let alone the target."'[1]

Norman and his men put up a good fight. They shot down a three-man team sent in to snatch the Governor, and kept the Argentine attackers at bay for what seemed like an eternity. Hunt took what shelter he could under the oak desk which is still in the Governor's study. Somehow, he managed to give a blow-by-blow account of the battle to the local radio station by telephone. But the outcome could not be in doubt. Hunt was not going to ask the marines to fight against hopeless odds, and at 8.30 a.m. he made it known to the Argentine commander that he was ready to surrender. The rest of Stanley was by now in Argentine hands too: one of the islanders, John Smith, wrote in his diary that there were Argentine amphibious vehicles 'rushing and roaring about all over the place, knocking down fences, breaking up the roads: troops and guns everywhere. It's like living a nightmare.'[2] At 10 a.m. Falkland Islanders who had been listening to their radio commentator, Patrick Watts, describing the course of the battle heard him announce that the Governor was on the telephone.

'Hello Islanders,' Rex Hunt told the radio audience, 'I hope you can hear me on the phone. The Argentine Admiral came along to me and I told him he had landed unlawfully on British sovereign territory. He refused [to leave], claiming that he was taking back territory that belonged to Argentina.... He appealed to me to cease the endless bloodshed as he had an overwhelmingly superior force. I said I couldn't argue with that, but I would not have agreed to a ceasefire had we had anything like comparable forces. I am sorry that it has happened this way. It's probably the last message I will be able to give you, but I wish you all the best of luck, and rest assured the British will be back.' Within minutes, five or six Argentine soldiers bustled into Watts's studio and made him run a tape which said in English and Spanish that the islands were now part of Argentina.[3]

And that was that. A sparsely inhabited British colony on the edge of the Antarctic, 8000 miles (nearly 13,000 km) from home, had been overwhelmed by a near neighbour, one of the largest countries in South America, which claimed it as its own. On that first morning a lot of people – perhaps most people – in Britain and Argentina must have believed that there was nothing whatever that Britain could do about it.

What followed, however, was not the shrugging-off of a *fait accompli*, but one of the most striking military conflicts of modern times. It was, by global standards, warfare on a small scale, and the cause may have seemed trivial to much of the rest of the world, but for Britain and Argentina it became a desperate struggle for fundamental interests. And for students of war it provided an extraordinary example of forces fighting at the extreme limits of their military capability.

THATCHER'S RESPONSE

The very last thing the British Prime Minister, Margaret Thatcher, expected was that her armed forces would be involved in fighting on the other side of the world. Her government was undermined by joblessness and political unpopularity at home. Defence planners, obsessed by the Cold War with the Soviet Union, had scheduled an end to the Royal Navy's capacity to range all over the globe. In future, they would concentrate on anti-submarine warfare in the North Atlantic. The government had even announced plans to abandon the one symbol of Britain's defence presence in the South Atlantic, the naval vessel HMS *Endurance,* which had been based in the Falkland Islands; she had been responsible for the protection of British interests in the Falklands and other dependencies in the region, like South Georgia. But the Falklands, with their tiny population of some 2000 people, were now seen as an awkward relic of empire. The islands were windswept, chilly for most of the year and largely unproductive apart from sheep farming and fishing. They had been permanently occupied by Britain since 1833, but it was an occupation persistently contested by nearby Argentina. The first instinct of Mrs Thatcher's government had been to try to come to an arrangement with Argentina that would at least leave open the issue of sovereignty, but the deeply pro-British islanders and the vigorous campaign of their allies in the House of Commons in London had soon put paid to that. Nevertheless, Mrs Thatcher's government continued to make it clear that the South Atlantic was low on its list of priorities.

All this must have given encouragement to the new military junta which seized power in Argentina in December 1981. The man nominally in charge was General Leopoldo Galtieri, but the naval chief Admiral Anaya was said to have lent his support to Galtieri only on condition that he committed himself to recovering the Malvinas – the Argentine name for the Falklands. After a few months of severe repression and economic mismanagement, the new government had become increasingly unpopular, and a military expedition against the tiny British garrison in the Falklands appeared a useful distraction. An invasion during the winter (from June onwards) would leave the British struggling with the fearsome South Atlantic weather if they did try to retaliate.

A series of Argentine challenges to British authority in South Georgia prompted Mrs Thatcher's government to send the patrol ship HMS *Endurance* to South Georgia and two submarines to the South Atlantic, with the prospect of them being joined by a third.[4] It soon became public knowledge that at least one was on its way. But far from deterring the Argentine military junta from putting to sea, reports of British naval movements appear to have spurred Galtieri to pre-empt their arrival and advance his date for the landings to 2 April.

By Wednesday, 31 March, Britain was receiving unmistakeable intelligence that an Argentine invasion fleet was heading for the Falklands, and that evening Margaret Thatcher called a meeting of her top advisers and ministers at the House of Commons. There was nothing Britain could do to stop the invasion: there was no Royal Navy surface vessel with the capacity to stop an invasion force and no submarine within reach of the islands, and the Stanley airport runway could not accommodate large troop-carrying jet aircraft. Rapid reinforcement of the tiny garrison was out of the question. Furthermore, most ministers took the view that a successful invasion by Argentina would be almost impossible to reverse and that an operation to reoccupy the island would be fraught with huge risks and costs in lives and matériel. Then, at this critical moment, the imposing figure of the First Sea Lord, Admiral Sir Henry Leach, appeared in the doorway. He had had trouble in persuading the Commons staff to give him access, but once admitted he made the most of it. He told the Prime Minister and the rest of the hushed gathering that the only realistic way of reoccupying the islands was to send a naval task force, and he could assemble one by the weekend. It would take three weeks to reach the Falklands, but once there, he assured her, British forces, which would be carried on amphibious ships with the task force, would be able to land and recover the islands. It would be difficult and dangerous, but, said Sir Henry, 'If Britain does not respond, it will be seen as a nation whose word counts for nothing.' Mrs Thatcher asked him what effect he thought the despatch of a task force would have on an Argentine admiral. 'I would return to harbour immediately,' he replied.

The Prime Minister may have had her own secret doubts about the massive risks involved in a military adventure of this magnitude. Britain's military strength had declined greatly in the previous 20 years, and its capacity to wield power the other side of the world was almost gone. But Leach's self-assurance and confident advice – even if Thatcher made allowance for the Royal Navy's natural urge to demonstrate its worth – must have helped fortify her resolve. What is certain is that from that moment she never wavered from the conviction that, if she could not persuade the Argentines to withdraw through peaceful negotiations, Britain would be in a military conflict which it had no choice but to win. The military implications of defeat for a large force afloat in the turbulent waters of the South Atlantic were unimaginable. The political consequences of defeat for a government as unpopular and apparently unsuccessful as Margaret Thatcher's would be disastrous. Armed with these certainties, she was now transformed into a leader whose iron will would utterly dominate the campaign and brush aside all those who voiced any doubts or reservations.

Even before the Argentine invaders had set foot on the Falklands, plans for the islands' reconquest were well under way. Leach and his staff put together a naval and amphibious force that was ready to sail on Monday, 5 April. Once Britain's defence establishment was alerted to a major emergency, its reaction was rapid and meticulous. Rear Admiral Sandy Woodward would command a naval force cen tred on the aircraft carriers *Hermes* and *Invincible*; Commodore Michael Clapp was to lead an armada of amphibious ships led by *Fearless* and *Intrepid*; and Brigadier Julian Thompson, a Royal Marine with a wealth of experience and a powerful intellect, was appointed commander of a landing force of three marine comman- dos and two parachute battalions. Moreover, that weekend a redoubtable sailor and navigator, Royal Marine Major Ewen Southby-Tailyour, was asked to brief the force commanders on the most suitable spots for an amphibious landing on the Falklands.

The final element in the construction of what was to turn into a national enterprise with almost unanimous popular support was the debate in the House of Commons on the day that followed the invasion and the surrender of Government House. That same day, 3 April, the Argentines landed a force in South Georgia and attacked the small force of British marines stationed there. There was a fierce battle, as there had been in Stanley: sustained fire from the Royal Marines brought down an Argentine Puma helicopter and killed most of the troops on board, while the Argentine frigate controlling the operation was holed by British anti-tank rockets. But further resistance was futile and the British commander, Lieutenant Keith Mills, surrendered 24 hours after the end of the fighting in the Falklands.

Press pictures of the Argentines in Stanley pointing guns at their Royal Marine captives lying on the ground caused huge resentment in Britain. Even if Mrs Thatcher had still been undecided, the wave of parliamentary fury right across the political spectrum would have left her no choice. Labour's left-wing leader, Michael Foot, said, 'We have a moral duty, a political duty and every other kind of duty to ensure that the Falkland Islanders' association with Britain is sus- tained.' The former Conservative right-winger Enoch Powell told the Prime Minister, whom the Russians had already dubbed 'The Iron Lady', that she would soon 'learn of what metal she was made'. Her Defence Secretary, John Nott, made a very different impression on MPs. One of his fellow Conservatives, Alan Clark, wrote: 'Poor old Notters on the other hand was a disaster. He stammered and stuttered and garbled. He faltered and fluttered and fumbled.'[5] But the overwhelming view of parliamentarians on all sides was that Argentina's action demanded a military response.

The die was cast. As the leading ships of the task force headed south in the first few days of April, the men aboard and most of the people at home knew that if Argentina was not now persuaded by this forthright demonstration of British power to abandon its occupation, the two countries would be at war. The fleet's first and only stop would be Ascension Island, a British dependency conveniently placed in the South Atlantic, just over halfway to the Falklands. There was a huge American base on Ascension, and the American Defence Secretary, Caspar Weinberger, an undisguised Anglophile, put its 10,000-foot (3000-metre) runway, its other military facilities and its huge stock of fuel at the disposal of the British. He caused deep unease in some quarters in Washington, which were anxious not to offend Latin American sensibilities by siding too obviously with the British. The US ambassador to the United Nations, Jeanne Kirkpatrick, led the other faction. Britain's ambassador in Washington at the time, Nicholas Henderson, describes her as 'probably the most influential member of the Latino Lobby. She did not consider Argentina was an aggressor: it was simply asserting a long stated claim to the islands.'[6] On a number of occasions she attempted to sabotage British attempts to win support at the United Nations, and even attended a dinner hosted by the Argentine ambassador on the day of the invasion.

THE VOYAGE SOUTH

Leading components of the task force – the carriers *Hermes* and *Invincible*, together with *Fearless*, the first of the amphibious ships carrying the spearhead troops of a possible landing force – reached Ascension Island on 10 April. As the task force headed south, the men aboard kept fit as best they could, running around the ships' decks in full combat kit, while their commanders pored over maps of the Falklands, searching for the best landing site and approach to Stanley.

Britain's other NATO and European allies did their best to help. France gave details of sales of its most advanced and dangerous anti-surface missile, the Exocet. This was a projectile that skimmed the surface of the sea and homed on to its target by radar, needing no guidance from some human operator. Once launched by a ship or an aircraft, the Exocet was on its own: the launching platform could turn for home. Argentina had a number of the missiles which could be fired from warships and – crucially – five, the French reckoned, which could be launched from their Super Etendard Mirage aircraft. Woodward quickly identified these as the most dangerous threat to his carriers and other warships. He would have submarines to protect him against naval attack, but his protection against air attack was less sure. *Hermes* and *Invincible* were carrying 30 Harriers armed with air-to-air missiles. Thanks again to Caspar Weinberger, the pilots would have the latest version of the American-made Sidewinder missile, the AIM 9L, to attack Argentine aircraft.

Woodward's anti-aircraft destroyers, like HMS *Sheffield*, were equipped with the Sea Dart, which was designed to lock on to approaching aircraft at medium range, around 30 miles (some 50 km) away. These destroyers had no close-range protection; only the Broadsword-class frigates, which carried the Sea Wolf, a more modern anti-aircraft missile, had the capacity to hit attacking aircraft close to. It was even claimed that they could intercept approaching missiles. Facing this uncertain pattern of air defence, the Argentines had an impressive array of some 100 fighter and strike aircraft, primarily American-designed Skyhawks and various versions of the French Mirage. But in the seas around the Falklands they would be operating at the limit of their range. It was clear that for both sides this would be a struggle with a highly unpredictable outcome.

By the end of April – just four weeks after the invasion – the Argentines had increased their garrison on the Falklands to some 13,000, a mixture of regular soldiers and marines and a large contingent of poorly trained conscripts. The British for their part had now embarked a fleet of some 25 warships and 45 transport and supply vessels, many of them, like the great white-painted liner *Canberra*, merchant ships that were dubbed STUFT for short – 'ships taken up from trade'. Partly at the urging of Brigadier Thompson, the final landing force would now be almost doubled in strength by the addition of another brigade, ferried out on the liner the *QE2*. Five Brigade, consisting of men of the Welsh and Scots Guards and the Gurkhas, would arrive off the Falklands around the end of May. Britain would attempt to land a fighting force of 8000 men to face 13,000 Argentinians.

The momentum towards armed conflict began to take on an aura of inevitability. But in spite of the parliamentary consensus, there were some convinced opponents of military action, even excluding the persistently dovish Labour MP Tony Benn. Some had their doubts about the rationale of risking so many lives to rescue a population of less than 2000 in a wind-ravaged territory of dubious economic value on the other side of the world. There were demands for a peaceful solution from newspapers like the *Guardian* and the *Sunday Times*. But most people were unhesitatingly committed to the principle that the Argentine aggression should not be allowed to succeed. Peace talks, conducted first by the Americans and then by the United Nations, constantly foundered on the failure to get agreement on the nature of any interim administration and the conditions for further negotiations on the status of the islands. The attempts of the US Secretary of State, Al Haig, at a compromise proved futile, and by the end of April, the United States had declared its support for Britain.[7] From this moment, Weinberger ordered that Britain should have access to any supplies it wanted, and if there was any delay he would want to know why. For the British ambassador, Nicholas Henderson, 'the most dramatic moment occurred when Weinberger took me aside at a party at the British embassy. He said he would be prepared to make a US carrier available to us in the South Atlantic if the military situation required it – an offer of spontaneous and practical generosity that must be unique in the annals of the Washington–London relationship.'[8] The offer was warmly received, but politely rejected on grounds of impracticality.

By this time, Woodward's main force had arrived off the Falklands. On 28 April, after some 21 days at sea, the fleet was now bouncing around in a turbulent South Atlantic 8000 miles (13,000 km) from home. A 200-mile (320-km) Total Exclusion Zone (TEZ) was declared around the islands. Britain announced that Argentine ships would be attacked if they entered it, and battle was joined almost immediately. On 1 May the task force made its presence felt with air attacks by Harriers on Stanley and Goose Green, and an attempt by a lone Vulcan bomber – flying from Ascension – to crater the Stanley runway. Refuelled en route by no fewer than 15 Victor tanker aircraft, it succeeded in making just one hole in the runway.

THE SINKING OF THE *BELGRANO*

Woodward now had the job of establishing an environment in which Thompson's force of marines and paratroopers could land on the Falklands with as few casualties as possible. The navy and its Harrier aircraft had to attempt to establish control of the airspace over the islands and the sea around them. And the first Argentine threat Woodward had to face was a naval one.

Late on the night of 1 May, two groups of ships appeared to be closing on Woodward's task force as it took up position 100 miles (160 km) or so north-east of the Falklands. The first was centred around the Argentine aircraft carrier *Venticinco de Mayo*, which was approaching from the north-west with carrier-borne strike aircraft apparently ready for launch. In fact, the carrier found itself becalmed that night and, unable to find enough wind to allow it to launch aircraft off its deck, it was powerless to strike the British fleet. But Woodward did not know this, and naturally regarded the ship as a grave threat. The second potential danger came from three warships to the south of the task force: the cruiser *Belgrano*, equipped with slightly longer-range guns than all the British ships, accompanied by two destroyers known to be armed with Exocet missiles, was spotted by a British submarine, HMS *Conqueror*. The three ships came within 40 miles (65 km) of the TEZ, steaming east, but then on the morning of the 2nd turned away west and pursued a zigzag course away from the British fleet. Woodward's worry was that *Belgrano* could at any time turn around and enter the TEZ

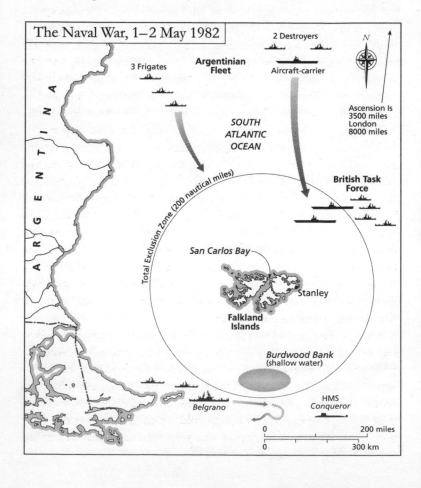

The Naval War, 1–2 May 1982

2 Destroyers

N

3 Frigates

Argentinian Fleet

Aircraft-carrier

A R G E N T I N A

SOUTH ATLANTIC OCEAN

Ascension Is 3500 miles London 8000 miles

Total Exclusion Zone (200 nautical miles)

British Task Force

San Carlos Bay

Stanley

Falkland Islands

Burdwood Bank (shallow water)

Belgrano

HMS *Conqueror*

0   200 miles

0   300 km

across the Burdwood Bank – water too shallow to allow *Conqueror* to continue shadowing her underwater. Whichever way he looked at it, the *Belgrano* and its escorts were a second serious menace to his task force.

Although both groups were just outside the TEZ, Britain now took action that was to lead to years of controversy. Woodward, nervous that his carrier force could be attacked within a day or two of its arrival by a pincer movement from north and south, appealed to London to be allowed to destroy the threat before it crossed into the TEZ. As he put it later: 'I needed to remove one of the claws [of the pincer] … and the *Belgrano* is the one we had firm contact with.' He urged London to authorize *Conqueror,* which was still shadowing the *Belgrano*, to sink her. At lunchtime on the 2nd the decision was taken at the highest level: Mrs Thatcher herself was consulted at her weekend retreat at Chequers. She and her ministers decided that the risks to the lives of British sailors outweighed any advantage that remained in keeping the door to peace open: the order was given to launch torpedoes. *Conqueror's* captain, anxious not to risk failure, used two well-tried Second World War torpedoes which had massive explosive power. They struck the *Belgrano* and she sank within 45 minutes, with the loss of 323 Argentine lives.

One Argentine officer aboard, Nestor Sensi, recalls: 'As soon as I got back to my cabin the first explosion occurred, it was a tremendous blast, it threw me to the floor. The noise was fantastic – it was loud, so very loud. And the smell, a penetrating smell – strong & sulphurous. I could feel it inside my nose. The ship died instantly. There was total darkness. Once I got back to my feet, I had to touch the walls to know where the door was.'[9]

One of the *Conqueror's* crew, Bill Budding, says there were mixed feelings aboard the British submarine: 'The immediate reaction from the control room team – who had done their job properly – was a cheer, and within 30 seconds there was silence in the control room, as people realised that the crew on board the *Belgrano* was over 1000 people, and it was very cold water, and they were a long way away from land … so it was very sobering after the initial euphoria of doing the job properly.'[10]

Rudolfo Hendrix, a 22-year-old midshipman on the *Belgrano*, remembers the chaos aboard the sinking cruiser: 'There were masses of injured men. Most of them had been burnt and there were men covered in oil. There was loads and loads of smoke and it was very difficult to walk on the deck because of the listing of the ship. When I got to my life raft, I asked a sailor to come with me again, and look for the people that were missing, including the commander. It was very dangerous because the temperature of the walls was very high, and they were disintegrating. I can't say how long I stayed there – but it was about 5 minutes – and in that kind of situation, that's a lot. I didn't have any mask or breathing apparatus but I could just about breathe.'[11]

Nestor Sensi managed to make it to a lifeboat: 'I thought that I could feel love towards the ship. I felt as if it was a relative who was dying. Once the ship sank, I could hear terrible explosions. And that is what really affected me. It was a tremendous noise in the middle of the sea. It was probably the engines that were exploding....'[12]

Another *Belgrano* crewman, Oscar Fornez, was in his liferaft in 30-foot (10-metre) waves: 'There were actually 16 of us in the life raft and we had to try and get away from the ship as quickly as possible. Otherwise, when the ship started sinking it would probably have taken us with it. And the wind was pushing us towards the ship. But suddenly – I don't know why – if it was a change in the wind or destiny itself, but a huge wave came towards us and took us in the opposite direction....'[13]

The subsequent controversy over the sinking of the *Belgrano* was heightened by British government ministers contradicting themselves about the cruiser's course and the threat she represented.[14] But, setting aside the war of words that was to follow, the effect of the sinking of the *Belgrano* was a victory for the Royal Navy. The rest of the Argentine fleet, including the carrier whose aircraft could have been lethal if the wind had allowed them to take off, returned home. It had been the first significant shedding of blood in the conflict. No one could now doubt that Britain and Argentina were at war.

Peter Walpole was an officer on the destroyer HMS *Sheffield*: 'I do remember … on reading the signal that said the *Belgrano* had been attacked and sunk … I do remember feeling a certain doom because to me it signalled the start of a major shooting war … to sink a major battle ship or a cruiser like the *Belgrano*, meant to all of us that the shooting was really under way for the big ships and that meant us….'[15]

Harriers from *Hermes* and *Invincible* were now strafing and bombing Argentine positions ashore. When they attacked the airport at the capital, Stanley, they faced Argentine surface-to-air missiles – as one British pilot was to learn to his cost in an attack in early June. Flight Lieutenant Ian Mortimore, flying his Harrier from *Invincible*, was sure he was well out of the way of the missile defences. But then: 'The first thing I saw was a tremendous flash. It was just as though somebody had shone a mirror, a huge mirror, into my eyes. There was nothing for a couple of seconds and then I picked up the missile…. There was an almighty explosion: the aircraft went head over heels and, being a bright lad, I guessed what had happened. It was a phenomenally violent explosion which really surprised me. It took the tailplane off. I was being thrown around a lot and I couldn't see anything…. I ejected immediately – just about as fast as I could.'[16] Mortimore parachuted into the sea and was in his dinghy for nine hours before being picked up by a British helicopter. Another Harrier pilot, Flight Lieutenant Jeff Glover, was tasked to take reconnaissance photos around Port Howard in West Falkland. 'Just as I was about to take pictures there were three loud bangs and the aircraft went out of control. It rolled very rapidly to the right, almost through 360 degrees…. I pulled the ejection seat handle. I heard the bang of the canopy exploding above my head, which is the normal way of ejecting…. I remember being upside down seeing the sea very close.'[17] At this stage, Glover appears to have lost consciousness, and he came to a little later under the water. He did not swim far before he saw a boatload of armed Argentines rowing towards him, and spent the rest of the short war in captivity.

But in the first air-to-air engagement of the war, on 1 May, Harriers proved their agility and the quality of their American-made

Sidewinder missiles by shooting down two Mirages and one Argentine Canberra.[18] Mrs Thatcher was later to write 'Without the Harriers ... using the latest version of the Sidewinder air-to-air missile supplied by Caspar Weinberger, we could not have retaken the Falklands.'[19]

THE ATTACK ON HMS *SHEFFIELD*

It was not until 4 May that the Argentine air force showed what it was capable of. At 8.45 a.m. two Super Etendard aircraft carrying Exocet missiles took off from Rio Grande in southern Argentina, and then refuelled in mid-air to give themselves maximum range. At 11 a.m. they briefly exposed themselves to British radar by climbing high enough to identify two British warships as targets, lock their Exocet missiles' radar on to them, launch the missiles and then turn and dash for home. HMS *Glasgow* detected the aircrafts' radar scanning their ship and loosed off a shower of chaff – a great cloud of small shavings to attract the missiles' attention and confuse the missiles' radar. Then *Glasgow* radioed a quick warning to the rest of the fleet. But the crew of the destroyer *Sheffield* was not so alert. The anti-air warfare officer was out of his seat taking a coffee break, and the radio operators failed to pick up any warning. *Sheffield*'s crew made no attempt to attack the aircraft with Sea Dart missiles and loosed off no chaff; they were not even called to Action Stations. The first they knew of their fate was when a crewman spotted an Exocet skimming straight at the ship a few seconds before impact.[20]

Peter Walpole was the signals communications officer on *Sheffield*'s bridge as the Exocet approached: 'It appeared to be stationary or suspended in air, but smoke or what seemed like smoke was coming from behind it: so the impression was of one of those speeded up films of a flower blossoming. The smoke was just billowing from behind and making it grow in appearance; it didn't seem to be moving anywhere ... and eventually we realised ... it was coming towards us and that it was a missile but that realization came very late. The *Sunday Times* quoted me as saying, "My God it's a missile" but I think I probably said, "What the fuck is that?"'

Remarkably, the warhead did not explode, but the half-ton (500-kg) missile was travelling at 700 miles an hour (1100 kph) and its impact took it right through the centre of the ship, as Walpole recalls vividly: 'It was a bit like your worst car accident but ten times worse in the sense of noise and pressure wave and the sound of the explosion. The sound was terrific and also the sense that just prior, a second prior, to the impact there was a perfect working ship and a second after it was irrevocably changed and immediately afterwards anything that was loose on the bridge was scattered in all directions. A tremendous amount of dust came out of the ventilation, and the place was instantly showered in paint fragments and dust.... So there we were with this tremendous noise and then afterwards the sound of alarm bells ringing....'[21]

Within seconds, there was a scene of horror at the spot where the missile's fuel caught fire. Many trapped in the galley died almost at once; the fire quickly consumed soft furnishings and the ship's insulation, giving out a great pall of noxious black smoke. Crewmen in the computer room sat at their posts until they were overcome by the fumes. The fire spread rapidly. *Sheffield*'s water main was punctured, which made fire-fighting even more difficult. After an hour, the destroyer's captain, Sam Salt, gave the order to abandon ship. The navy kept her afloat for another six days, but she finally sank on 10 May; 20 of her crew died and 24 were wounded.

The loss of *Sheffield* was a severe shock to the British. The first few days of the war had gone well for them: they had sunk a major warship, and were actively attacking land targets on the Falklands. The initiative was with Woodward and his task force. But now suddenly the Argentines had hit back. Two dedicated pilots armed with ultra-modern technology had demonstrated that it was not just the British who were able to operate in extreme conditions: the Argentine air force, unable to use the short runway at Stanley for its major strike aircraft, had shown that it could meet the challenge of operating at the very limit of its range from land bases in Argentina.

For the first time in recent history, the Royal Navy was operating without being able to detect any approaching air threat beyond the horizon – its last airborne early warning aircraft had departed with the scrapping of the carrier *Ark Royal* just four years before the Falklands War. The only good news for the British was the knowledge gained from the French that the Argentines had bought only five fully operational air-to-surface Exocets – the AM39s. That left them with three.

The struggle for air superiority now became the dominant concern not just of Woodward and his ships' captains, but of Julian Thompson as well. The landing force commander was insistent that he would not disembark his 3rd commando brigade unless Woodward could promise him control of the air. And in spite of the fact that Woodward now posted his anti-aircraft warships in pairs – type 42s with their longer-range Sea Dart missiles, and type 22s with their Sea Wolf close-range missiles – Thompson had serious doubts about their capacity to keep enemy strike aircraft away from his chosen landing zone on the Falklands. He had his doubts, too, about the Rapier anti-aircraft missile system which would be deployed in the hills around the landing beaches. It was unproven in the heat of battle, and Thompson knew the huge risks of landing troops without complete control of the air. He was right to be concerned, but ironically it was the navy and not his marines and paratroopers who would suffer most from being exposed to air attack.

On the advice of experts like Ewen Southby-Tailyour and others, Thompson and the amphibious force commander, Commodore Michael Clapp, had selected San Carlos Bay in the north-western tip of East Falkland as their landing spot. It was a deep-water inlet, virtually undefended by the Argentines, and surrounded by hills that could provide some protection against low-flying aircraft. The drawback was that San Carlos was some 50 miles (80 km) from Stanley: in between lay a great empty waste of difficult country. And Thompson knew that the real battle for the Falklands would have to be fought in the well-defended hills just to the west of the capital. He would have to rely on a shipment of heavy-lift helicopters for

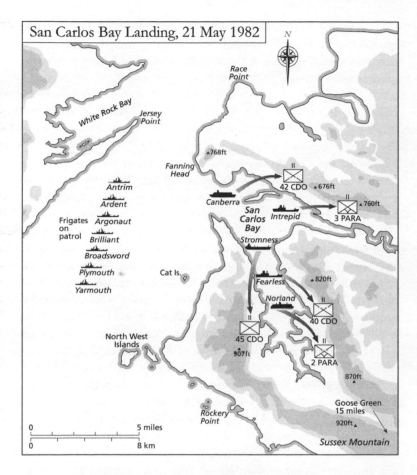

San Carlos Bay Landing, 21 May 1982

N

Race
Point

White Rock Bay

Jersey
Point

▲768ft

Fanning
Head

42 CDO
▲676ft

Antrim

Canberra

San
Carlos
Bay

Intrepid

▲760ft

3 PARA

Ardent

Frigates   Argonaut
on
patrol   Brilliant

Stromness

Broadsword

Plymouth

Cat Is.

▲820ft

Yarmouth

Fearless

Norland

40 CDO

North West
Islands

45 CDO

2 PARA

907ft

870ft

Rockery
Point

Goose Green
15 miles
920ft ▲

0   5 miles

0   8 km

Sussex Mountain

the transport of his troops from one side of the island to the other. He also knew that he would have to set aside his objections to landing his men without full control of the air. Time was too short and the amphibious force was now bouncing around in the choppy waters off the Falklands ready to land. There was a last-minute discussion between Thompson and Clapp about the best time for the landing. Thompson was concerned about the 'vulnerability' of the landing force. 'I wanted to land at last light, so that we would have darkness afterwards when the Argentine air force would be likely to attack. Clapp wanted to land at first light, so that the whole approach would be in darkness. We ended up splitting the difference and agreed to land in the middle of the night, which lasted a good long 14 hours.'[22]

'BOMB ALLEY'

And so it was that on the night of 21 May the British put into effect one of the most ambitious amphibious landing operations since D-Day in 1944. In numbers it was not remotely comparable, but the risks were high. An Argentine outpost on the Fanning Head at the entrance to San Carlos Bay was suppressed by a Special Boat Squadron raiding party, and under cover of darkness the big amphibious ships *Fearless* and *Intrepid* anchored off the bay in Falkland Sound. They ferried their troops into the bay in landing craft to secure the beaches, and then they and a whole flotilla of ships steamed into San Carlos Bay itself to begin the long process of unloading stores. Not everything had gone quite as planned. According to Commodore Clapp, 'We had found a Satellite Navigation system to help *Fearless* guide the amphibious force, but the thing couldn't take zig-zagging into account, and since we were zig-zagging to confuse any enemy submarines, we were unsure of our position, and arrived later than we intended.'[23] But the landings were largely unopposed, and as the night wore on the liner *Canberra* and the other ferries and supply ships pursued their unloading operation without let-up. And as sunrise came and went on that first day, the British began to hope that they might escape without aerial bombardment; but the Fuerza Aerea Argentina was not long in spotting its most inviting target yet.

From 10.30 a.m., some 26 Argentine aircraft managed to make low-level attacks on the British flotilla in and around San Carlos. Ten of them were destroyed, nine by Sea Harriers on patrol; but the planes dealt destruction on a nerve-racking scale. Four British warships were hit, but escaped with minor damage because the bombs were dropped from such a low level that they failed to fuse properly before they hit their targets. HMS *Ardent* was less lucky. At just before 2 p.m., two waves of Argentine Skyhawks delivered no fewer than seven bombs on to the frigate. One of the frigate's chief petty officers, Ken Enticknab, found himself lying on the floor of the dining hall.

'I had a quick look round and could see that my hand was injured. I had my anti-flash glove on and I could see just see a mess, a mass of blood. There was no pain, no pain at all. I thought: well, they can sew fingers back on these days, there's no problem…. I was unable to crawl out from whatever it was that was stopping me moving…. I could hear somebody moving around in the debris and he came up to me and said "You alright, mate?" I said, "Okay. Get this thing off my back." He was able to move it out of the way … we tried to stumble forward … we were gasping for breath and starting to choke…. I can remember what I was thinking. At that time my wife was five months pregnant with our first child and I wanted to get home.' In the end, the two men struggled out on deck and Enticknab jumped overboard and was rescued from the sea.[24]

Ardent's captain, Alan West, who in 2002 would become First Sea Lord, vividly remembers the chaotic scene on board as alarms sounded everywhere and his men fought desperately to keep the fires in the ship under control. 'I didn't need the alarms to tell me something was wrong,' he said. 'I'd just seen my Sea Cat missile launcher blasted 50 feet into the air: I knew there was something wrong all right.'

He also recalls how he struggled to look imperturbable so as to reassure those around him. He was the last to leave his ship before she sank 24 hours later with the loss of 22 lives.[25]

Under this terrifying bombardment, the unloading operation went on at full speed. By the end of the day, 3000 men and 1000 tons of stores had been disembarked. Admiral Woodward signalled home: 'It would be easy to lose my cool. But we always knew and accepted that it would be more expensive to take on the Argentine air force after the landing.' The landing force commanders complained about the inadequacy of the Rapier anti-aircraft missile system, which failed to do its job effectively. To Commodore Clapp,

'Rapier was no good up on the hilltops. If it had been sited on the shoreline looking up, it might have done better – it might have seen the planes better. But they came in so low their approach was difficult to spot.'[26]

For four more days the raids continued. One after another, British ships were hit and damaged by Argentine bombs. Time and again, the damage was limited by the failure of the bombs to detonate. But even the British expressed their admiration for the courage of the Argentine pilots who would fly their planes up and over the hills and then down to attack ships almost at deck height. The ships fired back with everything they had. Many had machine guns strapped to the rails, and men would grab them and swing them around each time they spotted an approaching aircraft. In the full five days, 17 British ships were hit; four sank, including *Ardent*. On 23 May HMS *Antelope* was struck by a bomb dropped by a plane which flew low over the ship and collided with its mainmast. The bomb failed to explode. But it did detonate when a pair of demolition experts attempted to defuse it inside the ship: *Antelope*'s captain, Commander Nick Tobin, said the two experts had been confident they could do the job, but after several efforts the bomb detonated and caused uncontrollable fires. 'There was only a millimetre in it either way when the bomb was being defused,' Tobin said. *Antelope* was soon consumed by fire, and sank in the centre of San Carlos Bay.

On 25 May HMS *Coventry* was the next ship to be destroyed. She was on anti-aircraft duty, accompanied this time by a Type 22 frigate which had the added protection of the Sea Wolf missile system to intercept aircraft and missiles on their final approach. *Coventry* herself successfully despatched two attacking Skyhawks with her medium-range Sea Dart missiles, but more aircraft came in and *Coventry* veered hard to port to try to avoid them – putting herself for a vital moment between the attacking aircraft and the frigate *Broadsword*, which was thus unable to fire the very Sea Wolf missiles which could have foiled the attack. Nineteen men were killed before *Coventry* sank. A crewman on board one of the Royal Fleet Auxiliary ships reported: 'We took most of the survivors on board that night

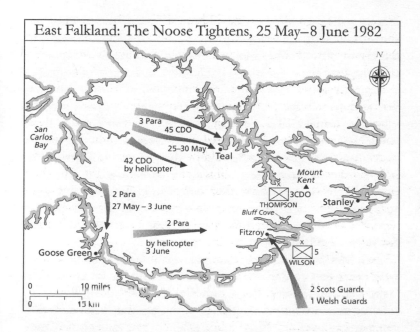

East Falkland: The Noose Tightens, 25 May–8 June 1982

and then got out of San Carlos water – forever I hope! Taking survivors on is a sickeningly sad business and I hope I never have to do it again, the burns, and the shock and the tears when they find that a chum didn't make it – war is horrible. The survivors bounced back remarkably quickly though but I'll bet that many are scarred mentally for life after their experience that evening.'[27]

That same day came one of the most costly attacks of all for the British. Two Super Etendards with Argentina's third and fourth air-launched Exocet missiles (the fifth and final one would be launched fruitlessly on 30 May) did a wide circle round to the north-west of the task force, approached the position where they supposed the carriers to be and loosed off their Exocets at two or three significant blips on their radars. The frigate *Ambuscade*, which was actually quite near the carrier *Hermes*, rapidly issued a warning and dispensed chaff which successfully confused the missiles. But one of the two missiles then veered left and picked up another target. It was a large one, but it was not a carrier: it was the defenceless container ship *Atlantic Conveyor*. The missile slammed into her hull and rapidly set fire to fuel supplies for vehicles that the ship was waiting to offload. The fires spread rapidly, and only 90 minutes after the Exocet hit her, the captain, Ian North, gave the order to abandon ship. Twelve men died, including North himself, who was the last to leave his ship: once in the water, he failed to find space in a liferaft. The material cost of the loss of *Atlantic Conveyor* was great, too, for she was bringing the shipment of troop-carrying helicopters that Julian Thompson had been depending on to lift his men forward towards Stanley. The navy had already managed to fly off its precious batch of reinforcement Harriers and one of the heavy-lift Chinook helicopters, but three more Chinooks and six Wessex Mark V helicopters plus a huge tented camp for 10,000 men went down with the ship.

Even Mrs Thatcher admits she had her moment of doubt during those nerve-racking days for the Royal Navy and the British government. On a visit to fleet headquarters at Northwood 'I did my best to seem confident, but when I left with Admiral Fieldhouse [the Commander in Chief, Fleet] and we were out of earshot of anyone else, I could not help asking him: "How long can we go on taking this kind of punishment?" He was no less worried.'[28]

But the five days of air attack had cost the Argentines dear too. By 25 May, they had lost around 30 aircraft, nearly half of their crack front-line force of fighter bombers, and – just as importantly – a large number of their best pilots. From now on, there was a noticeable drop in Argentine air assaults. The British had not won air superiority, but they – and a merciful bout of poorer weather – had succeeded in blunting the effectiveness of their enemy's airpower.

British commanders now found themselves enveloped in an increasingly bitter row about strategy. The chain of command stretched from Margaret Thatcher and her war cabinet through Lord Lewin, the Chief of the Defence Staff, and his service chiefs to Admiral Woodward and Brigadier Thompson in the South Atlantic. The chiefs were coming under pressure from Mrs Thatcher to pursue the campaign with urgency, which led to an open row between London and the operational commanders. The man in the front line, Brigadier Thompson, fought his corner hard.[29] He judged that he still did not have enough troops and helicopters on shore to fight the decisive battles in the mountains just west of Stanley where the Argentines had dug in the bulk of their troops, and argued that he should await the arrival of the second brigade, which was still travelling out on the liner *QE2*. To his superiors in London this strategy was over-cautious and unacceptable. By 26 May, top naval commanders in London were so exasperated that they signalled Woodward and ordered him to go ashore and 'shout at' Thompson until he moved his men out of the beachhead at San Carlos. Woodward did not need to; Thompson got the message. 'They were impatient in London, and I didn't help by telling them to stop being impatient. I was pretty pissed off but I was told to get on with it. After *Atlantic Conveyor* my plan was in tatters and I had to start again.'[30] Without helicopters, he had no option but to order his men forward on foot. Two of his units, 45 Commando Royal Marines and the 3rd Battalion, The Parachute Regiment, '3 Para', set out on the 50-mile (80-km) hike towards Stanley. He also ordered '2 Para' to attack and capture the town of Goose Green, less than 20 miles (some 30 km) away to the south.

THE BATTLE OF GOOSE GREEN

Goose Green was the largest settlement of islanders outside Stanley. There were over 100 people – mainly farmers, now augmented by some refugees from Stanley – living there, and the Argentines were reported to have sent fewer than 500 troops there. It looked like the obvious spot to go for an early victory that might placate London and boost the morale of the task force. 'I regarded Goose Green as a diversion from the task I really had, which was to head east for Stanley,' said Thompson. 'We were advancing in two directions and I thought that was a mistake, but I wasn't bitter about it: in the event it actually achieved rather a lot.'[31] But Goose Green was no

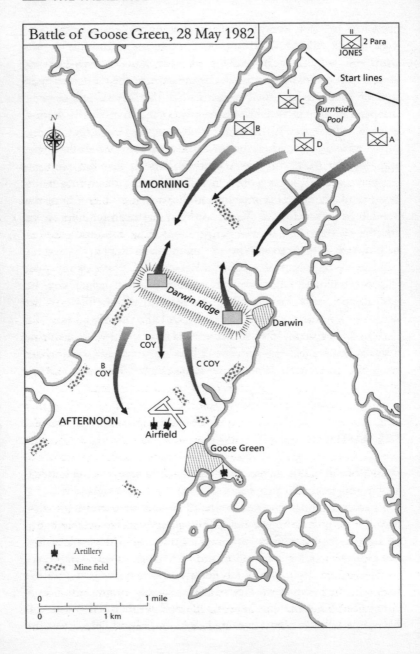

Battle of Goose Green, 28 May 1982

easy target: the settlement was on an isthmus only a mile (1.6 km) wide and 5 miles (8 km) long, with water on either side. A mile north of Goose Green was a ridge called Darwin Hill, on which the Argentines decided to make a stand. On 27 May Lieutenant Colonel H Jones led his men south from the San Carlos area and was appalled to hear a BBC radio broadcast indicating that he was heading for Darwin. He blamed the Ministry of Defence for leaking it, but remained confident that his battalion of Red Berets would be more than a match for the Argentines, even if they did reinforce their garrison. His orders contained the line, 'All previous evidence suggests that if the enemy is hit hard he will crumble.' There was actually little 'previous evidence' of this, but Jones no doubt hoped that a few hours of night-fighting, at which the paras excelled, would clear the Argentines out of Goose Green.

Jones sent his four companies off southwards at 10 p.m. on the 27th. One of his men, Paul Farrar, recalls the moment they plunged into the night. 'It is a distinct psychological jump as you cross the startline ... until you cross the startline you're somehow safe and sheltered from reality but the minute you're across it and advancing towards the enemy, then all of a sudden things come into very sharp focus and thereafter the training and indeed the leadership and the ability to proceed with the mission as stated takes over.'[32]

A Company followed the east side of the isthmus, C Company made for the centre, while D and B Companies took the west side. Most of the battalion met more resistance than they had expected, and by dawn A Company was severely pinned down by heavy fire from Darwin Ridge. Sergeant Major Barry Norman witnessed the fierce struggle for the ridge.

'Before you go in you put in a hand grenade or something to dis-organise the people in the trench and then, just like on television, you get in, bayonets fixed, automatic fire, to kill the people in the trench. If he hasn't got a weapon and he has got his hands in the air, we say he is giving up. If he has got a weapon and he hasn't got his hands in the air then we take it he's not going to give up and we shoot him. The fine line between life and death is either you kill him or he kills you. Once you are in a hand to hand fight, unless he is stood there with his hands in the air, you have got to assume he is about to kill you and do the necessary. And in that case it's kill him.'[33]

While this battle was going on, Jones, impatient that the battalion was still well short of its overnight objective, moved up to see what he could do himself. He was an unarguably brave but headstrong commander, who believed that there were times when a commanding officer should lead from the front. After watching A Company try in vain to break the resistance on the ridge, he then signalled to some of his staff to follow him, then moved off round to the right where a gully appeared to offer a way of creeping up on the enemy. But the gully had two sides to it, and there were Argentine trenches on both. So when Jones suddenly charged up its left-hand slope in an attempt to storm the defenders there, he came under fire from a dugout on the other side of the gully. The Argentine corporal in that trench, Osvaldo Olmos, remembers seeing Jones charge past him alone, leaving his followers in the gully below. Olmos said he was astonished at Jones's reckless bravery: his shots, fired from behind, may have been the ones that brought Jones down. Jones was posthumously awarded the Victoria Cross.

Barry Norman was just behind Jones when the CO charged off: 'I shouted at him to watch his back because I could see what was going to happen. He ignored me, or didn't hear me – I would think he actually ignored me – and charged up the hill…. You could see the rounds striking the ground behind him, coming up gradually towards him, and they shot him in the back…. He died. I felt slightly numb because COs are not supposed to die. The implication of the commanding officer taking on an enemy position from the front was comic book stuff you read about, and you don't think it should happen. My own opinion is that he shouldn't have been there, but being "H" Jones he was always going to be there because he was that type of CO.'[34]

Major Chris Keeble took over command and ordered his company commanders to put down a heavy concentration of fire in order to try to break Argentine resistance. A Company's commander also aimed anti-armour rockets at the Argentine trenches and successfully took most of them out that way. It was 11.30 a.m. when Darwin Ridge was finally cleared, but it had cost the lives of six people including the CO. The fighting was hard all along the line. C Company lost its commander as it pressed towards Goose Green. The two companies on the right, B and D, had to endure strafing by Argentine Pucara aircraft as they fought to fold back the western flank. The paratoopers' spirits rose in mid-afternoon when Harriers dropped cluster bombs on the Argentine positions. But by evening, Goose Green was still holding out against the British attack. Moreover, the civilian inhabitants of the place were now in great danger. Since British aircraft began attacking four weeks earlier, 115 of them had been cooped up by the Argentines in the local village hall. Some had been allowed back to their houses, but there were still around 80 in the hall. A battle for the settlement itself would seriously endanger their lives.

Keeble's men were exhausted, his timetable in shreds: a day and a night had not been time enough to win the battle. A cunning ploy now occurred to him which might get the Argentines to surrender. He wrote a letter to the commander, saying that they were now surrounded by the best unit in the British army. Keeble said his men were ready to fight on and would bring down a heavy bombardment on Goose Green; they would hold the Argentines responsible for any civilian loss of life unless they surrendered. Amazingly, the following morning the Argentines agreed to do just that.

It was an impudent gamble that worked miraculously: the paras were astonished to see no fewer than 1000 Argentines surrendering. The British attackers had been outnumbered by around three to one and it had been a costly battle. At least 55 Argentinians were killed, while the British lost 17 men and 36 were wounded. But the boost to British morale among the task force and at home was great. The commander of the other parachute regiment, Lieutenant Colonel Hew Pike, said, 'Goose Green was a moral turning point. Before it we understood we had to win: after it we knew we would.' Julian Thompson takes much of the blame for the high loss of life: 'I didn't give H Jones enough assets: I should have given him the light armoured vehicles. I was concerned they might have got bogged down and been a target for Argentinian attack. But actually they could have got there. I was wrong.'[35]

In the meantime, Thompson had been busy reaching forward with his main land forces towards Stanley. It was a daunting task. On 28 May an islander at Teal Inlet, around halfway between San Carlos and Stanley, saw some soldiers approaching and greeted them in Spanish; a moment later he was chatting delightedly in English to soldiers of '3 Para'. Three days later, 45 Commando Royal Marines arrived at Teal. The conditions were dreadful, with driving wind and snow squalls; the men's boots sank deep into the mud and some started to split open. Many marines ran out of fresh water and drank brackish stuff from the pools; they developed diarrhoea. 3 Para had one night in the freezing cold without sleeping bags. Their colleagues in 42 Commando were luckier: when the SAS discovered that Mount Kent – only 15 miles (24 km) from Stanley – was unoccupied, the whole of 42 was lifted forward with the available helicopters. After their victory at Goose Green, 2 Para were even luckier. A chance telephone call by one of the battalion's majors to the islander who managed Fitzroy settlement, 20 miles (32 km) south-west of Stanley, revealed that there were no Argentine troops there. The task force's only Chinook helicopter was deployed to ferry the whole battalion forward. Thompson now had his main fighting force on the western approaches to the mountain strongholds from which the Argentines hoped to protect Stanley.

Over the next few days, three other commanders arrived to help Thompson carry the load. Brigadier Tony Wilson was commanding 5 Brigade, whose troops were in San Carlos by the beginning of June; Major General Jeremy Moore would be in overall command of the land forces; and finally there was 'H' Jones's replacement as CO of 2 Para, Lieutenant Colonel David Chaundler, who dropped in – appropriately – by parachute. He had had to endure a flight of more than 12 hours by Hercules from Ascension, and when his flight safety officer pronounced on arrival over the Falklands that the weather, light and wind made a drop risky, Chaundler replied that he had not come all this way to take over command only to turn back home. He promptly jumped, and spent 20 freezing minutes in the water before being picked up.

Before the battle for Stanley could begin, 5 Brigade had to be brought forward. And in their haste to achieve this end, British commanders made a blunder that was to lead to the single biggest British loss of life in the whole war. It was decided that the three battalions of 5 Brigade would be ferried forward under cover of darkness to an area 20 miles (32 km) south-west of Stanley where they could land within a short march of the likely battlefield. Some were ferried in by landing craft to Bluff Cove, a shallow lagoon nearest to Stanley; others were taken to the deep-water harbour at Fitzroy. Among those destined for Fitzroy were the Welsh Guards: they were embarked on the landing ship *Sir Galahad*, and the plan was that they would leave San Carlos early enough on the night of 7–8 June to arrive at Fitzroy and disembark under cover of darkness. In the event, there were delays in their departure, but instead of postponing their trip till the next night it was decided to take the risk of them arriving in daylight. *Sir Galahad*, accompanied by *Sir Tristram*, did not arrive in Fitzroy until 7.30 a.m. Instead of disembarking immediately, the Welsh Guards were ordered to stay aboard until they could be ferried by smaller craft to Bluff Cove, which would save them several miles of marching. For several hours of daylight, the two ships sat within the view of Argentine troops on the mountains west of Stanley. It was only a matter of time before the Argentine air force was alerted. The commander of 42 Commando, Lieutenant Colonel Vaux, and his signaller, John Adams, were on one of those mountains that morning and Adams remembers Vaux remarking how foolish it was to have berthed two large ships so conspicuously at Fitzroy in full daylight.[36] Vaux said, 'We knew only too well how terrible the air threat could be: there was great consternation that two ships were unloading in full daylight.'[37] Ewen Southby-Tailyour, the Falklands anchorage expert, happened to be at Fitzroy and several times urged the British to empty the ships as quickly as possible. But they didn't. Around noon, with the horrified Vaux still watching from the hills, no fewer than eight Argentinian Skyhawks attacked.

Vaux later described how he'd watched, 'helpless with horror', as the Skyhawks rose upwards, 'and then swooped down upon the unsuspecting ships. A myriad of malevolent flashes preceded the great booming explosions…. *Sir Galahad* erupted in flames and billowing smoke.'[38]

Both ships were hit, but *Sir Galahad* was loaded with fuel and ammunition and quickly caught fire. Great sheets of flame and clouds of black smoke made rescue almost impossible. Small boats and helicopters managed to save most of the men aboard, but 49 died and another 150 were wounded, some with severe burns which would be with them all their lives.

Major Davies was a paratroop officer who watched the wounded being unloaded from the helicopters: 'It was only after a couple of loads that the enormity of the tragedy began to dawn on me…. I lost count of the men we took from the helicopters to the medical centre, which rapidly filled to overflowing. We had to take screaming, bleeding, badly burned men off stretchers and put them on the floor to free more stretchers for yet more wounded. The sight, sounds and smell of burning flesh were horrific. Thankfully the brain can delay the realisation of such horror and we ran with our smouldering loads, doused them with water and fitted intravenous drips with a vague oblivion.'[39] One of the Welsh Guards' platoon commanders, Crispin Black, witnessed the full horror of his own men being crippled in front of his eyes: 'It was the first time I'd seen people without arms and legs….'[40]

According to Commodore Clapp, the amphibious force commander, who had reluctantly agreed to take the risk of allowing the ships to move the troops to Fitzroy: 'Two of my staff and one of General Moore's aides were telling them to get off the ship. But they didn't and there was a tragedy. It seems the Welsh Guards had been told that they'd be transported to Bluff Cove [a point closer to their objective] and they decided to wait for that, but I would never have allowed the ships to take them there: they should have disembarked without delay at Fitzroy.'[41] But Crispin Black said later he 'always resented people who suggested that we didn't get off because we wanted the ship to take us somewhere else to avoid having to march an extra distance. That isn't true.... We thought we were safe in the bay.'[42]

On 21 June *Sir Galahad* was taken out to sea and sunk as a war grave.

The battle for Stanley was now about to begin. General Menendez had gambled all on entrenching his men in the small cluster of hills that lay between Stanley and Mount Kent, which the British had found unoccupied. The fighting was to be at night, an environment in which the highly trained paratroopers and marines excelled. To a raw recruit, fighting in the dark was frightening enough, but the advantage that surprise brought to the attacker at night made the task of the defender far more difficult. Even with night goggles and night sights, with which some forces on both sides were equipped, it was hard for the defenders to spot an attacking force stealing towards them. Some of the Argentines were tough, experienced marines and Special Forces who had been trained to fight at night were used to extremes of climate. But most were young conscripts, unused to the Falklands winter, largely untrained, struggling to survive in the trenches in deep discomfort and on poor rations. Michael Savage was a 19-year-old Argentine conscript on Mount Longdon. He had hardly been trained to use a rifle, and knew nothing of infantry tactics. He was fed just one meal a day. He went to the Falklands weighing about 130 lb (60 kg) and returned weighing under 90 lb (40 kg). He reckoned he was lucky to have survived the war.[43]

THE STRUGGLE FOR THE MOUNTAINS

Moore and his two brigade commanders, Thompson and Wilson, now put into effect a two-phase offensive for which Thompson had already submitted a battle plan. On the first night three of Thompson's battalions, 3 Para, 45 Commando Royal Marines and 42 Commando, would attack Mount Longdon, Two Sisters Mountain and Mount Harriet. If that first attack was successful they would launch 2 Para, together with troops from Wilson's 5 Brigade, onto the next group of hills – Wireless Ridge, Mount Tumbledown and Mount William. To reduce Argentine resistance, gunfire would be called in from the Royal Artillery's 105mm light guns behind Mount Kent and from naval warships offshore.

The costliest of the three battles that first night was 3 Para's attack on Mount Longdon, where the Argentines had stationed some of their marines. Its summit, like the others, was a daunting set of crags like great rocky teeth one behind the other. Each of these mountains was a formidable challenge for an assault force. The commander of 3 Para, Lieutenant Colonel Hew Pike, used rugby terms to set his men their objectives. Free Kick was the start line; the first two summits were named Wing Forward and Fly Half; and the final, eastern summit was Full Back. Pike planned to approach Longdon in complete silence, without an artillery barrage, and stage a surprise assault on it from the west and the north.

One soldier, Private Connery, was appalled at the orders his platoon was given to advance strung out in an extended line to avoid more than one person at a time being hurt in the Argentine minefield. 'I couldn't help thinking some bastard was on drugs and that they had turned back the clock and we should be lined up in red tunics.'[44] All went well until a corporal, Brian Milne, stood on a mine. It blew off his foot and the battalion's cover was broken. From then on it was a very hard-fought battle, with the paras clawing their way forward trench by trench.

An Argentine, Corporal Carrizo, said he had barely been able to rouse his sleeping men when the paras came at them: 'Everyone was in a panic. I ran for cover and crawled into a bunker with a Sergeant. Outside, the English were running past, screaming to each other and firing into tents and bunkers. I could hear my men being killed. They had only just woken up and were now dying. I could hear muffled explosions followed by cries, helpless cries.'[45]

There were acts of bravery on both sides. One of the most conspicuous on the British side followed hard on the moment when Sergeant Ian McKay was told by his platoon commander, who had just been shot in the leg, that he was now in command. His platoon was being held up by a single heavy machine-gun position, surrounded by rocks and defended by a group of Argentine riflemen as well. McKay gathered together a group of men and assaulted the position. Three men fell beside him, but MacKay charged on and destroyed the Argentines with grenades. But then at the last moment he himself was shot dead. He was posthumously awarded the VC.

A sergeant with 3 Para, Graham Colbeck, remembers how daylight revealed what he called 'the full savagery of the night's work. It was as though we walked through the chamber of horrors in a waxworks: here a grinning face on a pile of scorched flesh and clothing, and there a corpse with half a head…. We occupied enemy sangars and began to brew tea and eat chocolate as if breakfast surrounded by corpses was something we did every day.' The paras also took a large number of prisoners: 'The pathetic line of demoralised and bewildered boys were conscripts of the 7th Infantry Regiment sent to fight for an emotive cause which they had come to realise was not worth their lives. After searching the prisoners we gave them water and allowed them to clutch their rosary beads before they were taken away to join those captured during the night.'[46]

The battle for Longdon went on for ten hours. Even when they had captured the whole mountain, the paras then had to endure hours of shelling from the Argentines, who turned their artillery on their own positions. Twenty-three paras died in the attack on Longdon. Colbeck stopped by one dead paratrooper. 'The waterproof jacket which had covered his face had been blown aside and was flapping in the wind, and I paused to replace it.' It was the highest British death toll of any single land battle in the war. But they counted at least 50 Argentine dead.

The other two mountains that first night were attacked by Royal Marines. The first, Two Sisters, fell to 45 Commando, which suffered four killed and ten wounded. The second, Mount Harriet, was a classic example of a well-prepared and professionally executed night attack. Lieutenant Colonel Nick Vaux had spent the best part of the previous ten days patrolling the approaches to Mount Harriet, which stood at a strategic position dominating any approach to Stanley from the south-west. Each night several patrols went out to identify Argentine positions, map out minefields and, most importantly, choose an approach for the final assault that would catch the Argentines unawares. Artillery barrages were brought down on Harriet at varying times throughout those ten days, so that by the night of 11–12 June the Argentines had no reason to connect the final barrage with an assault. The Argentine minefields stretched around the approaches to Harriet from the west and south, but its south-east slopes were wide open. It was clear that any attack was expected from the west or south-west. Vaux ordered his men to reconnoitre an approach from the south-east of Harriet, the last thing the Argentines would expect. 'Once we found the end of their minefield, we could be sure that we had extra security and the further we went behind them the more disconcerting it would be for them when we attacked.'[47]

As darkness fell on the night of the attack on Two Sisters and Longdon, two of Vaux's companies, K and L, began a long march. They made a wide detour along a carefully prepared route around the south of Harriet and reached their start line way off to the south-east of the mountain. Vaux's other company, J, made up of marines who had been part of the original Falklands garrison, brought down heavy fire on the western slopes of Harriet, as if to cover an assault there. The two assaulting companies then crept up from the south-east and took the Argentines by surprise – although they still had a tough fight capturing the full length of the rocky summit. Corporal Newland, one of K Company's section commanders, identified an enemy position in some giant rocks ahead that was pinning down the attack. He put a full magazine on his gun and charged the main position, throwing two grenades into the trench in front of him. But he hadn't killed all the Argentines: one survivor managed to raise his rifle and put a bullet through both of Newland's legs. 'That Argentine died rather quickly,' Newland reported after he had been lifted out to hospital. As Argentine resistance crumbled, the marines witnessed Argentine officers firing on their own men to prevent them from surrendering. The marines took out the officers where they could, but they also had to fire on the luckless Argentine troops who had to put away their white flags and pick up their rifles for fear of being shot by their own officers.

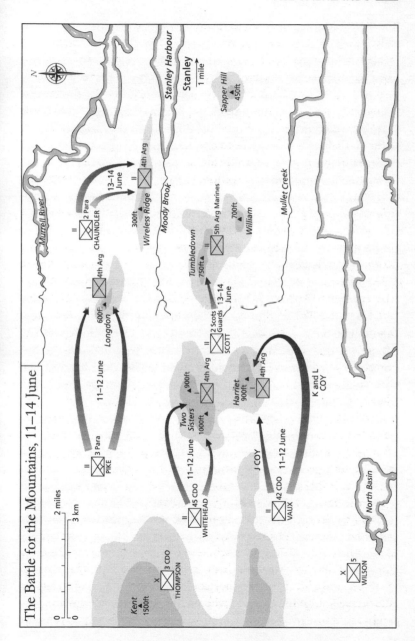

The Battle for the Mountains, 11–14 June

The Royal Marines succeeded in capturing Harriet with the loss of only 2 men; 26 were wounded.

Nick Vaux believes 'the Argentines were utterly unsuited to the form of warfare they had to fight. We of course took every advantage of this, but we could not help being very sorry for the enemy soldiers. They were quite appallingly led and trained.'[48] His own marines 'would never have lasted the three weeks they had to endure without shelter if they hadn't been well trained in survival skills. After the fighting it was found that 96 per cent of them had severe foot ailments, from frostbite to trench foot.'

Thompson reckoned that 'the attack on Mount Harriet was the most brilliant of all the attacks in the Falklands'.[49] British forces now had the first three mountains under their control: all that lay between them and Stanley now were three more hills, centred on Mount Tumbledown. Tumbledown was a substantial mountain: a long rocky ridge extended from west to east. It was defended by the best Argentine marines, fighting what they knew was their last-ditch stand before Stanley. The Scots Guards facing them had been on ceremonial duty at Buckingham Palace just eight weeks earlier. Moore ordered the Scots Guards to attack Tumbledown on the night of 13–14 June. They decided on an approach from the west that would allow them to fight their way along the ridge stronghold by stronghold.

Mike Scott, an officer with the Scots Guards, described the terrain and the conditions: 'I think one's got to remember, although it was June, that of course the seasons are reversed, and it was just on the edge of mid winter…. The great large tussocks of grass were difficult to walk over, and then you had these boulders, and rocks – the rock runs as they call them – which were rather like sort of rivers of rocks … very, very difficult to walk over. You had to look down and see where you were putting your feet each step…. Snow was coming horizontally at that stage; it was very difficult to see the chap practically standing next door to you.'[50]

The first assault up the western slope of Tumbledown was accomplished without difficulty by G Company. But then the momentum rapidly diminished as the Argentines targeted the platoons trying to fight their way along the ridge. The Argentines were well dug in and fought back fiercely, bringing sustained machine-gun and mortar fire down on the attackers.

Jim Mitchell of the Scots Guards recalls 'all hell' breaking loose:

'It was murder. We were coming under mortar fire, machine-gun fire, sniper fire. You name it, it was coming towards us. There's a saying, expect the unexpected. And that was unexpected. You cannot really describe it. Nobody could describe it if they've not been there. You could only hear the screams. People getting hurt. One of my section got hurt straightaway, as soon as we came under fire. But he didn't last that long. Oh, I was frightened but you just want to get on with it. It's more adrenalin than anything else….'[51]

For a time, the Scots Guards looked as if they might be hopelessly stalled. But then their 13 platoon had a lucky break. They had managed to climb up to the top of the ridge from the north side and found themselves looking down, undetected, on the main point of Argentine resistance. British artillery was now directed at the Argentine stronghold, and 13 platoon provided heavy covering fire as 14 and 15 platoons hacked their way through the Argentine positions. The Argentines fought back desperately, but the top of the ridge was slowly secured by the Scots. The battle had already lasted several hours, and it was not over yet. Another company was given the task of pressing the attack right to the end of the long Tumbledown ridge. Altogether it was 11 1/2 hours before Tumbledown was finally captured, and it left the Scots Guards with 7 dead and 43 wounded.

One Scots Guardsman who was on Tumbledown that night, Philip Williams, says the casualties' reactions varied depending on their cause. 'I can remember the different reactions from a casualty from the cold and the reaction of a gunshot victim seemed quite different. Well, the cold victim seemed to be more shocked and louder, and a lot more scared. And it seemed that the gunshot victims were very calm and very still, and not necessarily showing any fear. But very quiet.'[52]

The other attack that night – on Wireless Ridge to the north of Tumbledown and even nearer Stanley – was conducted by 2 Para, who had been flown east from Goose Green a few days earlier and were now commanded by Lieutenant Colonel David Chaundler. They were determined to try to avoid the high casualties they had suffered at Goose Green. An elaborate fire-support plan was laid down, and naval and artillery gunfire was brought down on the ridge before the attack went in. The paras were supported in their assault – which they mounted from the north side of the ridge – by two Scimitar armoured cars and two Scorpion light tanks of the Blues and Royals. Thompson corrected his earlier mistake and the Paras were supported by the armoured vehicles of the Blues and Royals. They proved a valuable additional source of firepower to the paras: by the end of the battle one Blues and Royals tank had fired off 17 boxes of 200 rounds each. The only significant hill between the British and Stanley now was Mount William, and the Gurkhas were tasked to clear it. But when they got there, they found the Argentine positions deserted. They had learned that the Gurkhas were on their way and decided not to fight.

One young, unnamed Argentine soldier wrote home after the battles in the hills west of Stanley: 'I fulfil the role of nurse and marksman. In my company there are many sick, with bronchitis, flu and fever, and the beginnings of frostbite.... I am tired, cold, unhappy; I swear that I can't take anymore, I can no longer see the time of departure and being back with you.

'I have a cave between the rocks, together with a soldier, who is called Toledo Ricardo, who is like bread from Heaven. My best friend here, where we share our sadness, necessities and fear. Don't call it cowardice, but a wish to live. Children, I am aware of the fact that this letter is sad and that it is going to worry you, but I want you to know how I am. Be strong, I will be with you soon like before.'[53]

SURRENDER

Argentine resistance suddenly melted away: with the Argentines now falling back into Stanley and its immediate surroundings, the road to the Falklands' capital was open. Max Hastings, reporting for the London *Evening Standard*, found himself enjoying a journalist's dream. He walked through no man's land along the road and into Stanley before the British moved up, and found the way clear. 'It was simply too good a chance to miss,' wrote Hastings, '... with a civilian anorak and a walking stick that I had been clutching since we landed at San Carlos I set off towards the town.' He walked past file after file of Argentine soldiers who 'looked utterly cowed, totally drained of hostility.... It was like liberating an English civilian golf club.'[54]

At 11 a.m. on the 14th the Argentines indicated they were ready to talk. Moore sent Menendez a message. 'I call on you as one military commander to another to lay down your arms now with honour to avoid more unnecessary bloodshed. This action will be understood by your countrymen and will not lessen the high regard in which the Argentine forces are held or the military reputation which you have maintained throughout the present conflict.'

Menendez passed on the British offer to Galtieri in Buenos Aires. The leader of the junta signalled back immediately that Menendez should continue the fight: 'Use all the means at your disposal. Continue fighting with all the intensity of which you are capable.' Menendez replied that he had no troops in defensive positions, no high ground left and no ammunition. He was given permission to open negotiations.

Moore did not insist on an unconditional surrender. The Argentines would be repatriated as soon as possible, and were all home by the middle of July. He walked to the building in Stanley where many islanders had gathered and said, 'Hallo, I'm Jeremy Moore. I'm sorry it's taken a rather long time to get here.' Some people cheered, some cried. Most just quietly took it on board that they were free again after 74 days of occupation. That evening Moore signalled home: 'The Falkland Islands are once more under the government desired by their inhabitants. God save the Queen.'

The British lost 255 killed in the Falklands War; 777 were wounded. Many of the British dead were taken home for burial; a few, including 'H' Jones, were buried at a neat military cemetery which looks over the bay at San Carlos. Thirty-six Harriers were lost and six ships, including the *Sir Galahad* and the *Atlantic Conveyor*, were at the bottom of the sea. The Argentines reported the deaths of 652 of their men, although many believe their losses were much higher. Three days after the defeat, Galtieri resigned and the junta collapsed. A democratic regime succeeded under President Alfonsin, and in 1990 diplomatic relations were restored with Britain.

Margaret Thatcher was re-elected in 1983 with a massive majority which many experts put down largely to the so-called 'Falklands Factor'. Thatcher herself emerged with hugely enhanced personal stature. Enoch Powell's question of 3 April was answered: she was now unquestionably the Iron Lady. But her government's diplomatic strategy came under severe criticism for sending the wrong signals to the Argentines before the war. Her Foreign Secretary, Lord Carrington, was widely recognized as having done the honourable thing by resigning three days after the Argentine invasion. The Franks Report, published a year later, was condemned in much of the press as an elaborate whitewash of the government's conduct of Falklands policy. Though full of disturbing evidence of lapses on the part of government, Franks concluded by ascribing 'No criticism or blame to the present government for the Argentine junta's decision to commit its act of unprovoked aggression'.

In the three years between 1983 and 1986 Britain spent in excess of £1 billion constructing a new airfield and military base at Mount Pleasant, 35 miles (56 km) south-west of Stanley. It costs the British government some £100 million a year to maintain a deterrent force in the Falklands to protect the islands and its 3000 inhabitants. The base houses 2000 troops and contract staff, which the British government has equipped with what it hopes will be enough firepower to warn off any further Argentinian attempt at invasion: a flight of RAF interceptor aircraft, an infantry company, a defensive screen of surface-to-air missiles and frequent visits by a naval frigate or destroyer, with a submarine always within reach of the islands. But the key deterrent is the full-length runway that could be receiving reinforcements of troops and aircraft within 24 hours. A successful invasion by Argentina – even with the maximum element of surprise – is almost inconceivable as long as that British commitment remains.

The Falklands War was a military operation of spectacular professional skill. The odds against success were significant, and the risks high. The campaign was not faultless, and the British were lucky that the bravery of the Argentine pilots was not matched by the effectiveness of their bombs: 6 ships were sunk, but another 11 escaped because bombs failed to explode. It could have been a far costlier war for Britain. If Woodward had lost one or both of his carriers, it could have been one of history's great military disasters. But in the event, Britain's armed forces delivered victory in two and a half months. There was something almost bizarre about a nation of 55 million people sending the cream of its armed forces to rescue a population of less than 2000 in remote islands on the other side of the world. If Margaret Thatcher had not been prime minister, it might not have happened. But it did. And with Argentina showing no sign of abandoning its claim to the islands' sovereignty, there will be no easy end to Britain's commitment to this tiny relic of Empire.

KUWAIT

In the early evening of 16 January 1991 Wing Commander Jerry Witts, of the Royal Air Force's 31 Squadron in Saudi Arabia, got an urgent call to report to his airbase in Dhahran. He knew instinctively that he was being summoned to go to war, and remembers being terrified as he drove in. He glanced at other motorists thinking, 'I wonder if they know where I'm going.'[1]

Witts's payload was a large canister slung under his fuselage. Called JP233, it was a uniquely British weapon which the Americans regarded as essential to the destruction of Iraq's airpower. The JP233 consisted of two pods. The rear one carried 30 runway-cratering bombs, each with two charges. The first would blast a hole in the runway's concrete. The second would go through the hole and explode to leave a large crater. The front pod carried 215 anti-personnel mines which would be scattered around the craters to explode at pre-set intervals. They would also explode if anyone or anything touched them. Witts would have only a few seconds to drop his lethal cargo directly on to the runway from a height of 200 feet (60 metres), and would be exposed to Iraqi air defence missiles and anti-aircraft fire as he approached and escaped from his bombing run. But if his and other Tornado missions were successful, they could help ground Saddam Hussein's air force in the opening hours of the war.

Jerry Witts was one of 700,000 servicemen and women who fought on the allied side in the struggle to liberate Kuwait, code-named Desert Storm. His was one of the most dangerous missions in a war in which allied generals anticipated tens of thousands of casualties. Saddam Hussein's invasion of Kuwait in August 1990

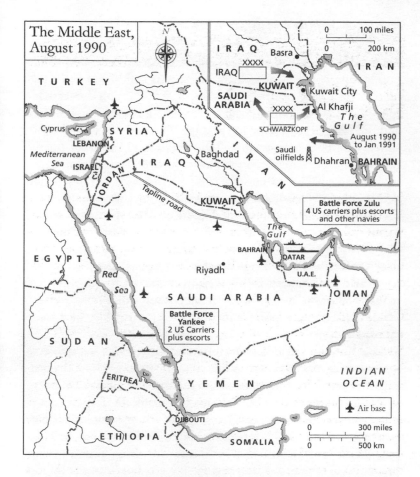

The Middle East,
August 1990

prompted the largest single build-up of international military force
since the Second World War, and no one knew for sure how high
the risk would be to allied troops. The generals' hope was that the
power and accuracy of their modern weapon systems and the sustained bombing of Iraqi troops on the ground would reduce their
enemy's capacity to cause high casualties among the allies. In the
event, the high-tech Gulf War would end in almost bloodless victory for one side and military humiliation for the other. But none of
this appeared certain to decision-makers before the fighting began.

SADDAM INVADES KUWAIT

Before August 1990, few people suspected that Iraq's dictator would invade Kuwait. President Saddam Hussein had already earned a reputation for brutal internal repression and ruthless diplomacy. He spent the 1980s leading his country through a bloody war with Iran and had enjoyed some support from the West and the Soviet Union, which were both anxious to contain Iran's fundamentalist Islamic regime. But the war ended in stalemate in 1988 and left Iraq bankrupt. A $30 billion surplus in 1980 had become a $100 billion deficit. By 1990, Saddam was engaged in an angry quarrel with his oil-rich neighbours, insisting that the oil price should be allowed to rise in order to boost Iraq's oil revenues. Saddam singled out Kuwait for his most aggressive demands, claiming that his small southern neighbour had stolen some of Iraq's oil from an oilfield near their joint border. In his view, Kuwaiti over-production had reduced oil prices and damaged Iraq's economy and its war effort. He demanded a large cash payment from Kuwait and an increase in oil prices.

The Kuwaitis decided they were on safe grounds to refuse to agree to Saddam's demands in full. The Americans, whose dependence on Middle East oil made security in the Gulf a matter of prime strategic importance, urged Saddam to pursue the dispute peacefully, and the US President, George Bush senior, wrote a personal letter to him. He said, 'We believe that differences are best resolved by peaceful means and not by threats involving military force or conflict. Let me reassure you that my administration continues to desire better relations with Iraq.'[2] Historians – with hindsight – point out that Bush chose not to warn that military action by Saddam would prompt a US military response. They suggest that the absence of any such warning may have sent Saddam the message that he could invade Kuwait with impunity. But it is more likely that neither the United States nor Kuwait really believed that Iraq would take the blatant step of invading its next-door neighbour. There were clear signs of a military build-up on Iraq's southern border by the middle of July 1990. But what happened in the early hours of 2 August took the rest of the world by surprise.

At 1 a.m. 2000 Iraqi tanks and 100,000 troops swept across the frontier and over-ran Kuwait. Most drove the 40 miles (64 km) to Kuwait City. Others landed by helicopter at strategic points all over the small Gulf state. There was some resistance: the brother of the Kuwaiti ruler was killed in a shoot-out in the palace. But by 3 August, Kuwait was in the hands of the Iraqi army. Its ruler, Sheikh Sabah al Sabah, escaped to Saudi Arabia. Saddam named Kuwait the 19th province of Iraq.

Some of Iraq's own soldiers were as surprised as the rest of the world. One of them, Abu Fatima, told the BBC: 'Kuwait was the first country that helped Saddam Hussein in his war with Iran, it helped him in everything. So when we received the order to mobilise toward Kuwait ... we asked some officers, "We can't be serious about invading Kuwait." Saddam's order to invade Kuwait was unbelievable, half the army could not envisage or expect such an invasion. Even when we entered Kuwait we could not believe we were actually invading it.'[3]

Over the next few months, the Iraqis did far more than just attempt to destroy Kuwait's capacity to produce any more oil. During their occupation, they looted almost anything of value. Kuwait's Central Bank was robbed of $2 billion-worth of gold. Jewels from the city's gem market, ferries, trawlers, airliners, hospital equipment, even hearses and seats from the stadium were stolen. Nineteen libraries were stripped of their books; even cinemas were vandalized.

There was some Kuwaiti resistance during the occupation. The Iraqis did not have it all their way, as Dr Badr Nasser Al Khalaf, who was in Kuwait for the worst of the Iraqi occupation, told us: 'I saw once with my own eyes an Iraqi soldier who had stolen a car. People chased him and when the resistance caught him they shot him, doused him with petrol and burnt him. There was a deep hatred for the Iraqis for the way they had treated the Kuwaitis.'[4]

Iraq's occupation of Kuwait was at once almost universally condemned. The United Nations Security Council Resolution 660 demanded an immediate Iraqi withdrawal from Kuwait, and

Western leaders were soon making it clear that they were ready for military action. The immediate thought was as much for the security of the world's oil supply as it was for the integrity of Kuwait. Saddam's action put Iraq, which already possessed 10 per cent of the world's oil, in control of another 10 per cent in Kuwait. Moreover, his military forces now stood on the border of Saudi Arabia, the richest oil producer on earth. A 200-mile (320-km) advance due south from Kuwait would see his troops over-run another 20 per cent of the world's oil in the Saudi oilfields around Dhahran. Saudi Arabia alone supplied around a quarter of all US oil imports. The Iraqi dictator's military adventure in Kuwait was bad enough: it violated a frontier and upset the already fragile stability of the Middle East. But the prospect of Saddam controlling the world's single most concentrated source of oil was intolerable, and Saudi Arabia's meagre defence forces would be hard put to stop him.

President Bush, a war veteran himself, had a natural caution about involving the United States in a military confrontation. But it wasn't long before he took a robust stand. Britain's Prime Minister, Margaret Thatcher, who met him in Aspen, Colorado on 2 August, was characteristically blunt and straightforward. Saddam had to be stopped, she said, and stopped quickly. Colin Powell, America's chairman of the Joint Chiefs of Staff, pointed out the geography to President Bush and asked him, 'Mr President, should we think about laying down a line in the sand concerning Saudi Arabia?' Powell reports that Bush thought for a moment and then said, 'Yes.'[5]

A few days later, he went further. When asked publicly for his reaction to Iraq's invasion of Kuwait, Bush replied, 'This will not stand.' He appeared to be setting the agenda not just for the protection of Saudi Arabia, but for the liberation of Kuwait. He may have hoped to do it by pressure, but his emphatic assertion implied that if Saddam could not be persuaded he would have to be forced.

The immediate imperative was to dissuade Saddam from extending his attack into Saudi Arabia. The only nation with the military resources to shift a credible deterrent force to the area within days was the United States. The US command responsible for the security of the Gulf was Central Command, under General Norman Schwarzkopf. A great bull of a man, with a large frame, a quick temper and a formidable intellect, he had been a lieutenant colonel in Vietnam and had seen how incompetent management and lack of public support had helped lose that war. Now the crisis was in the Middle East, and it just happened that in late July 1990 Schwarzkopf and his staff were in Florida, engaging in an exercise in which the Iraqis invaded Saudi Arabia. He was now to bring his formidable powers of leadership and judgement to focus on sustaining a coalition of no fewer than 38 nations from all around the world – including some Arab countries – in an effort to save Saudi Arabia and get Saddam Hussein out of Kuwait. His personality was to play as large a role in the Gulf War as that of Macarthur four decades earlier in Korea – or perhaps, in the age of television, an even greater role.[6]

OPERATION DESERT SHIELD

Schwarzkopf's strategy was to build such a large force on the ground and in the air that, if it did come to fighting, allied casualties would be as low as possible. That was the first and most important lesson of Vietnam. On 3 August Schwarzkopf was summoned to Washington to brief President Bush. Bush told his commander that the military response must make it clear to Saddam that any invasion of Saudi Arabia would mean war. Schwarzkopf warned the President that it would take four months to assemble a large enough force to stop the Iraqis over-running much of Saudi Arabia, and it would take as much as eight months or more to build up an army that would throw Saddam out of Kuwait.

But first Saudi Arabia had to be persuaded to accept the presence of American troops on its territory. On 6 August US Defence Secretary Dick Cheney and a top-level team that included Schwarzkopf arrived in the Saudi capital with an ambitious aim. They hoped to persuade the Saudi royal family, the guardians of Islam's holiest places, Mecca and Medina, to welcome foreign, non-Muslim troops on Saudi soil. Most of those troops would come from the USA, already deeply unpopular in the Middle East for being the closest ally of the Arabs' worst enemy, Israel. The team was led into the presence of King Fahd, and Schwarzkopf showed the King satellite images of the Iraqi build-up on the Kuwait–Saudi border. He then flipped through a set of charts to show the King how big a force he would have to introduce to be sure of defending the kingdom. Cheney finished off by saying to the King, 'If you ask us, we will come. We will seek no permanent bases. When you ask us to go home, we will leave.' The King turned away and talked with his senior princes, then came back to Cheney and said, simply, 'OK.'[7] Schwarzkopf recalls one prince urging the king to be careful not to rush into a decision. But the King sharply responded, 'The Kuwaitis did not rush into a decision and today they are guests in our hotels.'

Within hours, Schwarzkopf had under way the largest US deployment of force since the Vietnam War. The US air force despatched F15 and F16 fighters and strike aircraft. 120,000 troops were given their marching orders; and two US marine expeditionary brigades were sent by air – their heavy equipment followed by sea. The United States and Britain led the way with naval forces. British warships and Tornado aircraft were quick to arrive and the Americans rapidly stationed two carrier battle groups, one based on the USS *Independence* in the waters of the Gulf and the other on the USS *Dwight D. Eisenhower* in the Mediterranean. Each of these carriers – and there were to be six of them involved by the end of the war – carried more than 70 combat aircraft. The lesson of the Battle of Midway 50 years earlier had not been lost: the aircraft carrier was more than ever the key to the projection of military power.

More alliances soon formed, and within weeks naval forces from 14 other countries assembled as well: Argentina (Britain's opponent in the Falklands War only eight years earlier), Austria, Belgium, Canada, Denmark, France, Germany, Italy, the Netherlands, Norway, Poland, Portugal, Spain and Turkey, as well as Saudi Arabia's own navy. This was the basis of a coalition that would grow to a total of 38 nations, including substantial contingents from Arab nations such as Egypt and Syria, shocked and angry at Iraq's assault on an Arab neighbour. Forces even came from as far away as New Zealand, Australia, Senegal and Honduras.

Britain's military contribution was the second largest – less than a tenth the size of the United States' commitment, but still substantial. Whitehall planned to send 6000 people; the military asked for 10,000 and by February 1991 it was to reach a total of 45,000, the largest single force Britain had despatched abroad since the Second World War. The first ground contingent sent was the 7th Armoured Brigade, whose forbears had fought with Montgomery at Alamein and earned the nickname 'Desert Rats'. Now they were stationed in Germany, a legacy of the Cold War with the Soviet bloc which had evaporated in 1989. The brigade was commanded by Brigadier Patrick Cordingley; he and his force were given a fortnight to prepare to leave with their 117 tanks. Lieutenant General Sir Peter de la Billiére was appointed commander of all British forces in the Gulf. An ex-SAS officer, with eight years' experience of serving in Arab countries, he had begun his military career as a subaltern on the Imjin River in Korea 40 years earlier. His overall commander in London, Air Chief Marshal Sir Patrick Hine, says, 'Mrs T knew and trusted Peter de la Billiére: he had organised the SAS raid on the Iranian embassy in London. He had true leadership … he was not that inspirational but a very good overall commander whom everyone respected.'⁸

The new commanders' immediate task was to make sure their force could fight, so Britain's entire armoured strength in Germany was plundered for spare parts, working vehicles and skilled troops in order to make the Desert Rats fully operational. De la Billiére was soon to meet the formidable Schwarzkopf. 'A degree of formality persisted for a while,' he says, and he could see that Schwarzkopf could be 'very frightening' in his relations with his staff. But Schwarzkopf was meticulous in maintaining the most cordial of relations with America's allies: he and de la Billiére soon got along well. Unlike the Falklands War, in which Britain conducted its own independent national campaign, the command structure in the Gulf reflected the fact that this action had to be seen to be an international operation. Lieutenant General de la Billiére (of three-star rank), as commander of British forces in the Gulf, and his overall military commander at home, Air Chief Marshal Sir Patrick Hine (four-star), worked in close cooperation with the American commander-in-chief. De la Billiére was effectively Schwarzkopf's No.2 in the international coalition. Looking back, de la Billiére has no doubt that Schwarzkopf was a 'brilliant' leader.[9]

The American commander's first task was to manage the awkward business of introducing a massive force into a country that regarded Christians as infidels and pornography as a crime. The Saudis were appalled at seeing American women wearing T-shirts and driving cars. They complained that American troops were introducing the magazine *Playboy* to their country. Schwarzkopf had to set up military post offices to receive magazines that could not be delivered through the Saudi postal service. The Saudis even complained that a number of oil workers' wives who were entertaining the US troops were strippers, and Schwarzkopf and his staff had to spend precious time reassuring the Saudis that this was not so.[10] British forces had to play down their religious activities. Padres were told to wear special unobtrusive dog collars, and de la Billiére says the import of Christmas trees later in the year was 'OK, but low-key.'[11]

The commanders' other major preoccupation during the operation that came to be known as Desert Shield was the danger of Saddam using chemical or biological weapons. He was reckoned to have some 1000 tons of chemical weapons, and there were fears that he might have stocks of weapons armed with two deadly biological agents, botulinum and anthrax. These fears proved unfounded when it became clear after the war that his development of germ weapons had not got that far. But large numbers of British and American soldiers were injected with antidotes to the two biological agents, and chemical warfare training became a high priority for all forces. This inoculation programme led to the accusation after the war that troops were suffering from Gulf War Syndrome, a medical condition observed in a large number of Gulf War veterans in Britain and America which appeared to have been at least partly induced by the vaccines. The controversy remains unresolved at the time of publication.

There were discussions at the highest level about how Saddam should be deterred from using weapons of mass destruction. Some suggested a nuclear response: another suggestion, made by Schwarzkopf's air force commander, Buster Glosson, was the destruction of the huge dams on the River Euphrates that would result in the flooding of much of Iraq. This and other extreme measures were rejected by Washington for fear of causing major disruption in the fast-developing international coalition. A massive conventional response against high-value targets like oilfields in Iraq was preferred. Schwarzkopf, typically, put it in robust terms: 'We knew we would have mass casualties if they did use chemical weapons. So we transferred the message to Iraq that if you use chemical weapons we'll turn your country to rubble.'[12]

As summer turned to autumn and the build-up of forces proceeded, it soon became apparent that although Saddam was not going to invade Saudi Arabia, he was not going to be browbeaten into pulling out of Kuwait. President Bush made it clear that only a complete and unconditional withdrawal of Iraqi forces would be acceptable, and compared Saddam with Hitler. The Iraqi leader responded: 'Thousands of Americans whom you have pushed into this dark tunnel will go home in a dark coffin.'

Discussion between Schwarzkopf and his superiors in Washington soon turned into haggling about the size of force that would be required to eject Iraqi forces from Kuwait. The same dialogue took place between de la Billiére and London. Saddam's forces in and around Kuwait were now reckoned to be mounting towards the half million mark – on paper Iraq had the fourth largest military force in the world. Whatever the doubts among the experts about the quality of its equipment and its leadership and morale, the military commanders naturally planned for the worst. If the defensive Desert Shield was to turn into an offensive that would be called Desert Storm, they would need massive reinforcement. Schwarzkopf asked for another 150,000 men and 1000 tanks. De la Billiére asked for another brigade.

The discussions between the American commander and Washington became very heated. Schwarzkopf says he was 'seething' that he wasn't allowed to go to Washington himself and brief the Defence Secretary on the need for more troops. He was even told that there were some in Washington who regarded him as 'just another Maclellan'. This was a reference to the Union's General Maclellan in the American Civil War, who dithered outside the Confederate capital even though he had the larger force. An apoplectic Schwarzkopf said he would show them 'the difference between Schwarzkopf and Maclellan'. He had, of course, a smaller force than Saddam, and argued vigorously for an increase with Colin Powell, who visited his headquarters in Saudi Arabia on 22 October. Powell was persuaded, and between them they planned to present the President with a strategic plan for the liberation of Kuwait.[13]

The plan was for the war to begin with a long air campaign that would cripple Iraqi military and political installations in and around Baghdad and destroy the country's air force. It would also bombard Iraq's army in Kuwait and shatter its resolve in order to prepare the ground for an allied land offensive to dislodge Saddam. This offensive would take the form of a diversionary attack from the sea and across Kuwait's southern frontier, followed by a giant lefthook. This main punch, way off to the west of Kuwait, would be delivered by around 350,000 troops storming across the Saudi frontier into Iraq. This fast-moving armoured and helicopter-borne force would sweep forward as far as the River Euphrates and then swing eastwards into Kuwait itself and the approaches to Basra. The main target of this huge flanking force would be the four or five divisions of Saddam's Republican Guard, his highest-motivated and best-equipped troops, who were stationed north-west of Kuwait. The plan was ambitious and so was its price: Schwarzkopf and Powell said they would need almost to double their current level of 250,000 troops in the Gulf to achieve it.

On 30 October President Bush met with his advisers, including Powell, in the situation room at the White House. Bush leaned forward to listen carefully to Powell's detailed description of the plan for the attack, and when it was finished he said, 'OK, do it.'[14] The next day, Powell rang Schwarzkopf and told him, 'You are going to get everything you asked for and more.' Another 200,000 troops would be shifted to the Gulf, including an entire armoured corps from Germany – VII Corps, with 145,000 men and 1400 tanks.

De la Billiére for his part was now planning for Britain to deploy a division under Major-General Rupert Smith. Another brigade, commanded by Brigadier Christopher Hammerbeck, would join the Desert Rats. Up to now the plan had been for the British troops to fight alongside the US marines, whose main attack would be across Kuwait's southern border. Brigadier Cordingley and the US marines had trained together and developed close teamwork. This suited Schwarzkopf, too: the marines needed the British tanks to support their much lighter-armed attack through Kuwait's southern border. But de la Billiére was unhappy that Britain's force would not be in the main action – the big left hook into Iraq. And although Cordingley said he was 'desperately uncomfortable' with the idea of abandoning the marines and shifting to another front, and Schwarzkopf was reluctant to change the line-up, de la Billiére eventually prevailed. He argued that the heavy British armour would be much more usefully deployed where their range and strength could provide VII Corps with a flexible flanking force. He told the US commander, 'Our division is tailored for manoeuvre operations. If we don't use it for that, we'll be under-employing it and it'll be in a type of battle for which it is not trained.' It took de la Billiére a month to persuade Schwarzkopf to agree. But on 14 December he accepted that the change should take place. The new British division being created under General Smith's command would now join the main assault across the Saudi–Iraqi frontier.[15]

Critical to the success of Schwarzkopf's strategic plan was the diversionary operation intended to distract Saddam Hussein. A large amphibious force of 24,000 American marines was assembled in the Gulf and British minesweepers were tasked to go in and clear the approaches to the beaches on the east coast of Kuwait. Forces from Syria, Egypt, Saudi Arabia and exiles from Kuwait were to drive into southern Kuwait either side of the main land-based force of 70,000 US marines. US battleships would fire their 16-inch guns at Iraqi positions on the Kuwaiti shoreline. Provided that Schwarzkopf's air campaign had by now destroyed or grounded Saddam's air force, Iraq would have no way of locating the massive movement of Schwarzkopf's main forces north-west along the Saudi–Iraqi frontier. This huge deployment would only begin once the air campaign had effectively blinded Iraq.

Through December and the beginning of January, this fast-growing ground force was massing south of Kuwait. By the middle of January – just before the air campaign began – faced with half a million Iraqi troops in and around Kuwait, with 4000 tanks and more than 3000 artillery pieces, Schwarzkopf had amassed a force of 600,000 men, 3400 tanks and 1700 combat aircraft.

During the months of this huge build-up, a small group of air force planners had been laying the groundwork for the most high-tech air assault in history. Under Schwarzkopf's air commander, Lieutenant General Chuck Horner, Brigadier General Buster Glosson drew up the detail of Operation Instant Thunder. Around one-tenth of the bombs and missiles dropped in the air campaign would be PGMs – precision guided munitions. These 'smart' bombs were guided by laser designation to hit specific targets with almost total accuracy, which massively increased the effective destructive power of air strikes. In the Second World War it had taken 9000 bombs to be sure of destroying a target the size of a tennis court. By the time of the Vietnam War, it took 300 bombs to be able to do the job. In the Gulf, air force chiefs claimed one bomb would be enough to strike home. These munitions could be launched from an aircraft as far as 7 miles (11 km) away and still explode with deadly precision within 10 feet (3 metres) of their targets.

This technology allowed Glosson's team to draw up a list of targets in Baghdad, confident that there would be little of the so-called 'collateral' damage that had made bombing so indiscriminate in the past. Civilians living in the vicinity of a military target should be less at risk than before. The pilots too would face less danger, being able to drop their bombs from medium height – well over 10,000 feet (3000 metres). Only the British in their Tornados would have to fly in low over Iraqi airfields in order to be sure of dropping their canisters of JP233 in the middle of the runways.

Iraq had a large air force which included some of the most sophisticated Soviet-built jets. Horner's first task was to neutralize their radars and surface-to-air missile systems. The opening phase of the air war would also target major command centres in Baghdad. Schwarzkopf would launch long-range cruise missiles at major specific targets in the capital. These Tomahawk missiles, launched from warships in the Gulf and by B52 bombers, would use an onboard system called TERCOM – Terrain Contour Matching – to pick out enough features of the terrain to guide them to their target.

Glosson's team divided Instant Thunder into four phases. The first would attack command centres in Baghdad and Iraq's air defence system. The second would strike strategic targets, like factories suspected to be making chemical and biological weapons. The third would target infrastructure, like bridges and roads. And finally the air campaign would focus on Iraq's ground forces in and around Kuwait, to reduce their capacity to resist a ground attack. Schwarzkopf was anxious that the air campaign should target these Iraqi army positions from the first moment; Horner, his air force chief, believed that the other targets should initially have higher priority. It was to be a point of tension between them throughout the air campaign.

The prospect of having to fight to maintain his occupation of Kuwait did not appear to rattle Saddam Hussein. Nor did the virtual unanimity of the rest of the world's hostility to him. On 29 November the United Nations Security Council, impatient at the failure of diplomacy to shift Iraq from Kuwait, passed a resolution authorizing the use of 'all means necessary' to secure the withdrawal of the Iraqis, which the coalition took as a clear mandate for the use of force. The Security Council set a deadline of 15 January 1991. Just before the time for talking expired, the US Secretary of State, James Baker, met Tariq Aziz, Iraq's Foreign Minister, in Geneva. They had seven hours of talks which got nowhere. War was inevitable.

THE AIR WAR

Midnight on 15 January came and went. The ultimatum had run its course. The world had 27 hours to wait.

H hour, the hour for the strikes on the main strategic targets, was set for 3 a.m. on the morning of 17 January. At 2.38 a.m. eight Apache helicopters armed with an array of precision-guided missiles fired the first shots of Operation Desert Storm. Their target was two Iraqi radar sites that controlled the skies between the Saudi border

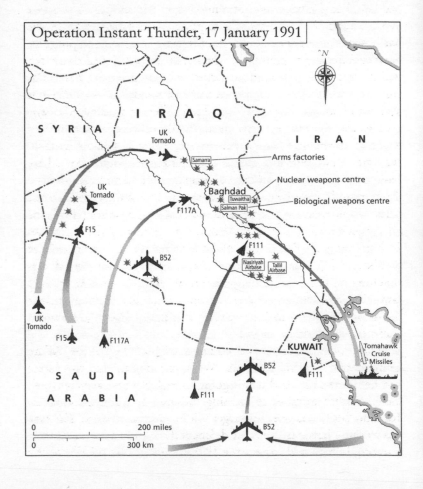

and Baghdad. Over the next four minutes, the Apaches loosed off 27 Hellfire missiles that homed in on the radars at two key sites in southern Iraq.

Thirteen minutes later, two F117a stealth fighter-bombers destroyed another radar site further north. A highway in the sky was now open for the main force to attack. More than 100 British and American aircraft sped through the gap in the radar defences and began the bombing of Baghdad.

What followed was not just the first allied military response to Saddam, but the beginning of a new era in the coverage of warfare in the media. TV correspondents placed in the front line of the battle were to supply not only live snapshots of fighting in progress, but continuous live pictures of the battle via satellite transmitters, which were now to become standard equipment in the field. The contrast with what had happened nine years earlier in the Falklands War could not have been more striking. Then there had been days, even weeks, to wait before pictures finally made it back from the battle front, and government censors had a captive flock of journalists who could film and report only what they were allowed to. Now new technology and the comparative lack of controls allowed the story to be beamed around the world in seconds. Details of the battle visible to correspondents in the field were instantly displayed on people's screens at home. When Peter Arnett of the American 24-hour news channel Cable News Network (CNN) reported the bombing of Baghdad live from his hotel room, the world was watching it with him. Even government ministers found it their fastest means of following events. And the first major military clash the whole world was able to watch as it happened was the air bombardment of Saddam's capital.

'There were hundreds and hundreds of planes up there,' Wing Commander Jerry Witts recalls. 'We were going to stuff this bloke and he deserved it. And it was going to be OK because we were all there.' Within minutes of crossing the border, Witts, piloting his Tornado GR1, was over his target – a major Iraqi airbase. His task was to cause havoc in Iraq's air defences by dropping his canister of cratering bombs and mines, the JP233, right in the middle of the runway. 'We ran at it and I couldn't see a thing. My navigator had it on the radar and the autopilot was doing the work. I threw all the switches and we let the thing go. It took a few seconds. It was like going over a cobbled road very quickly. It seemed very important to me to stay very low, because if anyone did start shooting that's where I wanted to be. All of a sudden we were up at about 800 feet and I was fighting like a dingbat to keep the plane down and get away as fast as we possibly could.'[16]

While the coalition air force was striking Baghdad and its air defences, cruise missiles were being fired from warships in the Gulf. After a short technical delay, launcher crews on the huge battleship *Wisconsin* fed in the ten-digit codes that would take the Tomahawks to their targets. Other cruise missiles were carried under the bellies of seven B52 bombers that took off from a base in Louisiana 15 hours ahead of H hour. The giant planes flew for 35 hours – to their targets in Iraq and back, a journey of 14,000 miles (some 23,000 km).

Those were the 'smart' weapon carriers – although the vast majority of the strike force, the F111s, the F15s and carrier-based aircraft, were carrying ordinary unguided bombs that they dropped as best they could from a safe height. Only 7 per cent of the bombs actually dropped were precision guided. Even the 'smart' bombs, however, could – and did – malfunction from time to time. During that first night of Instant Thunder, the worst collateral damage was done by a cruise missile. It was aimed at the telecommunications centre at Diwaniyeh but hit a building next door, killing 11 Iraqi civilians and injuring 49. In this new era of instant communication, Schwarzkopf was deeply aware of the need to persuade public opinion that the coalition was doing all it could to minimize the killing of civilians. Throughout the war he was constantly seen illustrating for the media the precision with which many allied aircraft could strike their targets. At one famous press conference, he showed pictures of an Iraqi truck driver just managing to cross a bridge before it was blown to pieces by a 2000-lb (900-kg) bomb. He was, said Schwarzkopf, 'the luckiest man in Iraq'. But stray bombs like the one that hit Diwaniyeh demonstrated that even at the end of the twentieth century technology could not be guaranteed to deliver 'surgical strikes' that would leave civilians unscathed.

Fighters were in the sky as well. Alan Miller piloted his F15 into Iraq hoping to get a bead on an Iraqi Mig 29; instead, he flew into a formidable anti-aircraft defensive screen of missiles and gunfire. He was alerted by signals in his cockpit to several Iraqi missiles aimed at him and immediately zigzagged across the sky, firing off chaff to attempt to distract them. He was lucky. He saw one missile zip past him just as he dipped his wing to avoid it. When another warning signal sounded, he put the plane into a dive, but soon found himself within reach of anti-aircraft fire and had to use his afterburner to climb steeply again. Miller returned to base feeling pretty chastened: he had spotted no enemy aircraft and had been lucky to escape with his aircraft in one piece.[17]

By morning, of all the 700 aircraft which had ventured into the heavily defended airspace over Iraq only two had been lost, including one shot down by one of the few Iraqi Mig 29s to venture into the air. The allied air campaign had got off to a promising start. With each night that passed, the threat from Iraq's air defences would be reduced. Over the entire air campaign, 36 coalition aircraft were shot down by missiles or anti-aircraft fire. Of Iraq's air force there was little to be seen. One or two fighters took off and chased the attackers, but they could claim only that one success.

The following morning, the coalition's top air strike planners, including Glosson, were congratulating themselves on the success of the first night of raids. They were gathered in the basement of the Saudi air force base in Riyadh when Norman Schwarzkopf walked in. He asked Glosson why his aircraft had not been attacking Republican Guard units as well as airbases and radars. Because it was important to attack Iraq's air defence first, replied Glosson.

'I said I wanted them [the Republican Guard] bombed from hour one, and that's what I want,' Schwarzkopf shouted back. 'You people have been misleading me. You're not following my orders. You're not doing what I told you to do.'[18]

Glosson tried to make it clear to his commander-in-chief that without Iraq's surface-to-air missiles fully neutralized it would be foolhardy to commit area bombing strike aircraft like the B52 in large numbers. But Schwarzkopf was implacable. His priority was to destroy what he could of Iraq's front-line troop concentrations before he ordered his ground forces to advance. Slowly over the next few weeks, the emphasis of the air campaign swung from strategic targets in Iraq to the front line, but it was never enough for Schwarzkopf.

There were, however, lighter moments: 'One of the things I wanted to do', says Schwarzkopf, 'was to blow up the statue of Saddam in Baghdad. We could've done that but the State Department said no because it wasn't a military target. The lawyers got involved and they wouldn't accept. I kept on asking Powell: "Are you sure I can't do it?" And he would laugh. It became a joke between us.'[19]

It took a few days for Iraq's air defence system to be effectively obliterated, and until that was achieved coalition aircraft faced some dangerous missions. A squadron of A6 attack aircraft from the US carrier *Saratoga*, commanded by Michael Menth, was directed to tackle the threat from Soviet-built Scud missiles based in western Iraq. Their target was the large base called H3, and the advice from air force chiefs was to drop bombs from the relatively safe height of 15,000 feet (4600 metres). But Menth believed the unguided 1000-lb (450-kg) bombs they were carrying would be hopelessly inaccurate if they were aimed from that height. He argued that attacking at low level would improve accuracy and avoid some of the more lethal Iraqi anti-aircraft missiles, like the Soviet-supplied SAM 6. Menth led his pilots in from two directions, but the Iraqis responded with such a fusillade of anti-aircraft fire and surface-to-air missiles that the squadron could do little more than race in, drop their bombs and run for it. One aircraft, piloted by Lieutenant Bob Wetzel, was destroyed when a missile exploded close to it and set fire to its tail. He and his bomb-aimer ejected and were captured on the ground near the Iraqi base. Another of Menth's A6s was severely damaged, but just succeeded in making it back to the *Saratoga*. When Menth returned, he strongly urged that no more low-level attacks should be attempted. His advice was rapidly adopted and the signal was sent to the US carrier fleet to abandon low-level attacks unless with express permission.[20]

Low-level attacks also took their toll of Britain's Tornado bombers. Their unique task was to help ground the Iraqi air force by cratering their runways. In the first five days of the air campaign, five Tornados were brought down by the Iraqis and more damaged. Ten crewmen were either killed or captured. It became clear after a day or two that the Iraqi air force had little intention of flying. The Iraqi airbases were huge; their runways were wide, and sand on the surface absorbed much of the impact of the British bombs – the Iraqis were filling in the craters within 48 hours. It quickly became evident to US and British air commanders that the Tornados were taking unnecessary risks. Sir Peter de la Billiére remembers Chuck Horner turning to him and saying, 'Peter, I admire the courage of your pilots but I'm a little concerned that they ain't achieving much in relation to the risks they're taking and the effort they're putting in.'[21]

RAF morale was badly shaken by the loss of men and aircraft. On 23 January Air Chief Marshal Hine decided to abandon low-level attacks. From then on, Tornados were tasked to attack from medium level, and Hine sent out a group of Buccaneer aircraft to act as laser designators for them. A Buccaneer would 'illuminate' the target, and the laser-guided bomb dropped by a Tornado would follow the laser to the spot it was marking.

The task of destroying Iraq's air force became the job mainly of the two most sophisticated US aircraft, the F111 bomber and the F117a stealth fighter-bomber. They were given the job of hitting the concrete shelters in which the Iraqi aircraft were concealed, and television viewers around the world were treated to nightly images of successful strikes. But detailed analysis after the war by the General Accounting Office (GAO) in Washington showed that the likelihood of a laser-guided bomb dropped by these aircraft hitting its target was only 40–60 per cent. And far from the air force's claim that a single laser-guided bomb could destroy a target, it actually took an average of four bombs to do it. The GAO estimates that 290 Iraqi aircraft (40 per cent of the air force's strength) were destroyed by coalition air attack. Of the rest, 121 escaped to Iran:

the fundamentalist regime there was no friend of Saddam's, but escape to an unfriendly neighbour seemed to some pilots better than almost certain destruction on their bases. Even so, another 300 aircraft managed to survive the war in Iraq.[22]

Air attacks on Iraq's command and control systems were crippling, but again not decisive. Throughout the war, Saddam Hussein managed to retain the capability to direct and redeploy his forces. Nor did attacks on the so-called 'leadership' targets, the palaces and command bunkers, cause the regime to collapse. The GAO's assessment of the attacks on Saddam's nuclear, chemical and biological targets is that only a tiny fraction of the targets were hit. The damage to Iraq's road and rail links was much greater: three-quarters of the bridges connecting central Iraq with the war zone around Kuwait were destroyed, and the railway was cut. The attacks on Iraq's troops in and around Kuwait proved much more difficult to assess. The attacks appear to have concentrated on the front line and Schwarzkopf was probably right in pressuring for more attacks on the Republican Guard, who were held back in reserve north-west of Kuwait. It was soon clear to coalition commanders that the air campaign was not going to defeat Saddam on its own and that only a ground offensive would decide the matter.

SCUDS

The arena in which the air campaign most blatantly failed was in countering what became Saddam Hussein's most effective weapon, the Scud missile. On 17 January – just a day after the air assault on him began – Saddam ordered eight Scud missile attacks on Israel, not a member of the coalition. Five scuds landed in and around Tel Aviv. There was initial panic that the missiles might have been fitted with chemical warheads. But they were not, and, miraculously, only two Israelis died in the impacts; four more died of heart attacks. The effect on the Israeli government, however, and on the coalition's prospects in the war was electric. The natural instinct of Yitzhak Shamir, Israel's right-wing Prime Minister, was to retaliate. Israeli aircraft were soon airborne and awaiting targeting orders for attack into western Iraq.

The coalition was thrown into crisis. Israeli participation – even if uninvited – in the war against Iraq would be a political catastrophe: the Arabs who were taking their positions in the front line against Saddam would quit in disgust. Washington was in no doubt about the need to hold the Israelis back. James Baker, the Secretary of State, was soon on the telephone to Shamir, urging restraint. An emergency consignment of America's brand-new Patriot missiles, said to have the capacity to intercept incoming Scuds, was despatched to Israel. The Patriots were rapidly scattered around vulnerable civilian targets in Israel and provided some reassurance. But they failed to intercept the Scud attack that came on 22 January: 96 people were injured when a missile landed on the Tel Aviv suburb of Ramat Gan, and more than 1000 homes were damaged.

For the Americans, stopping the Scuds became the top priority. It was clear that, although their military effect was negligible, they were politically deeply damaging. The Israelis had to be placated. They were already asking the Americans to persuade the Saudis to open their airspace to allow Israeli strike aircraft to attack Iraq – and an assault force of helicopter-borne Israeli troops was being stood by to fly into Iraq from the Negev desert. Speaking today, Schwarzkopf is in no doubt that the Israelis had to be stopped: 'There was no question [but] that the Arabs would've left the coalition had Israel got involved.'[23]

Somehow, the Americans persuaded Shamir to hold back, but they had to convince him that the coalition could do the task. Schwarzkopf was told to divert to attacking the Scud launcher vehicles as much of the air campaign that was needed to destroy them. Over the next few days, aircraft that should have been hitting Baghdad were redeployed to seeking out the Scud launchers in western Iraq. Boeing 707 aircraft with the JSTARS surveillance system – capable of picking up almost any kind of movement on the ground – were ordered in, and details of any suspicious object were passed on to the strike aircraft. Britain's SAS helicoptered in patrols that sought out the launchers on the ground. Everything possible was done to destroy Saddam's Scuds and to dissuade the Israelis from attacking Iraq.

One Iraqi soldier charged with handling the Scuds told the BBC after the war that the Iraqis had gone to great lengths to camouflage the missiles: 'The launchers were disguised, covered with leaves, mud and branches to blend them into where they were … they used to bring the missiles up in ordinary coaches: they had to take all the seats out and slide the missile in from the back so the American pilots would think it was just people travelling along.'[24]

Air Marshal Hine believes the military efforts had patchy results. 'We were conspicuously unsuccessful in using air attacks to destroy Scuds. They were very good with decoys – fakes that deceived us. But the SAS do appear to have had an effect: Scuds did stop being fired from our area of responsibility. The SCUD launchers would be in caves and emerge for a maximum of 45 minutes and then zip back inside. All we had to respond with was the SAS if they were very lucky, and JSTARS in a Boeing 707 which could pick up any launcher that was visible and report to the SAS. I don't know of any destroyed Scuds, but their campaign was probably deterred by the SAS and then finally given up.'[25]

Remarkably, in the course of the next few weeks of the air campaign the Scud attacks fell away dramatically and the immediate threat of Israeli intervention went away. The SAS and the relentless air attacks may have helped deter the Scuds, but after the war the GAO reported that there was 'no confirming evidence that *any* Scud launchers were destroyed'. Furthermore, the general conclusion after the war was that the Patriots, which had provided some reassurance in the feverish atmosphere of the first few days of the Scud attacks, were ineffective at intercepting any incoming missiles.

The narrow escape from Israeli intervention was not the only political embarrassment for the coalition's leaders during the air campaign. Their boast that they were staging surgical air strikes with their precision guided weapons was also being speedily eroded. The bombing was killing civilians and the world was watching. Four British Tornados – now staging medium-level attacks – launched bombs at a bridge near Fallujah. One malfunctioned, went astray and killed 130

▲ The Falklands, 2 April 1982. British Royal Marines are forced to lie down at gunpoint after the surrender to the Argentine invasion force. The marines fought to defend Government House, but the Governor, Sir Rex Hunt, decided further resistance was hopeless. This scene provoked fury in Britain.

▲ Three days after the Argentine invasion HMS *Invincible* sails from Portsmouth, on 5 April 1982. Together with the aircraft carrier HMS *Hermes*, *Invincible* formed the core of the task force that arrived off the Falklands at the beginning of May. Harrier aircraft were flown on to the carriers once they were at sea.

▶ The Argentine cruiser General Belgrano sinks in the South Atlantic Ocean just outside Britain's Exclusion Zone on 2 May 1982. She was torpedoed by the British submarine Conqueror when Thatcher endorsed the Royal Navy's view that the cruiser was a threat to the task force. In spite of the life rafts, 323 Argentine sailors died.

▲ Caught in Bomb Alley, 23 May 1982. The British frigate, HMS *Antelope*, was one of the victims of the Argentine air raids on the British landing force at San Carlos Bay. *Antelope* was hit by two bombs that failed to explode on impact but blew up when experts attempted to defuse them.

◄ RFA *Sir Galahad* ablaze at Fitzroy where Argentine fighter bombers caught her in full daylight loaded with troops she was ferrying up to the front. Forty-nine British soldiers died and 150 were wounded. It was the biggest blunder the British made during the Falklands War.

▶ RAF Harriers of No. 1 (F) Squadron on HMS Hermes. RAF and Sea Harriers took off the carriers' angled decks and provided vital air cover to the fleet and the troops ashore. Armed with the latest US sidewinder missiles, Harriers shot down large numbers of Argentine aircraft.

◀ Royal Marine Commandos 'yomp' towards Port Stanley in the Falklands. Deprived of their helicopter transport by a successful Argentine air strike, the marines had to struggle some 50 miles on foot. 3 Commando Brigade slept in the open, endured bitterly cold and wet conditions and were still ready to fight a battle at the end of it.

▶ The memorial to Lieutenant Colonel 'H' Jones on Darwin Ridge, East Falkland. He won a Victoria Cross when he was killed leading a charge up the slope from the left.

▲ Jubail, Saudi Arabia, October 1990. A column of Britain's 7th Armoured Brigade, which earned its nickname of 'The Desert Rats' during the Second World War, moves up towards the front line in the Gulf War. In February 1991 they were part of a giant offensive into Iraq that helped to shatter Saddam Hussein's grip on Kuwait.

▲ Baghdad, early morning on 18 January 1991. The skies above the Iraqi capital erupt with anti-aircraft fire as allied warplanes strike targets in the first moments of the Gulf War. The attacks were designed to weaken Saddam and his forces so that an allied assault on the ground would meet little resistance.

▲ A Tomahawk cruise missile lights up the night sky as it is launched from the deck of the battleship USS *Wisconsin* early in the morning of 18 January 1991. The missiles were designed to pick their way to their targets with pinpoint accuracy.

▼ Men of the US Army's 101st Airborne Division swoop deep into Iraq by helicopter and establish a position on 25 February 1991. They were part of the massive left hook with which the US-led coalition hoped to outflank Saddam Hussein's army, force it out of Kuwait and destroy it.

▲ An F-117A Nighthawk Stealth fighter-bomber, en route to Iraq from Nevada, is refuelled over Kansas by a KC-135 tanker. These aircraft were effectively invisible to Iraqi radar. More than 3000 anti-aircraft guns and 60 surface-to-air missile batteries protected Baghdad, but not a single Nighthawk was hit.

▶ 'Stormin' Norman', US General H. Norman Schwarzkopf, the overall commander during the Gulf War. His explosive temper terrified some, but he was popular with his troops and with other allied commanders.

▲ March 1991. An American soldier stands on a destroyed Iraqi tank celebrating the successful eviction of Saddam Hussein's army from Kuwait. Behind him Saddam's final act of vandalism, the destruction of Kuwait's oil wells, blackens the horizon.

◄ Highway of Death, 28 February 1991. The graveyard of hundreds of Iraqis and their vehicles on the road to Basra. Coalition aircraft caught them in the open, fleeing from Kuwait. The White House feared that this scene of annihilation would have a negative effect on world opinion.

people in a marketplace. And on 13 February a US 2000-lb (900-kg) bomb, guided with perfect accuracy on to its intended target, ploughed deep into a bunker in the Baghdad suburb of Amariyah. Coalition intelligence had identified it as a command bunker: actually it contained a large number of civilians, of whom 300 died in a scene of dreadful carnage. One civilian wounded by the bomb, Mohamed el Alwani, described to us the bloody scene:

'We got up to see if we could find our family but we couldn't get in: the flames from the fire were enormous, the fire was incredible. Everyone was dead ... there were skeletons lying around. During maybe five minutes the fire had burnt them completely. Outside I found my father screaming, "My kids ... my kids ... my kids." The civil defence had put a blanket over me and left me outside, so when I heard my father I got up and told him, "Dad, I am Mohamed." He embraced me and went with me in the ambulance to hospital.'[26]

The attack on the Amariyah bunker was a malfunction not of the bomb or its targeting system but of intelligence. The coalition made some play of accusing the Iraqis of deliberately crowding civilians into a military bunker; but in the end it simply apologised for a tragic mistake.

Saddam took one other stab at the coalition during the five weeks of the air campaign. On the night of 29 January an Iraqi mechanized division – a mix of tanks and infantry – and two more brigades thrust south across the Kuwaiti border into Saudi Arabia. Schwarzkopf's intelligence team had picked up the concentration before it crossed the border, but did not know what to make of it. A tape of the voice of a US operator watching his unmanned spyplane picking up the Iraqis crossing the border indicates the level of surprise that Saddam achieved: 'Holy crow, let's see what they are. Closer ... closer. They've crossed into Saudi Arabia. King Fahad's going to be pissed. Fahad baby's going to be pissed ... he's going to be hot.'[27]

The area immediately beyond the border was sparsely defended by detachments of US marines who had to pull back before the overwhelming weight of Iraqi armour. Four marines were killed in the first 'friendly fire' incident among American troops on the ground, when one unit fired at what it thought were the advancing Iraqis, only to hit its fellow marines. Another marine unit lost seven dead in a further friendly fire incident before they withdrew. Within hours, the Iraqi force had occupied Khafji, a Saudi town just 4 miles (6 km) from the border, whose population had already abandoned it because it was well within Iraqi artillery range from across the border. Only two marine reconnaissance teams remained in the town, and they hunkered down and reported on the strength and location of the occupying Iraqis.

Schwarzkopf and his team had been caught by surprise; Saddam had scored a useful piece of short-term propaganda. But he had committed only a relatively meagre force, with no sign of a follow-up. This was no large-scale invasion. He had seized a tiny portion of Saudi Arabia and given the coalition a fright. But his 5th Mechanized Division was now exposed to air attack by the allies, who had complete control of the skies. During the following two days, Horner's strike aircraft destroyed huge numbers of Iraqi tanks and armoured vehicles. Saudi and Qatari troops fought their way into Khafji and recaptured the town from the battered Iraqis. What had started looking like a bold initiative by Iraq had been exposed as an ill-conceived and reckless mistake. Schwarzkopf's fears that he faced formidable Iraqi resistance in Kuwait were sharply reduced.

But the coalition's commander-in-chief was taking no chances. Under cover of the five-week air campaign, he put his ambitious redeployment strategy into effect, and the great deception plan took shape. While visible preparations went on for a possible landing on the coast and marines exercised in the area immediately south of Kuwait, hundreds of thousands of troops, together with huge numbers of armoured vehicles and guns and lorry-loads of logistical supplies, moved west. Travelling in long lines up the road that would take them hundreds of miles from the sea, they were extending their front line beyond Saudi Arabia's border with Kuwait to where it abutted Iraq. The French, on the extreme left, and the US XVIII Airborne Corps had the furthest to go; VII Corps, with its heavy armoured vehicles, had the shortest distance to cover. It was a nightmare of logistical organization and manoeuvre: more than 30,000 vehicles fought for space on a single desert road. Britain's 1st Division alone had to shift no less than 24,000 tons of ammunition and over 200,000 gallons (900,000 litres) of fuel. By the middle of February, Schwarzkopf had some quarter of a million American, French and British troops with 1500 tanks – the coalition's heaviest armoured forces – lining the Iraqi border up to 200 miles (320 km) west of Kuwait. He was preparing to launch his left hook north into the Iraqi desert and then east into Kuwait.

By this time, Washington was becoming impatient for the ground campaign to begin. But Schwarzkopf was determined not to be rushed. When Powell told him he had informed President Bush that the attack would begin on 24 February, Schwarzkopf erupted: he replied that the weather looked very bad for the 24th and 25th, and he told Powell to make it clear to the President that it was militarily unsound to attack in bad weather. 'For Chrissake, Colin, don't you understand? My marine commander has come to me and said we need to wait: we're talking about marines' lives.' Even Powell lost his temper at this: 'Don't patronise me with talk about human lives,' he shot back. 'Don't tell me I don't care about casualties. What are you doing? Putting on some kind of show for your military commanders?' The row ended amicably when the weather prospects suddenly improved, and Schwarzkopf was able to confirm that 24 February was on.[28]

THE GROUND WAR, 24 FEBRUARY–28 FEBRUARY

The attack began at 4 a.m. that Sunday, the 24th. Schwarzkopf had arranged to stagger the assault in two stages. In order to maintain the fiction that the main weight of the attack would be against Kuwait itself, the troops on the far eastern flank, the US Marine Corps, were the first to move – against Kuwait's southern border. The Arab forces alongside them were held back for the first 24 hours. At the same moment, 200 miles (320 km) to the west, the French and the fast-moving troops of the US XVIII Airborne Corps launched themselves due north across the Iraqi desert, heading for the Euphrates. Schwarzkopf held his main armour – VII Corps, in the centre – behind the start line for the moment. They were scheduled to launch their attack on day two.

The marines feared they would meet robust opposition: Saddam's troops had built some formidable sand ramparts on the southern Kuwaiti border. The Iraqis had laid minefields, and in places they had dug ditches which they appeared to be planning to fill with burning oil. In the event, the two marine divisions – aided by an artillery barrage from the battleship *Missouri* in the Gulf – encountered little resistance and were soon reporting large numbers of Iraqis surrendering. There was no attack from the direction Saddam was expecting. 'The Iraqis were convinced we were coming from the sea,' Schwarzkopf recalls. 'They arranged themselves in a way to protect the beaches ... so we outflanked them. I had my troops where I needed them, the Iraqis didn't move, so it was the "I gotcha" moment!'[29]

Over on the western flank, Schwarzkopf's great left hook was soon well on its way to its goal. The French advanced towards As Salman, 70 miles (110 km) inside Iraq, and would capture it a day behind schedule, on the 25th. Before this happened, they were rapidly overtaken to their right by the men of the US 101st Airborne Division, flown in by male and female pilots in 300 helicopters. By the end of the first day, the 101st had seized a point codenamed Objective Cobra 90 miles (140 km) inside Iraq, halfway to the Euphrates. Their progress and that of the marines to the east was exceeding Schwarzkopf's expectations. Anxious to prevent the Republican Guard divisions escaping before his main force could destroy them, he decided to bring forward the time for VII Corps to start rolling its heavy tanks across the Iraqi border. Instead of sending them off on day two, he brought their start time forward to 3 p.m. on day one.

The various Iraqi divisions in the south of the country, way to the west of Kuwait and about 200 miles (320 km) from the Gulf coast, had been expecting a quiet time. They were deployed as a long-stop in case the anticipated coalition attack on Kuwait's coastline and

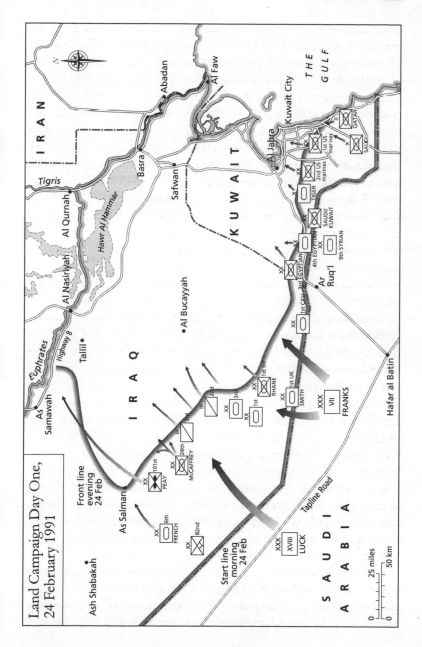

Land Campaign Day One,
24 February 1991

southern border spilt over into southern Iraq. Suddenly, in the middle of the afternoon of 24 February, they found themselves overwhelmed by one of the fiercest artillery bombardments ever. One pulverizing new weapon, the Multiple Launch Rocket System, could deliver a salvo of rockets from a multi-tube launcher in a few seconds: each rocket scattered 644 bomblets over a wide area, and the Iraqi troops must have felt they were being showered with hand grenades. This artillery barrage was the prelude to an advance by four heavy divisions. One mechanized and two US armoured divisions broke into Iraq on a 50-mile (80-km) front, with Britain's tanks following 21 hours later. Their Challengers and Abramses could utterly outgun and outperform the Soviet-supplied tanks of the Iraqi border divisions, and they were also expected to outmatch the more modern T72s of the Republican Guard, which were their ultimate target.

The 1st US Division smashed through the Iraqi fortifications just inside the border with mine ploughs that buried many Iraqis alive. At midday the following day, the 25th, the British pushed through behind them and swung east towards the Kuwaiti border, while the three US divisions in VII Corps headed north and then east towards the Republican Guard. Britain's General Rupert Smith made the 7th Armoured Division, the Desert Rats, his spearhead. The break-in to Iraq went faultlessly. The American 1st Division had cleared lanes through the minefields for them and marked them with tapes. 'Welcome to Iraq, courtesy of the Big Red One,' read the signs. Once out on its own in the desert, the first British unit to run into opposition was the Queen's Royal Irish Hussars. It was 4.30 p.m. The Iraqi position was a small one, and after an exchange of fire white flags soon appeared; the surrendering Iraqis were clearly already suffering from a severe lack of food and water. Smith gave his units a set of objectives codenamed after metals: one of them, Copper, proved a tougher Iraqi position than most. The Scots Dragoon Guards in tanks and the Staffordshire Regiment in Warrior armoured personnel carriers were directed to suppress it in a night attack. The tanks broke into the position first, and then the men in the accompanying Warriors waited for the shout: 'De-bus,

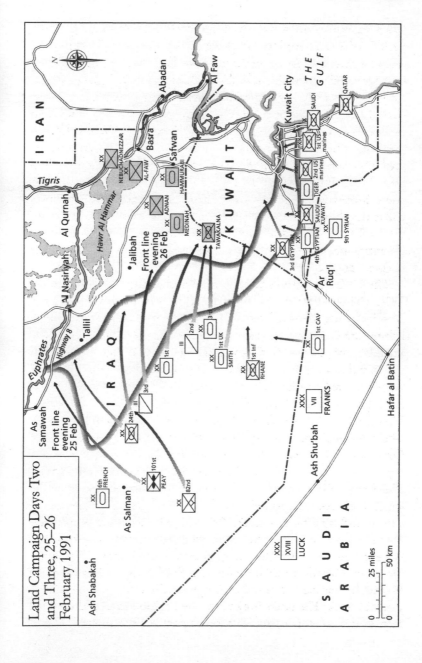

Land Campaign Days Two and Three, 25–26 February 1991

De-bus.' On went the brakes, and the men poured out of the vehicles and quickly overan the position. There was some hand-to-hand fighting in the one-and-a-half-hour battle, and five of the British soldiers were wounded.

Across the rest of the front, the Americans too made short work of the Iraqi strongpoints. At the end of their first day there were only 6 men reported killed and 27 wounded across the entire battlefield.

The heavy tank divisions of VII Corps moved slowly compared to the fast-moving airborne and lighter-equipped forces in XVIII Corps to their west. On the first night, General Franks, commanding VII Corps, called a halt to his tanks. He wanted to make sure they were all able to move forward at the same time the following morning, the 25th.

Schwarzkopf was in his war room at 4 a.m. on the 25th to assess the progress of Desert Storm. Resistance on all fronts was far weaker than he had expected, and the Iraqis indicated that they were about to abandon Kuwait by destroying the desalination plant. His troops were moving forward on all fronts, and reports everywhere spoke of Iraqi resistance collapsing. Speed was vital if he was to stop Saddam Hussein's Republican Guard escaping to fight another day. Schwarzkopf singled out Franks: he was the man holding up the advance by not spurring on his heavy tanks to meet the Republican Guard. He was scarcely able to contain his anger over the next couple of days at what he saw as the inexcusably cautious pace of VII Corps towards its objectives. The other units over to the west were soon on the Euphrates, in command of the road between Baghdad and Basra and attempting to deny the Iraqis an escape route.

As the offensive continued, the extent of the Iraqi collapse became almost pitifully apparent. Thousands were dying, tens of thousands were surrendering and even more men were simply fleeing. Captain Mujbil Habib of the 7th Division told us of the dismay among Iraqi troops.

'Morale collapsed towards the end because we were nearly defeated, our supplies wouldn't arrive. Communication was cut, so our divisions collapsed: it was very hard to evacuate the injured and the martyrs. Towards the end American forces used a scorched earth policy: they would use cluster bombs – the whole earth explodes and not a single human life remains. I saw this with my own eyes. They were using their overwhelming military power, planes, missiles: it was very ugly, they didn't have any consideration for human life.'[30]

Another soldier, Abu Fatima, remembers how the Iraqis would eat or drink anything they could find: 'The water was cut off, there was no water in Kuwait ... we started drinking water from car radiators. It was filthy water but we had to drink it.'[31]

At 1 a.m. on the 26th, a JSTARS aircraft, which could monitor any movement on the ground, picked up a growing exodus north from Kuwait City. It was clear that Iraqis were escaping in any vehicle they could find. Glosson tasked his F15Es and A10s to strike at the fugitive convoys with missiles and cluster bombs, and for the next 18 hours their attacks littered the road with shattered vehicles – and corpses. The main road from Jahra north towards Basra became known as the Highway of Death. On it and the smaller road that looped around and went north up the coast nearly 2000 vehicles were destroyed. Sergeant Sameeh Muden told us what it was like as he and some fellow soldiers tried to escape: 'A bloody massacre took place there. The planes were bombing everyone on the road, including civilians, the young, the old, anyone there. We had kids with us, there were Kuwaitis leaving on that same day, civilians, kids and families, planes were not distinguishing civilian from military, young from old. That same road we call it the "road of death". I lived under that bombing for more than four and a half hours.'[32]

Another Iraqi, called Sardar, described how the bombs literally set people on fire: 'We were driving along and we saw two big lorries that had been hit, burning ahead of us. The driver of one of the burning lorries had tried to get out. He had one hand on the steering wheel and was trying to open the door with the other, but he couldn't escape. So that hand had fallen down, but the other was still on the steering wheel and all his body was on fire – there were flames everywhere. I could see that the passenger next to him was also on fire but I couldn't really make him out. There were many injured people on the road. Some were slightly injured, some were badly injured, some were without arms or legs. When they saw our car, even though some of them were half dead, they tried to crawl towards us but they just couldn't make it. And anyway we didn't have any space for them. I knew no medical help – ambulances or whatever – would be coming to them but we just had to leave them.'[33]

Saddam Hussein was still able to fight back. On the evening of the 25th the Americans had just 30 seconds' warning of a Scud attack on Dhahran in Saudi Arabia. An attempt to intercept the Scud with Patriot missiles stationed near the base was a failure, and the Iraqi missile made a direct hit on a barracks: 28 US soldiers were killed and 98 wounded.

The war on the ground soon became little more than an Iraqi rout. There were moments when the American marines in Kuwait itself, or the British and Americans fast approaching Kuwait from the west, met small pockets of spirited resistance. But on the whole, the battles, if they can be called battles, to liberate Kuwait were almost bloodless. One of Britain's tank regiments, the Royal Scots Dragoon Guards, were apprehensive enough as they approached their first contact. Captain Charlie Lambert recalls how their advance into enemy territory started just before last light on the 25th.

'Little did we know at this stage how little resistance the Iraqis were going to put up. 24 section were able to provide the Battle Group with white light during an infantry dismounted attack, while 21 and 22 sections were involved in the collection and removal of prisoners. No one who saw those prisoners will forget how pathetic they were and how happy and grateful they were to be captured.'[34]

Captain Calcott's regimental medical aid post treated a number of Iraqi casualties, and was appalled by the condition of the prisoners. 'Many of them had not eaten for days and were rationed to one cup of water per day. When offered a cup of water, many just sipped it and passed it back assuming the cup was for the whole crew. Many had little muscle into which to inject pain-killing morphine. Others remained motionless and fearful as they were treated: I believe they dared not believe we really did care. One of them required urgent attention, but made a good recovery C squadron had seen him shot by his commanders in the neck while trying to surrender'.[35]

Many of the most damaging engagements – as at Khafji – were exchanges of friendly fire. One of the worst occurred on 26 February, when British troops moved on from successfully suppressing an Iraqi position at Brass to attack the next strongpoint, codenamed Steel. Suddenly, out of the sky two A10 aircraft, armed with Maverick missiles, launched an attack on what they thought were Iraqi T55 tanks. They had acquired their targets from heights well above 5000 feet (1600 metres), which made visual checks almost impossible. If they had been low enough to see the inverted Vs on the personnel carriers they would have known they were British – two Warriors manned by soldiers of the Royal Regiment of Fusiliers. The missiles were deadly accurate: 9 soldiers died and 11 were wounded. It was a dreadful mistake, aggravated by the reaction of the US air force chief, Chuck Horner, whose first explanation was that the accident had been caused by mines. De la Billiére remembers Horner being highly emotional and telling him that no blame should be attached to his pilots. It was by far the biggest single casualty toll the British suffered in the Gulf War. Britain's own divisional commander in the Gulf War, Major General Rupert Smith, explained that he too had had a narrow escape from being attacked by friendly fire: 'My ADC had just stopped our vehicle to check our position…. I heard my leading battle group calling an enemy target on the position I was on…. I was in front of the battle group instead of coming up behind them…. "I am the target you are calling," I radioed. "Roger out," came the reply. I then attracted the attention of my ADC in the turret of the vehicle by grabbing his leg and telling him to move out of there.'[36]

That same day, the 26th, the American forces in Schwarzkopf's left hook who had reached the Euphrates swung east towards

Kuwait and Basra. The priority now was for them to locate the Republican Guard divisions and destroy as much of their equipment as possible before they had a chance to escape. By mid-afternoon, the 3rd US Armoured Division had come up against the Tawakalna Division of the Republican Guard in the Iraqi desert just north-west of Kuwait. In the next 12 hours, the superior gunnery of the American Abrams tanks overwhelmed the T72s facing them, and by dawn on the 27th the Tawakalna was effectively annihilated.

But once again friendly fire took a severe toll, this time of a US cavalry unit. A squadron (equivalent to a British battalion) of Bradley armoured cars of the US 7th Cavalry was heading into the battle with the Tawakalna. They had an unfortunate history, having been with General Custer in the disastrous battle of Little Big Horn back in 1876. The victorious Indians had taken a heavy toll of them then, and in 1965 they had lost over 150 dead in an ambush in Vietnam. Their 4th Squadron commander in the Gulf War was Lieutenant Colonel Terry Lee Tucker. His Bradleys were operating in very poor visibility that Tuesday afternoon, and one of his troops suddenly ran into a line of tanks and armoured cars from Saddam's Tawakalna Division. Tucker's men came under murderous fire – not just from the Iraqis, but from a US tank unit as well. In the fog and confusion, the Bradleys had slewed around to the north and run partly across the approach track of the Abrams tanks, which were also bent on attacking the Tawakalna. For several frightening minutes the Bradley crews fought a savage close-quarters fight with Iraqis firing machine guns and rocket-propelled grenades, while tank rounds from their own side smashed into some of their vehicles. Tucker had to order his Bradleys to withdraw under cover of a smoke-screen. More than a dozen of his vehicles had been hit. Most were damaged by Iraqi fire, but three were destroyed by American shells.

Less than 24 hours later, on Wednesday the 27th, VII Corps confronted more Republican Guards. Around midday, tanks of the US 1st Armoured Division, advancing in much better visibility than the day before, spotted Iraqi tanks at a range of just under 2 miles (around 3000 metres). It was the Medinah Division of the Republican Guard, and about 150 Abrams tanks were soon engaging them. The American Abrams had a kill range of 6000 feet (some 1800 metres), and was able to fire on the move without its tank barrel being deflected from its target. The effective range of the Iraqi T72 was no more than 5600 feet (1700 metres), and then only when it was stationary. It was a wholly one-sided fight: 60 Iraqi tanks were destroyed, but not a single US tank was lost.

Saddam had one final shot in his locker, an act of vindictive vandalism that was to set the seal on the world's unanimous condemnation of his aggression against Kuwait. He ordered the destruction of Kuwait's oilfields. The inferno of blazing wells and the resulting pollution of air and water was one of the greatest man-made environmental disasters of the twentieth century.

In the middle of that afternoon, in Washington, President Bush called his senior advisers, including his military chief, Colin Powell, to the Oval Office. By now they had seen television pictures of the extent of the destruction and killing that had taken place on the so-called Highway of Death north of Kuwait City. Powell had already talked to Schwarzkopf about the scale of the Iraqi collapse: the US marines accompanied by the Arab forces had now reoccupied Kuwait City and virtually the whole of the rest of the Gulf state was free of Iraqi troops. Powell told Schwarzkopf, 'The doves are starting to complain about all the damage you are doing.' Schwarzkopf had no objection in principle, but asked Powell to keep the war going for at least another day. He suggested a 'five-day war' sounded good. Powell agreed.

In the meeting with Bush, Powell was able to say he had already consulted Schwarzkopf: 'Both Norm and I feel we're now within the window of opportunity to end this.' There was some discussion about the unfinished business of the other major war aim – the destruction of Saddam's military capability. Two of the four major Republican Guard units had been crippled, and they might catch more in the few hours before a ceasefire. But any further damage to Iraq's forces would mean the involvement of coalition forces in and around Basra and beyond. There was general agreement that pushing the campaign that far could damage the unity of the coalition, and that enough of the essential task of weakening Saddam's military strength had been achieved. No doubt the pictures of the Highway of Death made an impression as well. The President did not want America to appear a bully because it had gone on pursuing an army now in total retreat. Bush said he could announce a ceasefire that evening on national television. Powell agreed to consult Schwarzkopf, who, after a minute's thought, gave his approval. Bush announced that a ceasefire would become effective in Iraq and Kuwait at 8 a.m. the following day, the 28th. That would be midnight Eastern Standard Time in the USA.

In the few hours left before the firing stopped, coalition troops raced forward to seize what ground they could. The British covered 40 miles (64 km): in the small hours they were just inside the western edge of Kuwait. By 8 a.m. they were astride the Kuwait City–Basra road. One US journalist described the thousands of British flags on the advancing vehicles as 'a glorious flutter of reds and whites and royal blues. Like an avatar of the bygone empire, the British Army charged east, proudly, at full pelt.'[37]

Four days later, at 11 a.m. on 3 March 1991, Schwarzkopf arrived at the airfield of Safwan, just inside Iraq, to agree the terms of the ceasefire with Iraqi generals. The delegation from Baghdad was led by Saddam's army deputy chief of staff, Lieutenant General Sultan Hashim Ahmad. Before they went into a tent for the meeting, Schwarzkopf told him everyone would be searched.

'There is no need to search us,' said Ahmad. 'We left our weapons in the vehicles.... I refuse to be searched unless the senior participant on the US side is searched as well.'

Schwarzkopf shot back: 'I *am* the senior US participant.'

The Iraqis admitted to taking 41 prisoners, and Ahmad appeared astonished when he was told that the coalition had 60,000 Iraqi prisoners. 'His face went pale,' Schwarzkopf wrote later. 'He clearly had no concept of the magnitude of the Iraqi defeat.' But he appeared to agree to the American terms without demur. The only request he had was that Iraqi military helicopters should be allowed to continue to fly over the country in areas where roads and bridges were down. Schwarzkopf agreed: it seemed to him unreasonable not to.

'So you mean helicopters that are armed can fly in Iraqi skies but not the fighters?' asked Ahmad.

'Yes,' replied Schwarzkopf. He was to regret it. Within weeks, he says, 'we discovered what the son of a bitch really had in mind: using helicopter gunships to suppress rebellions in Basra and other cities'.[38]

Casualties on the Iraqi side of the Gulf War dwarfed the losses among coalition forces. Figures of 20,000 up to 100,000 are estimated for the number of Iraqis killed, with the lower end thought likelier. America's Central Command put the figure at 20,000 dead with anything up to 250,000 Iraqis wounded. Coalition forces lost around 250 killed in action and around 600 wounded. Astonishingly, the US losses of 152 dead from accidents and friendly fire incidents appear higher than the figure of 147 for those reported killed in action. But overall, the relative casualty figures make this one of the most one-sided wars ever fought. Some military historians have accused Schwarzkopf and his planning team of massive overkill. Clearly, with hindsight, the war could have been won with half or even a third of the strength of the troops sent in on the ground. But this was an age in which the Western democracies, and America most of all, insisted that the main purpose of their commitment of resources of money, technology and military tactics was to preserve the lives of their own troops. Against that background, no general was going to make do with any force other than the largest he could persuade his government to provide.

There was relief and some surprise that Saddam had at no stage ordered the use of chemical weapons. Tariq Aziz, his Foreign Minister, later imprisoned by the Americans, told BBC2 after the war, 'We didn't think it was wise to use them. That's all I can say: it was not wise to use them in that kind of war against that kind of enemy.' Asked if Saddam had been afraid of American nuclear retaliation, Aziz said, 'You can draw your own conclusions.'

For a brief moment after the war, most people genuinely believed that the 'New World Order' proclaimed by President Bush had really arrived. The Cold War was over and a uniquely wide coalition of nations had clubbed together to oust a grim dictator from a state he had seized by force. Once Kuwait had been liberated, its government was restored and the coalition dissolved with expressions of mutual admiration. There was little talk of pursuing Saddam to Baghdad and ousting his regime, because that would have been quite outside the UN mandate to Schwarzkopf's broad-based coalition and would have split it wide open. The bulk of the huge American force went home.[39]

But the new order quickly unravelled. The chaos that followed the collapse of Yugoslavia prompted nothing like the international consensus over Iraq. Peace in the Middle East briefly blossomed, then receded. As for Iraq itself, a revolt by the Marsh Arabs in the south led to massive repression and the draining of the marshes by Saddam. President Bush, who had openly encouraged the revolt, rejected pleas by the rebels to intervene in their desperate fight to stop Saddam crushing them. In the decade after the war Saddam continued to defy the United Nations and obstruct the work of UN inspectors in monitoring his weapons programmes. Sanctions and a few bursts of punitive military action did little to chasten Saddam, but caused much suffering among the Iraqi people.

But there was another, much more portentous, aftermath to the Gulf War of 1990–1. The influx of US troops into Saudi Arabia, and the fact that not all of them left the country immediately, enraged some militant Muslims, who found it intolerable that the 'land of the two mosques' had been profaned by American unbelievers. Shortly after the end of the war, the wealthy Saudi Osama Bin Laden founded Al-Qaeda. The aim of this terrorist organization was to reduce outside influence in the Muslim world, promote Islamic orthodoxy and attack American targets around the world. On 11 September 2001 Al-Qaeda struck: two aircraft were crashed into the twin Trade Center towers in New York.

By this time, the United States had a new President, George Bush's son George W Bush. He responded to the 9/11 attack by declaring a war on terror, which was soon to target Saddam Hussein's regime in Iraq. The pressure built up and President Bush, with the support of Britain's Tony Blair, tried but failed to recreate the kind of worldwide coalition that had backed the use of force in 1990–1. They decided to go it alone with a handful of military allies, which included no Arabs and few mainstream European nations. The invasion of 2003 was a quick military success, but its aftermath was hopelessly mishandled. Over the following years, increasing lawlessness, sectarian violence and attacks on the coalition forces left Iraq on a road to chaos.

By the end of the twentieth century, it had become clear that the nature of warfare was set to change fundamentally. There would still be a place for the massive all-arms panoply of major industrial war, with technology making it more and more possible for the stronger side to reduce the risk of its own casualties. But there would also be an increasing incentive for weaker sides to find alternative ways of pursuing their struggles. The implications for leadership, force structure and weapon system design will challenge defence policy priorities well into the twenty-first century.

NOTES

AMIENS

1 Nicholas Hobbes, *Essential Militaria* (Atlantic Books, London, 2003), p.117.
2 Hew Strachan, *The First World War* (Pocket Books, London, 2006), p.304.
3 Ibid.
4 Malcolm Brown, *1918 The Year of Victory* (Pan Books, London, 1998), p.4.
5 Ibid.
6 Ibid., p.23.
7 Ibid., p.25.
8 Field Marshal Douglas Haig, *The Private Papers of Douglas Haig 1914–19*, ed. Robert Blake (Eyre and Spottiswoode, London, 1952), p.291.
9 Ibid., p.294.
10 Martin Gilbert, *Winston S. Churchill*, Vol. IV (Heinemann, London, 1975) pp.77, 79.
11 Brown, p.48.
12 Ibid., p.39.
13 Ernst Jünger, *The Storm of Steel* (Constable, London, 1994), p.250.
14 Ibid., pp.254–9, *passim.*
15 Brown, p.45.
16 Ibid.
17 Gilbert, p.102.
18 Ibid., p.104.
19 Strachan, p.304.
20 Sir John Monash, *The Australian Victories in France in 1918* (Imperial War Museum, London, 1993), p.56.
21 Tim Travers, *How the War was Won* (Pen and Sword Military Classics, Barnsley, 2005), p.116.
22 J.P. Harris and Niall Barr, *Amiens to the Armistice: The BEF in the Hundred Days' Campaign* (Brassey's, London, 1999), p.71.
23 Sergeant H.L. Witherby, *Account of Operations Taken Part by the 20th Lethbridge Bty, Canadian Field Artillery, 5th Brigade, August 8–12th 1918* (Imperial War Museum, London), 79/46/1, p.1.
24 Brown, p.190.
25 Witherby, p.3.
26 W.H. Downing, *To the Last Ridge* (Duffy & Snellgrove, Sydney, 1998), p.135.
27 Brown, pp.197–9.
28 Witherby, p. 3.
29 Major D.D. Coutts DSO (Imperial War Museum, London), 96/51/1, p.76.
30 Witherby, p. 3.

31 J.R. Armitage, testimony appears on the website of the Australian War Memorial, Canberra. http://www.awm.gov.au/1918/battles/amiens.htm

32 Ibid.

33 Coutts, p.75.

34 Brown, p.199.

35 Witherby, p.4.

36 Coutts, p.76.

37 Quoted in *The Oxford Companion to Military History*, ed. Richard Holmes (Oxford University Press, 2003), p.45.

38 Travers, p.122.

39 Gary Sheffield, *Forgotten Victory: The First World War: Myths and Realities* (Review, London, 2002), p.241.

40 D.G. Denison (Imperial War Museum, London), p.191.

41 Ibid.

42 Witherby, p.9.

43 Ibid., pp.4–10.

44 The story of the 10th Essex appears in Michael Stedman, *Advance to Victory 1918*, (Leo Cooper, London, 2001), p.59.

45 Sergeant G. H. Robertson, http://www.awm.gov.au/1918/battles/amiens.htm

46 Hew Strachan relates in *The First World War* that at the Somme British battalions numbering 1000 men carried four Lewis guns and one or two trench mortars into action. By Amiens, battalions numbered 500 men and were typically equipped with 30 Lewis guns and eight trench mortars.

47 Coutts, p.76.

48 Lt. MacPherson, Royal Canadian Horse Artillery, witnessed this charge from 500 yards away. He wrote in his diary: 'I now know what it is to gallop through Machine Gun fire and it is not pleasant.' From his diary, Vol. 10, 8 August 1918, MG30 E23, Public Archives, Ottawa, Canada.

49 Appears at http://www.firstworldwar.com/diaries/augtonov.htm

50 Coutts, p.77.

51 Harris and Barr, p.108.

52 Trevor Wilson, *The Myriad Faces of War* (Basil Blackwell, Oxford, 1986), p.582.

53 Lieutenant Alfred Gaby of Tasmania won a Victoria Cross after he strode coolly along a German parapet firing his pistol into the defenders. An entire company of 50 men and four machine guns surrendered to him. From James McWilliams and R. James Steel, *Amiens 1918* (Tempus Publishing, London, 2004), p.124.

54 Travers, p.121.

55 Witherby, p.11.

56 Quoted in Barrie Pitt, *1918 The Last Act*, (Papermac, London, 1962), p.205.

57 Appears at http://www.firstworldwar.com/source/amiens_hindenburg.htm

58 Gregor Dallas, *1918 War and Peace* (Pimlico, London, 2002), p.57.

59 Erich Ludendorff, *My War Memoirs*, Vol. II, (Hutchinson, London, 1919), p.679.

60 Strachan, p.311.

61 Robert Asprey, *The German High Command at War*, (Warner Books, London, 1994), pp.449–50.

62 Brown, p.191.
63 Harris and Barr, p.2.
64 Appears at http://www.firstworldwar.com/source/amiens_gibbs.htm
65 Jünger, p.318.

MIDWAY

1 Jonathon Parshall and Anthony Tully, *Shattered Sword: The Untold Story of the Battle of Midway* (Potomac Books, Washington DC, 2005), p.125.
2 Michael Barnhart, 'Japan's Economic Security and the Origins of the Pacific War' in *Journal of Strategic Studies*, Vol. 4, 1981, No.1, pp. 97–124.
3 Walter Lord, *Day of Infamy* (Wordsworth Military Library, London, 1998), p.8.
4 Ibid., p.7.
5 Interview with WO Takeshi Maeda. Transcript courtesy of Jon Parshall.
6 Lord, *Day of Infamy*, p.24.
7 These figures are debated. We have used Paul Dull's seminal study *A Battle History of the Imperial Japanese Navy* (Naval Institute Press, Annapolis, MD, 1978). It is based on Japanese original material.
8 Lord, *Day of Infamy*, p.37.
9 Ibid., p.48.
10 Ibid., p.66.
11 Ibid., p.67.
12 Gordon Prange, *At Dawn We Slept* (Penguin, London, 1991), p.67.
13 Lord, *Day of Infamy*, p.71.
14 Ibid., p.90.
15 The story is hard to verify but is quoted in the official literature at the USS Arizona monument in Pearl Harbor.
16 Prange, *At Dawn We Slept*, p.403.
17 For an audio recording see: http://www.radiochemistry.org/history/video/fdr_infamy.html
18 Gordon Prange, *Miracle at Midway* (Penguin Books, London, 2002), p.6.
19 Ibid., p.9.
20 Ibid., p.35.
21 Mark Healy, *Midway 1942* (Osprey Publishing, London, 2005), p.15.
22 Samuel Morison, *History of United States Naval Operations in World War II, Volume IV: Coral Sea, Midway and Submarine Actions, May 1942–August 1942*, (Little Brown and Company, Boston, 1950), p.84.
23 Ibid.
24 Prange, *Miracle at Midway*, p.170.
25 Ibid., p.181.
26 Ibid., p.190.
27 Robert Cressman et al., *A Glorious Page in our History: The Battle of Midway* (Pictoral Histories Publishing Company, Missoula, MT, 1990), p.60.
28 Healy, p.54.

29 Prange, *Miracle at Midway*, p.199.

30 Parshall and Tully, p.200.

31 'The Tragedy of Midway', in NHK (ed.), *Pivotal Point of History, Vol. 4, Nagoya* (KTC Chuoh Publishing, Japan, 2001), p.181.

32 Parshall and Tully, p.149.

33 Cressman et al., p.84.

34 Prange, *Miracle at Midway*, p.238.

35 Ibid.

36 Walter Lord, *Midway: The Incredible Victory* (Wordsworth Military Library, London, 2000), p.86.

37 Ibid., p.139.

38 Masaji Fukuoka, *Sorrow of Reconnaissance Plane 'Chikuma' Witnessing the Tragedy of Midway Thrice* (1983), in Toshio Hashimoto et al. (1992), *Testimony: The Battle of Midway*, (Kojinsha, Tokyo, 1992), pp.52–3.

39 Prange, *Miracle at Midway*, p. 211.

40 Healy, p.61.

41 Prange, *Miracle at Midway*, p.217.

42 Pashall and Tully, p.183.

43 Ibid., p.188.

44 Prange, *Miracle at Midway*, p.246.

45 Interview with Sesu Mitoya. Transcript courtesy of Jon Parshall.

46 Cressman et al., p.96.

47 Parshall and Tully, p.236.

48 Lord, *Midway: The Incredible Victory*, p.173.

49 Transcript of interview with Kanao Ryoichi, courtesy of Jon Parshall.

50 Naoki Kohdachi, *Yoshino Haruo: Reflection of Pearl Harbour Attack Squadron after the War*, in Naoki Kohdachi, *The Portrait of Warriors* (Bunshun Nesko, Tokyo, 2004), p.16.

51 Prange, *Miracle at Midway*, p.266.

52 Ibid., p.274.

53 '*Banzai*' was a Japanese battle cry during the war. It literally translates as 'ten thousand years' and was used in the acclamation of the Emperors, similar to shouting 'Long Live the King' in the West. As a battle cry, *banzai* was an expression of the samurai's *gyokusai*, a determination to die rather than accept defeat. Later in the war Kamikaze pilots reportedly shouted banzai as they flew their aircraft into enemy ships.

54 There is some debate over this story, but it appears in: Mitsuo Fuchida, *Midway: the Battle that Doomed Japan* (US Naval Institute Press, Annapolis, MD, 1955), p.164.

55 Both of these observations are taken from Prange, *Miracle at Midway*, p.277.

56 Lord, *Midway: The Incredible Victory*, p.215.

57 Prange, *Miracle at Midway*, p.277.

58 Toshio Hashimoto, 'Hiryu Squadron – Our Fight and Death for Honour in Midway', in Toshio Hashimoto et.al. *Testimony: the Battle of Midway*, p.30.

59 Hiroshi Kamei, 'Surviving Hero from Midway', in Toshio Hashimoto et.al *Testimony: the Battle of Midway*, pp.234–5.

60 Ibid.

STALINGRAD

1 It is worth remembering that during the Second World War the German army relied overwhelmingly on horses rather than vehicles for transport.

2 Geoffrey Roberts, *Victory at Stalingrad* (Longman, London, 2002), p.23.

3 The elimination of the key political and military personnel of the Soviet State during Barbarossa is discussed by Jurgen Forster. The SS was 'charged with the elimination of the civilian cadres... the Army was to eliminate the "Jewish–Bolshevik intelligentsia" within the Red Army, the commissars, and the real or potential carriers of resistance.' This appears in David Cesarani (ed.), *The Final Solution* (Routledge, London, 1994), p.89.

4 Incredibly, the focus of armaments production had already been shifted away from the army to the airforce and navy in anticipation of the final showdown with the Anglo–Saxon nations. Hence the reason why the army ran into problems in the autumn.

5 Antony Beevor, *Stalingrad* (Viking, London, 1998), p.23

6 Simon Sebag Montefiore, *Stalin: The Court of the Red Tsar* (Phoenix, London, 2004), p.380.

7 Ibid., p. 387. This story appears in the memoirs of Beria's lieutenant, Sudoplatov, who was given the task of talking to the Bulgarian Ambassador, Ivan Stamenov.

8 Richard Overy, *Russia's War* (Penguin, London, 1999), p.154

9 Walter Goerlitz, *Paulus and Stalingrad* (Methuen, London, 1963), p.155.

10 This appears in Directive Number 41 of 5th April 1942. It is quoted in Hugh Trevor–Roper, *Hitler's War Directives, 1939–1945* (Sidgwick and Jackson, London, 1964), p.119.

11 The source for the diary of Wilhelm Hoffman is in fact the Soviet hero of Stalingrad, Chuikov, who claimed to have found the diary on the battlefield and to 'have [it] in my personal files'. It appears in Vasilii Chuikov, *The Beginning of the Road* (MacGibbon and Kee, London, 1963), p.248ff.

12 Overy, p.133

13 This is discussed in detail in Earl F. Ziemke and Magna E. Bauer, *Moscow to Stalingrad: Decision in the East* (Center of Military History, Washington DC, 1987), p.343.

14 Roberts, p.60.

15 Will Fowler, *Stalingrad: The Vital Seven Days* (Amber Books, London, 2005), p.23.

16 Montefiore, p.436.

17 Chuikov, p.68.

18 Interview with the authors, September 2005.

19 Fowler, p.33.

20 Stalin reiterated his determination not to evacuate people or machinery from Stalingrad when he talked to Yeremenko on the phone just before midnight on the 23rd. 'I do not want to debate this question,' shouted Stalin. 'The evacuation... will be interpreted as a decision to surrender Stalingrad. Therefore the State Defence Committee forbids it.' William Craig, *Enemy at the Gates: The Battle for Stalingrad* (Penguin, London, 2000), p.61.

21 Joel S. A. Hayward, *Stopped at Stalingrad: The Luftwaffe and Hitler's Defeat in the East, 1942–1943* (University of Kansas Press, 1998), p.189.

22 Montefiore, p.435.

23 Alexander M. Samsonov, *Stalingradskaya Bitva* (Nauka, Moscow, 1968), pp.152–3. Translated in Roberts, p.79.

24 Fowler, p.38.

25 Craig, p.67.

26 Interview with the authors, September 2005.

27 Alexander Werth, *Russia at War 1941–1945,* (E.P. Dutton Co., New York, 1964), p.508.

28 Chuikov, p.93.

29 Chuikov, p.80.

30 Montefiore, p.436.

31 Craig, p.100.

32 Chuikov, p.106.

33 Ibid., pp.221–2.

34 Andrey Khozyaynov was the only Soviet survivor of the battle for the grain elevator. His account appears in full in Fowler, p.56.

35 Hoffman, in Chuikov, *The Beginning of the Road,* p.248ff.

36 Bundersarchiv-Militarachiv, *Freiburg Im Breisgau,* RH 20-6/216, p.51.

37 Chuikov, pp.319–320.

38 The two journalists were Akulshin and Kuprin, who wrote for Pravda. This article appeared on 28 September and is quoted in Alexander Werth, *The Year of Stalingrad* (Hamish Hamilton, London, 1946), p. 231.

39 Konstantin Simonov quoted in Werth, *Russia at War,* p.417.

40 Chuikov, p.167.

41 Interview with the authors, September 2005.

42 Diary of Leutnant Joachim Stempel, 108th Panzer Grenadier Regiment, 14th Panzer Division, quoted in Fowler, p.123. See also *The Battle for Stalingrad – The Battle for the Factories,* compiled by Hans Wijers, which is full of testimony from the battle in which Stempel features prominently.

43 Chukiov quoted in Werth, *The Year of Stalingrad.*

44 Rolf Grams, Panzer Division, 1940–1945 (Bad Nauheim, 1957), p.54.

45 Chuikov, p.248ff.

46 Diary of Lt Weiner of the 24th Panzer Division, quoted in Alan Clark, *Barbarossa: The Russian–German Conflict, 1941–1945* (Weidenfeld & Nicholson, London, 1965), p.238.

47 Wilhelm Adam, *The Hard Decision* (East Berlin, 1967).

48 Fowler, pp.106–8.

49 Quoted in Walsh, p.96.

50 Fowler, pp.122–3.

51 Beevor, p.199.

52 Fowler, p.118.

53 Jeremy Noakes and Geoffrey Pridham, *Nazism 1919–1945, Vol. 3* (University of Exeter Press, 1988), p.842.

54 Beevor, p.234

55 Matthew Cooper, *The German Army 1933–1945* (Stein and Day, London, 1978), p.344

56 Richthofen's diary, quoted in Craig, p.159.

57 Out of 104 tanks in the 22nd Panzer Division, only 42 were combat ready. Ibid.

58 Memo from General Walter von Seydlitz–Kurzbach to Paulus, quoted in V.E. Tarrant, *Stalingrad: Anatomy of an Agony* (Leo Cooper, London, 1992), pp.142–3.

59 Horst Boog et al., *Germany and the Second World War, Vol. 6* (Clarenden Press, Oxford, 2001), p.1148.

60 Ziemke and Bauer, p.499.

61 Craig, pp.377–8.

62 Alan Bullock, *Hitler and Stalin: Parallel Lives* (HarperCollins, London, 1991), pp.870–1. The quote is taken from the minutes of Hitler's noon conference on 1 February. Minutes edited by Felix Gilbert in *Hitler Directs his War: Secret Records of his Daily Military Conferences* (Octagon, New York, 1950), pp.17–22.

THE IMJIN RIVER

1 Michael Hickey, *Korean War: The West Confronts Communism 1950–1953* (John Murray, London, 2000), p.10.

2 Max Hastings, *The Korean War* (Pan, London, 2000), pp.16–17.

3 Interview with General Lee Jae Jeon, Liddell Hart Archive, King's College, London, 'Cold War 17/1'.

4 Interview with Kim Oei–Hwan, Liddell Hart Archive, 'Cold War 17/9'.

5 Hastings, p.77.

6 Cabinet Records CAB128, 27.7.50, Public Records Office, London.

7 Interview with Charles Bussey, Liddell Hart Archive, 'Cold War 27/11'.

8 Interview with Robert Fountain, conducted by Max Hastings, appears in his *Korean War*, p.4.

9 Interview with Charles Bussey, Liddell Hart Archive, 'Cold War 27/11'.

10 Donald Knox, *The Korean War: Volume 1: Pusan to Chosin: An Oral History* (Thomson Learning, London, 1985), p.60.

11 Walton Walker's words to the staff officers of the 25th Division staff on 29 July 1950 are known as the 'Stand or Die Order'. It is preserved in the Truman Presidential Library and Museum. Full text is available at http://www.trumanlibrary.org/whistlestop/study_collections/korea/large/korea729_82.htm

12 Shepherd Oral History Transcript, US Marine Corps Museum.

13 Hastings, pp.118–9.

14 Knox, *The Korean War: Vol. I*, p.226.

15 Ibid.

16 Hastings, p.153.

17 Hickey, p.107.

18 Interview with Szu Chiin Chang in the BBC television programme *The War in Korea*, episode 3.

19 Interview with Kuo Fei Wu, in the BBC television programme *The War in Korea*, episode 3.

20 In 1950 Communist China had only existed for a year. China's steel production was crippled, and the country had almost no industry, and no military-industrial complex to produce weapons in large quantity. Roughly, a Chinese army had less than 10 per cent of the fire power of a US Corps. For example, it had only 36 artillery pieces of 76mm or larger, while a US Corps had over 300 guns of 105mm or larger. Nor did the Chinese have any tanks.

21 Hastings, p.187.

22 Ibid., p.189.

23 Interview with Major Edwin Simmons, Liddell Hart Archive, 'Cold War 27/10'.

24 Interview with Charles Bussey, Liddell Hart Archive, 'Cold War 27/11'.

25 Hickey, p.148.

26 Letter sent by MacArthur to Joe Martin, the Republican Minority Leader in the House of Representatives, and read out by Martin in the House on 5 April. A copy can be found at http://www.learner.org/channel/workshops/primarysources/cold-war/docs/maca.html

27 C. J. Bartlett, *The Global Conflict: The International Rivalry of the Great Powers, 1880–1990*, 2nd Edition (London: Longman, 1994), pp. 296–301. See http://www.trumanlibrary.org/whistlestop/study_collections/korea/large/index.htm to listen to Truman explaining his reasons for MacArthur's dismissal.

28 See http://www.americanrhetoric.com/speeches/douglasmacarthurfarewelladdress.htm for a recording of his speech and the transcript.

29 Hickey, p.179.

30 Matthew Ridgway, *The War in Korea* (Doubleday, London, 1967), p.171.

31 Interview with Raymond Frazier, Liddell Hart Archive, 'Cold War 27/15'.

32 Sir Anthony Farrar Hockley, interview with the authors, March 2005.

33 Interview with Toby Younger, conducted by Max Hastings, appears in his *Korean War*, p.435.

34 Guy Temple, interviewed for a BBC documentary broadcast on 26 February 2001, *Forgotten Heroes: Korea Remembered*, archive tape number 9509.

35 David Green, *The Korean War Memoir of a Gloucester, 1950–1953* (Pen and Sword, London, 2003), p.99.

36 D.E. Whatmore, Imperial War Museum, London, 93/29/1, pp.62–3.

37 Mervyn McCord, Royal Ulster Rifles, *Forgotten Heroes: Korea Remembered*, archive tape number 9509.

38 Interview with John Dyer, Royal Ulster Rifles, ibid.

39 Interview with Harry Gledden, Royal Northumberland Fusiliers, ibid.

40 This exchange is recorded in Hastings, p.257.

41 Hickey, p.223.

42 Interview with Hwang Chen in the BBC television programme *The War in Korea*, episode 3.

43 Sam Davies, *In Spite of Dungeons*, (Hodder and Stoughton, London, 1955), pp.19.

44 Green, p.100.

45 Guy Temple, *Forgotten Heroes: Korea Remembered*, archive tape number 9509.

46 F.E. Carter, Imperial War Museum, London, 99/3/1, p.27.

47 Sir Anthony Farrar Hockley, interview with the authors, March 2005.

48 Ibid.

49 Green, p.103.

50 Ibid., p.101.

51 Anthony Farrar Hockley, *The Edge of the Sword,* (Frederick Muller, London, 1954), p.89.

52 Hastings, p.266.

53 Anthony Farrar Hockley, p.89.

54 Farrar-Hockley is reported to have said the following about the Drum-Major during that moment: 'I could see his tall, lean figure, topped by a cap comforter ... he always played a bugle well and that day he was not below form. The sweet notes of our own bugle, which now echoed through the valley below him, died away. For a moment there was silence – the last note had coincided with a lull in the action. Then the noise of battle began again – but with a difference; there was no sound of a Chinese bugle. There are not many Drum-Majors in the British Army who can claim to have silenced the enemy's battle calls with a short bugle recital.' See The Glorious Glosters, Korea – 1950-51, Military History Webring:http://members.tripod.com/ ~Glosters/Imjin.html
See also: http://www.nationalarchives.gov.uk/battles/korea/battle.htm

55 Sir Anthony Farrar Hockley, interview with the authors, March 2005.

56 Brigadier Brodie said of the Battalion: "Nobody but the Glosters could have done it." See The Glorious Glosters, Korea – 1950-51, Military History Webring: http://members.tripod.com/~Glosters/Imjin.html

57 Roy Appelman, *Ridgway Duels for Korea* (Texas ACM University Press, College Station, 1990)

58 Ridgway, p.173.

59 General James A. Fleet at a conference at the IX Corps CP. Recorded in Billy Mossman, *United States Army in the Korean War. Ebb and Flow November 1950 to July 1951* (Center for Military History, Washington DC, 1990), p.441.

THE TET OFFENSIVE

1 Dr Henry Kissinger wrote that for Presidents Kennedy and Johnson 'Vietnam was the decisive battle that would determine whether guerrilla war could be stopped and the cold war won.' Kissinger, *Diplomacy* (Simon and Schuster, New York, 1994), pp.644–5.

2 'Dominoes' were first mentioned by President Eisenhower in relation to the strategic importance of Indo China at a press conference on 7 April 1954: 'You have a row of dominoes set up, you knock over the first one, and what will happen to the last one is the certainty that it will go over very quickly.' *Public Papers of the Presidents: Dwight D Eisenhower* (Office of the Federal Register, Washington, 1954), pp.381–90.

3 Quoted in Stanley Karnow, *Vietnam: A History* (Viking Press, New York, 1983), p.247.

4 General Philip Davidson, in *Vietnam at War*, (Presidio Press, New York, 1988), is in no doubt that Khe Sanh was intended by the North Vietnamese to provide them with a spectacular military victory.

5 Eric Hammel, *Siege in the Clouds* (Pacifica Press, California, 2000), p.26.

6 Ibid., p.80.

7 Ibid.

8 Michael Maclear, *Vietnam: The Ten Thousand Day War* (Avon Books, New York, 1982).

9 Quoted in a message marked 'Top Secret' to President Johnson on 3 February 1968. *Johnson National Security File*, Washington, 3 February 1968, Vietnam file 2A(2).

10 George Allen, *None So Blind* (Ivan Dee, Chicago, 2002), p.261.

11 The siege of Khe Sanh, which was such a dramatic and destructive prelude to the Tet Offensive, quickly became little more than a footnote. Within weeks of Tet, the siege was abandoned by the North Vietnamese, and the base was later vacated willingly by the Americans. The Visitors' Book in the museum there today is a monument to the human passion for rewriting history. Many Vietnamese and some American visitors describe Khe Sanh as a significant Communist victory, but a number of American veterans dispute this. One entry on 13 May 2003 reads: 'Don't believe the crap you read in this book: US Marine Corps kicked ass' – Ed Garr USMC.

12 Many of the tunnels have now been widened to admit well-fed western tourists, but some of the original tunnels survive.

13 *Vietnam: A Television History* (WGBH TV, Boston, 1983), interview with Duong Sang.

14 Christian Appy, *Patriots: The Vietnam War Remembered from All Sides*, (Viking, New York, 2003), evidence of Tran Thi Gung, p.16–19.

15 Ibid., evidence of Tran Van Tan, p.288–9.

16 Ibid.

17 Ibid., evidence of Scott Higgins, p.85.

18 Christian Appy, *Vietnam: The Definitive Oral History* (Ebury Press, London, 2003), p.291.

19 Ibid., p296.

20 Keith Nolan, *The Battle for Hue* (Presidio Press, California, 1983), p.17.

21 *Vietnam: A Television History*, interview with Myron Harrington.

22 Nolan, p.154–5.

23 *Vietnam: A Television History*, evidence of Tran Van Do.

24 Richard Hunt, *Pacification* (Westview Press, Boulder, Colorado, 1995), p.137. He goes on to say that by March 1968 things were better: 'It had become clear that pacification's demise had been greatly exaggerated.' But by that time, says Hunt, 'it did little to sway critics' (p.149).

25 *Pentagon Papers*, Vol.4 (Senator Gravel edition, Washington), p.556.

26 The (unnamed) major was quoted by Peter Arnett of the Associated Press on 7 February 1968.

27 The Gallup Poll: *Cumulative Index: Public Opinion 1935–97* (Gallup Press, Washington, 1999), March 1968 poll.

28 *Wall St Journal*, 23 February, 1968.

29 CBS TV News, 27 February 1968.
30 Johnson Papers (Washington), 4 March 1968, doc. 103, quoted at www.state.gov/r/pa/ho/frus/johnsonlb/vi/13695.htm

YOM KIPPUR

1 Abraham Rabinovich, *The Yom Kippur War* (Random House, New York, 2004), p.105.
2 In the last resort, Israel had nuclear weapons. Few doubted that she would use them if faced with destruction.
3 Interview with Avi Yaffe, conducted for the authors, April 2006.
4 The Israeli transcript of the meeting is quoted in Ahron Bregman's book *Israel's Wars* (Routledge, London, 2000), p.77.
5 Rabinovich, p.50. In an interview with Professor Avi Shlaim on 3 December 1996, King Hussein claimed that he had 'no idea' of any Arab plan to go to war. See 'His Royal Shyness: King Hussein and Israel', *New York Review of Books*, 15 July 1999.
6 Victor Israelyan, *Inside the Kremlin During the Yom Kippur War* (Pennsylvania State University Press, 1995), p.1. Israelyan was one of the officials at the meeting.
7 Israel's intelligence community was by no means united behind Zeira. Some had such doubts that they began collating evidence to challenge his assumptions, which came to light after the war.
8 Henry Kissinger, *Years of Upheaval* (Little Brown, Chicago, 1979), p.465.
9 Rabinovich, p.86.
10 Henry Kissinger, pp.450–1.
11 General Youssef Afifi, *Military Review January–February 2003*, pp. 58–9.
12 Saad Shazly, *The Crossing of the Suez* (US Mideast research paperback, San Francisco, 2003), p.56. See also Erich Helmensdorfer, *The Great Crossing* (R.S. Shulz, Germany, 1975), evidence of Egyptian sapper chief General Abdel Sattr Megahid. In fact, the Israeli oil-igniting system had fallen into disrepair and was anyway ineffective.
13 Interview with Awad Alam, conducted for the authors, April 2006.
14 Motti Ashkenazi article in the *Jerusalem Post*, October 1973.
15 Helmensdorfer, p.71.
16 Ibid., p.69.
17 Avigdor Kahalani, *The Heights of Courage* (Steimatzky, New York, 1988).
18 Yug Yuval, Israeli tank commander, quoted in the *Jerusalem Post*, 9 October 1973.
19 Quoted in Rabinovich, p.163.
20 Ibid., p.216
21 Helmensdorfer, evidence of Abel Moneim Masri, pp.92–4.
22 Avi Yaffe interview.
23 *Times* online, 10 October 1973.
24 Some sources have Israel losing up to 85 aircraft in the first few days.
25 Kissinger, p.492.
26 Shazly, p.250.

27 Colonel Shaul Shay, interview with the authors, May 2006.

28 Interview with Amnon Reshef, conducted by Abraham Rabinovich.

29 Interview with Rami Matan, conducted by Abraham Rabinovich.

30 Shazly, p.255.

31 *Sunday Times: Insight on the Yom Kippur War* (Andre Deutsch, London, 1974), p.165.

32 Interview with First Lieutenant Salama El Sayed, conducted for the authors, July 2006.

33 Article in *Yedioth Aharonoth*, 26 October 1973.

34 Shazly, p.271.

35 Kissinger, p.558ff.

36 Ibid., p579ff.

37 Israelyan, p.173ff, says Brezhnev was amazed at America's 'over–reaction', but, he says, 'only a few hours passed before we realised how we had miscalculated'.

38 Three Egyptian generals in, *The Ramadan War* (Dupuy, Virginia, 1978), assert: 'The enemy (Israel) accepted the ceasefire resolution because he was at the time staggering and on the brink of defeat'.

39 Awad Alam interview.

THE FALKLANDS

1 Graham Bound, *Falkland Islanders at War* (Leo Cooper, London, 2002), p.50.

2 John Smith, *Seventy–four Days: An Islander's Diary of the Falklands Occupation* (Century, London, 1984).

3 Patrick Watts, interview with the authors, January 2006.

4 Lawrence Freedman, *The Official History of the Falklands War*, Vol. 2 (Routledge, London, 2005), p.3.

5 Alan Clark, *Diaries* (Weidenfeld & Nicholson, London, 2000), p.313.

6 Nicholas Henderson, *Mandarin* (Weidenfeld & Nicholson, London, 1994), p.445.

7 US efforts to try to persuade Britain to accept a diplomatic solution were not abandoned altogether. President Reagan was still trying to persuade Mrs Thatcher to negotiate as late as 31 May. Her reply to him on the telephone was so furious that he held the receiver away from his ear so that his aides could hear her. Freedman, p.516.

8 Henderson, p.443.

9 Evidence of Nestor Sensi, Imperial War Museum sound archives, code 355.

10 Ibid., evidence of Bill Budding.

11 Ibid., evidence of Oscar Fornez.

12 Ibid., evidence of Nestor Sensi.

13 Ibid., evidence of Oscar Fornez.

14 It was also established that at the time it was attacked the *Belgrano* was steaming away from the British, but the Royal Navy argued she could have turned towards them at any moment. The Labour MP Tam Dalyell conducted a long campaign against the government, arguing that Mrs Thatcher ordered the sinking of the *Belgrano* in order to sabotage any peace initiatives. See Dalyell's book *Thatcher's*

Torpedo (Cecil Woolf, London, 1983), *passim*. Freedman says bluntly that this is not correct, p.315.

15 Evidence of Peter Walpole, Imperial War Museum sound archives, code 11369.

16 Michael Bilton, Spe*aking Out: Untold Stories of the Falklands War*, (Andre Deutsch, London, 1989), evidence of Ian Mortimore.

17 Ibid., evidence of Jeff Glover.

18 President Reagan's US government was quick to supply the UK with the latest version of the Sidewinder missile, the AIM 9L, which could destroy enemy aircraft in a head-on attack.

19 Margaret Thatcher, *The Downing Street Years* (HarperCollins, London, 1993), p.226. Mrs Thatcher later approved an honorary knighthood for Weinberger for the support he gave Britain during the war.

20 Lawrence Freedman's *Official History of the Falklands War* has a full account on p.299.

21 Evidence of Peter Walpole, Imperial War Museum sound archives, code 11369.

22 Major–General Julian Thompson, interview with the authors, September 2006.

23 Commodore Michael Clapp, interview with the authors, September 2006

24 Bilton, evidence of Ken Enticknab.

25 Admiral Sir Alan West, interview with the authors, April 2006.

26 Commodore Michael Clapp, interview with the authors, August 2006.

27 Letter from Jim aboard *RFA Fort Austin* to his friend Juantha Carberry, Imperial War Museum archive 96/18/1.

28 Margaret Thatcher, *The Downing Street Years* (HarperCollins, London, 1993), p.226.

29 Thompson, in the preface to the 3rd edition of *No Picnic*, (Cassell, London 2001), argues that there would have been less 'misunderstanding and friction' if there had been an 'overall commander–in–theatre'. It was only later that Major–General Jeremy Moore arrived to take the burden of liaising with London off Thompson's shoulders.

30 Thompson interview.

31 Ibid.

32 Evidence of Paul Farrar, Imperial War Museum sound archives, code 13008/2.

33 Bilton, evidence of Barry Norman.

34 Ibid.

35 Thompson interview.

36 John Adams, interview with the authors, January 2006.

37 Major–General Nick Vaux, interview with the authors, August 2006.

38 Nick van der Bijl and David Aldea, *5th Infantry Brigade in the Falklands War* (Pen and Sword, London 2003), evidence of Nick Vaux.

39 Ibid., evidence of Major Davies.

40 Ibid., evidence of Crispin Black.

41 Clapp interview.

42 Nick van deer Bijl and David Aldea, evidence of Crispin Black.

43 Michael Savage, interview with the authors, January 2006.

44 Hugh Bicheno, *The Unofficial History of the Falklands War*, (Weidenfled & Nicholson, 2006), p.221.

45 Ibid., p.222.

46 Imperial War Museum documents, ref. no. 91/19/1, evidence of Graham Colbeck, sergeant with 3 Para.

47 Vaux interview.

48 Ibid.

49 Thompson interview.

50 Evidence of Mike Scott, Imperial War Museum sound archives, code 13055/1.

51 Ibid., evidence of Jim Mitchell.

52 Evidence of Philip Willimas, Imperial War Museum sound archives, code 13045/3.

53 Imperial War Museum documents, ref. 'Item', letter from anon Argentine soldier, 10/June/82.

54 Max Hastings and Simon Jenkins, The Battle for the Faulklands, (Michael Joseph, London, 1983), pp.308–9.

KUWAIT

1 Charles Allen, *Thunder and Lightning: The RAF in the Gulf War* (HMSO, London, 1991), p.49.

2 Cable from State Department to US embassy Baghdad, dated 28 July 1990, quoted on www.meij.or.jp/text/Gulf War/uscable0728.htm

3 BBC2 Gulf War Anniversary, January 1996, evidence of Abu Fatima.

4 Dr al Khalaf, interview with the authors, October 2005.

5 Colin Powell, *A Soldier's Way* (Arrow Books, London, 2001), p.463.

6 Rick Atkinson, in his *Crusade: The Untold Story of the Gulf War* (Houghton Mifflin, New York, 1993), describes Schwarzkopf as 'the most theatrical American in uniform since Douglas Macarthur'.

7 Norman Schwarzkopf, *It Doesn't Take a Hero* (New York, Bantam Books, 1993), p.353.

8 Air Chief Marshall Sir Patrick Hine, interview with the authors, November 2005.

9 General Sir Peter de la Billiere, interview with the authors, March 2006.

10 General Norman Schwarzkopf, interview with the authors, December 2005.

11 De la Billiere interview.

12 Schwarzkopf interview.

13 Hine told the authors that when he had visited Powell earlier in the crisis, Powell had favoured sanctions against Iraq, which he reckoned would take two years to be effective. Hine told him he was being quite unrealistic.

14 Powell, p.489.

15 De la Billiere interview.

16 Allen, p.54.

17 Atkinson, p.42–4.

18 Ibid., p.106.

19 Schwarzkopf interview.

20 Atkinson, p.102.

21 Sir Peter de la Billiere, *Storm Command*, (HarperCollins, London, 1995), p.231.

22 General Accounting Office report, Washington, 1997.

23 Schwarzkopf interview.

24 BBC2, Gulf War Anniversary, January 1996, evidence of Samdar.

25 Hine interview.

26 Mohamed el Alwani, interview with the authors, November 2005.

27 US Marine Corps Video and Sound Archives, Department of Defense, Washington, for day of 29 January, 1991.

28 Powell, p.515.

29 Schwarzkopf interview.

30 Captain Mujbil Habib, interview with the authors, November 2005.

31 BBC2, Gulf War Anniversary, January 1996, Abu Fatima evidence.

32 Sergeant Sameeh Mohammed Muden, interview with the authors, November 2005.

33 BBC2, Gulf War Anniversary, January 1996, Sardar evidence.

34 *Eagle and Carbine,* regimental magazine of the Royal Scots Dragoon Guards, No. 20, September 1991.

35 Ibid., p.77.

36 General Sir Rupert Smith, interview with the authors, November 2005.

37 Atkinson, p.465.

38 Schwarzkopf, p.566.

39 Sir Patrick Hine told the authors of a remark Margaret Thatcher made to him after she had retired. She told Hine she was astonished that such a distinguished array of military minds had been against marching all the way to Baghdad. Hine interview.

FURTHER READING

AMIENS

Asprey, R., *The German High Command at War* (London, Warner Books, 1994)

Blaxland, B., *Amiens 1918* (London, Muller, 1968)

Brown, M., *1918 The Year of Victory* (London, Pan Books, 1998)

Dallas, G., *1918 War and Peace* (London, Pimlico, 2002)

Downing, W.H., *To the Last Ridge* (Sydney, Duffy & Snellgrove, 1998)

Drury, I., *German Stormtrooper* (Oxford, Osprey, 2003)

Gilbert, M. *Winston S Churchill Volume. IV* (London, Heinemann, 1975)

Haig, Field Marshal D., *The Private Papers of Douglas Haig 1914–19* ed. by Robert Blake (London, Eyre and Spottiswoode, 1952)

Harris, J.P. and Barr, N., *Amiens to the Armistice: The BEF in the Hundred Days' Campaign* (London, Brassey's, 1999)

Hobbes, N., *Essential Militaria,* (London, Atlantic Books, 2003)

Holmes (ed.), R., *Oxford Companion to Military History* (Oxford, Oxford University Press, 2003)

Ferguson, N., *The Pity of War* (London, Basic, 1999)

Junger, E., *The Storm of Steel* (London, Constable, 1994)

Ludendorff, E., *My War Memoirs, Vol. II* (London, Hutchinson, 1919)

Marix Evans, M., *Over the Top, Great Battles of The First World War* (London, Arcturus, 2002)

McWilliams, J. and Steel, R.J., *Amiens 1918,* (London, Tempus Publishing, 2004)

Monash, Sir J., *The Australian Victories in France in 1918* (London, Imperial War Museum, 1993)

Pitt, B., *1918 The Last Act* (London, Papermac, 1962)

Sheffield, G., *Forgotten Victory, The First World War – Myths and Realities* (London, Review, 2002)

Simkins, P., *The First World War: The Western Front 1917–1918* (Oxford, Osprey, 2002)

Stedman, M., *Advance to Victory 1918,* (London, Leo Cooper, 2001)

Stevenson, D., *1914–1918: The History of the First World War* (London, Allen Lane, 2004)

Strachan, H., *The First World War, Volume 1: To Arms* (Oxford, OUP, 2003)

Terraine, J., *White Heat* (London, Sidgwick & Jackson, 1982)

Travers, T., *How the War was Won* (Barnsley, Pen and Sword Military Classics, 2005)

Wilson, T., *The Myriad Faces of War* (Oxford, Basil Blackwell, 1986)

MIDWAY

Bicheno, H., *Midway* (London, Cassell & Co., 2001)

Cressman et al., R., *A Glorious Page in Our History: The Battle of Midway* (Missoula, MT, Pictoral Histories Publishing Company, 1990)

Dull, P.S., *A Battle History of the Imperial Japanese Navy* (Annapolis, US Naval Institute Press, 1955)Fuchida, M., *Midway: The Battle that doomed Japan.* (Annapolis, US Naval Institute Press, 1955)

Grove, P., *Midway* (London, Brassey's, 2004)

Hashimoto et.al., T., *Testimony: The Battle of Midway* (Tokyo, Kojinsha, 1992)

Horikoshi, J. *Eagles of Mitsubishi: The Story of the Zero Fighter* (London, Orbis Publishing, 1982)

Kohdachi, N., *The Portrait of Warriors* (Tokyo, Bunshun Nesko, 2004)

Lord, W., *Day of Infamy* (London, Wordsworth Military Library, 1998)

Lord, W., *Midway: The Incredible Victory* (London, Wordsworth Military Library, 2000)

Morison, S., *History of United States Naval Operations in World War II, Volume IV: Coral Sea, Midway and Submarine Actions (May 1942 – August 1942)* (Boston, Little Brown and Company, 1950)

Parshall, J. and Tully, A., *Shattered Sword: The Untold Story of the Battle of Midway* (Washington DC, Potomac Books, 2005)

Prange, G., *Miracle at Midway* (London, Penguin, 2002)

Prange, G., *At Dawn We Slept* (London, Penguin, 1991)

Wildenberg, T. *Destined for Glory: Dive Bombing, Midway, and the Evolution of Carrier Airpower* (Annapolis, US Naval Institute Press, 1998)

Wilmot, H.P. *Empires in the Balance* (Annapolis, US Naval institute Press, 1982)

STALINGRAD

Adam, W., *The Hard Decision* (East Berlin, 1967)

Boog et al., *Germany and the Second World War, Volume 6* (Oxford, Clarenden Press, 2001)

Bullock, A., *Hitler and Stalin: Parallel Lives* (London, Harper Collins, 1991)

Cesarani, D., (ed), *The Final Solution* (London, Routledge, 1994)

Chuikov, V., *The Beginning of the Road* (London, MacGibbon and Kee, 1963)

Clark, A., *Barbarossa: The Russian–German Conflict, 1941–1945* (London, Weidenfeld & Nicolson, 1965)

Craig, W., *Enemy at the Gates: The Battle for Stalingrad* (London, Penguin, 2000)

Erickson, J., *The Road to Stalingrad* (London, Cassell Military, 2003)

Fowler, *Stalingrad: The Vital Seven Days* (London, Amber Books, 2005)

Goerlitz, W., *Paulus and Stalingrad* (London, Methuen, 1963)

Hayward, J.S.A., *Stopped at Stalingrad: The Luftwaffe and Hitler's Defeat in the East, 1942–1943* (Lawrence Kansas, University of Kansas Press, 1998)

Mawdsley, E., *Thunder in the East: The Nazi–Soviet War 1941–1945* (London, Hodder Arnold, 2005)

Noakes and Pridham, *Nazism 1919–1945 Volume 3* (Exeter, University of Exeter Press, 1988)

Roberts, G., *Victory at Stalingrad* (London, Longman, 2002)

Sebag Montefiore, S., *Stalin: The Court of the Red Tsar* (London, Phoenix, 2004)

Tarrant, V.E., *Stalingrad: Anatomy of an Agony* (London, Leo Cooper, 1992)

Trevor-Roper, H. *Hitler's War Directives, 1939–1945* (London, Sidgwick and Jackson, 1964)

Walsh, S., *Stalingrad: The Infernal Cauldron* (London, Amber Books, 2000)

Weinberg, G., *World at Arms: A Global History of World War Two* (Cambridge, University of Cambridge Press, 1994)

Werth, A., *Russia at War 1941–1945,* (New York, E. P. Dutton Co., 1964)

Werth, A., *The Year of Stalingrad* (London, Hamish Hamilton, 1946)

Ziemke & Bauer, *Moscow to Stalingrad: Decision in the East* (Washington DC, Center of Military History, 1987)

THE IMJIN RIVER

Appelman, R., *Ridgway Duels for Korea* (Houston, Texas A&M University Press, October 1990)

Appelman, R., *South to the Naktong, North yo the Yalu* (Washington, Center for Military History, 1992)

Barker, A., *Fortune Favours the Brave: The Commonwealth Brigade in the Korea War* (London, Pen & Sword, 2001)

Davies, S., *In Spite of Dungeons,* (London, Hodder and Stoughton, 1955

Farrar Hockley, A., *The Edge of the Sword,* (London, Frederick Muller, 1954)

Gugeler, R., *Army Historical Series Combat Actions in Korea* (Washington, Center for Military History, 1987)

Hastings, M., *The Korean War* (London, Pan, 2000),

Hickey, M., *Korean War: The West Confronts Communism 1950–1953* (London, John Murray, 2000)

Knox, D., *The Korean War, Vol. 1: Pusan to Chosin: An Oral History* (London, Thomson Learning, 1985)

Malkasian, C., *The Korean War,* (London, Osprey, 2001)

Mossman, B., *United States Army in the Korean War: Ebb and Flow November 1950 to July 1951* (Washington, Center for Military History, 1990)

Peters and Li, *Voices from the Korean War: Personal Stories of American, Korean and Chinese Soldiers* (Lexington: University of Kentucky Press, 2004)

Ridgway, M., *The War in Korea* (London, Doubleday, 1967)

Rottman, G., *Inchon 1950: The Last Great Amphibious Assault* (London, Osprey, 2006)

Stewart (ed), R., *American Military History, Volume II, The United States Army, In A Global Era, 1917–2003* (Washington, Center for Military History, 2005)

The US Army Center For Military History Homepage: http://www.army.mil/cmh/reference/Korea/kw-remem.htm

THE TET OFFENSIVE

Allen, G., *None So Blind* (Chicago, Ivan Dee, 2002)

Appy, C., *Patriots: The Vietnam War Remembered from All Sides* (New York, Viking 2003)

Arnold, J., *Tet Offensive 1968: Turning Point in Vietnam* (London, Osprey, 1990)

Davidson, P., *Vietnam At War* (New York, Presidio Press, 1988)

Gardner, L.C., *Pay Any Price: Lyndon Johnson and The Wars for Vietnam* (Chicago, Ivan Dee, 1995)

Hammel, E., *Khe Sanh: Siege in the Clouds* (California, Pacifica Press, 2000)

Hammel, E., *Fire in the Streets: The Battle for Hue* (New York, Dell, 1991)

Hunt, R., *Pacification,* (Boulder, Colorado, Westview Press, 1995)

Nolan, K., *The Battle for Hue* (California, Presidio Press, 1983) Richard Hunt

Karnow, S., *Vietnam, A History* (New York, Viking Press, 1983)

Kissinger, H., *Diplomacy* (New York, Simon and Schuster, 1994)

Kissinger, H., *The White House Years* (Boston, Little Brown and Co, 1979)

Langguth, A.J., *Our Vietnam: The War 1954–1975* (New York, Simon & Schuster 2000)

Maclear, M., *Vietnam: The Ten Thousand Day War* (New York, Avon Books, 1982)

Oberdorfer, D., *Tet!* (NewYork, Doubleday, 1971)

Pimlott, J., *Vietnam: The Decisive Battles* (London, Guild, 1990)

Prados, J. and Stubbe, R., *Valley of Decision: The siege of Khe Sanh* (Annapolis, Naval Institute Press, 2004)

YOM KIPPUR

Badri, Gen H.E., Magdoub, Gen T. el, and Zohdy, Gen M. el din, *The Ramadan War* (USA, Dupuy Assoc, 1978)

Boyne, W., *The 2 O'Clock War* (New York, Thomas Dunne, 2002)

Dunstan, S., *The Yom Kippur War 1973*, Volumes 1 and 2 (London, Osprey, 2003)

Gamassi, Gen M.A.G., *The October War* (American University Cairo Press, 1989)

Helmensdorfer, E., *The Great Crossing* (Germany, R.S. Schulz, 1975)

Herzog, C., *The War of Atonement* (London, Weidenfeld and Nicolson, 1975)

Herzog, C., *The Arab Israeli Wars* (London, Arms and Armour Press, 1982)

Israelyan, V., *Inside the Kremlin During the Yom Kippur War* (US, Pennsylvania State University Press, 1995)

Kahalani, A., *The Heights of Courage* (New York, Steimazky, 1988)

Kissinger, H., *Diplomacy* (New York, Simon and Schuster, 1994)

Kissinger, H., *The White House Years* (Boston, Little Brown and Co, 1979)

Kissinger, H., *Years of Upheaval,* (Chicago, Little Brown 1979)

Rabinovich, A., *The Yom Kippur War* (New York, Random House, 2004)

Seale, P., Asad (Canada, Harper Collins, 1999)

Shazly, S., *The Crossing of the Suez* (San Francsiso, US Mideast research paperback, 2003)

Shlaim, A., *The Iron Wall* (New York, W.W. Norton & Company, 2000; UK, Penguin, 2001)

THE FALKLANDS

Anderson, D., *The Falklands War* (London, Osprey, 2002)
Bicheno, H., *The Unofficial History of the Falklands War*, (London, Weidenfeld and Nicolson, 2006)
Bilton, M., and Kosminsky, P., *Speaking Out: Untold Stories of the Falklands War*, (London, Andre Deutsch, 1990)
Bound, G., *Falkland Islanders at War* (London, Leo Cooper, 2002)
Dalyell, T., *Thatcher's Torpedo* (London, Cecil Woolf, 1983)
Freedman, L., *The Official History of the Falklands War* (London, Routledge, 2005)
Hastings, M. and Jenkins, S., *The Battle for the Falklands* (London, Michael Joseph, 1982)
Henderson, N., *Mandarin* (London, Weidenfeld and Nicolson,1994)
Nott, J., *Here Today Gone Tomorrow* (London, Methuen, 2003)
Smith, J., *Seventy-four Days: An Islander's Diary of the Falklands Occupation* (London, Century, 1984)
Thatcher, M., *The Downing St Years* (London, Harper Collins, 1993)
Thompson, J., *No Picnic* (London, Cassell, 2001)
Van der Bijl, N. and Aldea, D., *5th Infantry Brigade in the Falklands War* (London, Pen and Sword Books, 2003)
Weinberger, C. *In the Arena: A Memoir of the Twentieth Century* (Washington DC, Regnery Publishing, 2001)

KUWAIT

Allen, C., *Thunder and Lightning: The RAF in the Gulf War* (London, HMSO, 1991)
Atkinson, R., *Crusade: The Untold Story of the Gulf War* (New York, Houghton Mifflin, 1993)
Cordingley, P., *In the Eye of the Storm* (London, Hodder and Stoughton, 1996)
De la Billiere, P., *Storm Command* (London, Harper Collins, 1995)
Finlan, A., *The Gulf War 1990–1991* (London, Osprey 2003)
Freedman, L. and Efraim K., *The Gulf Conflict 1990–1991: Diplomacy and War in the New World Order* (London, Faber and Faber, 1993)
Nichol, J. and Peters, J., *Tornado Down* (London, Michael Joseph,1992)
Powell, C., *A Soldier's Way* (London, Arrow Books, 2001)
Schwarzkopf, N., *It Doesn't Take a Hero* (New York, Bantam Books, 1993)
Sultan, K. bin, *Desert Warrior* (London, Harper Collins, 1995)

ACKNOWLEDGEMENTS

We have so many people to thank for the shaping of this book – people who gave us access to every corner of these battlefields, who put us in touch with eyewitnesses, who regaled us with source material and who shared their expertise with us. Their kindness has enabled us to tell the story of these eight pre-eminent conflicts with the thoroughness and clarity they deserve.

Our biggest debt is to the BBC television production team who travelled the world with us. The project was launched by Sarah Hargreaves, who made the brave call that the success of the *Battlefield Britain* television series should be followed by *Twentieth Century Battlefields*. So BBC2 viewers again watched father and son telling the stories of eight more great battles in 2007. Executive producer Jane Aldous and series producer Danielle Peck again provided incomparable leadership, and we benefited from the enthusiasm and hard work of the programme producers they appointed: Renuka Chapman, Ben Lawrie, Johanna Gibbon, Dan Kendall and Paul McGuigan. We owe a lot to them and to the energetic research and curiosity of those who worked closely with them: Stephen Douds, Kinda Haddad, Claire Messenger, Hannah Robson, Nick Sturdee, Jihad Hashim and Catherine Abbott. We were also very lucky in the creative skill of the camera crews and the support of Ben Sutton, Sue Fowler and Basia Pietluch, and particularly with the patience of Helena Berglund, who had the herculean task of masterminding the schedule and providing the team with back-up over nearly two years.

On the ground we had valuable assistance from Hyun Sung Khang, who was our guide and mentor in Korea, Jiang Nguyen Hoang, who opened doors for us in Vietnam, and Svetlana Agartseva, Deputy Director of the Volgograd Museum, who was familiar with every feature of the Battle of Stalingrad. Captain Jim Philippson in the Falklands made sure we had all the military facilities we needed before he was posted to Afghanistan, where he was tragically killed in action only a few weeks later. Tony Smith guided us round the Falklands battlefields, as he has guided almost every veteran since 1982, and shared with us his encyclopaedic knowledge of every moment of the action. Keith Walker was our guide and security escort in Kuwait and Alon Farago won us access to wherever we wanted to go in Israel and the Occupied Territories.

Here in Britain we had expert help from Alastair Massie at the National Army Museum and Kate Snow, who conducted an exhaustive search of the Imperial War Museum archives to secure eyewitness accounts. We are grateful to the historians who gave their invaluable advice: Professor Hew Strachan, Jonathon Todd, Ashley Jackson, Jonathan Parshall, Anthony Tully, Alessio Patalano, Marcus Faulkner, Martin Marix-Evans, Graham Ong, Sam Raphael, Professor Avi Shlaim, Simon Dunstan and

Maj-Gen Julian Thompson. Any mistakes that have crept in are entirely our own.

The spectacular graphics provided by Red Vision in Manchester for the television series encouraged us to go for a rich armoury of maps to illustrate the strategy and tactics of each battle. Ricky Capanni of HL Studios took on the task and each map was crafted with meticulous care by Peter Wilkinson. We have been fortunate too in having Sarah Hopper secure an abundant supply of pictures to give readers a real sense of what these battles looked like. The outcome has been a book that is a massive credit to the imagination of our designer, Martin Hendry.

We have been doubly lucky with our editorial team. Martin Redfern, the inspired editor of *Battlefield Britain* at BBC Worldwide, has become an editorial director at Random House, but has found the time to maintain a creative overview of *The World's Greatest Twentieth Century Battlefields*. And Eleanor Maxfield has edited the book with a matchless eye for detail and flawless judgement.

Finally, we are hugely indebted to our family for enduring the constant strain we have put on their patience and goodwill. In particular we have to thank an extraordinary wife and mother, television journalist Ann MacMillan, and her sister, the historian Margaret MacMillan, for their deft contributions to the coherence and fluency of our narrative.

INDEX

PICTURE CREDITS

BBC Books would like to thank the following individuals and organisations for providing photographs and for permission to reproduce copyright material. While every effort has been made to trace and acknowledge copyright holders, we would like to apologize should there be any errors or omissions.

Abbreviations: t: top, b: bottom, c: centre, tl: top left, tr: top right, tc: top centre, bl: bottom left, br: bottom right, cr: centre right.

Plate section 1

1: Underwood & Underwood/Corbis; 2tl: Imperial War Museum (CO003014); 2bl: Imperial War Museum (CO2979); 2-3tc: Bettmann/Corbis; 3tr: Bettmann/Corbis; 3br: Imperial War Museum (6910); 4t: Bettmann/Corbis; 4bl: Imperial War Museum (Q9178); 5: Bettmann/Corbis; 6t: Corbis; 6-7b: AP/Empics; 7tl: AP/Empics; 7tr: Corbis; 7br: The Art Archive/National Archives Washington DC; 8: Naval Historical Center, Washington.

Plate section 2

1t: Topfoto.co.uk; 1b: Imperial War Museum (HU005150); 2tl: Mary Evans Picture Library/Weimar Archive; 2b: Mary Evans Picture Library/Alexander Meledin; 2-3t: Mary Evans Picture Library/Alexander Meledin; 3bl: RIA Novosti: 3br: Keerle Georges de/Corbis Sygma; 4t: Mary Evans Picture Library; 4b: Imperial War Museum (5319); 5t: AP/Empics; 5b: Hulton-Deutsch Collection/Corbis; 6-7t: AP/Empics; 6b: Bettmann/Corbis; 7cr: Hulton-Deutsch Collection/Corbis; 8t: AP/Empics.

Plate section 3

1t: Corbis; 1b: Micha Bar Am/Magnum Photos; 2t: Simonpietri Christian/Corbis Sygma; 2b: David Rubinger/Corbis; 3t: Simonpietri Christian/Corbis Sygma; 3b: Popperfoto.com; 4t: Philip Jones Griffiths/Magnum Photos; 5t: Henri Bureau/Sygma/Corbis; 5b: Abbas/Magnum Photos; 6t: AP/Empics; 6b: Philip Jones Griffiths/Magnum Photos; 7t: Bettmann/Corbis; 7c: Popperfoto.com; 7b: Philip Jones Griffiths/Magnum Photos; 8t: Bettmann/Corbis; 8b: Christian Simonpietri/Corbis Sygma.

Plate section 4

1t: Peter Turnley/Corbis; 1b: AP/Empics; 2tl: AP/Empics; 2b: AP/Empics; 2-3t: Bettmann/Corbis; 3br: AP/Empics; 4t: Imperial War Museum (FKD002343); 4c: Imperial War Museum (FKD002028); 5t: Jacques Langevin/Corbis Sygma; 5b: AP/Empics; 6t: AP/Empics; 6-7b: Empics; 7t: Imperial War Museum (FKD001241); 8t: Ken Clarke/T/D, Camera Press, London; 8b: Imperial War Museum (FKD001146).

All other pictures courtesy of BBC production team.